The Crisis Manual

P9-DNI-198

THE CRISIS

MANUAL

for Early Childhood Teachers

How to Handle the Really Difficult Problems

by Karen Miller

Photographs by Nancy Alexander
Illustrations by Rebecca Jones

gryphon house
Lewisville, NC

Copyright © 1995, 2002 by Karen Miller

Published by Gryphon House, Inc.

PO Box 10, Lewisville, NC 27023

800.638.0928 (toll free); 877.638.7576 (fax)

Visit us on the web at www.gryphonhouse.com

All rights reserved. No part of this publication may be reproduced, stored in a retrieval system or transmitted in any form or by any means, electronic, mechanical, photocopying, recording or otherwise, without the prior written permission of the publisher. Printed in the United States of America.

Cover Design: Graves Fowler Associates

Text Photographs: Nancy Alexander

Text Illustrations: Rebecca Jones

Reprinted August 2015

The Library of Congress has cataloged the first printing of this book as follows:

Library of Congress Cataloging-in-Publication Data

Miller, Karen, 1942-

The crisis manual for early childhood teachers : how to handle the really difficult problems / by Karen Miller : photographs by Nancy Alexander ; illustrations by Rebecca Jones.

p. cm.

Includes bibliographical references and index.

ISBN 978-0-87659-176-5

1. School children--Psychology--Handbooks, manuals, etc. 2. Early childhood education--Psychological aspects--Handbooks, manuals, etc. 3. Child care--Psychological aspects--Handbooks, manuals, etc. 4. Crisis intervention (Psychiatry)--Handbooks, manuals, etc. 5. Mental health counseling--Handbooks, manuals, etc. 6. Life change events--Study and teaching. 7. Social problems--Study and teaching. I. Title.

LB 1121.M55   1995   95-25908

370.15--dc20   CIP

TABLE OF CONTENTS

FOREWORD

The Crisis Manual for Early Childhood Teachers is an important and timely guide for teachers who must educate children faced with challenging situations.

The Crisis Manual is a valuable tool in helping teachers create a learning environment that acknowledges the various experiences and backgrounds of children while providing practical and insightful information. The environment in which children grow makes a substantial impact on how they respond and develop in the world. This guide can help caregivers and educators provide the environment that helps children be successful and well nurtured.

As an early childhood educator and advocate by profession, I want to thank Karen Miller for making this guide available. We must not only prepare our children to be the best they can possibly be, but also provide our educators with the necessary support and resources to help them with their critical task. It is obvious that a great deal of thought, research and personal experience have been invested in this guide.

BEA ROMER
First Lady of Colorado

ACKNOWLEDGMENTS

A book like this would be impossible to write without the collaboration of many respected professionals. It's truly an example of synergism with many minds contributing experiences and viewpoints to create something useful and practical. First of all, I'd like to thank the many unidentified people I have met at early childhood conferences, who in casual conversations about this project encouraged me and said, "Go for it! The field needs this." That encouragement meant more than I can tell you. Many of your stories are woven into this text.

Nancy Alexander, Executive Director of Child Care Services of Northwest Louisiana, Shreveport, LA

Joyce Allan, family therapist, Charlottesville, VA

Doretta Allison, teacher, Prince George's County Public Schools, MD

Jane Bingham, my neighbor and friend, psychotherapist and authority on child sexual abuse

Donna Bloomer, Early Childhood Specialist and Training Director, Bryan Centre, Hagerstown, MD

Carolyn Brooks and Betsy McAllister Groves, Directors of Boston City Hospital Women's and Infant's Program and Child Witness to Violence Program

Vicki Carrington, family child care provider, Steamboat Springs, CO

Tammy Chatterton, parent, Moses Lake, WA

Louise Derman-Sparks, Director of the Culturally Relevant Anti-Bias Education Leadership Project

Jane Erckenbrack, social worker, Washington, DC

Mattie and Dick Feldman, Bank Street College, NY

Polly Ferraro, Director of Child Development Services, Port Hueneme Naval Base in California

Bev Fuqua, teacher, North Park Elementary School, Walden, CO

Bobbie Grantham, Director of Educational Services, Children's Home-Chambliss Shelter, Chattanooga, TN

Sharon Greenlee, grief counselor and author of *When Somebody Dies,* Centennial, WY

Mary Gregory, family child care provider, Canyon Country, CA

Mary Hammond, The Heart Center, Salem, OR

Patty Hishke, Director of Bright Start Children's Centers, Inc.

Susan Huffman, teacher, Montgomery County Public Schools, MD

Cindi Hunt, Activities Coordinator for First Start/Parents as Teachers family support program, Canon City, CO

Sue Johnson Jacka, Vice President of Bright Start Children's Centers, Inc.

Betty Jones, mentor to everyone who passes through Pacific Oaks College

Barbara Kilkka, parent, Orchard Lake, MI

Carol Krysko, owner of Early Explorations, Encinitas, CA

Maureen Moreland, Executive Director of Parent and Child Services, Inc., Portland, OR

Mary Rivkin, Assistant Professor, Early Childhood Education, University of Maryland Baltimore County, Catonsville, MD

Hedda Sharapan, Associate Producer of Mister Rogers' Neighborhood, produced by Family Communications, Inc., Pittsburgh, PA

Hanne Sonquist, NAEYC Governing Board member and family therapist

Muffy Stright, owner of Aspen Child Development Centers, Denver, CO

Jacqueline Wallen, Associate Professor, Family Studies, University of Maryland, College Park, MD

Francis Wardle, Executive Director of The Center for the Study of Biracial Children, Denver, CO

Heather Wenig, teacher of toddlers in Kearney, NE

Karen Williams, University of Wyoming

I thankfully acknowledge the great, supportive team at Gryphon House.

Larry Rood, President of Gryphon House, is the person who had the initial vision for this book, based on many conversations he has had with individuals in early childhood.

Leah Curry-Rood, Vice President of Gryphon House used her lifetime of knowledge about children's literature to assemble the many fine children's books listed in the resource sections throughout the book.

Gryphon House editorial assistant, Mary Duru, was extremely helpful in finding numerous additional adult resources.

Finally, I am grateful for the infinite skills of Editor-in-Chief, Kathy Charner, in the huge task of pulling everything together to create a book that is useful and usable.

INTRODUCTION

It feels strange to be writing a book that I hope you'll never need. Unfortunately, that is not likely to be the case. More and more teachers report the increasing incidence of crises in children's lives. These crises interfere with the children's ability to learn. As much as we might like to shield children from unpleasant events and emotions, we cannot do so.

One frustrated kindergarten teacher expressed the feelings of many when she said, "I resent having to spend so much time nurturing these children and dealing with difficult behaviors. I got into this field to educate children, and I'm finding I can't do that because children are having so many problems in their lives." Even though we might empathize with this teacher's feelings, we know that developmentally appropriate curriculum must respond to the issues that interest and concern children at the present time. If a child is experiencing crisis in her life, "lessons" that come only from the teacher's agenda will not connect with the child's life. Indeed, children who are experiencing extreme stress and trauma in their lives, whether from community violence, the death of a loved one, a serious illness in the family, homelessness, living with substance abusers or any of the other crises discussed in this book, are at high risk for developing emotional and developmental learning delays.

The young child has not yet learned to keep certain topics at home and others at school. For him, life and school are more integrated than for older children. We have always known that we must deal with the whole child—both the intellectual and the emotional parts. The challenge is how. Few people working in early childhood have specific training in addressing psychological traumas of young children. Teachers are hesitant to get involved or talk about certain situations, fearing that they may do more harm than good.

However, early childhood teachers and caregivers can do a lot to help a child and the child's family deal with a crisis. During difficult times, the child's teacher is often the one stable element in the child's life. The child care center or home can be a kind of haven for the child where she can express herself and where there are caring individuals who listen and help her sort out what is going on in her life. This adult has an important role to play in responding to the child in a helpful and supportive way, thus increasing the child's coping mechanisms. The teacher can also interpret the child to the parents and help them see things from the child's perspective. Another important role is to help the parents recognize when further help might be needed and to direct them to other professionals.

In this book, I have included resources that might be helpful in dealing with various crisis situations. It is not likely that you will sit down and read this book from cover to cover. More typically, you will turn to various chapters as the need arises.

This is a "start book", a source book. I hope it gives you many points to think about as you approach a problem—a little background information, things to try, resources to help, numbers to call, people to talk to.

Each chapter has a few insights about child development. These are general statements about how a young child might perceive a situation. Principles cited in the chapters are summaries of information I found reflected in various resources for each topic.

As I pulled together the How to Respond section of each chapter, I found that I was repeating myself. Almost all crisis situations call for curriculum practices that allow the child to express himself, and most important, to be heard by caring, sensitive adults. Therefore, I created Chapter 23, Curriculum Ideas & Activities, which goes into greater detail by listing more specific activities that can be used in numerous situations.

Each crisis chapter offers a list of children's books that relate to the topic. Books are a wonderful resource and may allow you to bring up a topic in a neutral, nonthreatening way. Some books are appropriate to read to the whole group, others are better read one-on-one with a child. You will have to make that decision yourself, depending on what you know and feel about the situation. Examine several of the books listed before selecting the one you feel is most appropriate for the particular child and situation. Consider the level of the book. You might be able to simplify vocabulary from time to time, but check to see that the child is comprehending what the book is trying to convey. Do not assume that the situation has been handled adequately just because the child doesn't ask any questions when you're finished reading the book. Books should be used to open doors of communication with the child and let the child know that he is not alone in what he is experiencing.

It would be impractical to list every single book and resource on any given topic. In searching through books, articles and video tapes, I tried to select ones I thought would be most useful to you in your situation as early childhood educators. I looked for resources that are concise and offer practical strategies. Many of the books have extensive bibliographies and reference sections, should you wish to do more in-depth study. The organizations and hot lines listed in each chapter can also be very helpful to you in finding resources.

New materials are always being developed. I would be very interested in hearing from you if you come across a resource not listed here that you find to be particularly helpful so that I might consider it for future editions. Please write to me, Karen Miller, at P.O. Box 97, Cowdrey, CO 80434, or contact the publisher, Gryphon House Inc., PO Box 10, Lewisville, NC 27023. Also tell us about crises or difficult situations not covered in this book that you wish we would address.

One difficult thing about writing the book was dividing it into chapters, because rarely do crises happen in isolation. In addition, every individual child is different and every crisis is different. I encourage you to check related chapters. Ultimately, it is up to you to piece together the resources and the strategies that will work best in your situation.

Keep in mind that the best crisis management technique, no matter what the crisis, is to have a plan in place beforehand. Think about the eventuality. Do what you can to prevent it. But if a crisis occurs, act professionally and use the resources available to you in your community. Turn a crisis into an opportunity—to sharpen your skills, become more connected professionally, and add depth to your service. I am very conscious of the fact that many early childhood professionals already feel overwhelmed. You can't do it alone. Progress only happens in the context of society and within the support systems for you as a professional as well as for the families you serve. Chapter 1, The Caregiver's Role discusses ways to function effectively with others.

Finally, some of you might be asking, who is Karen Miller to be writing a book like this? I asked myself that question! I am not a social worker, a psychologist or a therapist. I have a Master's Degree in Human Development from Pacific Oaks College. My knowledge is not specialized, except in one area. I have visited over a thousand child care centers and family child care homes around the country and have talked to literally thousands of teachers and directors over the years. I know and have respect for the incredible complexity of your jobs. I believe I have a sense of what is useful to you. In reading through the piles of resources I assembled, I said to myself, "If I have trouble understanding or following this, so will an early childhood teacher," or, "If this makes sense to me, it will be helpful to others." So, in effect, I have attempted to accumulate and sift through the information available for you. I believe we should all continue stretching and growing, and working on this book has been a learning experience for me.

Everybody wishes there were some magic "right" words to say to help a child through a crisis. Of course, there are no perfect phrases. All we can do is our best. When a crisis is occurring in a child's life, an early childhood program can either add to the problem or help to alleviate it. The goal of this book is to increase the odds that a child will learn and grow, even in a crisis situation, because of the sensitive responses of caring adults. It is with abiding respect for the important work that you do that I offer you this book and hope that it is helpful to you.

Karen Miller

Karen Miller

1
PART

CRISIS AND THE CAREGIVER

CHAPTER 1

THE CAREGIVER'S ROLE

How can we be helpful? When do we step in? How much can we help? In our field, we talk about the fact that on any given day, an early childhood teacher or director must be an educator, a janitor, a plumber, a cook, a nurse, a psychologist, an all-around "fixer." More and more, we are finding that the job of social worker must be added to that list of assignments.

WHEN DOES A SITUATION BECOME A CRISIS

Early childhood teachers are generally accustomed to interacting with children, planning their activities, observing their play and helping them sort out social problems with others. However, we are often hesitant to intervene when it comes to situations involving the children and their families. We ask, "Is this my business? Should I be involved?" Sometimes it is difficult to decide if a situation has become a crisis and needs professional intervention. You might learn about a particular problem when the child is first enrolled or later, when the child or the child's parent says something to you about it. **As a rule of thumb, when you feel the child's physical or emotional development is in jeopardy, you have a responsibility to take further action.**

Generally speaking, if it concerns the child, it is your business. Children can't learn and benefit from the program when distracted by traumatic events in their lives. When you help a child with a problem, you become closer to the child. You can also help a child get on track mentally and emotionally while supporting and strengthening the family. You are the child's advocate.

Teachers say, "I don't want to make the situation worse by saying or doing the wrong thing." It is natural to worry about this. Here are a couple of things to keep in mind:

Realize that you don't have to be perfect. If you sense that you did the wrong thing, try again. Children respect honesty. You can say, "You know, I'd like to go back to what we said about.... I've had a few more thoughts about it."

Remember that you are not alone. When faced with a difficult or sensitive issue, always work as part of a team with other concerned individuals in your organization and community.

BE PART OF A TEAM

Synergism is an exciting concept. Basically, it is the idea that the whole is more than the sum of the parts. When people work together on a problem, exciting things can happen. With collaboration, you might accomplish things that no one could have accomplished working independently.

WORK WITH YOUR SUPERVISOR

It is important to work with your supervisor. Everyone involved with the family should be informed of the situation and what you think should be done. **If you work in a child care center, your program supervisor and director should always be consulted before you take any action. Never just go off on your own, because:**

Your director or supervisor might have more information that sheds new light on the situation and might be able to recommend helpful resources.

You need the support of the administration. You might need time and resources to deal with the problem, as well as encouragement and moral support. In order to stand behind you, your administrator needs to be fully informed about the situation—what led you to certain conclusions and what you plan to do.

Your director needs to be kept informed. Keep your director and/or program supervisor fully apprised of the situation. Let them know about any special approaches that you think should be used, such as reading special books to the child or encouraging the child to talk about a problem. Find out how they would like you to keep them informed—with written reports, verbal reports or forms.

There may be legal implications. Your administrator needs to be informed whenever there is the possibility of irate parents or loss of enrollment.

You should go through the proper channels. Work first with your immediate supervisor. You will accomplish much more in the long run if you avoid stepping on toes.

Respected colleagues can provide a second opinion. You might say, "I think I'm seeing this. What do you think?"

If you are a family child care provider, you probably work independently. **Seek information and support from your professional family child care association** or other professional groups you belong to in your community. Often the child care licensing office or local child care resource and referral agency can provide advice or information.

WORK WITH OTHER PROFESSIONALS

"A little bit of knowledge is a dangerous thing." Learn where your educational expertise ends and the specialized expertise of other professionals begins. As one early childhood teacher aptly stated, "I know what the norm looks like and when something seems unusual, but I don't know how to pinpoint a problem." Often parents will ask you for advice and referrals. In the Who Can Help section, we have listed the types of professionals to seek out for further assistance. Also check out the organizations and hot lines listed at the end of each chapter. Many national organizations are aware of local resources.

LEARN WHO'S OUT THERE

The first step in making a referral is knowing what each type of professional does and who is available in your community. Is this a problem for a pediatrician, a psychologist or a social worker?

Many families bring all problems to their child's pediatrician or family practitioner. If the doctor knows the child and the family well, this may be a good place to start. However, sometimes pediatricians only look at the medical side of a situation and fail to take the social and emotional aspects of the problem into consideration.

The following are types of professionals in your community who may be helpful.

- ◆ Health professionals: pediatricians, family practitioners, nurse practitioners, pediatric dentists.
- ◆ Public safety professionals: law enforcement officers, firefighters.
- ◆ Mental health professionals: child psychologists, social workers, family therapists, grief counselors.
- ◆ Regulatory agencies: child care licensing agents, health department inspectors.

♦ Educational and special needs professionals: public school Child Find personnel, school psychologists, physical therapists, occupational therapists, speech and hearing therapists.

♦ Local county or state social services agencies, child care licensing offices or child care resource and referral offices may be good starting points. Agency staff generally know of other services in the area and may also be able to provide specific information.

Compile a list of these professionals to have ready when needed.

FIND OUT FROM COMMUNITY PROFESSIONALS

♦ **The scope of their services**—who they serve and what problems they deal with.

♦ **Fees for various services** and whether financial assistance is available for families who need it.

♦ **Proper procedures** for contacting them. Must clients be referred by some other agency? In many cases the parent must make contact directly.

♦ **How you can be helpful** when working with them. What information do they need to know about the case? How can you be part of the follow-up or support team and carry out recommended activities or interventions?

♦ **What kinds of strategies, resources and consultation services** can they provide for parents and educators?

GET TO KNOW THEM

While creating a list of professionals in your area is a good start, it is advisable to get to know some of these individuals. Talk to other parents or early childhood professionals who have worked with these individuals to gather opinions.

Try to develop a pleasant and mutually respectful relationship with these individuals. That will make future working relationships much easier. Speak to them as one professional to another, exploring ways to work together to assure the welfare of children and families in the community. Here are a few ways to get acquainted:

♦ **Invite them to the center** to see your program and meet the children.

♦ **Invite them to present a program** at a staff meeting, inservice training or parent education program.

◆ **Invite them to attend professional meetings** of state and local early childhood professional associations, possibly presenting a workshop.

Many centers prefer to keep a list of professionals as a service for parents and don't necessarily recommend a particular individual. You might say, "Many of our parents use this dentist," or "We have worked with this person before and found her to be very helpful," but make it clear that the parents must choose the person they will feel most comfortable with.

USE GOOD PROBLEM SOLVING TECHNIQUES

Whether you and other staff members choose to work on a problem within your own organization or to involve professionals outside your organization, it helps to be systematic in your actions as you proceed. Here are some general problem solving strategies that work in most situations.

DEFINE THE PROBLEM

What is really concerning you? Try to get it down on paper in a succinct description. As you become more informed and insightful, you can go back and rewrite the description.

GATHER THE TEAM

Pull everyone together who is involved with the problem, including the lead teacher, any assistants, teachers from other classrooms who might be with the child for certain times of the day, the program supervisor or director, the parents and possibly other family members and any other professionals already dealing with the child.

GATHER INFORMATION

From the child's record and from other team members who are acquainted with the family, gather as much factual information about the situation as possible.

LEARN

Find out all you can about the topic or problem in general. Read and talk to other professionals. What does the research say? How do other children and families respond? What types of action have been successful for others?

SHARE INSIGHTS AND BRAINSTORM

Make sure you are all seeing the same thing. Does someone have a different viewpoint? List possible things to try. As you plan for possible activities and interventions see chapter 23 on curriculum and other chapters on specific crises. You will need to ask yourselves, "How can we help both this child and the other children in the group?"

DEVELOP A PLAN OF ACTION

From the list of options you developed while brainstorming, decide **what** you will try first, and **who** will do **what** and **when**.

KEEP OTHERS INFORMED

Decide how you will keep the people involved aware of any progress.

SET A TIME TO RECONVENE AND EVALUATE

If all goes well and the plan achieved the desired results, congratulate each other. If it didn't work as well as you had hoped, go back to the "drawing board" and decide together what to try next.

KEEP GOOD RECORDS

Document all of your meetings. Note the date and the people involved, decisions made, interventions tried and results obtained. This can be useful if future intervention is necessary, or if you ever need to explain what you did.

PRACTICE PROFESSIONAL ETHICS

When you are involved in children's lives you are often forced to make judgments about how to act. Sometimes the answers are not clear. You have responsibilities to your employer, to the child's family, to the other families served, to your funding sources, to the child and to yourself. Sometimes there are conflicting interests.

It is a great help if you have colleagues, such as your director or program supervisor, whom you trust and respect and with whom you can discuss the issue. It also helps if you have had opportunities to develop guidelines for responsible behavior ahead of time. The topic of ethics should be part of every early childhood teacher's education as well as job orientation.

The National Association for the Education of Young Children has developed a *Code of Ethical Conduct*, referenced at the end of this chapter, with input from early childhood professionals all over the country. These principles will help guide you as you decide what to do in any given circumstance.

Two major ethical considerations to keep in mind when you deal with children in crisis situations are:

The well-being of the child should come first in all considerations. The law requires that you report abuse or suspicion of abuse in any form. If you feel that the agencies that handle abuse cases do not do so adequately, you and your colleagues have an ethical responsibility to take steps to bring this to public attention so that the situation can be corrected.

Guard the privacy of the people involved. Confidentiality is critical. Only those directly involved with the problem should know the details. When others—such as substitute teachers or staff from other rooms in the center—are with the child, decide how much they need to know in order to interact appropriately. Do not pry into family affairs that do not pertain to the situation at hand. Only situations that affect the child directly or indirectly should be discussed. If other parents hear you gossiping, they are likely to conclude that you will also talk about them and might be hesitant to confide in you if they need help in the future.

There will be many times in your career when you will have to rely on your own personal and professional ethics to decide a course of action, such as when you and a parent disagree about discipline, when you question the actions of a colleague, when a child reveals that something illegal is going on at home, and when a parent uses you to unload personal problems.

WORK WITH THE FAMILY

You cannot help the child during a crisis without working with the family. An important aspect of the teacher's role is to help strengthen the bond between the parent and the child. Child care providers and teachers are temporary influences in children's lives. The family is there for keeps. Making families more effective is the best way to help children. Each chapter has specific suggestions for working with the parents. Here are some general principles:

DEVELOP A RAPPORT WITH THE PARENTS

Parents need to feel your respect before they can hear your suggestions and advice, starting with the very first meeting you have with them.

Take your time with the intake interview. Both the child's teacher and the director should be involved. Naturally, there will be forms to fill out and policies to go over, but take time to let parents tell you about themselves and their child. Every child is special. Ask them what is special about their child. Show your interest. Ask them what their goals are for their child and how they hope their child will benefit by attending the program. Use this opportunity to make them feel welcome in the facility. Discuss the ways you intend to communicate with them—daily notes, occasional phone calls, regularly scheduled parent conferences and special meetings whenever you or the parents feel the need.

Communicate the message that you consider this a team effort. Many early childhood teachers are surprised to learn that parents are often intimidated by them. Parents consider the teacher an expert on young children. They are in awe of their ability to get a whole group of children to cooperate when they can barely handle just one child. Some parents may know that they have real problems parenting this little human being and suspect that you see right through them. Communicate to them that while you know about child development in general and have training in handling groups of children, you feel they are the expert on this particular child. Together you can make good things happen for this child.

In addition to the intake interview, it is worth the time and effort it takes to get to know parents in relaxed social settings, such as picnics and spaghetti suppers. When adults have spent time together in friendly social surroundings it is easier to address problems when they arise.

HELP THE FAMILY WITH SEPARATION ISSUES

It is natural for parents and their children to have difficulty parting from each other, especially before they have an internalized reason to trust you. The adult can rationalize the separation and, of course, knows that it is temporary, but the child is losing his framework of trust and is entering a strange and exciting (but also frightening) new arena. If there has been a trauma in the family's life, separation can be particularly difficult, and the family will need sensitive support from you.

Encourage the parent to visit with the child and stay most of the morning. Some children eagerly join right in, but other children need a longer time to adjust. Most programs are now eager to work with parents as long as necessary, encouraging the parents to stay with the child for part of the day and gradually lengthen the times of separation until the child feels totally comfortable. While we naturally concentrate on the distress of the child, don't forget to offer empathy to the parent who may be better at masking emotions.

All of the following techniques have helped children through the adjustment process.

◆   **A transitional object** such as a favorite stuffed animal or a security blanket can help the child feel more secure in the new setting.

◆   **An object that belongs to the parent** such as a scarf, an old wallet, even an extra set of car keys can provide comfort by reassuring the child that the parent really is coming back.

◆   **Take a photo of the parent**, or have the parent bring in one. Place it on the wall at the child's eye level, where the child can go over to it, touch it, talk to it. Or laminate it and let the child carry it around all day. You could also punch a hole in it and pin it to the child's clothing.

◆   **Allow the child to telephone the parent** at work or elsewhere. At that time the parent can say, "I still love you, and I will be back for you."

◆   **Let the child pretend to call the parent** on a toy telephone. You play the part of the parent and answer from another toy telephone. This game of pretend will reassure the child that you, the teacher, know that she misses her parent and respect that feeling.

◆   **Let the child dictate a note to the parent**, telling the parent how he misses her and wants to be with her. Do not edit what the child wants to say. Give the note to the parent while the child is present. Again, this shows respect for the child's feelings.

◆   **Take a photo of the child having fun**. Give the picture to the parents. This will help the parents realize that the child was not miserable all day. The parents can use the picture to talk to the child about the fun she is having at the center.

◆   **Send a picture of yourself home with the child**. By putting it on the refrigerator or in the child's room, parents can use it to show the child that they like and trust you.

CONSIDER HOME VISITS

Home visits can help tremendously. Even if it is not possible for you to visit all the children in the program, consider visiting any child who exhibits intense anxiety at separation time. Explain to the parents that you are not coming over to check out their living quarters or conduct any type of inspection. Your purpose is to develop rapport with the child on his home turf, where he feels safe. While there you can meet the other family members and pets. Parents often feel more comfortable talking about their child over a cup of tea in their own kitchen. You also have the opportunity to present yourself as a supportive friend rather than the all-knowing educator.

BE AN INTERPRETER FOR THE CHILD

Often this means helping parents learn to see things from the child's perspective. You can offer insights and observations about how the child is reacting to a situation, sharing your knowledge of child development. Sometimes children will reveal feelings to you that they are unable to express at home. If you have a good relationship with the parents and they see you as having the child's interest at heart, you can easily share your insights with them. If a problem or crisis arises, you can call the parents, talk to them when they pick up the child or set up a parent conference. Discuss options with your director.

HELP PARENTS ADDRESS THE ROOT PROBLEM

Supporting parents might also mean getting them the help and intervention they need to become better parents. This is especially true in situations involving child abuse and substance abuse. In these cases, intervention is most often initiated by the administration of the program, in conjunction with other community resources. You can help by bringing the situation to the attention of the director.

Denial of the problem can be a strong obstacle to overcome. Remember that you can't do much about a problem until the parent admits there is one. When the problem or crisis is beyond their control, such as the death of a family member or a natural disaster, parents often welcome help and support. When parents are responsible for the problem, as in instances of abuse or neglect, finding the most effective way to intervene is more difficult.

TRY NOT TO BE JUDGMENTAL

Sometimes this requires overcoming your own feelings of resentment or even outrage at the actions of the parent. Seek support and personal advice when dealing with these emotions. Many centers are developing staff support groups to help employees cope.

When working with families, always focus on the mutual circle of concern for the child. Assume that parents do love their children. Talk to parents from the point of view of the child.

PROVIDE RESOURCES

Recognize the credibility of the written word. People often believe something if they see it in print, even though you are telling them the same thing. It's a good idea for child care programs to have a resource library with a variety of good books or pamphlets on hand to loan to parents. Have a list of books to recommend. Remember that parents are less likely to use resources if they have to go to a library or book store. The resource section of each chapter lists books that will be helpful to both parents and educators.

BE A GOOD LISTENER

Finally, don't feel that you always have to have advice or suggestions to offer the parent. Sometimes just listening to the parent talk is the most appropriate action.

ENJOY THE REWARDS

While many early childhood teachers list working with parents as one of the more difficult and frustrating aspects of their jobs, they also see it as one of the most rewarding. When you help families function effectively, you have a positive influence on a whole circle of people, and the effects last long after the child has left your program.

FOCUS ON THE CHILDREN

Your main function is to support the child by answering questions and giving information in appropriate ways to increase the child's understanding and emotional well-being. The curriculum chapter (see chapter 23) contains many strategies and activities to allow children to express themselves and be heard. Here are a few principles to keep in mind.

LEARN TO OBSERVE

The better you know the children, the more you can help them. Take time during your busy day to observe what is happening with the children. Be systematic in the way you observe. One way is to observe a different child each day. All day long, while you are engaged in other activities, follow this child with your eyes. When you get a chance, make notes about where the child chose to play, with whom, for how long, the child's use of language, conflicts that arose, and any other events of the day. If you do this, each child in your group will have an in-depth observation about every two weeks. Over time, you will learn a lot about that child's personality, skills, interests and play preferences. This will give you a good base line for comparison if a crisis occurs.

Date all observations and keep them in a notebook with a divider for each child, or keep a file folder for each child in the group. Of course, you can add notes and anecdotes at any time when something interesting happens.

When a crisis occurs in a child's life, be conscious of the child's behaviors, not just her words. Also be conscious of the content of play episodes, drawings, or stories. But be careful not to over interpret. Is the child using red paint because she is angry or just because she likes red? Is she loud and rambunctious as a response to tension, or is she just imitating the play of friends? When you overhear unusual play themes in the dramatic play area, make a note but try not to jump to conclusions.

BE ACCESSIBLE TO THE CHILD

The most important thing you can do to help the child during a crisis is to encourage him to talk about his feelings or to act them out through play so he can better understand them.

When you know the child has experienced some sort of crisis or trauma, learn as much as you can about what happened. Find out what the family has told the child, and what has already transpired between the child and adults who are close to her so you can be supportive.

Teachers often wonder if they should bring up the topic if the child doesn't do so spontaneously. Generally it is best to follow the child's lead and respond to any questions the child has. Sometimes just letting the child know that you know about the situation is helpful. Offer to talk about it any time the child wants to. You might bring up the topic in a neutral, nonpersonal way. For example, read a book about a similar problem to a small group, or have a puppet describe a similar situation in his life.

Stop what you're doing if the child brings up a tender topic. There will be more opportunities for this to happen in a loosely structured program with much free play time. If it is really not possible to interrupt what you are doing, make a date with the child. "I can't stop and talk to you right now, but let me clean this up, and then I really want to hear what you have to say. We can go over and sit under the tree and talk." Afterwards, thank the child for talking to you about what she had on her mind and tell the child that if she wants to talk again just to let you know.

Be conscious of nonverbal language. When a child says something, we sometimes involuntarily roll our eyes or send messages over their heads to other adults. Think about how this affects children—it can add to the pain and shame they feel. They learn quickly that some things should not be mentioned.
They may even feel that their problem should be a family secret.

In conversation with the child, remember good listening techniques.

- ◆ **Give the child time** to express himself and don't interrupt.
- ◆ **Paraphrase** what the child had to say so the child knows she was heard correctly.
- ◆ **Let the child know it's okay to have those feelings**, that feelings should not be a cause of shame.
- ◆ **Help the child feel that he is not alone**, that other children have felt like that in similar circumstances.
- ◆ **Avoid judgmental statements** such as "You shouldn't feel that way," or "I'm sure he didn't mean that."
- ◆ **Don't worry if you don't know the answer** to a child's questions.

It can be hard to know how to respond sometimes. Turning the question back to the child, "What do you think?" is one way to see what the child needs. If you don't know the answer, say so. Hedda Sharapan, in the booklet *Talking with Young Children About Death* (referenced in chapter 6 about death), suggests that a good question to ask children to get them talking is, "What do you wonder about?" Offer sympathy. Help put things in perspective. Be there. Be safe. Be accepting of the child's full range of emotions.

RECOGNIZE WHEN TO SEEK HELP

One important role of the early childhood teacher is to notice when something is not right with the child. When others in the child's life are distracted by traumatic events, they are less likely to notice subtle changes in the child's demeanor or behavior. The early childhood teacher, who is often with the child most of his waking hours, can notice changes and help the parents and others respond appropriately.

Sometimes it is hard to differentiate between a behavior that simply represents a normal phase of development or reaction of the child, and a behavior that indicates a more serious mental health problem that requires some professional intervention.

The When to Seek Help sections of the chapters in this book are sometimes repetitive. That is because children have a limited repertoire of behaviors to indicate that something is wrong. Their behaviors may indicate there is some type of problem, but you will have to probe further to figure out the specific problem. Because young children often cannot put into words what is bothering them, we have to be very astute in reading their behaviors. Common stress indicators in children include:

◆　**Regression**. Children under stress often revert to more immature behaviors, as though they were going back to a time when life felt safer. Among these behaviors are bed-wetting, loss of toilet habits, thumb sucking and baby talk. Keep in mind that regression in the face of stress is actually a normal reaction, not a pathological sign.

◆　**Change in behavior or mood**. A child might display uncustomary aggression, defiance, or conversely, become overly clinging and whining.

◆　**Depression**. A depressed child might lose interest in what is going on around him and isolate himself or be overly inhibited during activities or discussions.

◆　**Low self-esteem**. If a normally confident child seems to suddenly lack confidence or show low self-esteem, you need to investigate. Children display low self-esteem by giving up or crying easily, becoming frustrated very quickly, having frequent tantrums or behaving aggressively.

◆ **Unreasonable and extreme fears**. While almost all children develop some fears in the course of normal development, sometimes their fears are triggered by real events.

◆ **Problems with concentration**. When a child is overly worried about what is going on at home, she can find it difficult to sit through a circle time or complete a project.

◆ **Physical symptoms**. Stomach aches, head aches, inability to rest at rest time and sleeping too much are all symptoms of stress.

Practically all of these symptoms could be present in any child, and may be perfectly normal. So it is very important not to jump to conclusions. **The key is to know each child**. The operative word may be change. Is there a change in the child's behavior? Is the child displaying behaviors that are unusual for that child? It's like working on a puzzle. You need to find all the pieces and fit them together. You should have access to the records for each child in your care so that you know about her background and family situation, and what the child might have experienced before entering your care. Talk to people who know the child. When signs persist over a period of time and disrupt family life or normal classroom activities with peers, further action may be necessary.

Keep a journal. Make specific notes about the child's behaviors that concern you. Note exactly what the child did, the date, the time of day it occurred, who else was involved, how you responded and how the child responded. Sometimes a pattern will emerge that will give you clues. At the very least, you will have more specifics to discuss with the parent and other professionals. If you keep regular written observations of all of the children in your care, you will see more quickly when a change in behavior patterns occurs.

If you or the parent feel that the child is acting in extreme or unusual ways, seek help. The earlier you uncover problems, the sooner you can start to work effectively to resolve them with the child.

CONCLUDING THOUGHTS

Although many crises are the result of adult problems, children are deeply affected by them. Without sensitive adult intervention, clarification and talking, a child may suffer great psychological and cognitive damage as a result of the crisis. The early childhood teacher has, therefore, a dual focus. You have to deal with the child in your care, with the situation of the moment, responding in a way that will give the child strength and comfort. But you also have to look at the cause of the problem to prevent an ongoing string of crisis situations for the child. Within the context of your organization, you must also try to help the parent work on the problem. You can't do it all, of course. But you are likely to feel frustrated if you have no resources to offer the parent.

Remember that you are not trained to be a therapist. Getting involved in people's problems, analyzing their situation, offering advice can be seductive. It can make you feel competent and powerful, but it is not what you should be doing. Instead, educate yourself on the topic and realize that you are not alone. In your community, there are resources you can use and people you can turn to. Help the families in crisis connect with the professional help that they need.

Early childhood teaching is really a series of judgment calls. Every situation is different. There are no perfect answers. That is what makes teaching an art. The most important thing to get across to children is that people can survive hard times, and that you are there to help them.

RESOURCES

Child Care Law Center, 221 Pine Street, 3rd Floor, San Francisco, CA 94104. 415-394-7144. www.childcarelaw.org.

Feeney, Stephanie, and Kipnis, Kenneth. (1992). *Code of Ethical Conduct and Statement of Commitment*. Washington, DC: National Association for the Education of Young Children.

Katz, Lilian G., and Ward, Evangeline H. (1993). *Ethical Behavior in Early Childhood Education*. Washington, DC: National Association for the Education of Young Children.

CHAPTER 2

AVOIDING BURNOUT

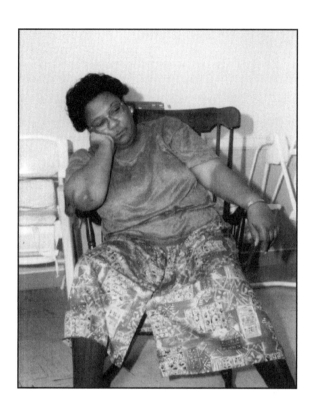

"In order for good things to happen for the children, good things have to happen for the staff."

This wise saying was expressed by Maureen Moreland, Executive Director of Parent and Child Services of Portland, Oregon. She maintains that people who work with children under stress need extra support to continue effectively in their jobs.

Sometimes people choose to work with young children because they believe childhood is a happy time of life and children are sweet, innocent, happy beings. These same people may be shocked when they realize this is not always so and may feel they must work all the harder to make everything right. When they discover they can't do that, disillusionment sets in.

Adults who work with children and families suffering from trauma can experience vicarious trauma. If the symptoms are ignored, these adults can experience serious psychological consequences, and programs can suffer from constant staff turnover, which seriously impacts the quality of their services.

Carol Brooks, co-director of the Women's and infant's Program, and Betsy Groves, Director of the Child Witness to Violence Program at Boston City Hospital, describe the effects of this vicarious traumatization on caregivers:

"It drains you. You feel incompetent. You feel frustrated and overwhelmed. You feel anger at the parents and families. You need a target or scapegoat for your anger. Anger at the department of social services is common. When you work with this type of family you begin to see this way of life as the norm. You feel 'survivor's guilt' in how you took your own good family for granted. You might have bad dreams, with a violent context. The boundaries of home and work may blur. It can affect your view of the world. You can feel helpless, hopeless and paralyzed."

Paula Jorde-Bloom, in the introduction to her book, *Avoiding Burnout: Strategies for Managing Time, Space and People in Early Childhood Education*, offers this definition of burnout:

"Burnout is a stubborn and elusive problem. It is characterized by a slow and progressive wearing down of the body and spirit. At its extreme, burnout has the power to render immobile otherwise healthy, competent individuals. Control slips away, the situation deteriorates, capacity to perform diminishes, and further stress results."

People working with children and families in crisis often feel that they are ineffective and wasting their time—that nothing they do makes a difference. They may feel unappreciated and unsupported. When people feel unprepared to deal with the situation, they also fear doing more harm than good and worry about being criticized. If many of the children in their care have severe problems, they can easily feel overwhelmed.

HOW PROGRAMS CAN HELP

It is not hopeless! There are things programs can do to support staff so they can develop personal and professional skills and strategies to address these problems head on.

PAY ATTENTION TO THE NEEDS OF STAFF

This seems like an obvious statement. However, when administrators encounter the enormity of problems faced by children and families, they sometimes fail to focus on their agents for change—the people working directly with the children. If you are a staff member feeling the threat of burnout, be your own advocate and talk to your supervisor. Tell your administrator what you need. Make some practical suggestions.

CONSCIOUSLY BUILD STAFF COHESIVENESS

When asked what keeps them in the field, people who have worked with young children for many years usually say first how much they enjoy working with the children. Often the next thing they talk about is their respect and affection for their coworkers. Family child care providers also often mention the warm and lasting friendships they have formed with other providers. The importance of this aspect of working in an early childhood setting cannot be overstated.

Friendships formed in the work place are personally and professionally rewarding. Adults working with stressed children need each other for a sanity check and general moral support. An empathetic look from across the room can do wonders to keep someone going. There are many ways to develop this.

Programs should have regular, weekly staff support meetings to evaluate and discuss events of the past week. Discussion should go beyond the mechanics of running a program, such as keeping the supply closet clean and preparing for the next parent event. Many administrators of programs with families in crisis have emphasized the importance of developing support groups among staff to discuss feelings and difficult situations that have developed.

Staff play days and retreats are a good idea. It is important to take time just to be together, have fun together, appreciate each other as individuals, outside of your professional roles. Laughing together makes it easier to communicate in times of stress. Staff members of the Parent and Child Services in Portland, Oregon take two such days a year in addition to their ongoing staff support groups. They have planned such events as a day-long riverboat cruise. Executive Director, Maureen Moreland, reports that such events are well worth the time and money spent.

When problems do arise among staff, inevitable in almost any early childhood program, do not ignore them and hope they will go away. Address problems and conflicts in positive, respectful ways. *Child Care Information Exchange* magazine (listed in the resource section at the end of the chapter) frequently has articles on supporting staff in their roles.

CLARIFY EXPECTATIONS

The seeds of burnout are often in what motivates people to help and expectations people have for themselves. It is not uncommon for people in the early childhood profession to have a "save the world complex." When expectations are too high, feelings of disappointment and disillusionment in the organizations and individuals around us can result.

Having a sense of mission helps. Does your school or center have a mission statement to describe why the organization exists and what you hope to accomplish? Working together to develop a mission statement can be a powerful way to build staff cohesiveness and mutual respect. Steven Covey's book, *First Things First*, describes a useful process of developing personal and professional mission statements. If you have a clear and realistic idea of what you expect to accomplish, you will be better able to measure your success and pat yourself on the back when you need to.

HAVE A PLAN

Just as you would prepare for a possible fire or other disaster, work as a group to develop a plan for how you will handle any crisis that may come up for a family or child. Who will do what? What people in the community would be available to you? What resources do you have? Being prepared can go a long way toward reducing the inherent stress in any situation.

Develop a crisis contact list of people and resources in the community for various crises addressed in this book. You could use this book as an outline to develop a "Just in Case" list.

HOW INDIVIDUALS CAN HELP

REMEMBER, YOU ARE NOT ALONE

First you need the support of your director and other staff members. Also, as mentioned in the chapter on the caregiver's role (see chapter 1), when you work with children and families, you should take advantage of the network of community professionals in related fields. Find out who else is working to support the needs of this family. Ask to be part of the team. Although this may take some extra time on your part, it may make you much more effective and less frustrated.

If you are a family child care provider, be sure to take advantage of your local professional association to put you in contact with other providers and services available to you.

PAY ATTENTION TO YOUR EMOTIONS

Remember that people must start with themselves when they develop strategies to deal with a crisis. It is essential to deal with the unfinished business you have on a personal level before you can be fully effective and professional in working with the children and families.

Working with children who are experiencing various crises or trauma in their lives sometimes reminds caregivers of painful experiences in their own childhoods. Talking about them in a support group with other staff can be very helpful. As suggested in many of the chapters, inviting a professional to speak about the psychological dynamics of many of the issues can help you understand yourself. If the problem is very painful, perhaps now is the time to join a support group or engage in therapy to come to terms with a painful past. Teachers have to first come to terms with their own feelings about these issues before they can help children.

Sometimes the most difficult situations to deal with professionally are those we have dealt with successfully in our own lives. We may be impatient with people who stay mired in the situation rather than taking corrective action, as we have. These close to home situations are also painful reminders of our own previous suffering. While we keenly empathize with someone's problem, we may be frustrated and impatient in allowing them to go through the process of solving it. Even worse is when they choose not to go through the process and stay stuck.

While keeping confidentiality and professional ethics in mind, seek out a level-headed and trustworthy colleague to discuss your concerns. This might be your director or program supervisor. Talking things out can clarify the situation and give you greater understanding and insight into what is going on. You need to be able to test and measure your responses against someone else.

KNOWLEDGE IS POWER

Educate yourself about the issues. The more you know, the more options you will have. Polly Ferraro, Director of Child Development Services at Port Hueneme Naval Base, says, "I nurture my staff by giving them training to get the skills they need to be successful with children."

Remember that there are many ways to learn. Some possibilities:

◆ Take a class.
◆ Attend conferences and workshops.
◆ Bring consultants in to talk with staff.
◆ Read articles, pamplets and books.
◆ Call local professionals and ask questions.
◆ Call hot lines and local contacts for advice.
◆ Visit other programs.
◆ Observe others in action.

ALL YOU CAN DO IS YOUR BEST!

Make all your decisions based on the best information you have at the time. Knowing you have given a situation your best effort allows you to rest easier.

Keeping a journal can be a very useful process, both in developing a systematic approach to a situation and giving yourself peace of mind. When you observe a child carefully, take notes on what activites you've tried and why. You will be able to look back and see how far the child has come.

If the situation does not improve, you will at least be able to see that you acted professionally. Your journal will help you analyze what went wrong and determine if there is anything you should do differently if you are confronted with a similar situation in the future.

DO SOMETHING

Be proactive. Combat the feeling of impotency by doing something that might contribute to correcting the situation, even if what you do is a small thing.

You can't solve all the problems of poverty or racism in this country, but you can improve life for one child or one family. Together with other staff you might have a clothing drive or raise funds for food or other assistance needed by families you serve.

BE AN ADVOCATE

While you recognize that you can't save the world, you can be part of a network of professionals and concerned adults that make up a larger voice. Join your local and national professional organizations such as the National Association for the Education of Young Children (NAEYC) or the National Family Child Care Association (NAFCC) and be supportive of their advocacy efforts both nationally and locally.

A sense of futility at not being able to alter society's course of direction can be a prime burnout factor. It makes us angry, and we want to blame someone or some institution. Rather than criticizing others, it is better to focus on the search for solutions. It's more helpful to look forward than backward.

One powerful way to advocate for children is to tell real stories either about how children benefited from skillful intervention or about how the system failed a child. The public—taxpayers and legislators—tend to respond better when a human face is put on the problem. Bea Romer, NAEYC Governing Board member and first lady of Colorado, reminds us that legislators are themselves parents and grandparents, and they care.

Often child care providers worry that they are doing more harm than good by reporting child abuse or domestic violence as they are mandated to do by law, because there is improper follow through. The child may be withdrawn from the program by angry parents and therefore experience the loss of a social network. If this happens, let people know about it, don't just accept it quietly. Talk to the agency involved. Request that the child remain in your program. Depending on the circumstances, let the funding sources—the legislators, the city officials, the tax payers—know. Write letters to the newspaper (always respecting the confidentiality of the children and family involved).

Also share the successes. A spontaneous letter to a legislator letting him or her know about how certain moneys have been spent to improve the lives of children can create further motivation to support such issues in the future.

TAKE CARE OF YOURSELF

There are many fine resources available on personal stress management. Proper diet, exercise and rest are all extremely important in maintaining physical and mental stamina. If you start to feel guilty about the time it takes to guard your own health, remember—if you give out, you're not doing anyone any good.

If you suffer some of the physical symptoms of stress such as stomachaches, headaches, heart palpitations and shortness of breath, your body is trying to tell you something important. Pay attention to these symptoms and see if you can find ways to deal constructively with them.

BUILD YOUR OWN PERSONAL POWER

The most important way to develop more power is to acquire more knowledge. It helps you assert yourself and act decisively. One wonderful resource is Maria Arapakis' book, *Softpower! How to Speak Up, Set Limits, and Say No Without Losing Your Lover, Your Job or Your Friends*.

INCLUDE TIME FOR PLAY

Realize that play has the same value for adults as for children. It can release tension and give us new ways to express ourselves. Have adult toys to play with in the teachers' lounge. You might include jigsaw puzzles, crossword puzzles and desk toys. Playing games helps avoid mental overload from stress and allows your mind to take a refreshing break.

Consider art therapy. Have art materials available in the lounge—fun stuff to doodle with. One group of teachers had a whole art corner set up in their lounge where they could finger paint, paint on an easel and draw to their heart's content. Their creations were proudly displayed on the wall and in the staff bathroom.

The staff bathroom is often the "humor center." Use a graffiti board or bulletin board to hold cartoons, philosophical sayings, compliments and other mood boosters.

Share the giggles and goosebumps, the funny and heart-warming things that happen every day. One director started each staff meeting by requiring that everyone share a giggle or a goosebump. Not only did this start the meeting off on a positive note, but knowing that they would have to come up with something, staff members found they were consciously looking for these moments and writing them down. This kept everyone in a more positive frame of mind.

Some schools and centers have a "Good Morning Book." Each staff person reads the page for the day when they sign in. The page tells them of any special events coming up that day or other details they should all know. You might include humorous sayings, cartoons and philosophical quotes for all to share. It's one more small thing that lends support.

STRIVE FOR SOME BALANCE

In can be difficult, but it is important not to let your work take over your whole life.

As a fun exercise, make a list of things you enjoy doing and that help you relax. The more the better. A good massage can do wonders! A long walk, a bubble bath, reading a novel, playing with the dog, playing a vigorous game of racquetball, painting a picture, playing the piano—all are examples of things people came up with that they find both enjoyable and relaxing. Doing these things is not self-indulgence. It is survival! Make a date with yourself at least once a week, and every day if possible, to do something that you enjoy. You deserve it!

While you're at it, develop your own support network. Personal relationships outside of work can be very nurturing and healing, helping you keep everything in perspective.

ANALYZE WHAT WENT RIGHT

When we work with stressed children and families in crisis, we ask ourselves many questions: "Did I handle this well?" "Was this activity really helpful?" "Why did that parent say that?" "What was going on with this child this morning?" "Did I really make a positive difference for this family?"

These questions are inevitable, and they help us to analyze and do our professional best. But don't forget to balance this self-analysis with self-praise. "Last year, this child was afraid to talk. Today he interviewed older kids about friendship." "Because of me, these children had a good morning and enjoyed laughter, music and creative play." "I helped this mother make a decision that will turn her life around."

We very rarely sit down and systematically analyze what went right. But you should identify strategies that seemed to work and give yourself the well-deserved pat on the back.

CONCLUSION

Don't accept burnout as a fact of professional life. It doesn't have to be. Instead, pay attention to the things that wear you down and address them individually and with your colleagues. Notice and value all the things that keep you going and keep you excited about your work. Keep growing, keep trying, keep laughing.

RESOURCES

STRESS MANAGEMENT AND BURNOUT-RELATED BOOKS

Arapakis, Maria. (1990). *Softpower! How to Speak Up, Set Limits, and Say No Without Losing Your Lover, Your Job, or Your Friends*. New York: Warner Books, Inc. The issue of assertiveness is updated in this book. While written with women in mind, there is much general wisdom for men as well. There is even a section called, "Letting go, cutting your losses to move on," which addresses life problems familiar to all.

Covey, Stephen R., Merrill, Roger A., and Merrill, Rebecca R., (1994). *First Things First*. New York: Simon & Schuster. This book goes beyond time management to life management. Philosophical and inspiring, it helps individuals anchor their values and priorities in life, with many useful exercises.

Hageseth, Christian. (1988). *A Laughing Place: The Art and Psychology of Positive Humor in Love and Adversity*. Fort Collins, CO: Berwick Publishing Company. Exploring the power of positive humor, the book is really an exercise in a positive approach to life. Fun to read and useful in daily life.

Hillman, Carolynn. (1992). *Recovery of Your Self-Esteem: A Guide for Women. New Techniques and Understanding for Women Who Want to Feel Better About Themselves More of the Time*. New York: Simon & Schuster. This book guides the reader through a process of self-discovery, with a particularly useful section, "Nurturing yourself in difficult situations."

Jorde-Bloom, Paula. (1982). *Avoiding Burnout: Strategies for Managing Time, Space and People in Early Childhood Education*. Washington, DC: Acropolis Books Ltd. Especially appropriate for program directors, this management book addresses the problems of everyday stress in serving children and families.

Kirsta, Alix. (1986). *The Book of Stress Survival: Identifying and Reducing the Stress in Your Life*. New York: Simon & Schuster. A comprehensive stress manual covering a wide range of topics, this book is attractive, easy to read and practical. It includes relaxation techniques, nutrition, dealing with problems, time management and meditation.

Schaef, Anne Wilson. (1990). *Meditations For Women Who Do Too Much*. New York: Harper San Francisco. The book is designed to read one page each day through the year and provides interesting thoughts for reflection. It is one way to nurture yourself and help keep things in perspective.

ADVOCACY RESOURCES

Goffin, Stacie G., and Lombardi, Joan. (1989). *Speaking Out: Early Childhood Advocacy*. Washington, DC: National Association for the Education of Young Children. A treasure of a book giving many practical starting points for having influence beyond the four walls of your program. It includes directions for how to write to legislators, and gives many actual examples of successful advocacy stories. Empowering!

Hatkoff, Amy, and Klopp, Karen K. (1992). *How to Save the Children: An Innovative Resource Guide Filled With Practical Ideas to Counter the Effects of Poverty and Neglect on America's Children*. New York: Simon & Schuster. A terrific book that shares hundreds of ways individuals can make a difference in the lives of children in large and small ways. It also lists national support agencies and numerous resources.

Schorr, Lisbeth B. (1988). *Within Our Reach*. New York: Doubleday and Company, Inc. This excellent resource contains ammunition that comprehensive programs for serving high risk families are effective and cost effective. Many successful programs are described, also giving you possible leads for people to talk to who have addressed similar problems.

Edelman, Marian Wright. (1992). *The Measure of Our Success: A Letter to My Children and Yours*. Boston: Beacon Press. This book is listed because of the inspiring professional and personal example of Marian Wright Edelman's work, and what she has accomplished in advocacy for young children.

MAGAZINE

Child Care Information Exchange, P.O. Box 2890, Redmond, WA 98073. This bi-monthly publication regularly publishes excellent articles on staff motivation and other staff management issues. Yearly indexes of all topics covered appear in their November issues. Subscription rate is $35 per year.

ARTICLE

Brooke, Gretchen, E. "My personal journey toward professionalism." *Young Children*. 49(6), September 1994, 69-71. The author describes the process she experienced in identifying herself as a professional. She specifically notes what happened that gradually made her feel professional.

PAMPHLET

The Full Cost of Quality Care. (1990). National Association for the Education of Young Children, 1509 Sixteenth Street, NW, Washington, DC 20036-1426. 800-424-2460. www.naeyc.org. This pamphlet is designed to familiarize parents and community leaders with the Full Cost of Quality campaign. $.50 per copy. Quantity discount $10 for 100 copies.

ORGANIZATIONS

National Association for the Education of Young Children (NAEYC), 1509 16th Street, NW, Washington, DC 20036-1426. 800-424-2460. www.naeyc.org.

National Association for Family Child Care (NAFCC), 5202 Pinemont Drive, Salt Lake City, UT 84123-4607. Accreditation information: 800-359-3817.
Membership: 602-838-3446. www.nafcc.org.

2

PART

CRISIS BY CRISIS

CHAPTER 3

CHILD ILLNESS & HOSPITALIZATION

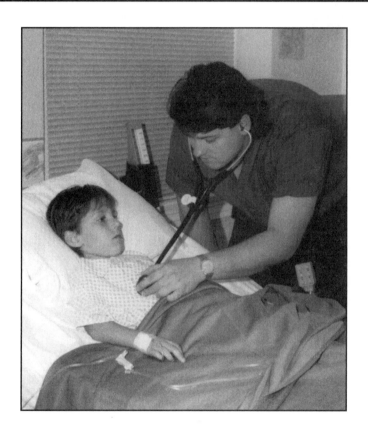

HERE'S AN EXAMPLE

Mark was first diagnosed with brain cancer as a four year old. Four years later, he is still alive, but has been in and out of the hospital numerous times and has also had a life-threatening bout with meningitis. When his hearing became impaired, his mother had to fight to keep him in his same school with all his friends, rather than have him transported to another town in their rural area where there was a special program for hearing-impaired children. She was successful. Throughout his illness, the support of his teachers and friends has made life worthwhile for him. The teachers and children benefited from seeing a video from the American Cancer Society to help them understand what was happening to Mark. The cassette tapes and large packages of cards and drawings they sent him while he was hospitalized made him feel like a valued part of the gang. Mark has learning problems and some behavior problems, however, he has a strong social network, many friends and feels valued and loved.

Illness & Hospitalization

ANOTHER CENTER DIRECTOR TELLS THIS STORY:

"My cook's eight year old son kept vomiting for no apparent reason. Finally after much medical investigation they did a CAT scan and found that he had a brain tumor. The surgeon took out as much as they could, but some of it was inoperable. Radiation caused him to lose his hair and he got huge and puffy. He was in a wheelchair for a while. He attended the center after school and in the summer when he felt well enough. The other children kept asking questions that were hard to answer: Why is he in a wheelchair? Why is he all puffy? Why did he lose his hair? Why does he have those stitches? The doctors gave him six months to live. When he told the other children he was going to die, the questions really started coming: Will I die too if I get sick? When I have the chicken pox does that mean I will die? Will I catch this from him and die? So I called the local number for the American Cancer Society and they came to the center and talked to the children about good cells and bad cells and what cancer cells are. They were a really good resource for us. We also found that the local hospital runs a similar service through their hospice unit. They have discovered that it is not only adults who need help in dealing with the reality of death and serious illness."

LET'S LOOK AT THE ISSUE

Any time a child is hospitalized is a stressful time for the family. The child will undoubtedly be anxious and may come face to face with some real fears. The parents' anxiety about their child's well-being as well as possible financial strains will also affect the hospitalized child and the other children in the family. The family routine is disrupted. One or both parents may have to take time off from work. If there are other children at home, they will miss their parents and have worries of their own. If the child is hospitalized over a long period of time because of a serious illness, the impact on the family will be even greater.

It used to be routine for hospital personnel to separate the child from the parent while most painful procedures were taking place. There has been much improvement in how hospitals consider the emotional well-being of both children and parents. Depending on the circumstances, parents are often allowed to stay with the child for comfort, even until the child is anesthetized in the operating room. Many hospitals allow a parent to sleep in the room with the child. Hospitals often offer preadmission visits to familiarize the child with his surroundings and explain all of the procedures he can expect. Play therapists or child life specialists often work with children ahead of time involving dramatic play with stuffed animals or other techniques to allow the child to play out fears and gain some sense of control. These measures are not universal, however.

In severe illnesses, such as cancer, where there are prolonged hospitalizations and repeated painful procedures, the child may suffer from Post-Traumatic Stress Disorder

(PTSD). The child, even when cured of the disease, may still suffer an emotional handicap, and the family may have lingering effects of anxiety, overprotectiveness and general stress.

Whether you are working with the child who anticipates or has recently endured a hospital stay, or for whom visits to the hospital are a regular part of his existence, or are working with other children in the family, there are things you can do to help the child and support the family.

INSIGHTS FROM CHILD DEVELOPMENT

Children feel helpless and vulnerable in a hospital. They are truly in a situation where they have no control or power. So they may act out—the one thing they have left—to show that they have power. Regression to younger behaviors is also a common and expected behavior.

Dramatic play is important. Children typically re-enact scenes from the doctor's office or hospital in their dramatic play. This is to be encouraged.

The child may think she caused the illness. The child might think she is ill because she was bad. Even if the child does not express this, it should be made clear to the child that she is not sick because of anything she did.

Children may ask the same questions over and over again.

Children understand little about how the body works. Children's ideas of what is inside their bodies are far from reality. Most of them think it is like an empty sack filled with blood, food and waste products. One common fear is that if there is a cut or an incision, everything inside of them will spill out.

Children need help with social relationships. Children who have been chronically ill for a long time and are now back with a peer group may need much help in social relationships. They have suffered social isolation from peers and have not had the practice of play and give-and-take with other children.

Other children may think the child's illness is contagious. Social development might also be impeded because other children think that they might catch the condition from the child.

The child's family may need help. As would be expected, how the parents cope with the child's illness has a great impact on how the child learns to handle the experience.

WHEN TO SEEK HELP

It is common for a child to want more attention and comfort after a hospital stay. For instance, they might become very particular about what they eat or what they will wear. A parent may think that the child is manipulative, but generally it's good to give the extra attention. However, if the parent feels that the child is not getting beyond the experience, and if, for that child it is unusual for the following things to occur, some professional counseling might be necessary.

◆ **Demands for attention.** The child's demands for attention and fear of separation seem excessive or continues longer than the situation seems to warrant.

◆ **Fears or sleep disturbances.** The child shows strong fears or continuing sleep disturbances.

◆ **Normal regression**—bed-wetting, loss of toileting habits, thumbsucking, baby talk—continues longer than the situation seems to warrant.

WHO CAN HELP

◆ Hospital play therapists and child life therapists
◆ Child psychologists
◆ The family's pediatrician
◆ Hospital social workers can help the families, especially in areas of financial concerns, and with other family needs.

HOW TO RESPOND

While it is certainly the parents' primary responsibility to prepare the child for the hospital stay, you also have a role helping prepare the child if the child is with you before the anticipated experience. Afterwards the child may be working through many of her recent experiences.

HOW TO RESPOND WITH THE STAFF

◆ **Learn about the condition**. Try to learn something about the child's condition so you have a better understanding yourself.

◆ **Communicate with the parents**. Find out from the parents what the child is going to experience so that you will be able to answer the child's questions honestly and sensitively.

HOW TO RESPOND WITH THE CHILD

◆ **Visit the child**. If the hospital stay is more than a day or two, a visit can be a wonderful way to say to the child and to the parents, "We care about you. You are important and cherished by all of us." You might bring pictures or homemade cards from the children.

◆ **Be honest with the child**. If the child asks you, don't tell the child that it won't hurt when it probably will hurt. It is better to say that it may hurt for a little while but the doctors and nurses will do everything they can to make the hurt go away as quickly as possible.

◆ **Acknowledge the child's fears**. Don't discount the child's fears by telling him there's nothing to worry about. Instead, let him talk about what worries him. Offer empathy, acknowledge his feelings and offer support.

◆ **Read a book to the child or to the group** about going to the hospital so the child knows she is not alone in what she is going through or in the feelings she is having.

◆ **Have a puppet, doll or stuffed animal** tell the children that he has to go to the hospital and he's frightened. See if the children know how to comfort the puppet. Let the puppet ask some of the questions and express some of the fears you suspect the child might have. If the child can put himself in the role of comforting the puppet, he might remember some of his own strategies later on. Perhaps the puppet could go to the hospital with him, or return to the group at the same time the child does. The puppet and the child can compare experiences.

◆ **Include appropriate accessories for dramatic play.** Small dolls and accessories depicting doctors, nurses, examining room equipment, ambulances and even wheelchairs are available. If you do not have or cannot purchase a set of these, perhaps you can improvise props and costumes for other small dolls. When children play with these small figures, the child becomes a giant, manipulating people and events in her imaginative play. This position of power can be of great benefit to a child.

◆ **Encourage dramatic play**. Provide dramatic play about hospitals and doctor visits. Include such things as play doctor's kits (either purchased or that you make up yourself), first aid kit supplies, examining tables, doctor's smocks, surgical masks, stuffed animals and dolls to be patients. Use this opportunity to incorporate literacy props into the children's play. Include magazines in the waiting room, clip boards, pamphlets from the doctor's office, prescription slips for the doctor to fill out, and, of course, checkbooks and receipts for when the parent pays the bill.

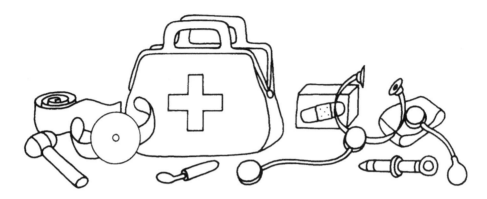

◆ **Help the child understand his illness.** Children need to learn basic facts about their illness, in ways they can understand, to reduce fears and imaginings.

◆ **Talk about how people show they care.** Ask the child to list all the people who care about him and help take care of him. Some will be family members, others will be health care providers, neighbors, friends and community people. Talk about relationships, how people help each other in many different ways.

◆ **Encourage the child's independence**. If a child has had a protracted illness, she may act more dependent than is appropriate for her age. Work on building independence skills—doing things for herself, helping you with classroom chores, and feeling satisfied at a job well done.

◆ **Support children's social interactions** by encouraging parallel playing, giving them ideas for how to enter play, and generally coaching them in social skills.

HOW TO RESPOND WITH THE OTHER CHILDREN

◆ **Send their greetings**. The children in the class could send their greetings to the hospitalized child by making a cassette tape recording of themselves. It might include a few of their circle time songs and poems.

◆ **Compile a book of photos**. A book made up of individual photos of their friends with dictated greetings from each child could cheer up a sick friend.

◆ **Make cards and drawings**. Encourage the children to make cards and drawings for their sick friend

◆ **Take a field trip to the hospital, emergency room or local medical clinic.** It can be interesting and beneficial for all children, even if no child in the group is anticipating a hospital stay. Many medical facilities now offer such tours. Meet with the people ahead of time to find out exactly what the tour entails. Talk about how children's questions might be handled. Ahead of time, make an experience chart letting children dictate to you what they already know about hospitals. This will let you know any misconceptions they have. You might read a book about the hospital or show them some pictures as well. Take a camera along on the trip. Afterwards, let children help you make a display of the photos you took and dictate what the captions should be. Focus on the helping and caring nature of the people they encounter. The more they know about what to expect, the less anxiety they will have.

◆ **Teach children about how their bodies work**. Then they can better understand when something goes wrong and needs to be fixed.

◆ **Discuss the child's condition**. In discussions with the other children in the group, stress that the child's condition is not catching and they cannot be harmed by playing with the child. Help them to understand some basic facts about the illness, if appropriate. You might involve the parents and the child himself to help explain to the other children what happened to him. Often they have the words worked out since they may have had to explain it many times before.

HOW TO RESPOND WITH THE PARENTS

◆ **Be supportive**. First just let the parents know that you are there to help, and tell them some of the things you might do in the classroom to prepare the child for the experience, or as follow-up activities.

◆ **Let them know about resources**. You may be able to let parents know about useful resources in helping to explain what lies ahead for the child.

◆ **Stay informed**. Ask parents to keep you informed about the child's condition.

WHERE TO FIND MORE INFORMATION

RESOURCES FOR CHILDREN

Books

Balter, Dr. Lawrence. (1990). Illustrated by Roz Schanzer. *Alfred Goes to the Hospital: Understanding a Medical Emergency*. New York: Barron's. A young boy, Alfred, has his appendix out in the hospital. The book shows Alfred's anxiety about going to the hospital and the procedures, including a blood test, before the operation—all handled respectfully by the nurse, with parents at his side. This book will help any child anticipating a hospital stay to know what to expect. All children, in fact, would find the book interesting. An informative section for adults is found at the back of the book.

Carlstrom, Nancy White. (1994). *Barney Is Best*. New York: HarperCollins. A child going to the hospital to have his tonsils removed insists on bringing a worn but beloved stuffed animal instead of a newer one.

Davidson, Martine. (1992). Illustrated by Marylin Hafner. *Maggie and the Emergency Room*. New York: Random House. Developed by the American Medical Association, this book shows what happens when a little girl needs stitches on her forehead.

Davidson, Martine. (1992). Illustrated by Nancy Stevenson. *Robby Visits the Doctor*. New York: Random House. Developed by the American Medical Association, this book describes a typical visit to the doctor by a young boy who has an ear infection.

Krisher, Trudy. (1992). Illustrated by Nadine Bernard Westcott. *Kathy's Hats: A Story of Hope*. Morton Grove, IL: Albert Whitman Publishers. Kathy's love of hats comes in handy when the chemotherapy treatments she receives for cancer make her hair fall out.

Lansky, Vicki. (1990). *Koko Bear's Earache: Preparing For Ear Tube Surgery*. Deephaven, MN: The Book Peddlers. Koko Bear goes through the process of having tubes put in his ears. Special notes are included for parents, to assist them in caring for children who need this procedure.

Pirner, Connie White. (1991). Illustrated by Nadine Bernard Westcott. *Even Little Kids Get Diabetes*. Morton Grove, IL: Albert Whitman Publishers. A little girl who has had diabetes since she was two years old describes her adjustments to the disease.

Roddie, Shen. (1993). Illustrated by Frances Cony. *Chicken Pox*. Boston: Little Brown and Company. A humorous look at chicken pox from a baby chick who suffers the discomfort of having chicken pox and tries everything to get rid of the itchy spots. Features movable tabs and flaps.

Rogers, Fred. (1986). *Going to the Doctor*. New York: Putnam Publishing Group. This book is a photo journal of a typical visit to the doctor; it will help children understand what to expect when they go to the doctor.

Rogers, Fred. (1988). *Going to the Hospital*. New York: Putnam Publishing Group. This book is a great way to give a child a chance to prepare for the experience of going to a hospital. It gives parents and/or caregivers and children a chance to talk about what to expect and offer reassurances. A book to read both before and after a hospital visit, for children to compare their story with the one in the book.

Sanford, Doris. (1992). *No Longer Afraid: Living With Cancer*. Sisters, OR: Questar Publishers. It may be hard to think of a children's book about cancer as uplifting—but this one is. Beautiful illustrations show a ten year old girl's progress through her illness, even receiving a horse from the Make a Wish Foundation. Though the story is about an older child, a young child would enjoy the book.

RESOURCES FOR ADULTS

Books

Bombeck, Erma. (1989). *I Want to Grow Hair, I Want to Grow Up, I Want to Go to Boise: Children Surviving Cancer.* NY: Harper & Row, Publishers, Inc. This is a heartwarming book about kids surviving cancer which includes stories of children who have every hope of living a full life. The book is a special gift edition prepared for the American Cancer Society, and is available free of charge to the families of children with cancer.

Rogers, Fred. (1983). *Mister Rogers Talks with Parents.* Winona MN: Hal Leonard Publishing Corporation. This general resource for parents has a chapter on hospitalization. Children's fears and general emotional development is one main theme of the book, so the chapter, read in the context of the whole book, is even better. The book is also available from Family Communications Inc., 4802 Fifth Avenue, Pitttsburg, PA 15213. 412-687-2990.

Booklets & Pamplets

American Cancer Society (ACS). *Back to School: A Handbook for Parents of Children with Cancer*, *Back to School: A Handbook for Teachers of Children with Cancer*, *Helping Children Understand: A Guide for a Parent with Cancer*, *What Happened to You Happened to Me* and *When Your Brother or Sister Has Cancer*. American Cancer Society, 1180 Avenue of the Americas, New York, NY 10036. 800-ACS-2345. www.cancer.org. A series of booklets available from the ACS which are written for parents, teachers and children. Some of the booklets have been written by children who have cancer. For a complete publications list call 800-ACS-2345 or your local chapter of the American Cancer Society.

Rogers, Fred. *When Your Child Goes to the Hospital*. Family Communications, Inc. 4802 Fifth Avenue, Pittsburgh, PA 15213. 412-687-2990. www.misterrogers.org. This eight-page booklet gives parents caring advice on ways to handle the situation ahead. It's a good resource to have on hand to give to parents. Your local hospital may have copies available to give to parents, or it can be ordered from Family Communications, Inc. The booklet is available in both English and Spanish. $.50 for individual copies. Bulk prices available.

Curriculum Materials

◆ **Plastic doll house people, furniture and accessories**, are available from school suppliers and in toy stores. Some include an impressive set of hospital play accessories—examining tables, wheelchairs, walkers and hospital beds.

◆ Most early childhood suppliers have **puppets that represent different occupations**. Such puppets will allow a child to role play people he is likely to encounter in his hospital experience.

◆ Most early childhood suppliers have **dress-up clothes** depicting nurses, doctors, police officers, and fire fighters as well as play doctor's kits.

Videos

Going to the Hospital, *Having an Operation*, *Wearing a Cast*, *A Visit to the Emergency Department* and *Going to the Doctor*, Family Communications, Inc., 4802 Fifth Avenue, Pittsburgh, PA 15213. 412-687-2990. www.misterrogers.org. Fred Rogers of Mister Rogers' Neighborhood television program has produced this series of five videos which are also available in Spanish. Most hospitals have the videos available for use with their child patients. There is also a series of three booklets, *Going to the Hospital*, *Having an Operation* and *Wearing a Cast* to accompany the videos. The videos are available from Family Communications, Inc.

Mister Rogers Talks About Childhood Cancer. Family Communications, Inc., 4802 Fifth Avenue, Pittsburgh, PA 15213. 412-687-2990. www.misterrogers.org. This video program and accompanying print materials for chil-dren and their parents feature Mister Rogers and familiar "Neighborhood" characters and puppets. The program for adults contains interviews by Fred Rogers with parents whose children have been treated for childhood cancer. This program is not on the consumer market but most cancer treatment centers have it. If not, it can be ordered from Family Communications, Inc.

No Fears, No Tears. American Cancer Society, 1180 Avenue of the Americas, New York, NY 10036. 800-ACS-2345. www.cancer.org. This video presents a range of technologies depicting how parents, professionals and children can work together to reduce anxiety and pain associated with painful procedures. The video is available from the local chapter of the American Cancer Society at a minimal cost. Call 800-ACS-2345 to obtain the number of your local chapter of the American Cancer Society.

When a Child Has Cancer: Helping Families Cope. American Cancer Society, 1180 Avenue of the Americas, New York, NY 10036. 800-ACS-2345. www.cancer.org. This video helps families cope with having a child who has cancer. It addresses all the stressful situations that the family may have to handle. The video is available from your local chapter of the American Cancer Society at a minimal cost. Call 800-ACS-2345 to obtain the number of your local chapter of the American Cancer Society.

Organizations & Hot Lines

Association for the Care of Children's Health, 3615 Wisconsin Avenue, Washington, DC 20016. The purpose of this organization is to ensure children's emotional well-being while they are being hospitalized. The organization has resources and supports available.

The Candlelighters Childhood Cancer Foundation (CCCF), PO Box 498, Kensington, MD 20895-0498. 301-962-3520. www.candlelighters.org. CCCF is a network of 155 self-help groups of parents of children with cancer which works to develop solutions to the problems of living with and treating childhood cancer. CCCF publishes a Youth Newsletter and a Quarterly Newsletter which may be received at no cost from CCCF. The American Cancer Society supports the work and publications of the CCCF through grants and donations.

Most major illnesses have national foundation offices and toll-free numbers to call. Many have specific resources for children and families (see the resource section at the end of chapter 4 for a listing). The child's doctor or local hospital libraries will probably have information about these organizations.

ILLNESS OF A FAMILY MEMBER

HERE'S AN EXAMPLE

Six year old Marsha has an older brother with cancer. He has had cancer for five years. She is his best friend. Often when he is feeling bad, only Marsha can make him feel better. When he won't eat, she can sometimes get him to take a few bites. Marsha is also the only one who will punch him when she's mad at him. The family is very proud of how she is "there" for her brother. However, Marsha has started acting out with her friends and being disruptive in class. It's as though she's saying, "What about me? When do I get to be the center of attention?" At home she has started to express resentment toward her brother. "Why is everyone always asking about Larry? Why does he always get all the attention and presents?" When people ask, "How's the family? How's Larry doing?" the mother reminds them that the family includes Marsha and she's doing really well, too. Marsha's caring, understanding parents are doing what they can to help her feel valued and important just for being herself. They try to include her teachers in this thinking so that Marsha can feel important at school. She knows that she matters to her brother and her family, and she is also learning that she is important just because she is who she is.

When someone in the family has a serious illness, physical or mental, the whole family can be thrown off balance. The person with the illness often becomes the center of attention, and younger children in the family tend to feel left out or even abandoned. Parents under stress may deny the seriousness of the situation. The demands of caring for a sick person at home can also take a toll on family members. There may be economic as well as emotional hardships. The family may become socially isolated. All of this can have a profound effect on young children.

When one parent is mentally ill, the children may have only the other parent to count on during times of need, and as a result might have to take on more responsibility than they are ready for. The social stigma connected with mental illness may further isolate the family.

It is a certainly a challenge for families to meet the needs of the sick member while keeping the healthy child's life as stable and normal as possible. This is an area where the child care provider or teacher can play a major role.

INSIGHTS FROM CHILD DEVELOPMENT

Understanding illness. Young children have a hard time understanding illness and disease. Because they can only really understand what they can perceive with their senses, it is difficult for them to understand microorganisms or internal organs.
Elementary school-aged children can begin to learn more about how the body works and what causes illness.

Self-blame. The child may feel responsible for the family member's illness.

Fear of developing an illness. Older children may be preoccupied with causality and experiment with cause and effect. They may question what caused the person to become ill and whether they, too, will become ill.

WHEN A PARENT OR GRANDPARENT IS ILL

Feelings of resentment. The child may feel resentment or anger and then shame for having those feelings.

Feeling abandoned. The child may feel abandoned, invisible, unimportant. Self-esteem suffers.

Feeling helpless. The child knows there is nothing she can do to make the situation better.

Illness of a Family Member

WHEN A SIBLING IS SERIOUSLY ILL

Loss of security. A sibling of the sick child may feel insecure. Because the parent is gone a lot (if the child is hospitalized) and because the parent's attention is focused on the ill child, the healthy child may feel unimportant, left out, even unloved.

Feelings of jealousy. When a child in a family becomes seriously ill, especially with a life-threatening disease, family members may overcompensate out of grief, showering the ill child with presents. The healthy sibling may feel resentful or jealous of the ill child. The child may even say, "That's not fair."

Retaliation. The sibling may even be mean to the child who is ill, to show his resentment.

Get into trouble at school. To regain her fair share of attention, the healthy child might get into trouble at school, in the neighborhood, or with caregivers.

Develop psychosomatic symptoms. The healthy child may develop psychosomatic symptoms or exaggerate minor physical complaints in order to get more parental attention.

Feelings of vulnerability. The healthy sibling may feel vulnerable and fearful that he too might become ill and have to go to the hospital.

Self-blame. Because of egocentric thinking, the sibling may think that she caused the illness by wishing that something bad would happen to that person. Or she may think the ill person is trying to get even with her for something she did.

MENTAL ILLNESS

Understanding mental illness. Mental illness can be especially confusing and difficult for young children to understand. There is often inconsistency in the way a mentally ill person responds to the child.

More difficult to explain. Since mental illness does not have visible symptoms other than the person's demeanor, it can be even more difficult to explain to a child. The adult could say, "Some illnesses show outside the body, some do not."

"Sick in their feelings." Eda Le Shan in her book, *When A Parent Is Very Sick*, describes mental illness to children as when someone is "sick in their feelings."

Feeling invisible. The child may feel unnoticed and uncared for when the parent is unable to focus on her.

♦ **Child develops aches and pains**. Stress may cause the child to develop aches, pains or stomach problems. These psychosomatic symptoms come with real somatic effects.

♦ **Child acts out**. The child may act out in extreme ways as a cry for attention. Behaving in an aggressive and angry manner, hurting other children, crying too easily in frustration—all may be signs that the child is not coping well and needs more help.

♦ **Child takes on more responsibility**. In some cases, especially in the presence of mental illness, a child takes on more responsibility than is appropriate or typical for her age, such as caring for younger siblings and preparing food.

WHO CAN HELP

- ♦ Hospital social workers
- ♦ Child psychologists or counselors
- ♦ Child life specialists or hospital play therapists
- ♦ Community mental health agencies

HOW TO RESPOND

HOW TO RESPOND WITH THE STAFF

♦ **Ask the family to keep you informed** about what is going on with the child. In case the child asks you for information about the illness, find out what the family has told her and be consistent in your explanations.

HOW TO RESPOND WITH THE CHILD

◆ **Reassure the child he did nothing to make the person sick**. Perhaps a puppet could voice this concern, feeling sad because someone in his family is sick and he feels responsible. Then you and the children can explain to the puppet that other people do not cause that type of illness.

◆ **Make the child feel special and important**. Since the child may feel forgotten or unimportant at home, do all you can to make the child feel special and important in your environment. Make her your special helper, play with her or ask her opinion.

◆ **The child could draw pictures or dictate stories for the ill person**. You can suggest this to the child and provide materials and offer to take dictation. This helps the child feel important, and that he is doing something. It is a useful way to help the child communicate with the sick person.

◆ **Talk about how all living things change**. Point out changes in trees, flowers and growing plants. Cut out and paste pictures of changes in nature. Collect pictures of how people change as they grow and develop. Discuss people's feelings about change. Some changes we have control over, some we do not.

◆ **Plan activities about feelings** (see chapter 23). Invite the child to talk about what she is feeling and be accepting and uncritical of what you hear. Offer outlets for anger such as clay, messy art, and outdoor play.

◆ **Encourage dramatic play**. It is one way children "talk it out" and come to terms with difficult situations. Make sure the child has plenty of opportunities to engage in socio-dramatic play. Do not dictate themes of play, but do provide props such as doctor's kits and dress-up clothes worn by hospital workers.

◆ **Offer puppets of doctors, nurses and other community helpers** to help the child recreate scenes from life and imagination.

◆ **Provide children with doll house-size people and furniture** that depict hospital equipment. Encourage children to express their feelings as they play.

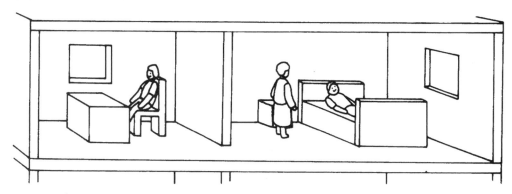

◆ **Encourage the family to give the child as much factual information as the child can understand**. You might be able to help them with this. Without factual information, children can imagine things are much worse than they are.

◆ **Involve the child**. If the ill person is being cared for at home, the child could be involved in appropriate ways in caring for the person. Perhaps the child could help bring the person food or add a pillow to make the person comfortable. The child will feel less helpless and more valued.

◆ **Prepare the child**. If a family member is seriously ill and might die, the family should prepare the child and let you know they have done so. You might be able to help them find words the child can understand (see chapter 6). Sometimes people hesitate to prepare the child, in case the person gets better. But the child can sense that something is terribly wrong by the tension in the household, visitors and phone calls. If they are not told the facts in ways they can understand, children are likely to feel even greater anxiety. Children need to know that they will be told when important things are happening.

◆ **The family should prepare the child for the experience of visiting a seriously ill person in the hospital**. It is best not to force a visit. In the classroom you could show the child books about hospitals (see the resource section in chapter 3).

◆ **Help the child get noticed in positive ways**. Send the parents upbeat reports, notes and art work. This may help the whole family feel more positively about things in general.

HOW TO RESPOND WITH THE OTHER CHILDREN

◆ **Promote friendships**. Do what you can to promote friendships with peers and strengthen the child's social ties outside of the family. Let the child feel important in her own social realm. You might encourage other parents to invite the child to their home to play or spend the night.

MENTAL ILLNESS

◆ **Provide security and predictability**. Because the child's home life may be very unsettled at this time, the child needs a sense of security and predictability in your environment.

◆ **Play and have fun**. The child should be encouraged to enjoy herself as much as possible.

◆ **Offer acceptance**. The child needs to know of your acceptance so he doesn't feel ashamed or embarrassed. The parent may be temporarily unable to nurture the child. Although you cannot substitute for the parent, you can help make the child feel valued.

RESOURCES FOR CHILDREN

Books

DenBoer, Helen. (1994). Illustrated by Janice Galanter Goldstein. ***Please Don't Cry, Mom***. Minneapolis, MN: Carolrhoda Books, Inc. Because his mother is sad all the time, Stephen and his father learn about depression and how to cope with his mother's illness.

Kohlenberg, Sherry. (1993). Illustrated by Lauri Crow. ***Sammy's Mommy Has Cancer***. New York, NY: Magination Press. This is a straight forward story that will help young children understand the changes in their lives when a parent is diagnosed with a life-threatening illness.

Sherkin-Langer, Ferne. (1995). Illustrated by Kay Life. ***When Mommy Is Sick***. Morton Grove, IL: Albert Whitman Publishers. A heart-wrenching story depicting what life is like for a young girl whose mother is often hospitalized with a chronic illness.

RESOURCES FOR ADULTS

Books

Fitzgerald, Helen. (1992). ***The Grieving Child: A Parent's Guide***. New York: Simon & Schuster Trade. Although this book deals primarily with helping a child understand death, there are useful discussions on dealing with illness in the family, preparing a child to visit someone who is seriously ill, giving the ill person a gift and debriefing after the visit.

Kubler-Ross, Elizabeth. (1985). ***On Children and Death***. New York: MacMillan Publishing Company, Inc. Although the book is about death, there is discussion of long-term illness and its effects on children. The focus of the book is on parents dealing with their own grief at the death of a child. However, relevant information is presented that would give the reader useful insights into children's thinking and how to support children.

Booklets & Pamphlets

Helping Children Understand: A Guide for a Parent With Cancer. American Cancer Society, 1180 Avenue of the Americas, New York, NY 10036. 800-ACS-2345. www.cancer.org. This free booklet outlines the steps parents can take to help their children understand what's happening to the parent with cancer and how to help the parent through this difficult time. The emphasis is on positive approaches that should help families strengthen ties and loving concern for each other.

When Your Brother or Sister Has Cancer. American Cancer Society, 1180 Avenue of the Americas, New York, NY 10036. 800-ACS-2345. www.cancer.org. This free booklet explains some of the thoughts and feelings children may have, including: worrying about what goes on in the hospital or clinic; worrying that you or your parents might get cancer; feeling sad, guilty or angry; feeling jealous and left out; and missing your parents.

Curriculum Materials

Small doll figures and puppets representing community helpers, including hospital and emergency medical personnel, fire fighters and police officiers.

Dress-up clothes depicting nurses, doctors, police officers, and fire fighters as well as play doctor's kits.

Organizations & Hot Lines

Many major illnesses have national support organizations which provide resource materials. For additional listings of organizations, contact a physician or check with the local hospital library.

American Cancer Society, 1599 Clifton Road, NE, Atlanta, GA 30329-4251. 800-227-2345. www.cancer.org.

American Heart Association, 7272 Greenville Avenue, Dallas, TX 75231. 800-242-8721. www.americanheart.org.

American Diabetes Association, 1701 North Beauregard Street., Alexandria, VA 22311. 800-232-3472. www.diabetes.org.

Alzheimer's Disease and Related Disorders Association, Inc., 919 North Michigan Avenue, Suite 110, Chicago, IL 60611-1676. 800-272-3900. www.alz.org.

American Lung Association, 61 Broadway, 6th Floor, New York, NY 10006. 212-315-8700. www.lungusa.org

The Arthritis Foundation, 115 East Eighteenth Street, New York, NY 10003. 800-283-7800. www.arthritis.org.

Epilepsy Foundation of America, 4351 Garden City Drive, Landover, MD 20785. 800-332-1000. www.epilepsyfoundation.org.

Lupus Foundation of America, Inc., 1300 Piccard Drive, Suite 200, Rockville, MD 20850-3226. 301-670-9292. www.lupus.org.

National Mental Health Association, 1021 Prince Street, Alexandria, VA 22314-2971. 800-433-5959. www.nmha.org.

National Multiple Sclerosis Society, 733 3rd Avenue, New York, NY 10017. 212-986-3240. 800-344-4867. www.nationalmssociety.org.

National Hospice Organization, 1700 Diagonal Road, Suite 625, Alexandria, VA 22314. 703-243-5900.

CHILD OR FAMILY MEMBER HAS HIV/AIDS

HERE'S AN EXAMPLE

Three year old Jonathan's mother has AIDS. She did not know that she had the HIV virus until long after she had given birth to Jonathan and she had already enrolled him in a local child care center. Jonathan has tested positive for the HIV virus, but as yet is showing no symptoms of AIDS. Realizing that the HIV virus is not spread by casual contact, his mother decided not to say anything to the director or staff of the child care center because she is afraid they would not allow him to continue to attend the program. She needs child care while she is still able to work, and she also wants Jonathan to continue to enjoy his friends and the benefits of the program as long as possible.

LET'S LOOK AT THE ISSUE

All people who have the HIV virus will eventually develop AIDS, which as of this writing, is eventually fatal. Finding that there is a child who is HIV positive in your program can cause staff members and parents to react in fear and panic.

According to the Centers for Disease Control and Prevention, as of December 1994, there were 5,734 cases of pediatric AIDS in infants and children under age thirteen reported across the country. There may be many more unreported cases of children who are HIV positive but not showing symptoms, or whose parents choose not to have them tested. It is possible that you might have a child who is HIV positive in your program and be unaware of it. The child may be asymptomatic and the condition could even be undiagnosed. Many parents of children who are HIV positive choose to keep it a secret because of the general fear and prejudice of uninformed neighbors, friends and employers. They fear becoming social outcasts, losing their jobs, even being the subjects of violence. Also, parents may feel guilty and ashamed and are, therefore, reluctant to reveal the condition.

If you have a child who is HIV positive or has AIDS in your care, you may also have a parent with AIDS. Working with the family may be difficult. AIDS can cause grief, guilt, depression. The parent may be too ill to fulfill normal parental duties. You may be dealing with foster parents, grandparents or other relatives instead of the biological parents, indicating that the child has already experienced separations. You can be sure there is stress in the family.

It is illegal to exclude a child from a child care program purely on the basis that the child is HIV positive or has AIDS. However, most children who have multiple symptoms of AIDS are not in regular child care settings because they are too ill. The child care setting poses too many risks for the child with AIDS because of his or her compromised immune system.

Being well informed about pediatric AIDS, and practicing excellent hygiene can go a long way to diffusing the initial fear that people express. However, even when staff members are informed and well educated about caring for children who are HIV positive and the child is showing no symptoms, there may be added stress on the caregiver. Extra vigilance in handwashing and general hygiene procedures should not cause undue stress, because it should be general policy for all staff under all circumstances. However, there may be an underlying sadness or anger at the parents (even if inappropriate) that must be handled. Since the primary caregiver, the health care worker and the facility director may, because of confidentiality policies, be the only ones to know about the child's special condition, the caregiver may feel isolated to an extent, needing someone to talk with. It is wise to be conscious of this and create avenues for the staff person to discuss and work through his or her feelings.

There are now child care facilities which have been set up specifically to care for children who have AIDS. Staff in these facilities are trained and prepared to care for children who are more severely impacted, and they often have support teams on staff such as a nurse, social worker, play therapist and occupational therapist. Usually local child care referral agencies, AIDS programs, a hospital pediatric AIDS unit or the department of health will know about these specialized care facilities.

Chapter 5

BASIC INFORMATION ABOUT AIDS

◆ HIV stands for Human Immunodeficiency Virus. Someone having antibodies for that virus is said to be HIV positive, which means their system has been exposed to that virus.

◆ A person who is HIV positive may appear perfectly healthy. Eventually a person's immune system will wear down and will no longer be able to fend off various infections. That is when AIDS begins.

◆ A person who is HIV positive but not yet showing symptoms of AIDS may still pass on the virus to someone else.

◆ AIDS stands for Acquired Immune Deficiency Syndrome. A person's immune system is no longer able to fend off germs that cause various infections, which eventually result in the person's death.

The four ways someone can acquire HIV/AIDS are:

◆ By prenatal or perinatal exposure. The virus crosses through the placenta from the blood of an HIV positive mother to the unborn infant, or the infant is exposed to the contaminated blood during the birth process.

◆ By being exposed to contaminated blood, either from a contaminated blood transfusion (very rare today), or by blood from the HIV positive person mixing with blood from an infected person through a wound or abrasion.

◆ Exposure to HIV contaminated blood from sharing unsterilized needles in intravenous drug use.

◆ Through sexual contact with a person who is HIV positive.

HIV/AIDS is **NOT** spread in these ways

◆ Saliva
◆ Mosquito bites
◆ Sharing eating utensils
◆ Sneezing or coughing
◆ Any casual, nonsexual contact such as hugging, dancing or playing

When a child has a family member with AIDS

When one person in a family has AIDS, the whole family will suffer stress. The very knowledge that AIDS is a long, painful and eventually fatal disease causes grief and stress among family members, no matter what the other circumstances of the family are. A child may reflect this stress in angry, frightened, withdrawn, confused behavior. Unfortunately, because many people choose to keep the existence of AIDS in the family a secret, you may not know what is causing the child's behavior.

HIV/AIDS

In addition to the stress of the illness, in a large percentage of families where a family member has AIDS, there are other behaviors that create a chaotic life style. Often one or more family members has been involved in intravenous drug use. With substance abuse there is an increased likelihood of domestic violence, child abuse, neglect, depression, all of which contribute to dysfunctional parenting. Shame, guilt, anger, frustration, and feeling hopeless and powerless are also likely to be present in the adults. Needless to say, all of this can make the family very difficult to work with. Be sure to connect with other support services working with the family as you interact with them.

For information on responding appropriately to other issues that may become part of the child's life, see chapter 4 on illness and chapter 6 on death.

When a staff person is HIV positive

Many people who are HIV positive or have AIDS choose to continue their employment as long as they are able. Adults who are HIV positive or have AIDS and work in a child care setting should be allowed to continue in their jobs as long as they meet regular performance standards for their work. Since HIV is not spread through casual contact and everyday activities, there is no reason a person cannot continue to work, provided he or she feels up to it.

Provide information and education for the rest of the staff and the parents to overcome fears and misconceptions, as well as social support for the individual. However, the individual's right to confidentiality should be maintained if they wish. Often people will choose not to share the fact that they are HIV positive for fear of ostracism and prejudice.

When they become ill with AIDS, teachrs should check with their physicians about the advisability of continuing to work in a child care setting or school where they may be exposed to more infectious germs than in other settings, putting themselves at heightened risk for infections.

BASIC FACTS ABOUT PEDIATRIC AIDS

A good source for additional information is *Serving Children with HIV Infection in Child Day Care* listed in the resource section at the end of this chapter.

◆   The great majority of children who have HIV/AIDS contracted it prenatally or at birth.

◆   Only about one-third of children born to HIV positive mothers will themselves develop AIDS.

◆   Almost all newborns born to HIV positive mothers will initially have the HIV antibodies, which they receive from their mothers, in their blood and test positive for HIV.

◆ With tests currently available, it is impossible to tell for sure if a baby has AIDS before the child is 15 to 24 months of age because it takes time before the baby's own immune system takes over.

◆ People who are HIV positive don't always have symptoms. It is impossible to tell whether or not an individual, child or adult, is HIV positive without a laboratory test.

◆ The individual is not said to have AIDS until specific symptoms of the disease emerge.

◆ Although in adults it can take ten years or more for HIV to turn into symptomatic AIDS, children with HIV become sick much sooner.

◆ While 82 per cent of children with HIV are diagnosed with AIDS by age three, some children do not develop symptoms until three or four years of age or older.

◆ The spread of the HIV virus is easy to prevent.

◆ There is no evidence that a child has ever contracted HIV/AIDS through casual contact with other children.

◆ Even biting is not considered a major risk. Toddler bites rarely draw blood. The contaminated blood of the HIV positive child must contact the blood of the other child for the second child to risk infection.

◆ Children may alternate periods of being well and feeling good with bouts of infection.

◆ A child who is HIV positive should not attend a regular child care setting if there is an outbreak of chicken pox or measles, or if the child with HIV infection has any condition that would normally preclude any child from attending (in compliance with state child care licensing regulations).

It is possible to prevent the spread of HIV/AIDS

The most important staff training issue is practicing excellent infection control procedures in the child care setting. These measures, of course, are important to reduce the spread of illness in general in your setting. So everyone benefits if training, and especially policies and practices are tightened up.

Stay informed. Since new information about HIV/AIDS is constantly being generated, child care providers should make every effort to stay informed about the latest findings. It is a good idea to assign one individual the responsibility for keeping up to date. Calling the National AIDS Clearinghouse or the other organizations listed in the resource section of this chapter on a regular basis, as well as paying attention to news releases are two ways to keep informed.

INSIGHTS FROM CHILD DEVELOPMENT

All children benefit. Children who are HIV positive or have AIDS and whose symptoms do not require exclusion under ordinary circumstances (such as excluding children who have a high fever or runny open sores) will benefit, like any other child with special needs, from developmentally appropriate early childhood education, social interaction and play with other children.

Vulnerable to illness. Because of the extent of their illness and their vulnerability to infection, children who have AIDS may be best cared for in specialized facilities that care only for children with AIDS. This decision must be made on an individual basis.

Learning disabilities and developmental delays. Since AIDS can and often does cause neurological damage, children often have learning disabilities and developmental delays. The learning program for each child must be individualized.

Behavior problems may also show up as a result of the neurological damage.

Stress in the family. Because there may have been a death or another ill person in the household, or because the child may have been removed from the family, the child may display anger, fear, sadness, anxiety, confusion and behavioral problems, all the general signs of stress within the family.

Child may lose developmental milestones. Because of the virus's effect on the nervous system, the HIV-infected child may lose developmental milestones previously attained.

Difficult to understand about germs and viruses. Children have a hard time understanding anything they cannot perceive with their senses. Therefore germs and viruses are difficult concepts, as well as trying to understand what goes on inside their bodies or how diseases are spread.

WITH CHILDREN WHO HAVE A FAMILY MEMBER WITH HIV/AIDS

Aura of fear. Children may have picked up from adults that AIDS is a terrible thing, and there may be an aura of fear around the discussion.

"Am I going to get AIDS?" Children are concerned about themselves first. They might ask, "Am I going to get AIDS?"

Fear of abandonment and loss. Any child who is aware that a loved one has AIDS or is HIV positive and also understands its seriousness will suffer emotional reactions. The fear of abandonment and loss, and the confusion resulting from the emotional turmoil in the household will affect the child's behavior.

WHEN TO SEEK HELP

When you know that a child in your care is HIV positive, be aware of signs of possible health deterioration. The family should be encouraged to seek specific medical intervention when any of these conditions appear:

◆ **Loss of developmental milestones** previously attained
◆ **Fever**
◆ **Chronic weight loss**
◆ **Frequent infections**
◆ **Thrush** (white patches in the mouth that appear in children six months of age or older). Thrush is usually not seen in healthy children after three months of age.
◆ **Skin rashes**
◆ **Signs of stress**. Also be sensitive to signs of stress in the child—sadness, isolation, anger, anxiety—and work closely with the family to comfort and reassure the child.

WHO CAN HELP

◆ Resource organizations listed in the resource section or this chapter
◆ Child life specialists and play therapists
◆ It is advisable to have a multidisciplinary team available for the consultation on each HIV/AIDS child. In addition to the parent or foster parent, include some of the following professionals on the team

       The child's pediatrician
       The family's social worker or an HIV case specialist
       A nurse
       An occupational therapist
       A physical therapist
       A nutritionist

HOW TO RESPOND WITH THE STAFF

◆ **It is possible to serve children with HIV/AIDS**. All staff members need to realize that it is possible to serve children with HIV/AIDS so that they receive positive benefits of early childhood education and social contact, and at the same time not jeopardize the health of other children or staff who come in contact with the child.

◆ **Policies**. All staff, volunteers and parents should be made aware of the center's written policies about serving children who are HIV positive, and about employing staff who are HIV positive. Implement all appropriate HIV related policies, and revise them as needed.

◆ **Essential issue**. Since any early childhood program in the country might, with or without their knowledge, be caring for a child who is HIV positive, this is an essential issue for staff training and parent awareness.

◆ **Respect the need for confidentiality**. Require staff to honor confidentiality. They should not discuss any child's or staff member's HIV status.

◆ **Work with a resource person**. Consider bringing in a resource person for staff and parent meetings occasionally so that all questions can be answered fully.

◆ **Develop a staff training outline and system** to make sure that every individual who works or volunteers has accurate information about the disease and knows precautionary measures to prevent its spread.

Staff training topics should include

> ◆ Information about infectious diseases in general and how they are spread
> ◆ The center's policies for exclusion of sick children for all illnesses, in compliance with your state and local child care regulations
> ◆ Current information about HIV/AIDS
> ◆ The differences between someone who is HIV positive and someone who has multiple symptoms of AIDS
> ◆ How the disease progresses in adults and in children
> ◆ How HIV/AIDS can be contracted
> ◆ How HIV/AIDS is not spread
> ◆ Precautionary hygiene measures to prevent the spread of the virus (practices that are required)
> ◆ The stress on the family caused by illness and how best to be supportive of parents and caregivers in their roles
> ◆ Community organizations and resources

HIV/AIDS

◆ **Caregivers need an outlet to discuss their feelings about this topic** in general, as well as specific feelings about infected children and parents in your program. Create opportunities for both informal and structured discussions at staff meetings with a psychologist.

◆ **Review frequently handwashing and diaper changing techniques** and other hygiene measures. An excellent guide is *Serving Children with HIV Infection in Child Day Care* listed in the resource section of this chapter.

◆ **Wear latex gloves when touching blood**. Consider keeping a pair of latex disposable gloves in your pocket so that you have them handy and can respond immediately if a child is injured and bleeds.

◆ **Frequent monitoring and training**. It is not enough to have excellent hygiene policies in place. It takes frequent monitoring and thorough training of all child care staff, new staff, substitutes and volunteers. It is easy for people to slack off. Post an illustration of the proper procedures at the diaper changing areas and sinks, and in the staff lounge. Develop a system for checking and monitoring each other to make sure the procedures are followed consistently by all people.

HOW TO RESPOND WITH THE HIV POSITIVE CHILD

◆ **Separation** is a big issue with children who have AIDS. They may already have been separated from their mother or their family. They may have been hospitalized. And they will certainly face major separations in the future. The mother may die before the child. So take great care in introducing the child and the parents or foster parents to the program.

◆ **Learning disabilities**. Keep in mind that children who have AIDS may experience neurological damage that creates learning disabilities. Revise your expectations of the child accordingly. Individualize your work through assessing the child's various skills and devise appropriate activities that challenge his current capabilities without frustrating the child. Let the child practice success.

◆ **Feeling powerless**. Since sick people, especially children, often feel helpless, create situations where the child feels less helpless. Offer the child choices and allow her to make decisions when appropriate.

> **Ask the child's opinion and preferences**, when appropriate. "Where do you think I should hang this picture?" "Shall we have snack inside or outside today?" "Do you think I should put out playdough or finger paint to play with today?"

Dramatic play. Allow much time and opportunity for dramatic play when the child can dictate the action and be the powerful star of his own dramas (see chapter 23). Any child who has been ill a lot with many visits to the doctor or hospital will probably enjoy playing doctor's office or hospital. Provide dramatic play props, uniforms, doctor's kits, examining tables and doctor's office settings. Take on a role yourself, if it seems necessary, to facilitate the play, but allow the child to direct the action. Children will also enjoy playing with doll house hospital furniture and people.

◆ **Puppets**. Doctor, nurse and other community helper puppets can encourage children to express themselves about illness.

◆ **Limits for behavior**. Be sure to set the same limits and expectations for behavior with this child as with the other children.

◆ **Reduce risk of biting**. Make special efforts to reduce the risk of biting, reducing frustration, crowding, fighting and aggression (see chapter 24).

◆ **Guilty**. Make sure that children do not feel guilty when they become ill. Let them know they did nothing to cause their illness.

◆ **Welcome the child back**. Make sure that the child is welcomed back warmly after having been ill and away from the program for a period of time. Help ease the child's social re-entry into the group.

HOW TO RESPOND WITH THE OTHER CHILDREN

◆ **How they can play together**. For children, focus on how they do not catch the disease rather than how it is contracted. "You can play with him, you can hug him, you can share toys with him and you can sit by him." With the children, make a list, or even an illustrated poster, of ways AIDS is not spread, including

- ◆ Playing
- ◆ Hugging
- ◆ Sharing food
- ◆ Sharing eating utensils, dishes
- ◆ Sitting in the same chair
- ◆ Drinking out of a water fountain
- ◆ Mosquito bites
- ◆ Dancing with someone

- ◆ Using the same telephone
- ◆ Using the same toilet

Stress that other germs that can make you sick in different ways might be spread in some of these ways, but not HIV.

◆ **Ask what they already know about AIDS**. Talk about it with the other children.

◆ **Teach all children not to touch someone else's blood**. Review with them what to do if someone gets hurt and is bleeding—call the teacher.

◆ **Talk about being sick and being healthy**. Engage children in talking about being sick and being healthy. Talk about, act out and illustrate things people do to stay healthy such as eating right, exercising, sleeping and washing hands. But do stress that children who are sick with AIDS did nothing to cause their illness.

◆ **With the children, rehearse basic hygiene routines** such as using a tissue, and washing hands after blowing their nose, going to the bathroom and before eating. Praise them for appropriate actions they do on their own as well as with prompting from you. Make posters and illustrations.

◆ **Cards and pictures**. When a classmate is ill and excluded from the program, the other children could make cards and pictures for the ill child.

HOW TO RESPOND WITH THE PARENTS OF THE CHILD WHO IS HIV POSITIVE

◆ **Added stress**. The child may be in a foster family or with the biological parent. In either case, the illness will certainly be a cause of added stress.

◆ **Look at the whole family situation**. Some children who are HIV positive or have AIDS may come from a chaotic family setting with dysfunctional parents who, because of substance abuse or other problems have been unable to be responsive and caring toward the child. They may abuse or neglect the child. All of this adds to the child's behavior problems. Be sure to rely on and work closely with the family's social worker and other professionals involved with the family.

◆ **Being supportive to the family** to help them learn how to be positive parents is even more important than usual if they have a child with HIV/AIDS. If you accept the parents and respect their difficulties and pain, you will be a valued social contact.

◆ **It is important to remember that these parents did not purposely infect their children**, nor did they purposely become addicted to drugs.

◆ **If a parent is a substance abuser**, the addiction must be treated effectively, with all the necessary social supports, before the parent can put the child first.

◆ **The biological mother and possible other family members may be sick** with AIDS or at least be anticipating the illness, facing their own deaths while trying to cope with the difficulties of caring for an ill child. Be aware of resources in your community which support people with AIDS and refer parents if they are not aware of them.

◆ **Foster parents, grandparents or caregivers** other than the biological parent who may have custody of the child will also need community support and understanding of their difficulties.

◆ **It is essential to respect the confidentiality** of the family. Many people choose not to reveal the child's condition for fear of stigma and retaliation by society. If you are in their circle of confidence it can be valuable for them to feel that they can talk to you without worry.

HOW TO RESPOND WITH THE PARENTS OF THE OTHER CHILDREN

◆ **All parents should be informed of your legal requirement** to accept children who are HIV positive.

◆ **Parents need to know that a child who is HIV positive may be in your care without your knowledge**, and that this is possible in any child care setting.

◆ **Give parents a copy of your written policies** about serving children who are HIV positive. Also inform them about your policies for exclusion of any child who shows certain symptoms of illness.

◆ **Parent meeting about the topic.** Have a parent meeting at least once a year to discuss the topic, how HIV/AIDS is not spread and what you do to prevent the spread of infection in your program. (Refer to *HIV/AIDS: A Challenge to Us All* listed in the video resource section of this chapter.)

◆ **Discuss the topic with parents** thoroughly and to their satisfaction during your intake interview. Offer to be available to answer any further questions they may have.

◆ **Talk openly and honestly with parents.** When parents threaten to withdraw their child because of your policies or knowledge that a child who is HIV positive is in your program, remind them that any child care program or family child care home might have such a child present with or without the knowledge of the administration. Because you are open about it and conscientious about staff training and hygiene practices, their child may actually be safer with you.

◆ **Honor confidentiality**. Do not comply with parents' requests or demands to know the identity of children or staff in your program who are HIV positive. Their knowledge of this may only lead to prejudicial action against the affected individual. At the same time, respectfully reassure them of your conscientious policies.

WHERE TO FIND MORE INFORMATION

RESOURCES FOR CHILDREN

Books

Giard, Linda Walvoord. (1994) Illustrated by Blanche Sims. *Alex, The Kid With AIDS*. Morton Grove, IL: Albert Whitman Publishers. This is a very realistic story about the adjustment of a kid with AIDS, and his very active classmates.

Hausherr, Rosmarie. (1989). Photographs by Rosemarie Hausherr. *Children and the AIDS Virus*. New York: Clarion Books. A very simple explanation of the body's immune system, and how it is attacked by the AIDS virus is included in this book. What to do to prevent the spread of the disease is also included. A special subtext with information for adults is provided.

Merrifield, Margaret. (1990). Illustrated by Heather Collins. *Come Sit by Me*. Toronto: Womens Press. Karen and Nicholas are best friends. Some children in the preschool are not allowed to play with Nicholas because he has AIDS. The book includes a parent meeting where parents get together and learn about AIDS. AIDS resources for parents and teachers are identified in the back of the book.

Quinlan, Patricia. (1994). Illustrated by Janet Wilson. *Tiger Flowers*. New York: Dial Books. When his Uncle Michael dies of AIDS, Joel's dreams and thoughts of his uncle provide consolation for Joel and his family.

Verniero, Joan C. (1995). Illustrated by Verdon Flory. *You Can Call Me Willy: A Story for Children About AIDS*. New York: Magination Press. This engaging story of Will, an eight year old living with AIDS, encourages compassion and understanding toward those with the illness. Children who have AIDS as well as those who do not will find their feelings validated by the sensitive story.

Books

Anderson, Gary R. (Ed.). (1990). *Courage to Care: Responding to the Crisis of Children with AIDS*. Washington, DC: Child Welfare League of America, c/o CSSC, (CWLA), Inc. *Courage to Care* provides a comprehensive review of the implications of AIDS on individuals, families and society. The book is the culmination of the contributions of 23 acknowledged experts in the field covering a broad range of care, services, training, education and preventive strategies. It identifies and describes pioneering programs to serve HIV positive children and their families. The book is distributed by CWLA-New England Office, 300 Congress Street, Suite 305, Quincy, MA 02169. 617-770-3008. www.cwla.org.

Barth, R., Pietrzak, J. and Ramler, M. (Eds.). (1993). *Families Living with Drugs and HIV: Intervention and Treatment Strategies*. New York: The Guilford Press. The importance of this book is in providing a multidisciplinary approach to substance abuse, particularly as it relates to HIV infection. The contributors are experts representing a broad cross-section of disciplines and agencies. The book focuses on the problems of drug and AIDS infected infants and their families.

Serving Children with HIV Infection in Child Day Care: A Guide for Center-Based and Family Day Care Providers. Washington, DC: Child Welfare League of America, Inc. This book will replace fear with knowledge of how to safeguard children, families and staff while meeting the special needs of children with HIV. It gives clear answers to questions about the disease, recommends policies and practices and discusses working with families and legal implications. The guide contains an excellent outline of staff training issues as well as illustrated charts on how to change a diaper and handwashing techniques. Straight-forward and reassuring, it is an extremely useful resource, that should be present in every child care facility. The book is distributed by CWLA-New England Office, 300 Congress Street, Suite 305, Quincy, MA 02169. 617-770-3008. www.cwla.org. It is also available from NAEYC, 1509 16th Street NW, Washington, DC 20036-1426. 800-424-2460. $9.95. www.naeyc.org.

Booklets & Pamphlets

Meeting the Challenge of HIV Infection in Family Foster Care. (1991). Child Welfare League of America, c/o CSSC, CWLA-New England Office, 300 Congress Street, Suite 305, Quincy, MA 02169. 617-770-3008. www.cwla.org. These guidelines are based upon medical knowledge of and legal requirements related to HIV infection which provide a basis for developing a family foster care approach. $10.95.

Myths and Facts: Caring for an HIV-Infected Child in Family Day Care. (1994). The Children's Foundation, 725 Fifteenth Street, NW, Suite 505, Washington, DC 20005-2109.

HIV/AIDS

The Children's Foundation worked with the Centers for Disease Control and Prevention (CDC) to develop guidelines for family day care and child care for children with HIV and AIDS to help providers meet new challenges.

Report of the CWLA Task Force on Children and AIDS: Initial Guidelines. (1988). Child Welfare League of America, c/o CSSC, CWLA-New England Office, 300 Congress Street, Suite 305, Quincy, MA 02169. 617-770-3008. www.cwla.org. These guidelines provide suggested administrative policies and program procedures for child welfare agencies that are serving the needs of children with AIDS. $8.95.

Curriculum Materials

The Project CHAMP—Children's HIV and AIDS Model Program—Materials. (1991). Child Welfare League of America, CWLA-New England Office, 300 Congress Street Suite. 305, Qunicy, MA 02169. 617-770-3008. www.cwla.org. The materials including a training curriculum and caregiver's handbook prepare caregivers to respond sensitively and competently to children infected by HIV and their families. Pilot tested in clinical and community settings, the materials include: *Caring at Home: A Guide for Families*, a handbook on coping with both the daily physical and psycho-social aspects of and caring for medically fragile children; and *Caring in the Community for Children with HIV: A Training Guide for Child Care Providers, Foster Families, Home Health Aides and Volunteers*, a curriculum guide for training caregivers and providers consisting of five modules which provide extensive information related to all aspects of pediatric HIV/AIDS disease. $49.95.

Videos

HIV/AIDS: A Challenge to Us All. A set of two videos, *Educating Our Children* and *A Parent Meeting*, plus a parent meeting handbook produced by the Pediatric AIDS Foundation, 2950 31st Street, Suite 125, Santa Monica, CA 90405. 310-395-9051. www.pedaids.org. The parent meeting video, 23 minutes long, shows an actual parent meeting held in an elementary school in which parents ask questions of a panel made up of a pediatrician, a psychologist, the school principal, a school director, the parent of an HIV-infected child and a pediatric AIDS specialist who describes HIV/AIDS in easy-to-understand terms. The handbook that accompanies the video gives useful guidelines for organizing your own parent meeting and using the videos. The video, *Educating Our Children*, shows children asking typical questions for their ages and appropriate adult responses. The entire package is extremely useful. The videos are available in English and Spanish and are free of charge.

Hugs Invited: An Educational and Training Series is a set of three videos *Caring for Infants and Toddlers with HIV Infection*, *Caring for School-aged Children with HIV Infection* and *Living with Loss: Children and HIV*. (1991). 15 min. each video. Child Welfare League of America, c/o CSSC, CWLA-New England Office, 300 Congress Street, Suite 305, Quincy, MA 02169. 617-770-3008. www.cwla.org. The series was developed to help health, social services and educational agencies educate and train families (birth, adoptive and foster), social workers, child care workers, home health aides, volunteers, and advocates to care for children and families infected by HIV/AIDS. The series was produced by the Child Welfare League of America in collaboration with Children's Hospital/National Medical Center. A discussion guide accompanies each video. $69.95 per video and guide.

With Loving Arms. (1989). 18 min. Child Welfare League of America, c/o CSSC, CWLA-New England Office, 300 Congress Street, Suite 305, Quincy, MA 02169. 617-770-3008. www.cwla.org. The video portrayal of three foster families caring for children with HIV helps to diminish the mystique and the fear of HIV transmission. This video will educate agency personnel, practitioners, caregivers and child advocates about the epidemiology of the disease and the need for loving stable home environments. Includes a discussion guide. $49.95

Organizations & Hot Lines

Child Welfare League of America, 440 First Street NW, 3rd Floor, Washington DC 20001-2085. 202-638-2952. www.cwla.org. The Child Welfare League of America (CWLA) is a primary source of information on issues including pending legislation, research and practice standards. CWLA publishes a bi-monthly journal, social legislation bulletin, quarterly magazine and a newsletter. Their comprehensive catalog has an extensive list of books and monographs.

The CDC National Prevention Information Network, P.O. Box 6003, Rockville, MD 20849-6003. 800-458-5231. www.cdcnpin.org. The Clearinghouse's expert multidisciplinary staff of reference specialists answer questions and provide technical assistance to public health professionals, educators and others working in the HIV/AIDS field. Using computerized databases and other resources, specialists respond to inquiries, make referrals and locate materials about HIV. Bilingual specialists are available to speak to Spanish-speaking callers. Their comprehensive catalog is designed to give you easy access to a wide range of materials and resources about HIV/AIDS.

Centers for Disease Control and Prevention National AIDS Hot Line, 800-342-AIDS (English Service). 800-344-7432 (Spanish Service). 800-243-7889 (Deaf Access/TDD). www.hshastd.org. The National AIDS Hot Line provides current, confidential information about HIV and AIDS to callers 24 hours per day. Hot Line information specialists provide details about HIV transmission, testing, counseling and prevention. In addition, callers can get printed materials on HIV and AIDS as well as referrals to local programs that provide health care, legal, and support services.

National Pediatric HIV Resource Center, Children's Hospital AIDS Program, Children's Hospital of New Jersey, 30 Bergan Street, ADMC #4, Newark, NJ 07103. 800-362-0071. www.pedhivaids.org. The Resource Center provides information about developing comprehensive services for children and families and for public policy issues.

National Resource Center on Women and AIDS, Center for Women Policy Studies, 1211 Connecticut, Avenue NW, Suite 312, Washington, DC 20036. 202-872-1770. www.centerwomenpolicy.org. The Center serves as a centralized source of information and plays a major role in defining key policy issues and developing strategies, including federal legislation, to advance women's issues in the federal AIDS policy agenda. Their extensive publications list includes a variety of issues affecting women.

National Training Center for Drug Exposed and HIV Infected Children and Their Families, 1800 Columbus Avenue, Boston, MA 02119. The National Training Center provides a training program that is designed to help professionals who serve or plan to serve HIV-infected and drug-exposed children and families. The Center is sponsored by The Foundation for Children with AIDS which has extensive experience in developing therapeutic child care, early intervention, counseling, case management and family support services. A manual with guidelines for providing services to children with HIV is available for $19.95. Center staff will conduct training at local sites.

Pediatric AIDS Foundation. 2950 31st Street, Suite 125, Santa Monica, CA 90405. 310-395-9051. www.pedaids.org. The Pediatric AIDS Foundation is a national organization confronting medical problems unique to children infected with HIV/AIDS. Through funding research the Foundation focuses on creating a future that offers hope through discovery of effective therapies and methods for blocking transmission from infected mothers to newborns. The Foundation has produced a set of videos, *HIV/AIDS: A Challenge to Us All*, which is available at no charge.

HIV/AIDS

CHAPTER 6

DEATH OF A FAMILY MEMBER OR FRIEND

HERE'S AN EXAMPLE

DEATH OF A PARENT

Five year old Brandon's mother had cancer. She was often in the hospital for longer and longer periods of time. Finally she died. But for weeks, the father, overcome with grief, could not bring himself to tell Brandon and went on with the funeral without his son. He wanted to wait until he could tell his child sensitively, discussing calmly what happened. In the meantime, Brandon sensed that something was terribly wrong. But nobody was telling him anything. At the child care center, the staff was aware of what happened, but felt it was not their place to break the news to the child, so they tried to carry on as though all was fine. All was not fine. Brandon, who had been a mild mannered little boy, became angry and aggressive and was hurting other children.

Finally, with encouragement and support from the child care staff, Brandon's father gathered his courage and took the time to tell his son what had happened. Brandon was confused and angry. For a while, feeling betrayed, his behavior at the center became even more aggressive. He began seeing a counselor who also helped Brandon's dad and the child care staff find ways to answer Brandon's questions and address his fears.

In the process, a bond of support was formed. The father often lingered at the center at pick up time, enjoying the feeling of friendship with the staff and playing with his child and the other children. Brandon's behavior improved with the love and attention from the staff and his dad. However, much confusion, resentment and anger might have been avoided had the father openly acknowledged his grief to his son and allowed Brandon to share in the initial grief and participate in the mourning process.

DEATH OF A PET

Squeeky, was a guinea pig who for years greeted children in the lobby of a child care center, and was a frequent visitor to classrooms. He even joined them on the grassy area of the playground from time to time. The children were very fond of him and would bring him veggie snacks from home now and then. One morning the director discovered that Squeeky had died during the night. She quickly consulted with each staff person as they came in and lesson plans were altered. In each classroom they read *The Tenth Good Thing About Barney* and then listed the things they liked best about Squeeky. A shoe box was filled with soft cotton and each classroom added special decorations. Right before lunch all the children assembled under a tree on the playground, sang songs and told the things they liked best about Squeeky. They helped dig a hole and placed Squeeky, inside his shoe box coffin, in the hole and buried him. Notes were sent home to the parents to let them know the proceedings of the day. The next day the staff was dismayed when several children dug up squeeky's body.

LET'S LOOK AT THE ISSUE

As much as we would like to shelter innocent young children from the concept of death and grief, we cannot. Death is a natural fact of life and in all cultures children will be exposed to it. In most cases the child will encounter death first by seeing dead bugs or small animals on the road, or by experiencing the death of a classroom or family pet. In other cases, the child first experiences the loss of a friend, family member or even a parent. In all these situations, the sensitive presence of a trusted adult and thoughtful discussion that addresses the child's questions, confusions and fears can go a long way toward helping the child deal with the situation in a healthy way. Because unresolved grief can be the cause of serious psychological problems at any age, it is important for the child to have help in dealing with feelings related to death.

One reason it is difficult to discuss death with children is because we often worry about how much of the topic to discuss. It is always good to follow a child's lead and respond to the child's questions and worries. Generally, children can be told facts about the death and what dead means. However, simply telling children the facts does not mean they will understand death.

People have different beliefs about the afterlife. Fred Rogers states in the introduction of his children's book, *When a Pet Dies*, "...I hope you'll find it possible to share your real feelings about a pet's dying. As for what happens after death, I believe that's best discussed in light of each family's traditions and beliefs." In the booklet, *Talking With Young Children About Death*, Hedda Sharapan addresses how to respond if you do not know the answer to a child's questions. She offers the very useful phrases, "No one knows for sure, but I believe..." or "You know, I wonder about that too."

INSIGHTS FROM CHILD DEVELOPMENT

Understanding death. Young children acquire an understanding of death in progressive stages. Children, ages five and younger, see death as neither final nor inevitable, nor can they understand the causes of death. They expect that people and animals can come back to life again. Usually between five and nine years of age, children can accept the idea that a person has died, but not accept that death ultimately happens to everyone, especially themselves. Children may ask over and over again what dead is. Do not be surprised if children repeat questions you thought they understood. Repeat the information you gave the child earlier, perhaps in a different way. In explaining what dead means, include the following: not moving, not breathing, not going to the bathroom, not feeling, not hurting, not being afraid.

Individual differences. There are no simple ways to help a child cope with death. Children as well as adults differ widely in their reactions to death. There are no timetables for grieving, adjusting to, or understanding death.

Fear of abandonment. Children may worry about being abandoned. "Are you going to die?" is a typical question of children, even when a pet dies. Sensing how dependent they are, children worry about who will take care of them if their parents die. Separation anxiety can become extreme. "I don't expect to die for a long, long time," is a good response.

Guilt and responsibility. A child's logic goes something like this: "When I am bad, like when I hit my sister, something bad happens back to me. I get punished. Something bad has happened to me. Grandpa died. Therefore, I must have been bad." Adults are often surprised that after a long illness of someone close to the child, the child still feels responsible for the death. "If I had behaved better, Grandma wouldn't have died." Young children also engage in magical thinking. They sometimes believe that wishing something would happen or thinking bad thoughts can cause things to happen. Or if they wished a sibling would disappear and the sibling dies, the child can feel responsible.

Curiosity about death. It is not uncommon for a child to dig up the body of a pet buried in the yard. They are curious about what happens to the body. Even after the child has participated in burying a pet or attending a funeral, the child might ask when the dead pet or person will return. Especially in preschool years children show a matter-of-fact interest in dead things—what they look like and feel like. Young children are also curious about how someone can breathe or eat or go to the bathroom after they are buried, or whether they will be cold or miss their friends.

Accurate information. The child should be told about the death as sensitively but as factually as possible, in response to their questions or concerns.

Need to feel included. Times of family crisis can actually be an opportunity for enhanced feelings of closeness and connection. In most cases it is best for the child to be included with talk, active remembering and shared feelings of sadness, as well as possible attendance at the funeral or memorial service.

Understanding cremation may be very difficult to explain to children. Be sure to emphasize that the dead body can feel nothing, no pain.

Use plain simple language. Young children have a very concrete understanding of language. Be careful not to use the common euphemisms surrounding death: "we lost him" or "gone to heaven." These phrases are confusing for children. It might also be a good idea to tell children that they might hear these phrases from other people and what the phrases mean.

Use dramatic play. It is typical for children to re-enact in their dramatic play the part of the death that they witnessed, whether it is the accident or hospital play, or most typically, the funeral or memorial service. This is healthy and good. Just as adults talk about the death over and over in processing their grief, re-enacting the death in play is a child's way of gaining greater understanding and acceptance of death.

Different response. Young children respond to death and grieve differently from adults. Children process their grief intermittently, pausing to be sad or to think about it and ask questions from time to time and then give their thoughts a rest as they return to play.

WHEN TO SEEK HELP

All of the following characteristics could be normal reactions. The difference is in the length of time these symptoms persist and in their intensity. The most important thing is to know the child well. If any behavior seems too extreme or seems to continue longer than the situation seems to warrant, encourage parents to seek the help of a trained therapist or grief counselor. A parent's denial can get in the way of a child wanting to talk about the death. So look at how the parent seems to be handling it as well.

Encourage parents to get professional help for the child if:

◆ the child seems intent on denying the death

◆ the child leaves the room every time the dead person's name is mentioned and cannot talk about feelings

◆ sleep disturbances continue for a long time

◆ separation anxiety becomes extreme

◆ the child shows heightened anxiety, clings more, whines more, cries more for long periods of time or if other fears become more intense, such as fear of the dark

◆ the child's anger does not dissipate and is hurting someone else, such as a sibling or a pet

◆ the child seems depressed or withdrawn for a long time

◆ regressive behavior is excessive or prolonged

Common signs of regression are normal. The child may retreat to a time when the world felt safer. Pay attention if these behaviors seem to continue for a long time:

◆ Toileting skills diminish

◆ Bed-wetting begins or re-emerges

◆ Thumb sucking becomes excessive or re-emerges

◆ The child starts talking baby talk

◆ The child crawls after having walked

WHO CAN HELP

In many communities there are grief counselors. Seek out someone who is not only familiar with the processes of grieving but also knows child development and can work effectively with very young children.

◆ Local hospice organizations often provide grief counseling after a death, or would be able to tell you who does in your community.

◆ Funeral directors sometimes provide grief counseling.

◆ Community mental health agencies may have someone specially trained in grief counseling

◆ The clergy has been traditionally where religious families turn for help. Like any other profession, some are better than others at explaining abstract concepts to young children.

◆ Private therapists who specialize in child therapy can be very helpful.

HOW TO RESPOND

HOW TO RESPOND WITH THE STAFF

◆ **Become acquainted with children's books** dealing with death and life cycles in nature (see the resource section at the end of this chapter).

◆ **Talk about death**. Many adults, including those who work with young children, have not themselves come to terms with the concept of death. In order to help children sift through their conflicting and confusing feelings about death, the adults guiding them must understand their own feelings. Discuss your feelings about death with your supervisor or trusted colleagues, or include this topic in staff training.

◆ **Meet with a grief counselor**. In some situations, it can be helpful for a grief counselor to come in and have a meeting, or a series of meetings, with the staff.

HOW TO RESPOND WITH THE CHILD

Help the child feel secure

◆ **Give the child reminders that he is loved** and will be cared for. Name the people who are there for him.

◆ **Give the child a special "lovey."** It might help to give the child a special "lovey"— a special stuffed animal just for herself—to carry around and keep her company. This may help the child feel special and cared for.

◆ **Maintain stability for the child**. When a child has experienced a death, try to keep as many things in her life the same. This gives her security and reassurance.

◆ **Give the child extra attention**. Grieving children, no matter how they are acting, need extra attention. All adults in the child's life should make an effort to spend time with the child and be there to talk, answer questions, and give reassurance and love. Give the child a special assignment she can do with you, like rearranging a learning center or going with you on an errand.

◆ **Allow the child to express his emotions**. The child may have felt helpless during all the events that have been going on around the death. By encouraging the expression of emotions and involving the child in activities, you will help move him from this passive, helpless state to one of actively coping.

◆ **Make your lap available** if the child needs it. "I know sometimes you will feel sad and might want to just sit close to me."

◆ **Talk about death** in an appropriate context, for example, when discussing life cycles in nature. Point out that every living thing has a beginning, a time in-between—for some things, like people, this is a long time, for others, like butterflies, this is a short time—and an ending--death.

◆ **Answer only what is asked**, or turn the question around first, "What do you think?," to see what the child is really asking.

◆ **Ask the child questions**. Are there words you don't understand? Hedda Sharapan suggests inviting the child to tell you if she is hearing any words she does not understand. Or ask the child, "What do you wonder about?" This might help open up discussion when a child is hesitant to bring up the topic.

◆ **Answer the child's questions as often as asked**. Don't be surprised when questions are repeated.

◆ **Read carefully selected children's books about death**. Read to the whole group and to the child individually.

Help the child address feelings of guilt

◆ **Explain that the child did nothing to cause the death** if the child seems to be expressing guilt. Adults must point out, repeatedly sometimes, that the child did nothing to cause the death. Then explain as factually as possible why the person or pet died. The child should hear that death is not a punishment.

◆ **Sing with the children**. You could sing, read the words or talk about Fred Rogers' song, "Wishes Don't Make Things Come True." They need to hear from you that just thinking something doesn't make things happen, that everybody has "bad" thoughts sometimes, but that doesn't make them "bad." Children should also be told that nothing they can do or wish will cause the person or pet to come back to life.

◆ **Explain what will happen at the funeral or wake**. If the child is to attend the funeral or wake, it is important that someone close to the child prepare the child ahead of time by explaining the things that will happen, what the child will see, what people will say and how people will act. (Check with the child's family to see if they want you to help with this.)

◆ **Be available as an adult friend** to take the child out of the funeral home for a break from time to time, or to visit with the child and then take the child home for the rest of the wake, depending on your relationship with the family.

Focus on feelings

◆ **Let the child feel his sorrow**. Adults are often intensely uncomfortable with children's sorrow. We want to fix it for them right away. We want children to be happy. Be careful that you do not deny children's feelings of sorrow. Let them express their sorrow in many ways. Only then can they move through the sorrow to accepting the death. Instead of trying to get a child to stop crying, by distracting the child or telling the child to stop crying, simply comfort the child. "Sometimes it helps to cry when you feel very sad. I am here to take care of you and you can sit next to me when you feel sad and want to cry."

◆ **Do not try to hide your own feelings of sadness**. It is important for children to see that real people express real feelings.

◆ **Empathasize with the child**. Let the child know you understand her feelings and accept them as natural. Invite the child to express herself in many different ways such as talking, artwork, play or stories.

◆ **Acknowledge the anger part of grief**. Offer the child the opportunity to express anger of this type by doing such things as scribbling, painting, making a mess, pounding clay or play dough, making loud noises or hitting pillows or a punching bag. Talk with the

child about the anger he is feeling so that the child is not ashamed of the feeling.

◆ **Use puppets**. Have puppets on hand so the children can talk through them. Sometimes it is easier for a puppet to express angry feelings than for the child to say it himself. The child might be more willing to talk openly to a puppet than to an adult. Children can use puppets to talk to the deceased and say things they wish they had said when the person was alive.

◆ **Tell children that although they feel bad now, they won't always feel so bad**.

Focus on happy memories

◆ **Remember together the enjoyable things** the child did with the deceased one.

◆ **Write a letter to the deceased**. Offer to help the child write a letter to the deceased. If necessary, take dictation.

◆ **Make a book or scrapbook**. Help the child make a book or scrapbook about the deceased. The child could illustrate it, if he is able to make representational drawings, or find pictures in magazines of what the person or pet liked to do.

◆ **Give the child an object belonging to the person who died.** It can be comforting for a child to have an object that belonged to the person who died, as a token to help the child remember the person.

Death of a parent, sibling or grandparent

The death of a parent is the most devastating loss a child can experience. The whole family will need your empathy and support. The death of a sibling can cause profound or subtle changes in the way a child's parents relate within the family. For some children the death of a grandparent may be the first loss of a family member. Find out how close the child was to the grandparent. The child's grief reaction, of course, will depend on how close the child was to the grandparent.

◆ **Maintain close communication**. If a family member is dying, maintain close communication with the family members so that you know what the family is telling the child and can help them understand the child's point of view.

◆ **Attend the funeral**. This shows visible support to the family and the child, and may let the child know that you know about what happened.

◆ **Talk to the child about his or her concerns**. The child's first fear is that he might be left alone, that the other parent might die. Adults should tell the child again and again that they are loved and cared for. The child may also feel anger at being abandoned.

◆ **Watch for feelings of guilt**. The child may have wished the parent, sibling or grandparent dead at one time and now feels responsible. Or the child may feel guilty for being unkind to the person. It's even possible that the child will feel she caused the death in some way. The child may also feel guilty for having felt jealous of the attention received by the deceased.

◆ **Respond to the child's needs for reassurance**. When a sibling dies it can be very scary for a child, because of their closeness in age. The child may feel that he will die soon as well. He may need frequent reassurance.

◆ **Help the child establish her own identity.** A child may need to work on establishing her own separate identity, "Who am I?" Sometimes a child may feel he must become a replacement of the dead sibling in order to console grieving adults.

◆ **Answer questions about age**. How old is old? Avoid saying, "Grandma was old and that is why she died." To a young child, a teenager is old! The child may ask the parent or you, "Are you old?" Try to reassure the child that you expect to live for a long time.

Death of a pet

◆ **Treat the grief seriously and respectfully**. Grief at the death of a family pet can be just as intense as the loss of any loved one and should be taken seriously. Very often, the death of a pet is the child's first exposure to death of someone they love. Regard this very painful experience as a learning opportunity.

◆ **Provide dramatic play opportunities**. Provide dramatic play of a veterinarian's office, including a doctor's kit, stuffed animals, cages, and an examining table.

◆ **Talk about the death with the child**. Perhaps share a similar experience that happened to you.

◆ **Do something symbolic,** such as plant a tree or some special flowers in memory of the pet.

HOW TO RESPOND WITH THE OTHER CHILDREN

◆ **Read children's books**. Select one or more of the books listed in the resource section. Reading a book about death, such as *Lifetimes,* when children have not experienced a death directly can be a good way to bring the concept into the child's awareness, before intense emotions are involved.

◆ **Talk about death before it happens**. As a routine part of your curriculum, include discussions of what being dead means. It is important to talk about death before children actually encounter death on a personal level.

◆ **Take nature walks**. It can provide ideal opportunities to routinely point out things in nature that are dead. Talk about the difference between dead bugs and live bugs. If you encounter a dead bird or small wild animal, let the children look at it (from a distance of a few feet). Point out how it is not moving or breathing or afraid because it doesn't feel or think anymore. Rather than aversion, try to show sadness and respect.

◆ **Take advantage of the death of a classroom pet**. It can be a good educational experience. Have a funeral for a classroom pet that dies. Let the children decorate a box, dig a hole, bury the box, sing a song and tell stories or memories about the pet. Ritual is important. The children may re-enact this in their play.

◆ **Find out how things decay**. To help children understand what happens to a body of a buried pet after death, you might let them see something else decay, such as a pumpkin or a piece of fruit. You could put this in a heavy, zip-close plastic bag or a sealable plastic container and examine it every few days. Try not to express revulsion, but help children see it as a process of nature. Think about what would happen if things did not decay when they died.

Death of a classmate or friend

◆ **Answer the children's questions**. When a classmate or a child's friend dies, he may fear that the same things might happen to him.

◆ **Explain sensitively and factually** why the child died, and that this is unlikely to happen to him.

◆ **Make a group scrapbook**. The class could make a group scrapbook about their friend and their memories and give it to the family.

◆ **Help children think of ways to respond**. The children might like to do something symbolic like plant a tree or some flowers to help them remember their friend.

HOW TO RESPOND WITH THE PARENTS

◆ **Ask the family to tell you as much as they can** about the circumstances surrounding the death and what the child experienced and what was told to individual children so that you can respond appropriately.

◆ **Show your support of the family by attending the funeral** or wake, if you knew the individual. Perhaps you can be the one to help with the child during the service.

◆ **Notify the other parents in the program** about the child's death. Also tell the other parents the follow-up activities you plan to do with the children and how they might answer some of the questions.

WHAT NOT TO DO

◆ **Do not avoid acknowledging or talking about death** with children.

◆ **Do not assume that children will understand death** if they are told "the facts."

◆ **Do not tell the child how he should be feeling or reacting**.

◆ **Do not act surprised if a child does not appear sad or unhappy**.

◆ **Do not impose your religious beliefs on the child**.

◆ **Do not use the word "sleep" when explaining death**. "Grandma has gone to sleep," might make the child afraid to go to sleep.

◆ **Do not tell a child someone died "because he was sick."** The child may fear that whenever she or someone else becomes ill, that person will die. Let the child know that most of the time when people get sick they get better again.

◆ **Do not tell the child someone died because they were old**. To a very young child, a teenager is old.

◆ **Do not use euphemisms**. Saying "We have lost Grandpa," is very upsetting to a child. "Then let's find him! Why aren't we doing something?" Children's literal interpretation of language makes phrases like, "departed" confusing and distressing to children. Saying something like, "Your sister was so good, God decided to take her to heaven to be with Him," might make the child determined to be very bad so that God doesn't come after him too! In fact, saying that God took someone to be with Him in heaven might make the child very resentful of God.

◆ **Do not tell a child "be a big help"** to your parent(s) at this special time.

RESOURCES FOR CHILDREN

Books

Balter, Lawrence. (1991). Illustrated by Roz Schanzer. *A Funeral for Whiskers*. New York, NY: Barron's Educational Series, Inc. A beloved family cat dies. The family grieves together and parents sensitively answer young Sandy's typical expressions about death such as "Will you die?", "Won't she miss me?" and "I want her to come back." They have a funeral for Whiskers and remember the good times. This book could be read to the whole group of children or could be left out for children to page through at other times. There is a very helpful section for adults at the end of the book explaining children's typical reactions to death and appropriate adult responses.

Brown, Margaret Wise. (1965). *The Dead Bird*. New York, NY: HarperCollins. This children's classic is a good discussion of what "dead" is—cold and stiff with no heart beating. It also shows the children having the ritual of a funeral, imitating what they had seen adults do when someone dies.

Clifton, Lucille. (1983). Illustrated by Ann Grifalconi. *Everett Anderson's Goodbye*. New York, NY: Henry Holt and Company. *Everett Anderson's Goodbye* is a touching portrait of a little boy who is trying to come to grips with his father's death. We see him struggle through many stages, from denial and anger to depression and, finally, acceptance.

Greenlee, Sharon. (1992). Illustrated by Bill Drath. *When Someone Dies*. Atlanta, GA: Peachtree Publishers. This beautifully illustrated book sensitively addresses the complex feelings people have when someone they love dies, such as emptiness and loss, anger and worrying that others might die too. The book also offers suggestions about what to do, starting with "go ahead and cry."

Hines, Anna Grossnickle. (1991). *Remember the Butterflies*. New York, NY: Dutton Publishers. This is both a lovely nature book and a story that will help children think about death as a natural evolution.

Krementz, Jill. (1981). *How It Feels When a Parent Dies*. New York, NY: Alfred A. Knopf. Eighteen personal stories by children ages seven to fifteen are included in this book. They share their feelings about how it feels when a parent dies. Most of all they share that there aren't any right or wrong feelings, that acknowledging how you feel helps the most.

Maple, Marilyn. (1992). Illustrated by Sandy Haight. *On the Wings of a Butterfly: A Story About Life and Death*. Seattle, WA: Parenting Press, Inc. Beautiful watercolor illustrations accompany this story about the friendship between a young girl dying of cancer and a caterpillar preparing to become a monarch butterfly. The two friends share their quiet fears and questions as they ponder life and death, and finally embrace the unknown together.

Mellonie, Bryan and Ingpen, Robert. (1983). *Lifetimes*. New York, NY: Bantam Books. A beautiful book that looks at the cycles of life in the natural world. It opens the door for discussion about the difference between things that are alive and things that are dead.

Miles, Miska. (1985). Illustrated by Peter Parnall. *Annie and the Old One*. Boston: Little Brown. A young Navajo girl does not want her grandmother to die. In this lovely multicultural story, about death, the grandmother explains the ways of nature and that one cannot stop time. A story for elementary school-aged children.

Varley, Susan. (1992). *Badger's Parting Gifts*. New York, NY: William Morrow and Company. The animal friends are sad when old Badger dies, and their reactions are very reflective of how people grieve when friends die. Badger's animal friends all get together and talk about the good times and their happy memories of time spent with Badger, "Badger's parting gifts." This is one healthy response to death that we can help children experience. The book might be an ideal introduction to such an activity.

Viorst, Judith. (1971). Illustrated by Erik Blegvad. *The Tenth Good Thing About Barney*. New York, NY: MacMillan Publishing Co. Inc. This book explores the feelings of grief a child experiences when a favorite pet dies.

RESOURCES FOR ADULTS

Books

Centering Corporation. (1989). *Dear Parents: Letters to Bereaved Parents*. Omaha, NE: Centering Corporation. This is a book of fellowship and pain, of common feelings and expression. The letters are casual, yet powerful in their messages.

Fernside, A Center For Grieving Children. *Dealing with a Death and Grief at School*. Cincinnati, OH: Fernside, A Center For Grieving Children. This handbook for teachers and school staff discusses how to explain a death, answer questions, assist individual grieving students, a grieving class, a crisis plan and includes a lists of books and other resources.

Fitzgerald, Helen. (1992). *The Grieving Child, A Parent's Guide*. New York, NY: A Fireside Book, Simon & Schuster, Inc. If I had to pick just one resource to recommend about children's understanding of death, this would be it. It is very readable and very real and contains many useful understandings and useable strategies. Helen Fitzgerald, a grief counselor, talks about many different situations you might encounter including a sudden death, suicide, death of a parent, and the death of a sibling. She has all the words worked out for us, which helps tremendously.

Goldman, Linda. (1994). *Life and Loss: A Guide to Help Grieving Children*. Muncie, IN: Accelerated Development. Member of Taylor and Francis Group. This guide covers loss of precious things, death and grief. The discussion of harmful myths and how to correct them is excellent. The guide goes beyond understanding grief to understanding the child. The guide is also available from The Centering Corporation, 7230 Maple Street, Omaha, NE 68104. 402-553-1200. www.centering.org.

Grollman, Earl A. (Ed.) (1995). *Bereaved Children and Teens: A Support Guide for Parents and Professionals*. Boston: Beacon Press. An excellent resource that summarizes current thinking on helping children cope with death.

Grollman, Earl A. (1991). *Talking About Death: A Dialogue Between Parent and Child*. Illustrated by Susan Avishai. Boston: Beacon Press. This is a dual-purpose book. There is an illustrated section intended for an adult to read to a young child. The following section for parents elaborates on each page of the children's story, providing an explanation of the child's behavior. There is an extensive reference section listing children's books for all levels, adult resources and organizations and support groups.

Johnson, Joy. (1978). *Children Die, Too*. Omaha, NE: Centering Corporation. A small, sensitive book for parents who have experienced the death of a child. Available in both English and Spanish.

Prestine, Joan S. (1993). *Helping Children Cope with Death: A Practical Resource Guide for Someone Special Died*. Columbus, OH: Fearon Teacher Aids, A Paramount Communications Company. This is a 61-page teacher's guide companion to the children's picture book, *Someone Special Died*. It is a very useful guide, giving the teacher or parent actual words and phrases they might use to explain death and the feelings around it. There are specific activity suggestions to help children deal with the various feelings about death. It also includes a helpful resource section. The classroom teacher would find this book very useful and readable.

Rogers, Fred and Head, Barry. (1993). *Mister Rogers Talks With Parents*. Winona, MN: Hal Leonard Publishing Corporation. This book describes the understanding of children which forms the core of Mister Rogers' communication. The book is also available from Family Communications, Inc., 4802 Fifth Avenue, Pittsburgh, PA 15213. 412-687-2990. www.fci.org.

Booklet

Rogers, Fred and Sharapan, Hedda. *Talking with Young Children About Death: A Message from Fred Rogers*. Pittsburgh, PA: Family Communications, Inc. Funeral

Directors who are members of the National Funeral Directors Association may have this booklet on hand to give to families. Or, it can be ordered from Family Communications, 4802 Fifth Avenue, Pittsburgh, PA 15213. 412-687-2990. www.fci.org. $.50 per copy. Bulk prices available.

Videos

Death of a Goldfish. Family Communications Inc., 4802 Fifth Avenue, Pittsburgh, PA 15213. 412-687-2990. www.pbs.org/rogers. www.fci.org. 30 min. This classic Mister Rogers' Neighborhood program explores with children the difficult subject of death. *Death of a Goldfish* can be shown to young children in schools, libraries, churches and funeral homes. The presence of an adult who can help children deal with the feelings it may evoke is recommended.

Talking With Young Children About Death. Family Communications Inc., 4802 5th Avenue, Pittsburgh, PA 15213. 412-687-2990. www.fci.org. 28 min. Fred Rogers converses with his colleague, Hedda Sharapan about the *Death of a Goldfish* video, described above. It is a good video to use for staff training or perhaps at a parents' night meeting.

How Children Grieve. The Dougy Center: The National Center for Grieving Children and Families, 3909 SE 52nd Avenue, P.O. Box 86852, Portland, OR 97286. 503-775-5683. www.dougy.org. 30 min. The video is an inspiring presentation which explains the principles of support and the various ways in which children grieve.

ORGANIZATIONS & HOT LINES

The Compassionate Friends, P.O. Box 3696, Oak Brook, IL 60522-3696. 877-969-0010. www.compassionatefriends.org. Believing that the pain caused by the death of a child is best understood by other bereaved parents, this is an organization to support parents who have had a child die. They also reach out to bereaved siblings. There are local chapters all over the country. Call the number listed above to find your local chapter. They have a useful pamphlet, *Suggestions for Teachers and School Counselors*, as well as other pamphlets for a nominal cost.

The Centering Corporation, 7230 Maple Street, Omaha, NE 68134. 402-553-1200. www.centering.org. This organization offers many resources to parents, teachers and children who are affected by the death of a loved one. Their resources include:

> *The Class in Room 44: When a Classmate Dies*
> *I Heard Your Mommy Died*
> *I Know I Made It Happen: A Gentle Book About Feeling Guilty*
> *Grief Comes to Class*

Call or write for a complete publications list or to order materials.

The Dougy Center: The National Center for Grieving Children and Families, P.O. Box 86852, Portland, OR 97286. 503-775-5683. www.dougy.org. Named after a thirteen-year-old boy who died of a brain tumor, the Dougy Center is a support center for grieving children and for those who are a part of their lives. It is the first center in the U.S. to work primarily with children grieving the death of a family member or close friend. The center has also provided training sessions that have spawned over 42 similar groups in cities around the country. To locate the center nearest you, or for information about starting a center in your area, contact The Dougy Center. A publications list including books, videos, staff training manuals, and activity books for children is available.

Fernside, A Center for Grieving Children, 2303 Indian Mound Avenue, Cincinnati, OH 45212. 513-841-1012. www.fernside.org. Fernside provides direct services to grieving children through support groups and also provides support and help to people in other locations who are interested in starting similar centers. They have helpful pamphlets you can request such as *How A Teacher Can Help a Grieving Child, How to Tell a Child About Death*, and *How Can I Help a Grieving Child*. They have also published a children's workbook, A Book For You From Kids Like You, which can be ordered from the above address for $12.50. It has drawings and quotes from Fernside kids and pages to write and color on, so each child can make it her own, covering the topics of feelings, questions, changes, school, special days, and memories.

National Hospice and Palliative Care Organization, 1700 Diagonal Road, Suite 625, Alexandria, VA 22314. 1-800-658-8898. www.nhpco.org. Hospices provide care for terminally ill patients. As part of their services, often local hospices also provide grief counseling to families and children. If they do not provide this service directly, they will probably be able to provide a referral, telling you about other professionals in the community who do. Look in your phone book or call the 800 number listed above to locate your nearest hospice.

SIDS Alliance, 1314 Bedford Avenue, Suite 210, Baltimore, MD 21208. 800-221-SIDS. www.sidsalliance.org. Sudden Infant Death Syndrome (SIDS) or crib death is the major cause of death of children between the ages of one week and one year in the United States. The SIDS Alliance focuses its efforts on providing support to families who have suffered this tragedy, encouraging research about SIDS and educating professionals and the general public about SIDS. The SIDS Alliance offers over 30 publications ranging in price from $.20 to $3.00 and have bulk prices available. Call the 800 number listed above to find out how to contact a local chapter or for its publications list. Their titles include:

> *Sudden Infant Death Syndrome: Siblings and Grief*
> *Is There Anything I Can Do To Help? Suggestions for Friends & Relatives*
> *Talking to Children About Death*
> *From a Childcare Provider's Point of View*
> *What Childcare Facilities Should Know*
> *Grief of Children*

Death of a Family Member

SEPARATION & DIVORCE

HERE ARE TWO EXAMPLES

Five year old Jared was driving the teachers and the director crazy with his generally obnoxious behavior. He was very hungry for attention, positive or negative. He always wanted to be first, and the center of everything that was going on. He frequently argued with other children. If any new adult—parent, teacher or visitor—entered the classroom, Jared would try to get their total attention. Jared was especially demanding of one father who frequently volunteered in his daughter's classroom. Jared was always clinging to him and climbing all over him. This father handled the situation very appropriately, becoming a buddy to Jared without allowing himself to be distracted from the other children. Then suddenly Jared mellowed out and became much easier to get along with. The change was so remarkable that the teacher mentioned it to the mother one day when she came to pick Jared up. "Well, it's probably because his dad and I have gotten back together again," she responded. They had been separated for six months, and nobody had mentioned anything to the child care staff! The teachers and director were quite frustrated and felt that they might have handled situations with the child differently if they had known, offering him more of the emotional support he needed.

When parents don't get along, they sometimes find it hard to resist making negative remarks about each other to the staff. The staff may even be the target of their rude or angry remarks, simply because they are the ones who are handy when the parent is feeling frustrated.

One father frequently made snide remarks about his ex-wife in front of his four year old son, often on the subject of money or how the child was dressed. Little Matthew whined a lot, cried easily and had difficulty making friends, reflecting low self-esteem and a feeling of powerlessness. The father was also rude to the director when he learned that his ex-wife had been informed of a change in the child's classroom situation but he had not. This caused the director to sharpen her policies of communicating with both parents in cases when there was joint custody of the child. But she also took the father aside and informed him that she and her staff would prefer that he not speak negatively about his ex-spouse in front of the child. The director doubts that her admonitions will have much effect. She wishes she had been able to be proactive rather than reactive in this situation.

LET'S LOOK AT THE ISSUE

Other than the death of a parent, divorce may be the most devastating thing that can happen to children. So many things in their lives change. Usually one parent is physically absent from the home. Depending on circumstances, they may have to move. Money may become a problem, and a previously nonworking parent may have to go to work outside the home, causing changes in child care arrangements.

Divorce is not a one-time problem or event. It goes on and on, starting with family stress and arguing, and progressing to the separation, custody battles, family adjustments, difficult feelings at visitation time, difficulties with other family members, parents dating, remarriage and step families. Conflict between parents sometimes increases after the divorce has taken place, with negative consequences for the children. Families going through divorce usually feel some degree of pain and tension.

Joint custody is becoming a common practice. Parents with joint legal custody share in the decision making process on issues relating to the child, such as religious training, schooling and medical care. Parents with joint physical custody share in the actual physical care of the child, with the child spending part of his time in both residences. The best way parents can help their children make a positive adjustment to the divorce is often very difficult for them: they must try to get along, be civil to each other in the child's presence and not criticize each other.

Whether a child care arrangement is new or the child has already been in the program, the child care program may be the most stable element in the child's life and the teacher can be influential in the child's positive adjustment. The child care setting or school, because it is neutral ground, often becomes the place where children are transferred from one parent to another and where messages can be left. Remember that it can be very helpful to parents to have you there in a supportive stance. But both parents, and above all, the child, must be made to feel respected and supported. Avoid taking sides or representing one parent to the other.

INSIGHTS FROM CHILD DEVELOPMENT

Seeing parents as a unit. As Vicki Lansky states in her book, *Vicki Lansky's Divorce Book for Parents* (see the resource section at the end of this chapter), parents are a package deal to their children, who tend not to think of their parents as separate beings with their own interests and needs.

Will you stop loving me? Children may fear that if their parents stopped loving each other, they can stop loving them too. They do not understand that a husband's and wife's love for each other is different from the love that parents feel for their children.

Feelings of denial. It is common for the child to deny the problem initially, as though he does not understand the information. The parent might need to repeat the message numerous times.

Guilt and responsibility. Young children, because they are egocentric and believe that everything happens for or because of them, often feel that they caused the parent to leave or that they are responsible for their parents fighting. The guilt they carry erodes their self-esteem.

If they are very, very good, then... When children feel they caused the divorce, they sometimes think they can "uncause" the divorce by being very good and loveable, by getting sick, by becoming a problem at school or by doing other things to demand the attention of both parents.

Feeling powerless. A child's self-esteem often suffers when she fails to reunite her parents. She may feel unimportant because she is not her parents' primary concern.

Need for extra attention. Insecure children often demand extra attention from the newly single parent, who frequently has much less time and mental energy to devote to the child. As the parent struggles to develop independence and self-esteem, the child is sometimes left in the wake.

Parenting problems. Parents often have diminished parenting skills during and immediately after a divorce. They are preoccupied and children may have less supervision and less attention.

Feeling abandoned. Children might feel abandoned by the absent parent and fear that the other parent will leave as well. To make matters worse, parents sometimes offer their young child no explanation when they hire a sitter and go out for the evening, thinking that the child is too young to need an explanation. This heightens the child's feeling of abandonment and can make the child even more fearful and insecure.

Change-over day. In situations of joint physical custody, the change-over day—when the child changes from one residence to the other—can be difficult as the child gets her bearings in the new environment and tests limits. This is especially true for younger children.

Aggression and anger. When it comes to dealing with conflict, children often imitate the actions of those around them. Children who have witnessed domestic violence are more likely to be physically aggressive.

WHEN TO SEEK HELP

All of the following behaviors could simply indicate normal, healthy reactions of a child to a difficult situation. To determine when these behaviors indicate a need for special intervention and professional help, consider the individual child. If the behaviors continue for a prolonged time or are very unusual for that particular child, consult with others and consider recommending that the child get help.

◆ **Regression**. Children under stress sometimes want to return to a time when they felt safer or more loved. They may act out this longing with such behaviors as thumb sucking, using immature speech patterns, bed-wetting and increased clinging.

◆ **Lowered self-esteem**. Some children with low self-esteem engage in antisocial behaviors—bickering with friends, withdrawal, aggression, temper tantrums.

◆ **Depression**. Extreme sadness, withdrawal, listlessness, lack of concentration and involvement in activities, are all symptoms of depression in children. If such symptoms last for a prolonged time, they are signs that the child needs special help.

◆ **Acting out**. The child may behave aggressively and get into frequent trouble at school—perhaps hoping to divert the parents' attention back to himself.

◆ **Sickness**. The child may feign illness or develop a real illness or injure herself to get the parents to focus on her rather than their conflict.

Separation & Divorce

WHO CAN HELP

- A family counseling agency
- Marriage and family therapists
- Clergy members
- Custody mediators

HOW TO RESPOND

Offering stability, friendship and support to both the child and the parents can help during the stress of a divorce.

HOW TO RESPOND WITH THE STAFF

- **Discuss positive terminology**. Encourage people not to use the term "broken home."

- **Examine unrelated issues**. Don't assume that all the child's difficulties are solely the result of a divorce. Some issues might be totally unrelated.

HOW TO RESPOND WITH THE CHILD

- **Be available to the child**. Let her know that you are aware of the situation and that you are available to talk and listen. But do not intrude or pressure the child to open up.

- **Encourage expression**. Do a lot of activities about feelings to let children know that everyone has a range of feelings and emotions and to help them talk about them. They should feel free to express their emotions (see chapter 24).

- **Work on accepting change**. Talk about change and do activities to reinforce the idea that change is part of life.

- **Discourage self-blame**. Children need to be reminded that they are not to blame for their parents' divorce or separation. The parents are the best people to get this message across, but the teacher or child care provider can help, too. Children also need to hear that they can't do anything to bring their parents back together.

- **Reinforce parental love.** Parents never stop loving their children. Emphasize to the child that although people can stop being a husband or a wife, they never stop being a daddy or a mommy.

◆ **Stress love and safety**. The child must be told by parents, with the message possibly reinforced by you, that they will be taken care of and protected and loved, no matter what the adults decide to do about their living arrangements.

◆ **Draw pictures of loved ones**. Point out to children all the different people who love them and take care of them (including yourself). Perhaps encourage children to draw pictures of all the people in their lives who love them.

◆ **Provide consistency**. It may be best if the child does not change classes or teachers at this time. The younger the child, the more this is true.

HOW TO RESPOND WITH THE OTHER CHILDREN

◆ **Teach family words**. Discuss words related to family: newlyweds, mother, father, sister, brother, grandparent, aunt, uncle, cousin, nuclear families, single-parent families, stepfamilies. Build vocabulary. Talk with the children about all kinds of families.

◆ **Display children's books**. Select ones that represent all different kinds of families.

HOW TO RESPOND WITH INFANTS AND TODDLERS

◆ **Notice infant stress**. Infants and toddlers cannot understand what is going on, but they definitely feel the stress. They may exhibit more anxiety at separation and may need extra physical contact and comforting.

◆ **Provide stability of care**. Do not change teachers for the baby while the family is in this transition. Stability of care with a familiar, loving caregiver is very important.

HOW TO RESPOND WITH THE PARENTS

◆ **Keep informed**. Get the message across to parents that the director and teacher should be informed of any major changes at home that might affect the child's behavior at school. This message might be included in the written policies of the program and restated from time to time in newsletters or other material sent home. "We can be most supportive to you and your child if we understand what is going on," would be one way to put it. Assure parents of confidentiality.

◆ **Support parents**. Parents feel vulnerable during this time. They may even fear your criticism. They need your support, respect and acceptance as human beings and as parents at this time.

◆ **Stay neutral**. Do your best not to get in the middle or take sides. If a parent needs to vent anger, discourage him or her from doing so in the presence of the child. Often parents think children don't understand or aren't paying attention because they have heard it all anyway. But children are not served well by hearing negative things about either parent. Point out to the parent that the child really needs to have positive feelings about both parents. If appropriate, suggest that the parent talk to you in private, or suggest another professional, such as a family counselor, who the parent might talk to.

◆ **Present child's point of view**. Your role is to present the child's perspective to the parent and make the parent aware of how to avoid possible damage to the child. Share insights about what the child might be thinking if the child reveals something to you.

◆ **Offer resource books**. If appropriate, recommend helpful reading materials for adults and children (such as those listed in the resource section at the end of this chapter) and refer parents to other community resources.

◆ **Make the transfer process smooth**. The child care setting is often the transfer point for children who are in the care of both parents, with one parent dropping off the child and her things in the morning, and the other picking the child up in the afternoon. Try to develop systems for this so that there is less likelihood for missed messages or lost possessions. Keep it as smooth and as comfortable as possible, for the child's sake.

◆ **Note changing residences**. Keep track of which days the child resides with the mother and which days with the father. You may need to call home in case of illness or emergencies, or to send written messages concerning the program.

◆ **Keep records of legal custody arrangements**.

◆ **Communicate with both parties**. Make sure both parents receive all written communications about the program, such as written policies, notices of conferences, invitations to special events and changes in the child's teachers or classrooms.

WHERE TO FIND MORE INFORMATION

RESOURCES FOR CHILDREN

Books

Goff, Beth. (1969). Illustrated by Susan Perl. **Where Is Daddy? The Story of a Divorce**. Boston, MA: Beacon Press. A touching and affectionate book, *Where Is Daddy* is the story of a little girl whose world is turned inside-out when her parents divorce.

Hogan, Paula Z. (1992). Illustrated by Dora Leder. *Will Dad Ever Move Back Home?* Austin, TX: Raintree Steck-Vaughn Publishers. When a child is bitterly unhappy that her divorced parents no longer live together, she and her family discover the importance of her directly expressing her feelings.

Ives, Sally Blakeslee, et. al. (1985). *The Divorce Workbook: A Guide for Kids and Families*. Burlington, VT: Waterfront Books. This book will help children explore and understand some of the many emotions triggered by the separation and divorce process.

Lindsay, Jeanne Warren. (1991). Illustrated by Cheryl Boeller. *Do I Have A Daddy? A Story About a Single-Parent Child*. Buena Park, CA: Morning Glory Press. A single mother explains to her son that his daddy left soon after he was born. Includes a section of suggestions for answering the question, "Do I Have A Daddy?"

RESOURCES FOR ADULTS

Books

Bienenfeld, Florence. (1994). *Helping Your Child Through Your Divorce*. Alameda, CA: Hunter House, Inc. The author describes how to help children adjust to divorce. Emphasis is placed on developing a closer relationship with the child, relating more positively to the other parent and sharing parenting after divorce.

Grollman Earl A. (1975). *Talking About Divorce and Separation: A Dialogue Between Parent and Child.* Boston: Beacon Press. This excellent resource is helpful for both parents and children. The first section, which is illustrated, is designed for an adult to read to a child. The second section shows the children's text and discusses its significance with the parent.

Lansky, Vicki. (1991). *Vicki Lansky's Divorce Book for Parents: Helping Your Children Cope With Divorce and its Aftermath*. New York: NAL Dutton. This is a useful book for parents going through the process of divorce. Throughout, the focus is on how their children are perceiving the situation and how to put aside animosities while in the presence of children. In typical Vicki Lansky style, it is easy to read and very practical, with many parents sharing their experiences. A good book to recommend to parents.

Ricci, Isolina. (1982). *Mom's House, Dad's House: Making Shared Custody Work*. New York: MacMillan Publishing Company, Inc. This sensitively written book articulates practical and systematic guidelines for parents who are already divorced, supporting the idea that divorced parents can cooperate and build two homes for their children, even when they are not on friendly terms.

Rogers, Fred and Head, Barry. (1993). *Mister Rogers Talks With Parents*. Winona MN: Hal Leonard Corporation. The authors discuss divorce in the "Very Hard Times" chapter of the book. They acknowledge and respond to the feelings of parents, speaking directly to them.

Teyber, Edward. (1992). *Helping Children Cope With Divorce*. New York: Free Press. Written for parents, this book has distilled children's major problems around divorce in the various chapters, providing an excellent overview.

Wallerstein, Judith S. and Blakeslee, Sandra. (1990). *Second Chances: Men, Women & Children a Decade After Divorce*. New York: Ticknor & Fields. The authors share observations taken from their groundbreaking research project that followed families for fifteen years after the divorce. The focus is on what happens to the children and the circumstances that allow for the best adjustment. It's a very readable book providing vignettes from the lives of the individuals studied and would be valuable reading for parents with children who are considering a divorce. It also provides insights for adults working with children.

Articles

Frieman, Barry, B. "Separation and divorce: Children want their teachers to know." *Young Children*. 48(6), September 1993, 58-63. The article provides an extensive overview of the effect of divorce on children. Helping to meet the emotional needs of these children is an integral part of an educator's job.

Booklets & Pamphlets

Nuta, Virgina R. *Stress and the Single Parent*. National Committee to Prevent Child Abuse, Fulfillment Center, 1 Community Place, South Deerfield, MA 01373-0220. 800-835-2671. www.channing-bete.com. This pamphlet suggests ways single parents can reduce stress created by financial pressures, challenges of daily living, emotional distress and isolation.

Rogers, Fred and Grollman, Earl. *Talking with Families About Divorce*. Family Communications, Inc., 4802 Fifth Avenue, Pittsburgh, PA 15213. 412-687-2990. www.fci.org. There are few more stressful times for children than separation and divorce. In this booklet, the authors discuss some commonly asked questions that parents face at this difficult time. $.50 per copy. Bulk prices available.

Videos

Mister Rogers Talks With Parents About Divorce. Family Communications, Inc. 4802 Fifth Avenue, Pittsburgh, PA 15213. www.fci.org. 60 min. This video was originally prepared to precede a week of programs on "Mister Rogers' Neighborhood" television program, featuring a theme of divorce. Fred Rogers, Earl Grollman, author and counselor and Susan Stamberg, moderator interact with a studio audience of adults about various children's issues on the topic of divorce. Also included is footage of children at a divorce counseling center and their parents talking to Fred Rogers. Winner of several awards, it is an excellent video to have in a training resource library.

Organizations & Hot Lines

American Association of Marriage and Family Therapy, 112 South Alfred Street, Alexandria, VA 22314. 703-838-9808. www.aamft.org. This organization can provide a listing of trained marriage, family and child counselors in your area.

Alliance for Children & Families, 11700 West Lake Park Drive, Milwaukee, WI 53224. 414-359-1040. www.alliance1.org. Family Service America, Inc. (FSA) supports a network of 290 nonprofit, community based, family counseling and support services. Although each agency is unique, offering diverse services, all provide counseling to individuals and families. Most agencies also offer educational programs on family topics, such as courses on parenting skills, couples communication and coping with divorce. FSA also has a wide range of resources available such as books, videos and workshops. Member agencies undergo a rigorous accreditation process to assure that their programs meet standards of quality. Call the toll- free number for their catlog and a listing of the FSA agencies that are in your area.

Parents Without Partners, Inc., 1650 Southdixie Highway, Suite 500, Boca-Raton, FL 33432. 1-800-637-7974. www.parentswithoutpartners.org. Parents Without Partners, Inc. is an international, nonprofit membership organization devoted to the welfare and interests of single parents and their children. Single parents may join one of more than 500 local chapters. For additional information contact the local chapter in your area.

Chapter 7

CHAPTER 8

AFTER THE DIVORCE

HERE'S AN EXAMPLE

Martin, a successful businessman, was married for twelve years to Yvonne, an alcoholic. They had four children, all boys. They were ages 10, 7, 4 and 18 months when Yvonne left, leaving Martin to raise them. The divorce was finalized and Martin received sole custody of the boys. Visits to their mother turned out to be extremely difficult for the boys. After several years, visits became infrequent and then stopped altogether.

In the meantime, Martin had difficulty developing a relationship with another woman. Although he had no difficulty finding women to date, relationships with them never lasted. When they encountered his troop of rambunctious and by now hostile sons, they would disappear, some after just a few dates. Because his very demanding job required long and sometimes unpredictable hours, he hired live-in caregivers to drive the boys to and from their schools and child care center, and provide evening and weekend supervision. However, the boys were such a handful that the caregivers never lasted very long. Martin felt that the boys almost made a sport out of getting rid of any woman who entered their lives, be it a girlfriend or a caregiver.

Staff members at the child care center where the two younger boys were enrolled were concerned that the children did not have positive female role models in their lives and went out of their way to give them a lot of attention. The boys adjusted very well. The director also gave Martin the names of several family therapists, which Martin gratefully accepted. They continue to lend support and caring to this family.

After the Divorce

When divorced parents get on with their lives and develop new relationships, their children—who may still be struggling with their grief, anger and fears about divorce—have a new and complicated adjustment to make.

Young children often find it easy to get attached to a parent's new partner. However, when a parent has a series of new relationships, the child may feel confused and anxious. The child may re-experience grief and feelings of guilt and rejection with each break-up, and may even learn to distrust people.

A parent's dating may cause feelings of jealousy and resentment in the ex-spouse. Sometimes the ex-spouse uses the child as a spy to gain information and even coaches the child in ways to sabotage the new relationship. This is always damaging to the child, placing the child in the middle, increasing the child's feelings of guilt and potentially destroying the child's relationship with the other parent. Also, while the dating parent is caught up in the joy of a new relationship, he may not be as emotionally available to the child and may not notice that the child is uncomfortable with the situation.

As a general rule, the younger the child at the time of the remarriage, the easier the child adjusts to the new parent. Each blended family develops its own dynamics and experiences problems common to all families, such as sibling rivalry, as well as those common to blended families. For example, the child may have had a special, close relationship with the divorced parent, and now resents the new adult partner. The new parent as well as the biological parent may hesitate to discipline the child consistently, fearing the child's disapproval. The child may become angry and demanding.

There are no easy answers. Once again, it is best for the child if both of her biological parents treat each other with respect in her presence.

INSIGHTS FROM CHILD DEVELOPMENT

Wishful thinking. The child may harbor a fantasy that his parents will get back together again. The new partner and the new marriage makes this impossible. The child sometimes resists and feels angry and betrayed.

Loyalty to the parents. A child may want to like the stepparent, but her loyalty to the biological parent may cause her feelings of guilt and confusion.

Fitting in to the new family. "Will my dad still love me if he has another family?" "Why did he need other kids, wasn't I enough?" The child may feel displaced by new siblings.

Time alone with their biological children. It helps if parents can manage to spend special one-on-one time with their biological child, to reassure him that he is still special and to reduce problems of rivalry.

Time alone with stepparents. It is also good for stepparents to spend time alone with stepchildren, doing something fun together, to build a relationship.

Creating new traditions. Stepfamilies should create their own traditions and celebrations to develop feelings of comraderie.

Avoiding the negative. The stepparent should avoid speaking critically of a child's biological parent.

WHEN TO SEEK HELP

All of the following behaviors could simply indicate normal, healthy reactions of a child to a difficult situation. To determine when these behaviors indicate a need for special intervention and professional help, consider the individual child. If the behaviors continue for longer than the situation seems to warrant or are very unusual for that particular child, consult with others and consider recommending that the child get help.

◆ **Regression**. Children under stress sometimes want to return to a time when they felt safer or more loved. They may act out this longing with such behaviors as thumb sucking, using immature speech patterns, bed-wetting and increased clinging.

◆ **Lowered self-esteem**. Some children with low self-esteem engage in antisocial behaviors—bickering with friends, withdrawal, aggression, temper tantrums.

◆ **Depression**. Extreme sadness, withdrawal, listlessness, lack of concentration and involvement in activities are all symptoms of depression in children. If such symptoms last for a long time, they are signs that the child needs special help.

◆ **Acting out**. The child may behave aggressively and get into frequent trouble at school—perhaps hoping to divert the parents' attention back to himself.

◆ **Sickness**. The child may feign illness, develop a real illness or injure herself to get the parents to focus on her rather than their conflict.

◆ Family therapists
◆ A family counseling agency

HOW TO RESPOND

HOW TO RESPOND WITH THE STAFF

◆ **Describe family background**. Staff should be aware of the living arrangements of the child, and other details of the family situation.

◆ **Stress confidentiality**. Re-emphasize to staff the importance of confidentiality. When encouraging parents to reveal situations in their lives that might affect children's behavior, assure them of their privacy.

◆ **Teach limit setting**. Urge staff not to become sounding boards for parents' complaints about each other. While some of this is inevitable, encourage staff to set limits and suggest to parents the name of local counseling services instead. Encourage teachers to role play with words they might use with the parent. "This is really a hard time for you. While I care about you and your son, and will help you in any way I can to make his life stable, I'm not qualified to give you advice. Here's a place where other parents have found some useful information and help..."

HOW TO RESPOND WITH THE CHILD

◆ **Offer security**. While the child struggles to find his place in the new family or relationship, your classroom is one place he can feel secure in his position. Plan group-building activities, helping children to value each other.

◆ **Encourage doll house play**. A dollhouse with miniature people might have real appeal. The child can then create a perfect world where she feels more in control of the situation. Have some extra dolls to represent new grandparents, siblings and parent figures.

After the Divorce

◆ **Do puppet shows**. A couple of puppets could talk about their feelings of rejection or jealousy when someone new comes into their parent's life and ask the audience for advice.

◆ **Be accepting** of all the feelings expressed by the child. Resist countering, "You shouldn't feel that way, I'm sure your stepfather really..." These judgmental sounding phrases will only make the child feel guilty, angry and ashamed. Instead, give the child many ways to express feelings. Use creative art, sensory materials and play. You can talk about how people have all different kinds of feelings, and that this is OK. The child might learn she is not alone in having these feelings. Read a story, such as *Good Times, Bad Times, Mummy and Me* (see the resource section at the end of this chapter) that illustrates it is possible to have different feelings about the same person.

◆ **Destroy the myth** of the "wicked stepmother." Avoid reading fairy tales that reinforce these myths. If a child is exposed to these stories, counter them immediately. "It's not fair to say that stepmothers are all bad, is it? Stephanie has a stepmother and she's really nice. Stephanie, tell us some of the things you and your stepmother have done together."

HOW TO RESPOND WITH INFANTS AND TODDLERS

◆ **Offer security**. Infants and toddlers need the security of a stable caregiver. Consider having the teacher move up with the infants as they mature and become their toddler teacher and later their two's teacher. The added security of someone who knows and loves them can provide a young child with security.

HOW TO RESPOND WITH THE OTHER CHILDREN

◆ **Stop children from taunting**. If you hear a taunt, "You don't have a daddy," or questions like "Who is that lady? I thought that other lady was your mommy," explain to the children that there are all kinds of families.

◆ **Make a family book**. Create your own "All Kinds of Families" book with the children. Let them look through old catalogs and magazines and cut out pictures of people to represent their families. You could start the book with the words, "A family is a group of people who love each other and take care of each other." Then page by page, describe each child's family. "Mark lives with his mother and his grandmother and his cat, Fluffy. Julie's family has two sisters and one brother and a daddy. Julie's mother lives in another house but they spend time together too."

HOW TO RESPOND WITH THE PARENTS

◆ **Encourage communication**. Encourage parents to let the child's teachers know when something emotionally taxing may be going on in the child's life. Emphasize to parents that you do not wish to be intrusive, but that teachers need to know about such things in order to respond to the child appropriately and supportively.

◆ **Find out about the family**. Find out what each child's family situation is. Who does she live with? Is there a stepparent? Does the child have regular contact with the non-custodial parent? As you would for other children, try to get to know or at least recognize any relative who might pick the child up.

◆ **Be sensitive about family events**. Make it clear in your invitations that any significant adults in the child's life are welcome at program events.

◆ **Reinforce relationships**. If the stepparent drops off and picks up the child, try to make her at ease. If the child appears happy to see the stepparent at the end of the day, reinforce the relationship by commenting on the child's positive response.

◆ **Set limits**. Stop parents immediately if they start complaining about an ex-spouse in the child's presence.

WHERE TO FIND MORE INFORMATION

RESOURCES FOR CHILDREN

Books

Adoff, Arnold. (1973). Illustrated by Arnold McCully. ***Black is Brown is Tan***. New York, NY: HarperCollins Publishers. Children, grandparents, aunts and uncles are all the colors of the rainbow, and the whole family is filled to overflowing with love.

Benamin, Amanda. (1995). ***Two's Company***. New York, NY: Penguin USA. The idyllic existence which Maddy and her mother share is not the same when Simon comes into their lives.

Galloway, Priscilla. (1980). ***Good Times Bad Times, Mummy and Me.*** Toronto, Canada: Womens Press. A little girl in a single-parent family describes how she hates her mother who is busy while her grandmother takes care of her, but then decides that she does love her mother.

Kroll, Virginia. (1994). Illustrated by Stacey Schuett. ***Beginnings: How Families Come to Be***. Morton Grove, IL: Albert Whitman Publishers. Parents and children discuss how their families come to be, covering birth families and various kinds of adoptive families.

Simon, Norma. (1976). Illustrated by Joe Lasker. *All Kinds of Families*. Morton Grove, IL: Albert Whitman Publishers. This book explores in words and pictures what a family is and how families vary in makeup and lifestyles.

Simon, Norma. (1976). Illustrated by Dora Leder. *Why Am I Different?* Morton Grove, IL: Albert Whitman Publishers. Differences in physical appearance, personality and culture as presented in this book help children come to terms with their own self-image and self-respect.

Willhoite, Michael. (1990). *Daddy's Roommate*. Boston, MA: Alyson Wonderland. This story is told by a little boy whose parents are divorced and whose father is gay.

RESOURCES FOR ADULTS

Books

Burns, Cherie. (1986). *Stepmotherhood*. New York: First Perennial Library.

Heegard, Marge. (1993). *When a Parent Marries Again: Children Can Learn to Cope with Family Change*. Minneapolis: Woodland Press. This workbook is designed to be used with children who are encouraged to draw their own pictures on each page. Thus each page provides a teacher or parent with issues to be aware of and that can be discussed with children.

Kaplan, Leslie. (1986). *Coping with Stepfamilies*. New York: Rosen Publishing.

Mala, Burt. (1989). *Stepfamilies Stepping Ahead*. Lincoln, NE: Stepfamily Association of America, Inc., 650 J Street, Suite 205, Lincoln, NE 68508. 800-735-0329. www.stepfam.org

Prilik, Pearl. (1990). *Stepmothering: Another Kind of Love*. New York: Berkley.

Savage, K. & Adams, P. (1988). *The Good Stepmother*. New York: Crowne Publishers.

Teyber, Edward. (1992). *Helping Children Cope with Divorce*. New York: Free Press. Written for parents, this book has distilled children's major problems around divorce in its various chapters, providing an excellent overview. The last four chapters focus on child-rearing after divorce, including problems of stepfamilies.

Wallerstein, Judith S. and Blakeslee, Sandra (1990). *Second Chances: Men, Women and Children a Decade After Divorce*. New York: Ticknor & Fields. This book shares observations and insights taken from a groundbreaking research project that followed families for fifteen years after the divorce. The focus is on what happens to the children and the circumstances that allow for the best adjustment. Some of the vignettes show children's emotions and responses to parents' dating and remarriages.

Videos

Remarriage and After, Stepfamily Association of America, Inc., 650 J Street, Suite 205, Lincoln, NE 68508. 800-735-0329. www.stepfam.org. 30 min. Told from the vantage point of both stepparents and mental health professionals, the video describes the realities and rewards of combining two families. Themes include learning to let go of unrealistic ideals and demands, keeping boundaries and redefining family roles.

Organizations & Hot Lines

Alliance for Children & Families, 11700 West Lake Park Drive, Milwaukee, WI 53224. 414-359-1040. www.alliance1.org. Family Service America, Inc. (FSA) supports a network of 290 nonprofit, community based, family counseling and support services. Although each agency is unique, offering diverse services, all provide counseling to individuals and families. Most agencies also offer educational programs on family topics, such as courses on parenting skills, couples communication, and coping with divorce. FSA also has a wide range of resources available such as books, videos and workshops. Member agencies undergo a rigorous accreditation process to assure that their programs meet standards of quality. Call the toll- free number for their catalog and a listing of the FSA agencies that are in your area.

Parents Without Partners, Inc., 1650 Southdixie Highway, Suite 500, Boca-Raton, FL 33432. 1-800-637-7974. www.parentswithoutpartners.org. Parents Without Partners, Inc. is an international, nonprofit membership organization devoted to the welfare and interests of single parents and their children. Single parents may join one of more than 500 local chapters. For additional information contact the local chapter in your area.

Stepfamily Association of America, Inc., 650 J Street, Suite 205, Lincoln, NE 68508. 800-735-0329. www.stepfam.org. The Stepfamily Association of America is an educational resource for individuals who want to learn about stages of stepfamily development. The Stepfamilies quarterly newsletter includes research, book reviews and information for professionals who work with stepfamilies. A catalog of resources including books, audio tapes, and videos is available.

After the Divorce

CHAPTER 9

NATURAL DISASTERS

HERE ARE TWO EXAMPLES

Mary's family child care home is not far from the epicenter of the 1994 major earthquake in Northridge, California. Because earthquakes do occur in that area, Mary had received training on earthquake survival from her local family child care professional association. She and the children had often practiced their "earthquake drill," crouching under her massive dining room table. A day after the 1994 quake, she was open for business again, her home having received only minor damage. Parents bringing children that day reported that their children were experiencing some sleep disturbances and anxiety, but otherwise had "hung in there" and helped their families clean up. Mary said that at her home, the children's favorite game became "earthquake." Spontaneously, they would start stomping their feet, shaking and shrieking and then gleefully crawling under the table, where they would crouch and giggle. They played this game over and over again. Mary feels that because they had practiced earthquake readiness and that their families remained stable during the earthquake, the children did not experience undue emotional trauma.

One newscaster reported after a large earthquake that his three year old daughter refused to sleep in her own bed for several days after the quake. She shook her finger and said, "Naughty, naughty bed!" She thought that her bed had caused the quake because that's where she was when it occurred!

Natural Disasters

Earthquakes, floods, fires, mud slides, hurricanes and tornados are experienced by people everywhere. The randomness of these occurrences makes them all the more frightening and devastating to victims. Unlike many personal disasters, which develop over a long period of time and are somewhat predictable, natural disasters are **always** unexpected.

Children are greatly influenced by the behavior of the adults around them in times of disaster. This type of trauma, though frightening for everyone, is not usually as psychologically devastating to children as community or domestic violence, for instance, because the child's trust in his family and neighbors is not affected.

Like other types of personal trauma, being the victim of a disaster involves loss and separation. There is an economic impact. There are long-term repercussions. A natural disaster is a "life marker," and people sometimes organize their memories in terms of "before the fire, after the fire."

Whatever the situation, stress will be felt by the adults, and that stress is likely to continue as people struggle to put their lives together—dealing with transportation problems and financial difficulties. When adults are distracted, they often have less emotional energy left over for the children. Children may feel angry or emotionally abandoned when important adults in their lives are so focused on other things.

If there is a positive side to natural disasters, it is that people often come together to deal with the resulting problems. Children will observe people helping people, and community helpers doing their jobs. Natural disasters often bring out the best in people. And they sometimes bring families closer, because when people lose possessions and are grateful just to be alive, they think again about what is really important in life.

"Be prepared!" is the consistent advice for families, child care programs and schools. All state licensing regulations require that schools, centers and child care homes show disaster plans and escape routes for fire and other disaters. But having it in the regulations and posting a chart on the wall is not enough. True preparation requires a well thought out plan for your particular location, assignments of who will do what, systems for contacting parents and frequent rehearsals with the children.

INSIGHTS FROM CHILD DEVELOPMENT

Natural disasters are even more frightening for children. Natural disasters that terrify adults are even more frightening for children who really have no understanding of what causes these events.

Adults must address their own fears. How children respond depends on how family members and other adults respond. Adults need to address their own fears as best they can.

The event may not be as traumatic as others in a child's life. Though frightening, natural disasters may not be as emotionally traumatic as community or domestic violence.

Children may think they caused the event. The child might think he did something to cause the problem. Some children feel shame or guilt. They might think they caused the event because they wished it would happen.

Children need reassurance. Adults experiencing a natural disaster are understandably upset and may act in a way that children are not accustomed to seeing. Children may need to be reminded that they did not cause the adult's anxious or irritable behavior.

Self-esteem may suffer. Children's self-esteem can suffer as a result of feeling powerless and helpless.

WHEN TO SEEK HELP

Watch for signs of extreme stress in children. While all children who have experienced a natural disaster will show some of these behaviors, if these behaviors persist with the same intensity or increase, the child may need professional help.

◆ **Long-lasting sleep disturbances**. It is common for children to want to sleep with parents after a terribly frightening event, and often parents prefer this as well.

◆ **Fearfulness**

◆ **Extreme separation anxiety**

◆ **Heightened aggression**

◆ **Exaggerated regression**. The child may turn to thumb sucking, bed-wetting or baby talk, in an attempt to feel safer.

In allowing regression you can reassure them, "Sometime you will feel comfortable again. But now we'll help you get through this."

◆   Local professional contacts such as your licensing office, a local branch of an early childhood professional organization or a local child care resource and referral agency will likely have guidelines for disaster preparedness and know where specific training is offered.

◆   Your local Red Cross chapter will have information on disaster preparedness.

HOW TO RESPOND

HOW TO RESPOND WITH THE STAFF

◆   **Design a broad disaster plan** to accommodate staff needs. Include this as part of staff orientation programs.

◆   **Practice disaster drills** and variations so that children and staff members know what to do. One center gave each person an envelope to open at 2:00 in the afternoon with a note saying such things as, "Earthquake. You are injured and cannot leave the room." This may work well with older children who can easily separate fantasy and reality. Another center did something similar, using a local boy scout troop to play the part of children in a disaster scenario.

◆   **Recognize that staff may experience inner conflict**, knowing they should remain with children at the center but wanting to be home with their families. Talk about this ahead of time. One center's plan is that staff members who have young children at home may leave. Discuss if you can cover for one another while a few staff members go to find out about their own children. It's an ethical concern.

◆   **Encourage staff to create their own family plan**, knowing that they may have to remain at work. Suggest they plan for other family members to be with their children.

HOW TO RESPOND WITH THE CHILDREN

Some people wonder if they should encourage children to talk about the event or act it out in play, fearing that they will intensify or prolong the children's fears. Generally, this is not the case. The children are already thinking about it. Talking about it may relieve some of their anxieties and show them that they are not alone in their feelings. You may also be able to clear up any misconceptions they have about the event.

Natural Disasters

◆ **Conduct drills**. Knowing what to do in the event of an emergency makes children feel safer and more in control. Talk about what you will all do if a particular event happens again.

◆ **Provide stability and routine**. It's important to make children feel safe and create stability and routine in their lives as quickly as possible after the disaster.

◆ **Re-enact the event**. Let children re-enact the event in their dramatic play. This is the way many children work it through and gain a sense of power and control over the situation.

◆ **Encourage miniature play**. Offer children small dolls, cars, blocks and doll house furniture to recreate in miniature the scene or event that they experienced in real life. This makes children feel less helpless.

◆ **Arrange group time** or circle time. Encourage children to talk about the disaster while others are listening. They can discover that they aren't the only ones who were scared or whose parents were distressed by the event.

◆ **Work on creative movement**. Encourage the children to use creative movement to express feelings about the event.

◆ **Share your own feelings** about the event. Be real. Talk about how you coped.

◆ **Do art activities**. It might help children to draw or paint pictures of their experience. Very young children might just scribble. If so, you might ask the child to tell you about the scribbles and take dictation, if you think it is appropriate.

◆ **Write in journals**. Older children could make an illustrated journal about the event. They could dictate their story for you to record, draw pictures and put in small souvenirs.

◆ **Read books about the event**. If you can't find any, make your own book about it. Let the child help.

◆ **Discuss community helpers**. Point out all the people in the community who helped out—police officers, fire fighters, Red Cross workers, counselors, neighbors, teachers and hospital workers. Talk about how people come together in times of crisis to help each other.

◆ **Talk about helping others**. Ask the children how they might help others during different types of disasters.

◆ **Plan activities about feelings**. Do lots of activities about feelings to allow the children to express how they felt in the situation. Offer many different modes. (See chapter 23 for activity suggestions.)

◆ **Include clay, sand or water play**. Children can use these materials to recreate a natural disaster in their play.

◆ **Talk about the good part**. Children need to know they are survivors. If you concentrate on something good that happened, the children will focus less on the negative.

Possible words to use

◆ "You are safe now."
◆ "I am sorry that it (the flood, fire, earthquake) happened."
◆ "It wasn't your fault."
◆ "Things may never be the same, but they will get better."

HOW TO RESPOND WITH THE OTHER CHILDREN

◆ **Talk with the other children**. If not all children were involved, talk to them about what happened to their friends. Exaggeration, even among four year olds, can make the situation much worse than it really was.

◆ **Encourage altruism**. You may have an opportunity to involve the children in altruistic, empathetic activities. Encourage them to think of ways they can help their friends who were affected.

HOW TO RESPOND WITH INFANTS AND TODDLERS

◆ **Watch for heightened separation anxiety**. Infants and toddlers show heightened separation anxiety after experiencing a disaster.

◆ **Be patient**. Sleep disturbances, fearfulness, regression in toileting are all common reactions. Urge parents to show extra patience.

HOW TO RESPOND WITH THE PARENTS

◆ **Explain your disaster plan**. Parents should supply the materials for their child's "earthquake kit" and provide the center with current information such as phone numbers and emergency contacts.

◆ **Encourage them to be good role models**. Let parents know that children usually do as well as the adults around them when a disaster happens. If the parents fall apart and show great fear and anxiety, so will the children. If the parents are able to put the event behind them, the children are also likely to recover faster.

◆ **Remind them to keep their children's needs in mind**. During a disaster, they may forget the importance of comforting their child.

◆ **Learn about each family**. You need to learn about every family's situation so that you can respond to the children appropriately.

WHERE TO FIND MORE INFORMATION

RESOURCES FOR CHILDREN

Books

Harshman, Marc. (1995). Illustrated by Mark Mohr. *The Storm*. New York, NY: Cobblehill Books. Though confined to a wheelchair, Jonathan faces the terror of a tornado all by himself and saves the lives of the horses on the family farm.

Polacco, Patricia. (1994). *Tikvah Means Hope*. New York, NY: Doubleday Books for Young Readers. After a devastating fire in the hills of Oakland, California, a Jewish family and their neighbors find symbols of hope amidst the ashes.

Simon, Seymour. (1991). *Earthquakes*. New York, NY: Morrow Junior Books. Seymour Simon examines the phenomena of earthquakes, describing how and where they occur and how they can be predicted.

Stewart, Dianne. (1993). Illustrated by Jude Daly. *The Dove*. New York, NY: Greenwillow Books. A visiting dove provides the answer to Grandmother Malokos' problems when floodwaters destroy her crops.

Stolz, Mary. (1988). Illustrated by Pat Cummings. *Storm in the Night*. New York, NY: Harper Trophy. While sitting through a fearsome thunderstorm that has put the lights out, Thomas hears a story from Grandfather's boyhood.

Books

Heegard, Marge. (1992). *When Something Terrible Happens: Children Can Learn to Cope With Grief Workbook*. Minneapolis, MN: Woodland Press. This workbook, which incorporates an art therapy approach, is one book of a series entitled Drawing Out Feelings. As an activity book it is designed for children to draw on the pages, but children also could draw on sheets of paper. Though the workbook is written for children, six to twelve years of age, the book contains insights for working with younger children as well.

La Greca, Annett M. and others. (1994). *Helping Children Prepare for and Cope With Natural Disasters: A Manual for Professionals Working With Elementary School Children*. Coral Gables, FL: Author. The manual is based on reseach conducted following Hurricane Andrew in the Departments of Psychology at the University of Miami and the Florida International University. The research was funded by The BellSouth Foundation. Single copies of this manual can be obtained at no charge by writing Annette La Greca, University of Miami, Department of Psychology, P.O. Box 248185, Coral Gables, FL 33124.

Nordgren, J. Chris, (1994). *Children and Disaster: A School Counselor's Handbook on How to Help*. Vermillion, SD: University of South Dakota. This handbook addresses key issues which need to be considered by school counselors when helping children cope with a disaster. Emphasis is placed on distinguishing milder normal reactions which do not need referral for intensive help from those reactions which are more severe and require referral for therapeutic intervention from a professional trained to treat traumatic stress responses. To order copies contact Disaster Mental Health Institute, University of South Dakota, 414 East Clark, South Dakota Union 114, Vermillion, SD 57069, 605-677-6575. www.usd.edu/dmhi.

Booklets & Pamphlets

Helping Children Cope With Disaster. Federal Emergency Management Agency, P.O. Box 70274, Washington, DC 20024. The Federal Emergency Management Agency's (FEMA) Family Protection Program developed this pamphlet in cooperation with the American Red Cross' Community Disaster Education Program. Both are national efforts to help people prepare for disasters of all types. For more information on how to prepare for and respond to disaster, contact your local or state office of emergency management and your local Red Cross chapter. Ask for "Your Family Disaster Plan", or write to FEMA at the address listed above.

CHILD ABUSE

HERE'S AN EXAMPLE

When Darla, four years old, came in to the child care center on a Monday morning, the director noticed that the whole left side of her chin was bruised and purple. When the director asked her what happened, Darla said, "My mom pushed me down on the carpet." The director looked up at the mother and asked, "Is this true?" The mother said, "Oh yeah, it's just a rug burn." It was obvious to the director that it was more than a rug burn. The bruise went all the way up into her cheek area. The director called Child Protective Services (CPS) and found out that they had an open abuse case on this family. When CPS came out to the center, they asked the seven year old brother what had happened. He said he wasn't there and didn't know what happened. When the CPS worker called from the director's office, she was heard to say, "Well, we have another complaint of abuse about Darla." The director thought, "Another complaint of abuse? Why aren't we doing something about this, and why didn't they let us know?"

The outcome was that the mother was required to take parenting classes. However, the mother was very frustrated with the child care center for reporting it. (Since the brother was questioned at the center, the parent knew where the complaint originated.) Darla's mother withdrew her from the center. So the center never knew how the family was doing, was unable to be supportive to the child or the parent and the child lost her friends and social setting.

Child Abuse

The director complains, "We never get the follow-up. And when we make the call as mandated reporters, CPS calls the home and says, `We have had a complaint about you. We will be at your house at 1:00 on Tuesday to check things out.' So by that time, it's going to look fine. We later get a letter from CPS saying in effect, `We find at this time that there is no cause for investigation.' In the meantime we lose the enrollment and the child isn't helped. Although the parent is never supposed to know who reported it, they usually figure it out. Even though we'd like to stay involved with the child, there are several things going against us. First of all, the parent would fear that we would be doubly suspicious and go over every inch of the child's body every day, and probably we would! Second, the staff bears a lot of frustration and outrage against the parent. How could they do a thing like this to a child? So it is very difficult."

LET'S LOOK AT THE ISSUE

Child abuse is a complex problem which cannot be addressed or solved by a single individual or agency. It is a community problem which requires a community response to support families so they will stop their abusive ways of handling stress and solving problems. As an early childhood professional, you have an important role to play on the team of professionals that addresses the problem.

The director in the example expressed the frustration of many teachers and administrators that they feel they often do more harm than good when they report abuse. Sometimes the intervention is inadequate, and they lose the child. Social service agencies are trying hard to address the rising tide of abuse in communities. If you have similar stories to tell, tell them. Speak to the supervisor of the agency involved. Speak to others. Write letters. Work to improve the situation. But the fact remains that no matter what, you are required to report any form of child abuse, or suspicion of abuse.

Your role includes identifying and reporting suspected abuse, providing a safe haven for the child while in your care, and providing case managers with pertinent information about the child and what you know about the abuse. Ideally, your role will also include working with other professionals in a treatment plan for the child, continuing to lend support to the child and the family, and giving feedback to case managers about the child's and the family's progress.

As the director in the example indicated, it can be very difficult to work respectfully with parents while you are outraged at their actions. It is no easy matter breaking the cycle of abuse. For instance, simply teaching parenting skills or stress management techniques is usually not enough. Child abuse is very often connected with or compounded by substance abuse. Poverty and family stress can also be complicating factors. Often these parents were never parented themselves. They have no positive role model to call to mind. Add to that the fact that the great majority of people who physically or emotionally abuse their children were themselves abused as children, and it is apparent that intervention needs to happen with a team of trained professionals with different areas of expertise.

From a proactive, or preventive point of view, child care programs can serve to support families and parents, relieving stress, confirming their role as parents, and ultimately preventing situations that lead to abuse such as low parental self-esteem, isolation and lack of good parenting strategies. This is accomplished by providing a warm, welcoming, fun and respectful atmosphere. Reach out to parents. Share positives about their child. Let them know they are important. Develop an atmosphere of empathy, support and friendship.

If there is a bright side to discovering child abuse it is that once discovered or uncovered, help can be given. It is ideal when the early childhood education setting can be positioned as a support to parents, helping to relieve their stress and understand their child's behavior and needs, and to learn positive techniques for discipline.

TYPES OF ABUSE

Child abuse is often broken down into the following three broad categories: physical abuse, sexual abuse and neglect. (Sexual abuse is discussed in chapter 11.) The *Coordinated Response to Child Abuse and Neglect: Basic Manual* published by the U.S. Department of Health and Human Services gives concise descriptions of all kinds of abuse.

Physical Abuse

Personal injury (for example, bruises and fractures) resulting from punching, beating, kicking, biting, burning, or otherwise harming a child. Although the injury is not an accident, the parent or caregiver may not have intended to hurt the child. The injury may have resulted from harsh discipline or physical punishment that is inappropriate to the child's age or condition.

The injury may be the result of a single episode or of repeated episodes and can range in severity from minor bruising to death. Any injury resulting from physical punishment that requires medical treatment is considered outside the realm of normal disciplinary measures. A single bruise may be inflicted inadvertently; however, old and new bruises in combination, bruises on several areas of the face, or bruising in an infant suggests abuse. In addition, any punishment that involves hitting with a closed fist or an instrument, kicking, inflicting burns or throwing the child is considered child abuse regardless of the severity of the injury sustained.

Omissions by the parents or other responsible persons that could cause serious behavioral, cognitive, emotional or mental disorders.

In cases of neglect, the most successful models of intervention programs work intensively with the whole family and endeavor to build a positive, secure attachment between the parent and the child. Since the abusers most often have very low self-esteem and associate intimacy with pain, the intervention programs work to support the parent to have successful relationships with their children. As the parent learns to read their child's cues, play interactively and elicit positive responses from their child, the parent's self-esteem and confidence as a parent gradually increase. When the parent feels nurtured and respected by the staff they can then begin to listen and learn. This takes much sensitivity and empathy as well as specific training.

Child abuse may occur in a home where other grave problems are also present. Very often when there is spouse abuse (domestic violence), there is also child abuse. Substance abuse is often involved. They are adults who, for one reason or another, are beyond their limits of stress. In most cases, adults do not get out of bed in the morning with the intent to abuse their children in the coming day. It is the accumulation of intolerable stressors and a lack of coping skills that lead them to the harmful actions. They need help. The children need help. But first, the abuse must be stopped.

INSIGHTS FROM CHILD DEVELOPMENT

INFANTS AND TODDLERS

◆ **Betrayed trust**. When an infant is abused by a parent or trusted caregiver, basic trust is betrayed.

◆ **Limp and nonresponsive**. Infants may become limp and nonresponsive, as though they have shut down and stopped trying.

◆ **Sleep disturbances**. Infants may have sleep disturbances and increased crying, which in turn, adds stress to the family and the potential for more abuse.

◆ **Developmental delays** are created both by possible physical damage to the child and by the destruction of the child's curiosity and initiative. They are less likely to explore, play with objects, experiment with cause and effect because of severe punishment, and lose the cognitive benefits of these activities.

◆ **Language delays** emerge in physically abused, ignored babies.

Physical abuse

◆ **Aggressive and hostile**. Physically abused children sometimes become aggressive and hostile toward other children. They identify with the powerful aggressor in their lives.

◆ **Withdrawn and fearful**. Other children may become withdrawn and fearful.

◆ **Act out**. Children may act out abuse they have experienced in their dramatic play, to help them feel a sense of power and control over the situation.

◆ **Social skills**. Children's social skills are often inadequate because they have not had the model of problem solving and empathy at home.

◆ **Suffer from separation**. If you are dealing with a child who has been removed from the home, you have some added, complex problems. Although the child may be safe from physical harm, the child is likely suffering emotionally from separation, loss of trust and the daily awareness that she could be removed from her present home. This can affect the child's ability to develop trusting relationships with teachers, caregivers or friends.

Neglect

◆ **Erosion of self-esteem**. Negelct results in the erosion of a child's self-esteem. The child feels worthless, like he is a burden.

◆ **Antisocial behavio**r. Antisocial, hostile, angry, aggressive behavior can also result from neglect.

WHEN TO SEEK HELP

SIGNS OF PHYSICAL ABUSE

◆ **On the body**. Physical signs on the child's body including welts, bruises, marks, bites, or burns on any part of the child's body such as the face, lips, mouth, back and buttocks. Be especially suspicious if there are both new and old bruises on the child, or if there are marks in the shapes of objects such as extension cords used for beatings.

◆ **Unexplained or vague injury**. The child acts confused or flustered and is not able to explain the mark, or is inconsistent in what he says about it.

Child Abuse

◆ **Covering up marks**. The child wears a lot of clothing in warm weather, possibly covering up marks.

◆ **Ignoring a problem that requires medical attention**. The parent continues to ignore an obvious physical problem that needs medical attention.

◆ **Injuries more common after weekends or vacations**. The child comes back from vacation or a weekend with an injury. Are symptoms of abuse worse after the child has been home for a while?

◆ **The parents frequently keep the child home**.

SIGNS OF NEGLECT

There are fewer clear indicators of neglect.

◆ **Aggressive or withdrawn**. The child may be aggressive or passive and withdrawn.

◆ **Low self-esteem and poor social skills**. The child usually exhibits low self-esteem and poor social skills.

◆ **Overly compliant**. The child may be overly compliant, listless, apathetic or depressed.

◆ **Poor expressive language skills**. The child may have poor expressive language skills.

◆ **Listen to how the parents talk to the child**. Often the most obvious clue is hearing inappropriate, humiliating remarks to the child coming from the parent such as name calling and frightening threats.

◆ **Listen to the child's pretend play**. Sometimes the child will reflect these remarks in her pretend play when she is playing the role of parent. Be careful not to jump to conclusions based on this alone.

WHO CAN HELP

◆ The agency in your area that deals with child abuse reports. Check the phone directory under the name of your city or county for one of the following listings, or ask the telephone information operator who to call in your area.

Department of Child Protective Services
Department of Social Services
Public Social Services Department
Department of Protective Services
Social and Rehabilitative Services
Bureau of Children & Family Services

◆ Law enforcement agencies
◆ Mental health centers
◆ Family therapists
◆ Social workers
◆ Child psychologists

HOW TO RESPOND

HOW TO RESPOND WITH THE STAFF

◆ **Regular inservice training**. All staff must be aware of how to recognize all types of suspected child abuse. Regular inservice training on this topic should be provided.

◆ **Find out the proper procedures** for reporting suspected child abuse in your state. It would be a good idea to obtain a copy of the state law to have in the center. This can be obtained through the local department of social services, city or county attorney's office, the law enforcement agency in your area or the state attorney general's office. You need to know who should report abuse, who to call, what needs to be reported, what type of information they need and what will happen. Sometimes the law requires both an oral and a written report.

◆ **Training session**. Invite a representative from the agency that would receive an abuse report to an inservice training session to describe what happens when a report is filed. What happens next?

◆ **Report suspected abuse immediately**. If you make the report of suspected abuse in good faith, meaning you have reason to suspect there may be abuse, and it turns out not to be substantiated, you are legally protected. You cannot be sued. In most cases your report may be made anonymously, but it is usually better if you identify yourself, so follow-through is more likely. Consult your director and staff procedures before filing a report.

◆ **Give the agency as much information as possible** about why you suspect the abuse and where the victim is, as well as where you think the perpetrator is at the time.

◆ **Remember, your report is not an accusation**. It is a required attempt to find out if abuse is taking place, so that if it is true, efforts can be made to intervene on behalf of the child and start the helping process.

◆ **Work with other professionals**. If abuse is substantiated you can express an interest in working with other professionals on a multidisciplinary team to benefit the child and support the family. Since child care professionals are often forgotten when a team is formed, it is good for you to take the initiative and express interest. You may have direct opportunities to help the child and family, and you may learn strategies for dealing with the situation from the advice of the other members of the team. Further, your input and feedback can give them valuable information in addressing and resolving the problem.

◆ **Seek professional counseling**. If you or any of your staff were yourselves abused or neglected as children, talk about it to try to come to terms with it, and if needed, seek professional counseling. This is necessary before one can deal with it in children.

Barriers to reporting abuse

(Adapted from *The Role of Educators in the Prevention and Treatment of Child Abuse and Neglect*)

◆ **Fear that the child may be pulled out of the program**. This is a legitimate concern for child care centers in circumstances where parents have other options for care. If parents are told with sensitivity of the report, the center might eventually be seen as an ally rather than an enemy, communicating to parents the desire to support the parent in the difficult task of looking after young children.

◆ **Fear for personal safety**. Sometimes the reporter is afraid that violent parents may come after them. It is true that parents who have been accused of abuse will usually feel anger. In actuality, although some parents will shout and accuse, they rarely act out against the reporter, even when they know the reporter.

◆ **Fear of causing trouble and stress** for the family. Teachers hesitate to report if they are not absolutely certain abuse is taking place because they do not want to cause trouble and stress for the family. If parents know that you are required by law to report even suspicions of abuse, they may even express appreciation, if they are innocent, appreciating your vigilance.

◆ Teachers may **worry about contradicting cultural norms**. One teacher described a family who had recently come to this country. "In their country hitting the children severely is accepted practice," she said. "What right do I have to tell them to change their cultural values?" The fact is that in this country hitting children in such a way is illegal.

◆ A director or administrator may discourage reporting, **not wanting to make waves or risk losing the enrollment**. This is illegal. It is important that administrators stand behind classroom staff in reporting abuse. Teachers whose administrators do not report may be held liable for the unreported abuse or neglect. While some states allow anonymous reporting, the teacher would not be protected as there would be no proof (i.e., a name) that he or she had ever reported.

◆ **More reluctant the second time**. People who have had a bad experience when reporting suspected child abuse may be reluctant to become involved a second time. There may be distrust of the agency investigating and treating the abuse, feeling that the previous case was not handled well. These concerns are real and often valid. Based on your previous experience you might request that a supervisor intervene. Child Protective Services (or other designated agencies) are constantly working to upgrade the quality of their responses. In any case, early childhood teachers and staff must report abuse, regardless of their concerns or previous experience. In addition, while reporting does not guarantee that the situation will improve, not reporting guarantees that the child will continue to be at risk if the abuse or neglect exists.

◆ **Frustrated at lack of follow-up**. People are frustrated at the seeming lack of follow-up. Confidentiality laws and policies often make follow-up impossible for the program. However, educators may offer to keep in touch with the agency during the treatment phase to help the child as much as possible and can request information about the disposition of the case, emphasizing their concern for the child. Some state laws will allow release of information from the protective agency (often Child Protective Services) to other professionals when the individual is a member of a multidisciplinary team.

HOW TO RESPOND WITH THE CHILD

◆ **First, a child needs to feel safe**. First and foremost, a child needs to feel safe in your setting. He needs to know that the adult will protect him from outside dangers and from aggression of other children. A consistent routine with few surprises is also recommended.

◆ **Safe, dependable relationships**. The child needs to feel safe in relationships as well. She should have the same caregiver every day, who knows her well and on whom she can depend. A small group of children is best, so the child can learn slowly to build social relationships and the give-and-take of problem solving without being overwhelmed by too much competition.

◆ **Do not act shocked or disgusted**. When a child reveals something to you, do not act shocked or disgusted. The child will assume it is because of him that you are responding in this way.

◆ **Respond to the child in a supportive way**. "I'm glad you told me. You did the right thing. I'm sorry this happened to you."

◆ **Tell the child it is not her fault**.

◆ **You cannot promise not to tell**. Tell the child you will get him help so that the hurting stops. "We'll find somebody who can teach your mommy to do other things when she is angry."

◆ **Try not to be critical of the parent to the child**. While you can say, "It's not okay for adults to hurt children," avoid saying, "Your daddy was bad."

◆ **Give the child many ways to express herself**. It might help to draw or paint about it. Very young children might just scribble. Or you can ask the child to tell you about the scribbles and take dictation, if you think it is appropriate.

◆ **Activities about feelings**. Have many activities and discussions about feelings to teach children that the whole range of feelings is acceptable and there are appropriate ways to express themselves (see chapter 24).

◆ **Dramatic play**. Allow for much dramatic play and try not to edit or intervene too much.

◆ **Build friendship skills**. Work on building friendship skills and teaching children to compromise and resolve conflicts in peaceful ways (see chapter 24).

◆ **Treat the child with kindness, respect and empathy**. In all situations, and especially when you are disciplining the child, treat the child with kindness, respect and empathy. Do set limits, but by your model, show that a person does not have to use violence or humiliation to solve problems.

HOW TO RESPOND WITH THE PARENTS

◆ **Include information about the prevention of child abuse**, such as one or more of the pamphlets listed in the resource section of this chapter, in registration packets, newsletters, free literature displays in your lobby and other communications with parents. Let them know you care deeply about this issue and are a resource for them.

◆ **Community support**. Make parents aware of other community support services such as Alcoholics Anonymous, shelters, health care and respite care that may reduce some of the stress they are experiencing, before problems develop.

◆ **Parent support**. Consider finding a facilitator and offering parent support groups or free parenting classes in your building in the evenings for parents, if that is practical in your situation.

◆ **Required by law to make a report**. When and if a parent finds out that you made the report you can say, "We made the report because we are required by law to do so, even if we merely suspect abuse. We also made the report because we care about your child and we care about you. We want you to get the help you need."

◆ **Parenting the parent is often the most needed response**. Often the parents were themselves abused as children. They may even feel jealous or resentful of their own children who are getting kind attention from professionals when they themselves still feel needy. This huge issue is out of the direct responsibility of the teacher or caregiver, but you might be a valuable resource on the team as you help that person understand and respond to the child, and empathize.

WHERE TO FIND MORE INFORMATION

RESOURCES FOR CHILDREN

Books

Freeman, Lory. (1982). Illustrated by Carol Deach. *It's My Body*. Seattle, WA: Parenting Press, Inc. The author's thoughtful approach prepares children for appropriate responses to physical assault without provoking damaging guilt feelings.

Freeman, Lory. (1986). Illustrated by Carol Deach. *Loving Touches*. Seattle, WA: Parenting Press, Inc. A book for children about positive, caring and appropriate kinds of touching. It teaches respect for one's own and other's bodies.

Girard, Linda Walvoord. (1985). Illustrated by Helen Cogancherry. *Who Is a Stranger and What Should I Do?* Morton Grove, IL: Albert Whitman Publishers. The emphasis in on how to deal with strangers in public places, on the telephone and in cars. It gives clear pictures of situations in which the best thing to do is run away or talk to another adult.

Kehoe, Patricia. (1987). Illustrated by Carol Deach. *Something Happened and I'm Scared To Tell: A Book for Young Victims of Abuse*. Seattle, WA: Parenting Press, Inc. In this story the young victim of sexual abuse is able to talk about the abuse and recover self-esteem.

Stanek, Muriel. (1983). *Don't Hurt Me, Mama*. Morton Grove, IL: Albert Whitman Publishers. This book offers children a look at the very scary topic of abuse. It also gives them some warning signs about conditions that foster an abusive situation.

Books

Child Abuse

DePanfilis, Diane and Salus, Marsha K. (1992). *A Coordinated Response to Child Abuse and Neglect: A Basic Manual*. Washington, DC: U.S. Department of Health and Human Services, Administration for Children and Families, National Center on Child Abuse and Neglect. This first volume in the *User Manual Series* lays a foundation of knowledge upon which other manuals in the 19-volume series build as they address more specialized topics. One strong point stressed throughout the series is that open and continuous communication between Child Protective Services and all other professionals involved, including early childhood and child care professionals, is critical for the success of intervention. It contains an excellent selected bibliography of resources for those desiring more in-depth information. 64 pages. Single copies are free and may be ordered in bound format or unbound for photocopying. To order call 800-FYI-3366.

Koralek, Derry. (1992). *Caregivers of Young Children: Preventing and Responding to Child Maltreatment*. Washington, DC: U.S. Department of Health and Human Services, Administration for Children and Families, National Center on Child Abuse and Neglect. *Caregivers of Young Children* is a guide in the *User Manual Series* designed for early childhood education professionals responding to child maltreatment in caregiving situations. Topics include: roles and responsibilities of caregivers, how to recognize and report child maltreatment, working with parents, caring for maltreated children and prevention. 80 pages. Single copies are free and may be ordered in bound format or unbound for photocopying. To order call 800-FYI-3366.

Magid, Ken and McKelvey, Carole A. (1989). *High Risk, Children Without a Conscience*. New York: Bantam Books, Inc. Focusing on children who have attachment disorders, this riveting volume exposes how child abuse and neglect lead to a child's failure to bond, and the subsequent development of psychopathic behaviors.

Schorr, Lisbeth B. and Schorr, Daniel. (1988). *Within Our Reach: Breaking the Cycle of Disadvantage and Despair*. New York: Doubleday & Company, Inc. This book describes many programs that already exist in this country that are successfully treating some of the more complex social problems, including child abuse and neglect. A good book to read for a social overview, and providing you with good material to quote.

Tower, Cynthia C. (1992). *The Role of Educators in the Prevention and Treatment of Child Abuse and Neglect*. Washington, DC: Department of Health and Human Services, Administration for Children and Families, National Center on Child Abuse and Neglect. *The Role of Educators* is a guide in the *User Manual Series* for school personnel on responding effectively to child abuse and neglect. Topics include: why educators should be concerned with child maltreatment, how to recognize and report child maltreatment, what happens when a report is made and prevention strategies. 82 pages. Single copies are free and may be ordered in bound format or unbound for photocopying. To order call 800-FYI-3366.

Booklets & Pamphlets

Broadhurst, Diane D. *Educators, Schools, and Child Abuse*. National Committee to Prevent Child Abuse, Fulfillment Center, 1 Community Place, South Deerfield, MA 01373-0200. 800-835-2671. www.channing-bete.com. With the information in this booklet, both administrators and teachers have the information they need to help protect children, from setting policies to following through with the family. 31 pages. $5.75

Catalog of Videotapes and Other Media on Child Abuse and Neglect. National Cearinghouse on Child Abuse and Neglect Information, 330 C Street SW, Washington DC 20447. 800-FYI-3366. www.calib.com/nccanch. This catalog provides descriptions of 136 videotapes, audiotapes, anatomical dolls and other types of media. The listings in this publication are grouped according to the audience and topic, with materials for professionals, parents, children and public awareness. 52 pages. $6.00.

Consortium of Clearinghouses on Child Abuse and Neglect. National Clearinghouse on Child Abuse and Neglect Information, 330 C Street NW, Washington DC 20447. 800-FYI-3366. www.calib.com/nccanch. Newly revised, this booklet describes the product and services of the 15 national clearinghouses and resource centers in the Federal Consortium of Clearinghouses and Resource Centers on Child Abuse and Neglect. 19 pages. Free.

Child Abuse and You. Childhelp USA, 1345 El Centro, Hollywood, CA 90028. 1-800-422-4453. www.childhelpusa.org. A brief overview of all types of child abuse as well as how to report abuse and what happens when you do. 13 pages.

Cohn, Anne H. *An Approach to Preventing Child Abuse*. National Committee to Prevent Child Abuse (NCPCA), Fulfillment Center, 1 Community Place, South Deerfield, MA 01373-0200. 800-835-2671. www.channing-bete.com. This booklet presents the National Committee to Prevent Child Abuse (NCPCA) official model for community action to prevent child abuse. It reviews and extensively documents what is known about the causes and prevention of child abuse, including ethnic and cultural influences. 59 pages. $5.75. Bulk prices available.

Donovan, Helen. *Act Now to Prevent Child Abuse*. National Committee to Prevent Child Abuse, Fulfillment Center, 1 Community Place, South Deerfield, MA 01373-0200. 800-835-2671. www.channing-bete.com. This booklet suggests community responses to child abuse and prevention of abuse. A good resource to use when addressing local community groups. $.35. Bulk prices available.

Garbarino, James, and Garbarino, Anne. *Emotional Maltreatment of Children*. (2nd. ed.). National Committee to Prevent Child Abuse, Fulfillment Center, 1 Community

Place, South Deerfield, MA 01373-0200. 800-835-2671. www.channing-bete.com. This useful booklet fills an important gap, since so little is written about emotional abuse. Since emotional abuse almost always accompanies any other type of child abuse it is important that it not be glossed over. The emotional scars of abuse are the longest lasting. 31 pages. $5.75. Bulk prices available.

It Shouldn't Hurt to Be a Child. National Committee to Prevent Child Abuse, Fulfillment Center, 1 Community Place, South Deerfield, MA 01373-0200. 800-835-2671. www.channing-bete.com. It provides a good overview of issues around child abuse and prevention. Lists national organizations. 13 pages. $1.00. Bulk prices available.

Jaudes, Paula, and Mitchell, Leslie. *Physical Child Abuse*. National Committee to Prevent Child Abuse, Fulfillment Center, 1 Community Place, South Deerfield, MA 01373-0200. 800-835-2671. www.channing-bete.com. Teaches readers to identify the less obvious indicators of physical abuse and gain a better understanding of factors leading to such abuse. Also discusses programs available to help both the abuser and the abused child. 36 pages. $5.75. Bulk prices available.

Splash Water On Your Face. National Committee to Prevent Child Abuse, Fulfillment Center, 1 Community Place, South Deerfield, MA 01373-0200. 800-835-2671. www.channing-bete.com. This pamphlet gives parents some simple suggestions for cooling down instead of lashing out at their children. An excellent resource to routinely tuck into enrollment packages or parent newsletters. $.35. Bulk prices available.

"Think You Know Something about Child Abuse?" Questions & Answers. National Committee to Prevent Child Abuse, Fulfillment Center, 1 Community Place, South Deerfield, MA 01373-0200. 800-835-2671. www.channing-bete.com. This pamphlet contains excellent questions and concise answers. A brief resource to use for staff training and parent nights. $.35. Bulk prices available.

Videos

Scared Silent. (1992). P.O. Box 933022, Los Angeles, CA 90093. 50 minutes. $8.50. Hosted by Oprah Winfrey, this video profiles six true stories of sexual, physical and emotional abuse told by the offenders and their victims. A very good resource to have on hand for staff training and parent meetings to understand the causes and prevention of child abuse. Send check or money order to the address listed.

Organizations & Hot Lines

Check your telephone directory for any local child abuse hot lines or resource agencies not listed here.

Childhelp USA National Headquarters, 1345 El Centro, Hollywood, CA 90028. 1-800-422-4453. www.childhelpusa.org. In addition to sponsoring the National Child Abuse Hot Line, this organization conducts research and treatment for child abuse victims in conjunction with the University of California. They have information pamphlets, posters and audio and video cassettes on the topic.

Child Welfare League of America, 440 First Street NW, 3rd Floor, Washington, DC 20001-1085. 202-638-2952. www.cwla.org. The Child Welfare League of America (CWLA) is a primary source of information on issues including pending legislation, research and practice standards. CWLA publishes a bi-monthly journal, social legislation bulletin, quarterly magazine and a newsletter. Their catalog has an extensive list of books and monographs.

Alliance for Children & Families, 11700 West Lake Park Drive, Milwaukee, WI 53224. 414-359-1040. www.alliance1.org. Family Service America Inc. (FSA) is a nonprofit organization which supports a large network of agencies that counsel families on a range of family issues. Call the toll free number for a listing of the FSA agencies in your area and a publication list of books and videos. The information and referral line service is available in both English and Spanish.

Kempe Children's Center, 1825 Marion Street, Denver, CO 80218. 303-864-5252. www.kempe.org. This organization was begun in 1972 to provide a clinically based resource for training, consultation, program development and evaluation, and research in all forms of child abuse and neglect. The Center has extensive publications and audio visual catalogs. The Center also provides training and consultation on a contractual basis.

Military Family Resource Center, Crystal Square Four, Suite 302, Room 309, 1745 Jefferson Davis Hwy, Arlington, VA 22202. 703-602-4964. www.mfrc.calib.com. The Military Family Resource Center (MFRC) is a part of the National Clearinghouse on Child Abuse and Neglect Information and provides material specific to abuse occurring in military family settings.

National Child Abuse Hot Line 800-4-A-CHILD. www.childhelpusa.org. The Hot Line is organized by Childhelp USA Information and is staffed around the clock by crisis intervention counselors.

National Clearinghouse on Child Abuse and Neglect Information, 330 C Street SW, Washington, DC 20447. 800-FYI-3366. www.calib.com/nccanch. The Clearinghouse is a service of the National Center on Child Abuse and Neglect (NCCAN) and promotes cooperation among the many organizations working to end child maltreatment. The Clearinghouse also provides services and products in a variety of areas including training support, networking, directories, catalogs, literature reviews, and computerized services. A CD-ROM is available for direct access to many of the Clearinghouse's data-bases. Call for a comprehensive listing of services and publications, many provided without charge.

National Committee to Prevent Child Abuse, 200 South Michigan Avenue, 17th Floor, Chicago, IL 60604. 312-663-3520. www.preventchildabuse.org. Founded in 1972, the National Committtee to Prevent Child Abuse (NCPCA) is an organization committed to the prevention of child abuse in all of its forms. Training and technical assistance provides local chapters with a variety of resources. NCPCA has a catalog of useful resources on parenting, discipline, stress management and child abuse. Many resources are available in both English and Spanish.

National Council on Child Abuse and Family Violence, 1050 Connecticut Avenue, NW, Suite 300, Washington, DC 20036. www.nccafv.org. The Council supports a resource center on family violence and family preservation services which provides educational materials, program and resource development consultation, technical assistance and training to agencies and volunteers. The National Family Violence HelpLine supported by the Council gives referral assistance to domestic violence victims.

National Family Violence Hot Line. 1-800-422-4453 (child abuse). www.childhelpusa.org. The Hot Line is organized by the National Council on Child Abuse and Family Violence.

CHAPTER 11

CHILD SEXUAL ABUSE

HERE'S AN EXAMPLE

Four year old Kathleen had attended the center for over a year. In the last month or so her teacher, Trudy, discovered Kathleen engaged in sexual play with other children. At first Trudy considered this the normal exploratory play of four year olds. Several times other children came to Trudy and complained that Kathleen pulled their pants down and touched them. Trudy responded by telling the children that their private parts were their own and that they did not have to let other children touch them. She also told Kathleen to stop this type of play immediately. However, the problem only seemed to increase. In fact, Trudy noticed that other children now seemed to enjoy sneaking off with Kathleen to engage in sexual play. Trudy felt the situation had gone beyond the level of curiosity play. She decided to talk about the situation to her director.

Trudy and the director arranged a conference with the mother. The mother, a professional woman, became irate and hysterical when they described what was going on. When the director asked the mother if she thought there might be any sexual abuse occurring in the child's life, the mother turned around and accused the center, and Trudy in particular, of perpetrating the abuse.

Kathleen's mother called her attorney and the local child abuse authority. The director called the center's attorney and the same authority. Trudy went on paid leave while an investigation ensued. This investigation showed that there was indeed child sexual abuse, but the perpetrator was the father and not a staff member. The parents withdrew Kathleen from the center, so Trudy and the director had no way of knowing if the child received the necessary intervention. In the meantime, Trudy, back on the job, reports that the play of the other children has returned to normal.

The entire incident was very upsetting to everyone involved. The center received negative publicity and lost a few children. The director lost much sleep as well as revenue. Trudy's professional reputation was put on the line. At times, Trudy asked herself if she really had done the right thing in bringing the situation to the attention of the director. She hopes that the abuse of Kathleen will stop and that Kathleen and her family will receive the help they need.

LET'S LOOK AT THE ISSUE

In our example, the major mistake of the director and teacher was to attempt to talk to the parent first. The law states that teachers must report any suspicion of sexual child abuse. It is not the responsibility of the child care provider or teacher to conduct an investigation.

Sexual abuse has undoubtedly been around since the beginning of time. Within the last decade and a half, the problem of child sexual abuse has received more recognition than ever before. This problem is not limited to a particular social class or group of people.

Child sexual abuse is defined as contact or interaction between a child and an adult where the child is being used in a sexual manner by the adult. Sexual abuse includes a wide range of sexual activity ranging from nonviolent, nonphysical offenses such as exposure to offenses involving physical (and sometimes violent) contact. Examples include fondling, oral or genital contact, vaginal and anal stimulation and penetration, and exploitation of children through pornography and prostitution.

In a great majority of all child sex abuse cases, the perpetrator is known to the victim. Many times the abuse takes place within the family. Both boys and girls are victimized by men and women. Sexual abuse occurs most often in the perpetrator's or the victim's home. Usually the abuse is followed by threats or bribes to coerce the child to keep it secret. A typical pattern of sexual abuse begins with the perpetrator befriending the victim, unless a relationship is already established, such as with a relative or babysitter. The friendship is solidified as the perpetrator gives extra attention to the child. After a period of time, the perpetrator sexually assaults the child. This assault is usually followed by a bribe or threat. Examples: "I'll go to jail if you tell," or "We can't be friends anymore if you tell."

Excessive sexual knowledge. A certain amount of sexual play or exploration is normal in young children. It becomes a "red flag" when it seems excessive and indicates sexual knowledge beyond what is typical of young children. This behavior may indicate that the child has witnessed sexual activity rather than experienced it directly, but there is still cause for concern.

Egocentric thinking. Because children are egocentric in their thinking, they often assume blame for sexual abuse. If people react with disgust or anger when children tell them about it, the child may assume that the adult is angry at him rather than at the situation.

Feelings of guilt and fear. The child might feel guilty or frightened for telling. The child may have been threatened. "If you tell I won't love you." "If you tell, mommy will go to jail and you'll be all alone." "If you don't tell, I'll give you presents..."

Fear of reporting the incident. Young children rarely report sexual abuse to an adult. They may fear that they will not be believed or that they will be blamed.

Difficulty with sequential events. Reporting the incident is also difficult because children usually can't tell a sequential story until about age five. Even then, sequencing of events is still difficult. They will often start out by describing what is most important to them.

Recalling details. Young children may remember fewer details, but what they recall is just as accurate as children of older ages.

Lowered self-esteem and depression. Child victims of sexual abuse often suffer from lowered self-esteem and depression. They may withdraw and participate less in the activities around them.

Feelings of anger. The sexually abused child may express anger toward others around him—including the other caring adults in his life who are in no way involved in the abuse. In the child's mind, these adults are all-powerful and he may feel that they should know about and fix the problem.

Preoccupation with sex play. It is not uncommon for a sexually abused child to become "sexualized"—overly interested in sex and seductive with other children and adults. One child can draw a whole group of children into repeated sex play, so the situation must be dealt with, not ignored.

Child Sexual Abuse

Normal needs for touching and closeness. All young children need touching, nurturing and physical closeness with their caregivers. A place where little children cannot be hugged, rocked and held is not a good place for them. Staff should talk about what is appropriate touching and what is not. Let the child take the lead. Hug the child when the child wants a hug, not when the adult needs a hug.

WHEN TO SEEK HELP

Any or all of the following might be signs that sexual abuse is occurring in the child's life.

◆ **Genital or rectal problems**—itching or pain in the genital or rectal areas, soreness when sitting or walking, blood on underwear, bruises in genital area or problems going to the bathroom. A young child might simply say, "It hurts" while pointing to the genital area. Evidence of physical trauma to the genitals, anus or the mouth is another sign.

◆ **Sleep problems** such as nightmares, bed-wetting or being afraid to go to bed. Nap time may be difficult.

◆ **Regression**. Noticeable, continuous regression of any kind in developmental milestones such as speech patterns or toileting.

◆ **Precocious sexual knowledge**. The child's vocabulary might include words not normally used by young children. Unusual interest in sexual matters.

◆ **Sexualized behavior**. The child might be inappropriately affectionate, seductive or even sexually aggressive.

◆ **Re-enactment**. Children often act out in play situations what they are unable to express verbally. So pay special attention to the child's role playing and dramatic play with dolls. You might notice a child playing out sexual acts normally beyond the experience of a young child.

◆ **Unusual or bizarre sexual themes** in art or stories generated by the child.

◆ **Restlessness or withdrawal**. There is often a lot of sadness in children who have been abused.

◆ **Fear of a particular person or gender.**

◆ **Reluctance to undress.**

◆ **Poor social relationships with other children**. Low self-esteem.

Child Sexual Abuse

◆ **Indirect hints**—allusions to problems at home.

◆ **Revelation**. The child might actually come out and tell an adult about the abusive situation. More common statements are, "My brother wouldn't let me sleep last night." "My babysitter keeps bothering me." "I know somebody who is being touched in a bad way." "I have a problem, but if I tell you about it, you have to promise not to tell anyone else."

◆ **Unusual absences**. An abusive parent might keep the child home a lot and may discourage peer relationships.

◆ **Some children show no signs**, physical or behavioral, while being abused. It is not uncommon for abused children to do well in school, the one place where they feel safe.

Remember that with the exception of the child's reporting of the incident, all of these behaviors may indicate other problems not related to sexual abuse. While you must not jump to conclusions, you must take some action to verify your concerns.

WHO CAN HELP

◆ The agency in your area that deals with child abuse reports. Look in the phone directory under the name of your city or county for one of the following listings, or ask the telephone information operator who to call in your area.

Department of Child Protective Services
Department of Social Services
Public Social Services Department
Department of Protective Services
Social and Rehabilitative Services
Bureau of Children & Family Services

◆ Law enforcement officers
◆ Mental health centers
◆ Family therapists
◆ Social workers
◆ Child psychologists
◆ Rape crisis centers
◆ Shelters for battered women and their families

Child Sexual Abuse

HOW TO RESPOND WITH THE STAFF

◆ **Have a staff meeting with a professional**. It is possible that some staff members were themselves victims of sexual child abuse, so it is advisable on a routine basis to have a staff meeting about the topic under the guidance of a trained professional. The topic should be thoroughly discussed, and people who were victims should be encouraged to work privately with a trained counselor.

◆ **Teachers are required by law to report cases of child abuse**. Since the particular authority to whom you should report sexual abuse varies from place to place, find out ahead of time who to call in your area. Have the name of the agency and if possible the name of a particular person within that agency, as well as the phone number on file. Consult with your supervisor before you take this action. However, if your supervisor advises against calling and you feel strongly that this abuse is taking place, you should still call. If you report suspected abuse "in good faith," meaning that you have a valid reason to suspect it, you are protected from personal lawsuits.

◆ **Remember, it is not your role to conduct an investigation**. However, be fully cooperative with any investigation conducted by the proper authorities.

◆ **Deal with your own anger** by talking in confidence to someone you trust (perhaps the director of your program, a colleague or a trained counselor).

◆ **Do not talk about the situation to others** not directly involved with the child. Respect the child's privacy.

Preventing sexual abuse in the child care setting

Although the vast majority of sexual abuse happens in the home of the perpetrator or of the child, it is possible for it to occur in any setting. There are things you can do to reduce the possibility of sexual abuse in your setting.

◆ **Hire staff carefully**. Do a thorough background and reference check on all individuals. Many states now require fingerprint and criminal record checks of child care employees. Recognize, however, that only a small percentage of perpetrators of sexual abuse have a criminal record.

◆ **Provide thorough orientation and training** for all new employees, substitutes and volunteers in your program. State specifically that you will not tolerate any form of abuse. Describe the professional behavior you expect. Emphasize discipline policies and ways to treat children with kindness and respect. These policies should be in writing and employees should sign a form when they have read them.

◆ **Encourage parents to train their child in personal care**, especially wiping after going to the bathroom. Although you will occasionally have to help the child, you should also encourage them to do it themselves.

◆ **Include the topic of sexual abuse in staff orientation**.

◆ **Assign a supervisor or staff buddy** to all new employees. Avoid having a new staff person work alone with any group of children.

◆ **Do not allow people who are not regular employees**, such as dance instructors, volunteers, entertainers or visitors to be alone with a group of children without a trained staff person present.

◆ **Supervise all staff**. Supervisors should visit classrooms without notice at all different times of the day, especially at nap time. Find errands that will take you into rooms for legitimate reasons at unexpected times.

◆ **Create an atmosphere that is supportive of open communication**. The supervisor should be ready to talk with people in private at any time.

◆ **Children's needs come first**. Even though it may feel uncomfortable for one staff person to be reporting a **suspicion** of abuse by another staff person, help the total staff to realize that **everyone** is responsible for ensuring that children have a good experience in the program. The rights and needs of children must come before staff loyalty to each other.

◆ **Maintain an open door policy for parents** of children enrolled in your program. They must be given the freedom to visit unannounced at any time. On the other hand, all other adults should be accompanied by a staff person on any visit.

◆ **Make sure children are supervised at all times**. Remember, the perpetrator of sexual abuse does not have to be an adult. Sometimes older children force younger children to engage in sexual acts when an adult is not present. Do not leave children alone while napping. Do not allow children to go into the building alone to use the bathroom while everyone else is outside. Pay special attention to transition times when children are moving from one place to another or using the bathroom.

◆ **Make sure children can be seen at all times**. Take a look at your environment to make sure there are not places where children can sneak off together out of view of adults. While children in child care need alone spaces, it is possible to arrange these so that the child feels separate from the group while adults can still see the child and supervise.

◆ **Do not allow field trips to staff homes** unless there is a legitimate reason (such as the staff person lives on a farm) and other staff and parents accompany the group.

◆ **Field trips should be planned well in advance** and have a specific educational focus. Parents should be informed about all the particulars of the field trip—times, destinations and purpose. Stick to your planned schedule as closely as possible and do not allow spontaneous side trips. Always make sure all children are accounted for.

◆ **Make sure your center or child care home is secure** and no "unscreened" adult could enter the building or play yard unnoticed.

◆ **Provide general educational programs for parents and staff on child abuse**. Both parents and staff could be included in the same training sessions. Make sure that sexual abuse is included in the topics covered.

◆ **Stop any abuse you see**. If you actually discover a situation where an adult or older child is sexually abusing a child, tell the abuser to stop immediately. Take the child with you. Report the abuse to your supervisor. If you retreat, you may be considered part of the abuse.

If you are a supervisor and there is an allegation of child sexual abuse by one of your staff:

◆ You must notify authorities.

◆ The employee could be suspended with pay while an investigation takes place, providing the individual is totally cooperative in all matters pertaining to the investigation.

◆ You may decide to suspend the employee without pay.

◆ Cooperate fully with the agency doing the investigation.

◆ Do not become defensive. Let the authorities know you are genuinely concerned and will work to correct any problems they find. Maintain your professional demeanor.

◆ Ask what the investigative process will be. If parents are to be interviewed, ask if you can inform the parents that an investigation is in progress so that they know you are aware and concerned.

◆ If an individual child or children have been named as victims, be sure to be supportive of the families and children involved. Maintain their privacy as much as possible.

◆ Notify the rest of the staff that allegations have been made. It is not necessary to give all the details. Ask other staff members individually and privately if they have any information that may assist in the investigation. Refer any witnesses to the investigating agency. In order to limit rumors and exaggerations, give the staff periodic status reports.

◆ If the allegations turn out to be true, terminate the staff person immediately. Be honest with your parents and describe what steps you have taken to correct the problem. They will probably appreciate your candor and realize that you are not trying to hide anything.

HOW TO RESPOND WITH THE CHILD

A child's long-term recovery from the trauma of sexual abuse depends very much on the sensitive and open responses of parents and caregivers.

If a child tells you about abuse

◆ **Believe the child**. Young children rarely lie about sexual abuse.

◆ **Don't promise you won't tell**. You can promise the child that she will be protected. Tell the child that you and others will do everything you can to prevent this from happening again. Praise the child for telling you and emphasize that it is not her fault and that she is not "bad."

◆ **Don't react with horror or disgust**. The child will assume your response is directed at him, not the perpetrator. Guard your facial expression as well as body language. React calmly and respond with empathy. Comfort the child and say you are sorry that happened to him. Be a good listener. Make yourself accessible to the child to talk one-on-one if he needs to in the future.

◆ **Avoid criticizing the adult**. Don't say, "Your daddy is a bad person." Concentrate on the child.

If you have a child in your program who has been sexually abused

◆ **Let the child know that you know**. After the case has been investigated, or if the child is new in your program, do not pretend that nothing happened. Let the child know you are aware of what happened and that you are there to listen if she wants to talk about it. The child must know she is not alone.

◆ **Be part of the team of professionals**. As the child's teacher, you are in a circle of adults close to the child. Work with the other professionals to gain insights about the child and the situation and to respond in a supportive way.

◆ **Document everything**. Write down and date what the child said and did. Do this "journal style." Note as many details as you can, including the time of day and the circumstances surrounding any incident. This will help you avoid conjecturing and jumping to conclusions.

◆ **Stop sexual play immediately**. If you discover the child in explicit sexual play, you have to stop the play. A response suggested by Hertha Klugman in Scholastic's *Learning Through Play: Dramatic Play Book* is to say to the children involved, "I'm glad the two of you are friends, but in our room people don't touch each other's private parts. What are some other things that friends do together?" Find an activity that the pair seems particularly interested in and help them get involved. When they are engaged in appropriate play, you can withdraw but try to maintain an observing eye.

HOW TO RESPOND WITH THE PARENTS

◆ **Have a parent meeting on the issue of child abuse** (including child sexual abuse) as part of routine parent educational events. Have brochures and hot line phone numbers available in the center and include information on child abuse and sexual abuse occasionally in your newsletter. Let parents know that you are on top of this issue.

◆ **Be honest with parents**. If there has been an allegation of child sexual abuse by a staff member, be up front with parents. As you would with the press, give them only pertinent facts and information that relate to their children, and do not speculate or share hunches. Instruct the staff not to gossip. A parent meeting with a local expert on the issue of child abuse can clear up a lot of confusion and give parents important information.

◆ **Parental denial is a strong tendency** in families where sexual child abuse may be going on, as in our example when the nonperpetrating parent is unable to acknowledge and accept the reality of the situation. In other cases, a parent may have been aware of the situation but be unable or unwilling to accept and deal with it.

◆ **Many perpetrators of sexual abuse were themselves victims of abuse**.

◆ **Work closely with other professionals** for guidelines on how to interact effectively with families in the midst of this trauma.

WHERE TO FIND MORE INFORMATION

RESOURCES FOR CHILDREN

Books

Dayee, Frances S. (1988). *Private Zone*. New York, NY: Warner Books. This is a book you might read to a child or a small group of children, especially if there has been an incident of sexual abuse in the child's life.

Freeman, Lory. (1982). Illustrated by Carol Deach. *It's My Body*. Seattle, WA: Parenting Press, Inc. The author's thoughtful approach prepares children for appropriate responses to physical assault without provoking damaging guilt feelings.

Girard, Linda Walvoord. (1984). *My Body Is Private*. Morton Grove, IL: Albert Whitman Publishers. In the context of a loving family, a little girl talks about what private means. She learns to resist a touchy uncle. A "Note to Parents" page gives helpful information about the topic of sexual abuse in general.

Porett, Jane. (1993). *When I Was Little Like You*. Washington, DC: Child Welfare League of America. This book is designed to help even small children understand what sexual abuse is. The author tells the child reader about an incident that happened to her as a child and gives the child two main strategies to say a loud, clear, "No!" to the abuser and to tell an adult they trust, emphasizing that sexual abuse is not the child's fault.

Sanford, Doris. (1986) Illustrated by Graci Evans and Ruth Gregory. *I Can't Talk About It*. Portland, OR: Multnomah Press. At her grandmother's beach cottage, Annie reveals her father's sexual abuse of her to a magic dove who says all the right things and helps her heal and learn to trust again. Lists guidelines for adults to help sexually abused children. Not a book that you would read to the whole group at story time, this book could be helpful when you are working one-on-one with a child you know has been abused.

Sanford, Doris. (1993). Illustrated by Graci Evans. *Something Must Be Wrong With Me: A Boy's Book about Sexual Abuse*. Sisters, OR: Heart to Heart, Inc. An elementary school-aged boy is taken advantage of sexually by his coach, whom he admires. Finally Dino gets the courage to tell his mother. He is hurt, angry, confused, sad and embarrassed all at the same time, but finds a sympathetic response from his mother while they inform the police.

RESOURCES FOR ADULTS

Books

Adams, Caren and Fay, Jennifer. (1990). *No More Secrets: Protecting Your Child From Sexual Assault*. San Luis Obispo, CA: Impact Publishers, Inc. An excellent book for adult reading, written to help adults understand sexual abuse and to find the right words to use with children.

Behrman, R.E. (Ed.). (1994). *The Future of Children, Sexual Abuse of Children*. Los Altos, CA: The Center for the Future of Children. This 250-page volume is a thorough and scholarly, yet readable investigation of all aspects of child sexual abuse. Chapters written by leading experts include immediate and long-term impacts of child sexual abuse, reporting and investigating, prevention of child sexual abuse and characteristics and treatment of offenders. This report is volume 4, number 2 in the Summer/Fall 1994 issue. To order contact The Center for the Future of Children, The David and Lucile Packard Foundation, 300 Second Street, Suite 102, Los Altos, CA 94022. 415-948-3696.

Black, Claudia. (1981). *It Will Never Happen to Me.* New York: Ballantine Books. The primary focus of this book is adult children of alcoholics. There is a section in the "Family Violence" chapter that discusses sexual abuse.

DePanfilis, Diane and Salus, Marsha K. (1992). *A Coordinated Response to Child Abuse and Neglect: A Basic Manual.* Washington, DC: U.S. Department of Health and Human Services, Administration for Children and Families, National Center on Child Abuse and Neglect. This first volume in the *User Manual Series* lays a foundation of knowledge upon which other manuals in the 19-volume series build as they address more specialized topics. One strong point stressed throughout the series is that open and continuous communication between Child Protective Services and all other professionals involved, including early childhood and child care professionals, is critical for the success of intervention. It contains an excellent selected bibliography of resources for those desiring more in-depth information. 64 pages. Single copies are free and may be ordered in bound format or unbound for photocopying. To order call 800-FYI-3366.

Faller, Kathleen Coulborn. (1993). *Child Sexual Abuse: Intervention and Treatment Issues.* Washington DC: U.S. Department of Health and Human Services, Administration for Children and Families, National Center on Child Abuse and Neglect. This guide in the *User Manual Series* addresses the needs of professionals such as child protection workers, legal system professionals, and health care professionals who encounter child sexual abuse in the course of their work. It is also a valuable resource for educators and parents. Single copies are free and may be ordered in bound format or unbound for photocopying. To order call 800-FYI-3366.

Koralek, Derry. (1992). *Caregivers of Young Children: Preventing and Responding to Child Maltreatment.* Washington, DC: U.S. Department of Health and Human Services, Administration for Children and Families, National Center on Child Abuse and Neglect. *Caregivers of Young Children* is a guide in the *User Manual Series* designed for early childhood education professionals responding to child maltreatment in caregiving situations. Topics include: roles and responsibilities of caregivers, how to recognize and report child maltreatment, working with parents, caring for maltreated children and prevention. 80 pages. Single copies are free and may be ordered in bound format or unbound for photocopying. To order call 800-FYI-3366

Tower, Cynthia C. (1992). **The Role of Educators in the Prevention and Treatment of Child Abuse and Neglect**. Washington, DC: Department of Health and Human Services, Administration for Children and Families, National Center on Child Abuse and Neglect. *The Role of Educators* is a guide in the *User Manual Series* for school personnel on responding effectively to child abuse and neglect. Topics include: why educators should be concerned with child maltreatment, how to recognize and report child maltreatment, what happens when a report is made and prevention strategies. 82 pages. Single copies are free and may be ordered in bound format or unbound for photocopying. To order call 800-FYI-3366.

Articles

Corbett, Susan Miller. "Children and sexuality." *Young Children*. 46(2), January 1991, 71-77. The director of a child care center discusses the need to be staightforward in communicating with parents about normal sexuality in children. Samples of letters and newsletters are included in the article.

Booklets & Pamphlets

Broadhurst, Diane D. *Educators, Schools, and Child Abuse*. National Committee to Prevent Child Abuse, Fulfillment Center, 1 Community Place, South Deerfield, MA 01373-0200. 800-835-2671. www.channing-bete.com. With the information in this booklet, both administrators and teachers have the information they need to help protect children, from setting policies to following through with the family. 31 pages. $5.75

Catalog of Videotapes and Other Media on Child Abuse and Neglect. National Cearinghouse on Child Abuse and Neglect Information, 330 C Street, SW, Washington, DC 20447. 800-FYI-3366. www.calib.com/nccanch. This catalog provides descriptions of 136 videotapes, audiotapes, anatomical dolls and other types of media. The listings in this publication are grouped according to the audience and topic, with materials for professionals, parents, children and public awareness. 52 pages. $6.00.

Conte, Jon R. *A Look at Child Sexual Abuse*. National Committee to Prevent Child Abuse, Fulfillment Center, 1 Community Place, South Deerfield, MA 01373-0200. 800-835-2671. www.channing-bete.com. The 52-page booklet reviews and summarizes current understandings of child sexual abuse. Emphasis focuses on the definitions and characteristics of child sexual abuse and discusses treatment and prevention efforts.

Ryan, Gail and Blum, Joanne. (1993). *Childhood Sexuality: A Guide for Parents*. Kempe Children's Center, 1825 Marion Street, Denver, CO 80218. 303-864-5252. www.kempe.org. This 43-page booklet discusses the normal development of sexuality during childhood. This booklet will help parents become more comfortable and confident in acknowledging and responding to their children as they learn about their sexuality. $11.00.

Sexual Victimization of Children. National Committee to Prevent Child Abuse, Fulfillment Center, 1 Community Place, South Deerfield, MA 01373-0200. 800-835-2671. www.channing-bete.com. The 16-page booklet expains forms of sexual exploitation and abuse, common characteristics of child molesters and physical and behavioral signs that may indicate a child is being exploited. Tells readers what to do if they suspect or know of victimization.

Spelman, Cornelia. *Talking About Child Sexual Abuse*. National Committee to Prevent Child Abuse, Fulfillment Center, 1 Community Place, South Deerfield, MA 01373-0200. 800-835-2671. www.channing-bete.com. This is an indispensable pamphlet for all parents. It identifies the signs and behavior in children that may indicate abuse and outlines an approach for discussing abuse with a child. It also provides instructions for reporting suspected abuse and offers guidance to adults who were sexually abused.

You're in Charge! National Committee to Prevent Child Abuse, Fulfillment Center, 1 Community Place, South Deerfield, MA 01373-0200. 800-835-2671. www.channing-bete.com. This coloring and activities book balances the need to protect young readers from sexual abuse with the need to protect their innocence. Painstakingly researched and written, and thoroughly reviewed by experts, it helps children in the early elementary grades understand when the behavior of others is inappropriate, and tells them what to do in case of abuse or attempted abuse. A Spanish edition is available.

Curriculum Materials

Talking About Touching: Child Abuse Prevention Curricula. Committee for Children, 568 First Avenue S., Suite 600, Seattle, WA 98104-2804. 800-634-4449. www.cfchildren.org. This personal safety curricula teaches children assertiveness, decision making skills and effective use of community resources to reduce their risk of abuse. Lessons on physical abuse and neglect, as will as lessons on sexual abuse and environmental safety, provide an integrated learning approach. Different curricula sets are designed for preschool/kindergarten, elementary (grades 1-3) and elementary (grades 4-5). Free previews are available on all curricula and accompanying videos.

Videos

Confronting Child Sexual Abuse: Video Training Series. (1993). Produced by Kingsley Communications for the Child Welfare League of America. Child Welfare League of America, c/o CSSC, New England Office, 300 Congress Street, Suite 305, Quincy, MA 02169. 617-770-3008. www.cwla.org. Three videos, 3 hours, 23 min. $495. This training series provides an in-depth view and practical help for staff to serve as effective advocates on behalf of sexually abused children. A discussion guide accompanies the series.

Identifying, Reporting and Handling Disclosure of the Sexually Abused Child. Committee for Children, 568 First Avenue S., Suite 600, Seattle, WA 98104-2804. 800-634-4449. www.cfchildren.org. 25 min. $125. This training video for professionals shows examples of common behavioral indicators of child sexual abuse. It provides clear guidelines on reporting responsibilities for mandated professionals. It also models appropriate responses to a child's disclosure of sexual abuse. The Committee for Children also provide staff training sessions. Fees are determined according to the type and length of training.

Scared Silent. (1992). P.O. Box 933022, Los Angeles, CA 90093. 50 minutes. $8.50. Hosted by Oprah Winfrey, this video profiles six true stories of sexual, physical and emotional abuse told by the offenders and their victims. A very good resource to have on hand for staff training and parent meetings to understand the causes and prevention of child abuse. Send check or money order to the address listed.

Organizations & Hot Lines

Check your telephone directory for any local child abuse hot lines or resource agencies not listed here.

Child Welfare League of America, 440 First Street NW, 3rd Floor, Washington, DC 20001-2085. 202-638-2952. www.cwla.org. The Child Welfare League of America (CWLA) is a primary source of information on issues including pending legislation, research and practice standards. CWLA publishes a bi-monthly journal, social legislation bulletin, quarterly magazine and a newsletter. Their catalog has an extensive list of books and monographs.

Alliance for Children & Families, 11700 West Lake Park Drive, Milwaukee, WI 53224. 414-359-1040. www.alliance1.org. Family Service America Inc. (FSA) is a nonprofit organization which supports a large network of agencies that counsel families on a range of family issues. Call the toll-free number for a listing of the FSA agencies in your area and a publication list of books and videos. The information and referral line service is available in both English and Spanish.

Kempe Children's Center, 1825 Marion Street, Denver, CO 80218. 303-864-5252. www.kempe.org. This organization was begun in 1972 to provide a clinically based resource for training, consultation, program development and evaluation, and research in all forms of child abuse including sexual abuse. The Center has extensive publications and audio visual catalogs. The Center also provides training and consultation on a contractual basis.

National Child Abuse Hot Line: 800-4-A-CHILD. www.childhelpusa.org. The Hot Line is organized by Childhelp USA Information and is staffed around the clock by crisis intervention counselors.

National Clearinghouse on Child Abuse and Neglect Information, 330 C Street SW, Washington, DC 20447. 800-FYI-3366. www.calib.com/nccanch. The Clearinghouse is a service of the National Center on Child Abuse and Neglect (NCCAN) and promotes cooperation among the many organizations working to end child maltreatment. The

Clearinghouse also provides services and products in a variety of areas including training support, networking, directories, catalogs, literature reviews, and computerized services. A CD-ROM is available for direct access to many of the Clearinghouse's databases. Call for a comprehensive listing of services and publications, many provided without charge.

National Committee to Prevent Child Abuse, 200 South Michigan Avenue, 17th Floor, Chicago, IL 60604. 312-663-3520. www.preventchildabuse.org. Founded in 1972, the National Committtee to Prevent Child Abuse (NCPCA) is an organization committed to the prevention of child abuse in all of its forms. Training and technical assistance provides local chapters with a variety of resources. NCPCA has a catalog of useful resources on parenting, discipline, stress management and child abuse. Many resources are available in both English and Spanish.

National Council on Child Abuse and Family Violence, 1050 Connecticut Avenue, NW, Suite 300, Washington, DC 20036. www.nccafv.org. The Council supports a resource center on family violence and family preservation services which provides educational materials, program and resource development consultation, technical assistance and training to agencies and volunteers. The National Family Violence HelpLine supported by the Council gives referral assistance to domestic violence victims.

National Resource Center on Child Sexual Abuse, 107 Lincoln Street, Huntsville, AL 35801. Specializing in the topic of child sexual abuse, this organization keeps a listing of publications and curricula. They are not a hot line for reporting abuse. Rather, they serve as a networking center and provide technical support to all professionals who work with sexually abused children and their families.

CHAPTER 12

DOMESTIC VIOLENCE
WITNESSING SPOUSE ABUSE

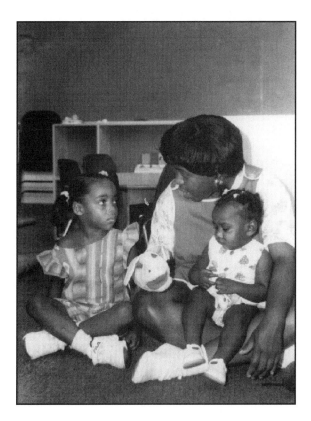

HERE'S AN EXAMPLE

Monica, a quiet, fearful four year old, was acting particularly nervous one morning. During their morning circle time when all the children sit down together to plan the day she blurted out, "I just wish my daddy would stop hitting my mommy." Her teacher, Diane, was taken aback and didn't know how to respond. All the children became quiet and looked at her. Diane said to Monica, "I'm really sorry that happened, Monica. I wish he wouldn't hit her too." After the children left, Diane called the local social worker in the small rural community where they live. The social worker was already aware of the domestic violence and substance abuse in this family. There had been numerous previous incidents. Nobody had given this information to the teachers. As far as Diane could tell, nothing had happened. Monica mentioned this type of thing several times in later months, so the abuse seemed to be continuing. Each time, Diane reported it. Finally Monica and her sister were withdrawn from the program and the family moved away.

LET'S LOOK AT THE ISSUE

"A safe and nurturing family environment ought to be the basic right of any child. When a child loses the sense that the home or family is a safe, loving refuge, the child loses a critical pillar of a stable and enriching life. A crime against one's own family—against a spouse or a child—shatters the trust upon which healthy families are built. It causes psychological and emotional damage that often cannot be repaired. It can be the most damaging and debilitating force in a child's life." —Colorado Governor Roy Romer, November 1994.

The greatest percentage of violence witnessed by children is domestic violence. It is also the single major cause of injury to women. Nearly half of the men who abuse their wives also abuse their children. Whether or not they are personally the target of abuse, watching their mothers be beaten by their fathers is extremely traumatic for children.

The causes of domestic violence are complex and interrelated. Very often, substance abuse, addiction to alcohol or drugs, is a companion. Domestic violence is always associated with low self-esteem and intense feelings of rejection on the part of the perpetrator. It is about power and control. It is usually, but not always, the man (the husband or boyfriend) who beats the woman.

It is often a repeated cycle. The child who sees his father beat his mother is going to see this as an acceptable way of life. Children growing up in such homes do not know what a healthy relationship is. Boys often become abusers themselves, identifying with their fathers. Girls often become victims in their own adult relationships, seeing violence as a normal fact of life that women must simply put up with, or even see it as a proof of affection. "I know he cares about me because he hits me."

Because the effects of witnessing domestic violence are so profound on children, the National Center for Child Abuse and Neglect (NCCAN) describes it as emotional child abuse. If it is classified as child abuse, does this mean that as mandated reporters, if a child reports to a teacher witnessing such an event, the teacher must report it? Probably. Check with your state agency for investigating child abuse and your state child abuse law.

Often spouse abuse is guarded as an ugly family secret. Children learn very early not to talk about it. However, young children aren't very good at keeping secrets, and the teachers of young children are more likely than the elementary school teacher to hear reports about battering. While a teacher may be saying to herself, "I don't want to be hearing about this," there is a need to break the silence around this issue. Finding the support for this family in crisis can be the beginning of their recovery. You can make a difference.

INSIGHTS FROM CHILD DEVELOPMENT

This kind of violence is very damaging. It robs the child of the feeling of personal safety, since it is perpetrated by someone the child knows. Fear and vulnerability replace the basic trust they need to thrive and develop. The child has no solid base, nobody he can truly depend on to make his world stable.

A child loses the sense that the world is a safe place. A child's emotional development occurs within the context of the family. It is there that the child learns to interpret the emotions of others and identify her own responses, all within an environment of nurturing and support. When this disappears, the child loses the sense that the world is a safe place and that there is sense in people's actions. The family plays a crucial role in supporting the child in recovery from trauma. In cases of spouse abuse, this support becomes unavailable.

Children have the psychological choice of remaining helpless or identifying with the aggressor. It is not surprising that some children find it safer to identify with the powerful one. The outcome is that these children (frequently boys) become more violent and aggressive in interactions with others.

Aggression has been their only model in problem solving and they adopt this method themselves to get what they want. This mode of interaction gets in the way of developing solid friendships and good peer relationships, an important factor in resiliency against stress.

Children may become fearful and withdrawn. Some children, usually but not exclusively girls, become fearful and withdrawn. They try very hard to blend in and not make waves, not get noticed. They see the world as a hostile place.

Young children often blame themselves for causing a parents's anger. They do not have the skill to see situations from someone else's point of view and assess incidents that led up to the violence. Their self-esteem suffers.

Older children may blame themselves for not intervening or preventing the attack. They feel helpless and ashamed.

Children may "tune it out." They learn not to feel, not to empathize.

Children often have difficulty concentrating at school, thinking instead about what might be going on at home. This has a major impact on the child's ability to learn.

Children who accompany their mothers to take refuge in shelters continue to have problems, even in a safe environment. They suffer from the trauma of moving and losing their familiar surroundings, their points of reference, their favorite objects and toys and their friends. Especially school-aged children miss the social supports of peers they knew in the neighborhood and at school.

Domestic Violence

Children may suffer from post-traumatic stress, resulting from feelings of being overwhelmed and helpless.

The adults may not be able to help their children. It is not surprising that when adults are traumatized by violence they may be less sensitive to their children. They fail to act as moderators for the child, helping the child make sense of it, as they might in other frightening situations.

Young children may accept family violence as a normal way of life. However, when they go to school, make friends, visit other homes, they learn that this is not the way it is in all families. Then children may feel embarrassed and angry. It is not uncommon, however, for these families to be very isolated. Children are sometimes not encouraged to have friendships or participate in school activities.

There may be severe problems in these families. Families where there is spouse abuse are deeply troubled families where there is often loud verbal fighting, and separation and divorce (see chapter 7 on separation and divorce).

WHEN TO SEEK HELP

◆   **The young child might tell you of the incident**. Or, you might see re-enactments in the child's dramatic play.

◆   **The child tries not to make waves**. Tries not to be noticed.

◆   **The child becomes aggressive**.

◆   **The child becomes excessively fearful**. They might have more difficulty separating from the parent.

◆   **Children develop sleep disorders**, wake up frequently or have nightmares.

◆   **School-aged children have trouble concentrating** and school work suffers.

◆   **Sad demeanor**. Flat affect.

WHO CAN HELP

◆   Law enforcement agencies
◆   Local social service agency (in some places called Child Protective Services)
◆   Shelters and safe houses for battered women
◆   Rape crisis centers

◆   Local mental health or family counseling centers and domestic violence prevention programs

◆   Child psychologists

HOW TO RESPOND

HOW TO RESPOND WITH THE STAFF

◆   **Offer support for the staff** to work through the overwhelming nature of these stories and to support each other. Some staff may have experienced similar scenes as a child and need to deal with that in order to be effective and professional with the child.

◆   **Offer staff training** about the dynamics of domestic violence. People often need help in understanding why a woman (or man) could allow such abuse to go on, especially in the presence of a child. "Why doesn't she just leave him?" is often a question. They must learn not to blame the victim and explore how to be most supportive.

◆   **Be sure to connect with the administrator** and decide how to proceed when you encounter an incident of a child reporting spouse abuse.

◆   **Work with other professionals**. The early childhood program, working in collaboration with other community support agencies, can be a helpful agent in supporting this family. You can encourage them to seek help, let the parents know how it impacts the child, and help parents with parenting skills.

HOW TO RESPOND WITH THE CHILD

◆   **Be a caring, empathetic, listening teacher**. Establish a good relationship with the child. This is vital. The child can learn to use a secure and trusting relationship with an adult. You can become one stable place for the child.

◆   **Avoid embarrassing the child.** Children get trained early not to say anything and to pretend all is fine. Avoid embarrassing the child in front of other children when this topic is discussed. Remain available to the child, and encourage the child to talk to you about it.

◆   **Let the child know you are available**. If you learn of it from someone else, while you don't want to pry, let the child know that you know about what went on and that you are available to talk if he wants to. Make yourself accessible to the child.

◆   **Be open and empathetic**. If the child reveals it to you, be open and empathetic to what the child was feeling. "I'm sorry this happened." Be careful not to show shock or disgust when the child talks about it because the child may interpret that as criticism of her rather than your reaction to the situation and be embarrassed to share anything more.

◆ **Validate the child's feelings**. Let the child know that her feelings of fear, pain and anger are normal and understandable in such situations. Let them know that it is okay to have those feelings.

◆ **You can't promise you won't tell**. "It's not okay for daddies to hurt mommies. I will tell someone who will try to help him learn to do other things when he is angry and not hurt people."

◆ **Let the child know that he did not cause the violence**. Be sure to communicate to the child that they did not cause one parent to attack the other. This can be difficult when it was an argument about the child that started the violence, as it sometimes is. Let the child know that there are many ways to express anger and that he did not cause the violence.

◆ **What can he do if it happens again?** Help the child think about what he can do if it happens again—ways to cope with traumatic situations. Help him plan a strategy. Which adults can he talk to? How can he maximize his own personal safety? Is there a safe place the child can go? To his room? To a neighbor's house?

◆ **Teach the child how to call 911** when violence starts if it is possible to do it from another room in the house, or from a neighbor's house.

◆ **Give the child many expressive opportunities**. Give children many constructive opportunities to express their feelings, by drawing about it or just using materials to express emotions as in creative movement and playing with clay. Children may also feel some relief when they act it out in their dramatic play.

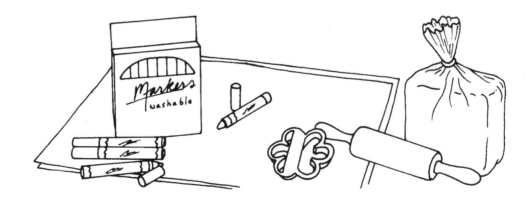

◆ If a child becomes more aggressive, **work to help the child learn ways to channel aggression and anger** (see chapter 24).

◆ If the child is withdrawn, consciously **include the child in fun activities and give the child encouragement to express feelings**. Also facilitate that child's friendship with at least one other child.

◆ **Reinforce the child's feelings of competence and self-esteem**, since witnessing domestic violence often makes him feel guilty, vulnerable and helpless.

◆ **Help the child feel powerful**. Give the child lots of ways to have power in the classroom environment. Ask the child's opinion about where to put things. Involve the children if you change the room arrangement. Have materials available where she feels powerful—big blocks, clay, art or riding toys.

HOW TO RESPOND WITH THE OTHER CHILDREN

◆ **Teach all children about using 911**.

◆ **Talk about anger**. Talk a lot about different ways to deal with anger.

◆ **Set clear boundaries of safety** and interactions, so the child will not have to test them so often. Set basic ground rules.

◆ **Build a sense of community** in the classroom. Caring for each other, helping each other, talking things over, problem solving together.

◆ **Provide time, space and equipment for lots of dramatic play**. Don't edit their play. If you are uncomfortable about the play, discuss it with your supervisor. However, stop children's play if it becomes sexual.

◆ **Offer to write down their stories on a routine basis**, without judgment or editing. Then, if traumatic events occur, this will be an easy, everyday avenue of expression.

HOW TO RESPOND WITH THE PARENTS

◆ **Have information and pamphlets** available for all parents about domestic violence and safe houses in your area as well as general family counseling services. You could place pamphlets in a display rack in your lobby, include them routinely in enrollment packets and mention the programs occasionally in your newsletter.

◆ **Talk with the parent**. If you know that one parent has been the victim of spouse abuse that the child has witnessed, talk to that parent about how such scenes affect children. Perhaps the parent is unaware that the child is also traumatized. Sometimes this is the push that is needed to get that parent to seek help or to leave for safe shelter.

◆ **Know about available resources in your community**, such as counseling services and safe houses. Find out if there are any fees, how people can connect with them and the scope of their services.

◆ **Work to build the self-esteem of the victim parent.** If you sense that this person tries hard to be a good parent, mention that. Offer warmth and friendship and a feeling of respect.

◆ **Focus on the mutual concern about the child**. In dealing with the parent, focus on the mutual circle of concern about the child. Assume that parents do love their children. Talk to them from the point of view of the child. Become an advocate for the child.

◆ **Try to understand the parent's position**. Working with the parents, try to eliminate the question, "How could they...?" from your mind. It is unproductive. Be available for the parent. Make them feel comfortable in your setting. Talk. Share. Try to understand the parent and his or her situation. Being able to talk to a trusted person about it helps.

HOW TO RESPOND WITH INFANTS AND TODDLERS

For children under the age of two, direct work with the parents is the most helpful strategy.

◆ **Even very young children are aware of the situation**. Parents may think a young infant is oblivious to fighting and is therefore not affected. This is not true. The child is aware of tension and becomes more tense herself. She may cry more, and have sleep and feeding problems, which in turn increase tension in the parents which may lead to more abuse. Therefore, counsel the parents that fighting and tension in the child's presence does affect the child, and encourage them to get help in working out their problems.

◆ **Parents may have less emotional energy left for the child**. When a parent is stressed out because of the threat or actuality of abuse from a spouse, there is less emotional energy to be responsive to an infant. Depending on the severity, this can interfere with bonding and can lead to attachment disorders and neglect. Therefore, be a consistent loving caregiver to the child.

WHERE TO FIND MORE INFORMATION

RESOURCES FOR CHILDREN

Books

Davis, Diane. (1985). Illustrated by Marina Megale. ***Something Is Wrong at My House***. Seattle, WA: Parenting Press, Inc. This book about parents fighting encourages children in violent homes to express common feelings of anger, fear and loneliness. It offers children ways to cope with the violence they see and helps break the cycle of domestic violence.

Lee, Ilene and Sylvester, Kathy. (1993). ***When Mommy Got Hurt: A Story for Young Children of Battered Women***. Kansas City, MO: R and M Press, Inc. A young child moves into a shelter with her mother after her father has been abusive. There is a discussion about the positive steps the abusive father must take so that the violence will stop.

Otto, Maryleah. (1988). Illustrated by Clover Clarke. ***Never, No Matter What***. Toronto, Canada: Womens Press. *Never, No Matter What* is a story for children that focuses on a child whose mother chooses to leave an abusive family situation and goes to a women's shelter. Included is a question and answer page for adults and children.

Paris, Susan. (1986). Illustrated by Gail Labriski. ***Mommy and Daddy Are Fighting: A Book for Children About Family Violence***. Seattle, WA: Seal Press Feminist.

RESOURCES FOR ADULTS

Books

Black, Claudia. (1987). ***It Will Never Happen to Me***. New York: Ballantine Books, Inc. The focus topic of this book is adult children of alcoholics. There is a very good chapter on dealing with violence within an alcoholic family, offering potential victims practical advice about what to do and where to go.

Eth, Spencer and Pynoos, Robert S. (1985). ***Post-Traumatic Stress Disorder in Children***. Washington, DC: American Psychiatric Press, Inc. Chapter Two deals with children traumatized by witnessing acts of personal violence. Other chapters give the broad picture of post-traumatic stress caused by different situations in children's lives.

Jaffe, Peter G., Wolfe, David A. and Wilson, Susan K. (Eds.). (1990). **Children of Battered Women**. Thousand Oaks, CA: Sage Publications, Inc. Summarizes major research studies related to children witnessing violence in the home and how it impacts their development.

Maracek, Mary. (1993). Illustrated by Jami Moffett. *Breaking Free from Partner Abuse: Voices of Battered Women Caught in the Cycle of Domestic Violence.* Buena Park, CA: Morning Glory Press. Filled with personal stories and poetry, this book is useful to understand the perspective of the battered woman. While there is no discussion on the effects on children, there is a useful bibliography at the end.

Osofsky, Joy and Fenichel, Emily. (1994). *Caring for Infants and Toddlers in Violent Environments: Hurt, Healing, and Hope.* Arlington, VA: Zero to Three National Center for Clinical Infant Programs. Offers caregiving strategies and support for very young children who are witnesses to or victims of community violence, family violence, and abuse. Available from Zero to Three National Center for Clinical Infant Programs, 2000 Fourteenth Street North, Suite 380, Arlington, VA 22201-2500. $4.50.

Booklet

The Impact of Domestic Violence on Children. American Bar Association Service Center, 750 North Lake Shore Drive, Chicago, IL 60611. 800-285-2221. www.abanet.org. $6.00. Specify order reference number 549-0248.

Organizations & Hot Lines

Domestic Abuse Intervention Project, 202 East Superior Street, Duluth, MN 55802. 218-722-4134. www.duluth-model.org. This project offers training materials and consultant services to assist agencies in developing a community-coordinated response to domestic violence.

National Council of Child Abuse and Family Violence, 1155 Connecticut Avenue, NW, Suite 400, Washington, DC 20036. The Council supports a resource center on family violence and family preservation services which provides educational materials, program and resource development consultation, technical assistance and training to agencies and volunteers. The National Family Violence HelpLine supported by the Council gives referral assistance to domestic violence victims.

National Coalition Against Domestic Violence, 1201 East Colfax Avenue, Suite 385, Denver, CO 80218-0749. 303-839-1852. www.ncadv.org. The Coalition provides technical assistance and information through printed materials, national directories, and monographs which focus on specific issues as family violence in rural communities.

Pennsylvania Coalition Against Domestic Violence, 6400 Flank Drive, Suite 1300, Harrisburg, PA 17112. 800-537-2238. www.pcadv.org. This organization houses the National Resource Center for Domestic Violence which provides comprehensive information and resources, policy development and technical assistance designed to enhance community response to and prevention of domestic violence. Resource packets are available on a range of topics including the impact of domestic violence on children.

Domestic Violence

CHAPTER 13

SUBSTANCE ABUSE IN THE FAMILY

HERE ARE TWO EXAMPLES

Andrea's father, an airline pilot, enrolled his four year old daughter in a child care center. Andrea adjusted quickly and showed a great deal of independence and maturity. A very bright little girl, she quickly became a leader in her classroom and was eager to take on responsibility and help the teachers.

Several weeks later the staff was surprised to hear that Andrea's father was going through the process of a divorce. He told the director that Andrea's mother was a substance abuser and had been through rehabilitation programs four times, but couldn't seem to overcome her addiction. He said his wife had been an alcoholic ever since he had known her, and that she goes into rehab programs with the best of intentions. When she drinks, however, she becomes abusive and violent. He said it didn't matter to her right now whether he had Andrea or not, so he was asking for sole custody. When the director asked how Andrea handles all of this, the father replied, "Well, her mother has been sick all of Andrea's life. It's just the way things are. We just keep telling her that Mom has to go in the hospital for a while to get better."

Like many children of alcoholics, Andrea compensates by being very responsible and independent. The teachers responded to her situation by making sure Andrea had lots of

Substance Abuse in the Family

time to play, be silly and just act like a typical four year old. They also arranged lots of informal times to be with her so she could express herself.

At this point, Andrea is doing fine in the classroom and her dad appreciates the understanding and support he finds at the child care center.

A staff member in her mid-twenties asked her director if she knew of anyone she could talk to about her alcoholic mother. She said she had always coped well with her mother's alcoholism, and was proud of how she had taken care of her younger brother and learned to cook at an early age. Caring for children in a child care setting seemed to be a natural job for her. But now some of her childhood experiences were troubling her and she found it especially difficult to interact with parents she suspected were substance abusers. The director put her in contact with Adult Children of Alcoholics, where she has been able to meet with others and work through some of her feelings.

LET'S *LOOK AT THE ISSUE*

It is a myth that people who abuse drugs or alcohol only hurt themselves. Probably no group is more aware of this fallacy than the people who work with their children and see the damage to their self-esteem and general development.

Our country has declared a "War on Drugs," but victory seems a long way off. The problem of alcohol and drug abuse in our society is so pervasive that at any given time, virtually every teacher will have children from homes where substance abuse is a way of life. We are all too aware of the subversive damage this does to children's self-esteem, emotional development and sometimes physical well-being.

Should teachers be doing anything in classrooms to address the issue directly? Can a teacher in any way influence what goes on in a child's home, or the child's attitude and ability to resist alcohol and drugs later in life? Some programs are intervening successfully by dealing with the whole family and its support system. We can all learn from them, but it's certainly not easy! Substance abuse is a whole family issue and the only way to intervene effectively is to deal with issues of the whole family, supporting a parent's very difficult recovery in the context of their whole social survival.

More realistically, the classroom teacher's role is to provide the child a safe place, supporting the child's emotional well-being and intellectual growth while others in the professional team see that the family receives intervention. The teacher might be the person to serve as a supportive and sensitive model to help the parent learn how to interact effectively with the child and to give suggestions for pleasurable things to do at home with the child, building a positive relationship between parent and child.

As stated in the video, *Putting the Family Together Again*, described in the resource section at the end of the chapter, when people are addicted to alcohol or other drugs, the addiction is the most important thing in their lives. All of their thoughts are directed to where they will get their next "hit." Parents who are addicted to drugs must first be supported in their recovery from addiction before they will be able to focus on proper parenting of their young children. This does not mean they don't love their children, but that the addiction dominates all of their thoughts and actions.

It is possible that teachers or other caregivers will be unaware of addiction problems in a child's family. People become skilled at hiding their addiction and family members, even young children, learn to help hide the secret. Some children, especially those who have taken on compensating responsibilities at home, do very well in school. School or child care settings become the place where they feel safe and where they can shine for their abilities. However, these children also need special support from their teachers.

When there is substance abuse in a home, there are often other problems affecting the child such as physical and sexual child abuse, domestic violence, neglect, unemployment, poverty, and homelessness. Substance abuse is at the root of many of our most complex social problems.

INSIGHTS FROM CHILD DEVELOPMENT

Self-blame. Children often feel they are to blame for the family member's substance abuse. They may believe that the person is drinking or taking drugs because their behavior upset him.

Loss of self-esteem. The child suffers a subsequent loss of self-esteem because of guilty feelings. A child's self-esteem may also suffer because she believes, "If daddy really loved me he wouldn't drink."

Feelings of confusion. Because substance abusing parents are inconsistent in their responses to children, children are often confused and frustrated.

Lack of attention. Children who are raised in a home where substance abuse is present, even if only one parent is a substance abuser, often suffer from parents not being there for them. The substance preoccupies the adults. The lack of focused attention on the child can cause the child to have diminished self-esteem.

School as a place of consistency. Children of alcoholics often do surprisingly well in school because it is the one place where they can thrive, where there is consistency.

Keeping quiet. Children in alcoholic families usually learn very early not to express or even acknowledge their feelings.

Developmental delays. If children have been prenatally exposed to drugs or alcohol they may suffer a wide range of developmental problems including delays, hyperactivity and behavior disorders (see chapter 16 on children with special needs).

WHEN TO SEEK HELP

◆ **Recurrent themes of drugs, alcohol or family violence** revealed in the child's dramatic play, stories or drawings

◆ **Signs of neglect**—child improperly dressed, dirty, hungry

◆ **Signs of physical or sexual abuse**

◆ **Excessive acting out**, "confirming" what the child feels to be other people's low opinion of him

◆ **Lack of attachment** to family members

◆ **Hyperactivity**

◆ **Nonexpressive behavior**. The child seems very nonexpressive. Some children learn early on: don't talk, don't trust, don't feel.

◆ **Regressive behaviors**

◆ **Frequent absences**

WHO CAN HELP

◆ Local chapters of Alcoholics Anonymous (AA), Al-Anon, Alateen, Adult Children of Alcoholics (ACOA) and Adult Children Anonymous (ACA)
◆ Substance abuse counselors
◆ Maternal substance abuse treatment programs
◆ Mental health centers
◆ Family therapists
◆ Hospitals that provide detoxification and rehabilitation services

◆ Look under "Alcoholism Information & Treatment" in the Yellow Pages of your phone book for a listing of local resources and treatment programs.

HOW TO RESPOND

HOW TO RESPOND WITH THE STAFF

◆ **Start with introspection**. In today's society, many people have some form of substance abuse in their own families. It's important to be acutely aware of these issues so that you can moderate your responses to situations. It might be most helpful to do this in a staff meeting or workshop with someone specially trained in issues of substance abuse.

◆ **Find out about alcoholism**. Read up on the topic. Possibly attend AA or Al-Anon meetings to know the dynamics of the disease and how it affects families.

◆ **Be aware of your mandated responsibilities** if you suspect child abuse or neglect.

HOW TO RESPOND WITH THE CHILD

◆ **Develop consistency and security**. Keep the daily schedule of routines stable and the number of staff members who interact with the child to a minimum. Maintain small group sizes.

◆ **Be dependable**. Because the child may have inconsistency and broken promises at home, be dependable. Stick to any promises you make to the child. Let her know what to expect ahead of time.

◆ **Let the child know he is not to blame**. If a child talks to you about a parent's substance abuse, reinforce that he is in no way to blame for the abuse. Also stress that he cannot stop the parent from drinking or using drugs.

◆ **Work to develop trust**. Be careful about teaching a child to speak out against alcohol or drugs for it may backfire and create angry feelings in the adults at home. Rather, focus on giving the child a stable, accepting environment where she can feel free to play and trust.

◆ **Build self-expression skills**. Provide many open-ended art experiences, block play, and opportunities to dictate stories of their own making. Let the children know you value their thoughts and think they have good ideas.

◆ **Encourage dramatic play**. Provide many opportunities for dramatic play, with both dress-up and housekeeping corner equipment, and with small dolls either in a doll house or in the block corner. This gives children opportunities to play out scenes and put themselves in positions of power. While their play may be informative, avoid over interpretations.

◆ **Work on feelings**. Do a lot of activities about feelings to show children that everyone has a range of feelings and it's okay to express them (see chapter 24).

◆ **Read some of the books** listed at the end of this chapter to the child. Give the child the opportunity to talk about them.

HOW TO RESPOND WITH THE OTHER CHILDREN

◆ **Foster an atmosphere of playfulness**. Life outside your classroom may appear very serious to the child. Use and encourage humor in the form of silliness and laughter (never teasing).

◆ **Help form friendships**. A child may have difficulty forming friendships and entering play with other children. Gentle coaching from the teacher can be helpful.

HOW TO RESPOND WITH INFANTS AND TODDLERS

◆ **Recognize vulnerability**. Infants and toddlers of substance abusing parents are at extreme risk. Their emotional development may be greatly affected. When parents are addicted and "high," or looking for their next "fix," they cannot be responsive to their baby's cues and offer warm, nurturing care. The child fails to develop basic trust. The world is not a safe, predictable place for the baby. Neglect is common because the parent is distracted. Physical abuse is common because the parent's tolerance is lowered. Immediate and comprehensive intervention is necessary.

◆ **Children may have physical and neurological damage**. Children who have been prenatally exposed to drugs and/or alcohol can suffer a whole range of effects, from invisible ones to severe physical and neurological damage. The impact on the child has to do with the particular drug, the amount, and the time and duration of the exposure during pregnancy. Effects are often long lasting and impact the child at each stage of development through adulthood.

Fetal Alcohol Syndrome

Prenatal exposure to alcohol can lead to Fetal Alcohol Syndrome (FAS). FAS can include the following characteristics in children:

◆ Mental retardation
◆ Hyperactivity
◆ Over sensitivity to touch or other stimulation
◆ Facial and physical anomalies
◆ Problems in attention and learning
◆ Seizures

However, not all children prenatally exposed to alcohol will exhibit these characteristics.

Fetal Alcohol Effect

Fetal Alcohol Effect (FAE) exists when a child may have some of the characteristics listed above, but not enough to qualify for a diagnosis of FAS. Developmental delays and hyperactivity can be part of FAE.

Because there is such variability in how FAE or FAS effects individual children, each child needs to be looked at individually. Therapists, together with parents and teachers, should consider each symptom and work up an individual plan for the child.

HOW TO RESPOND WITH THE PARENTS

◆ **Notify your director** if you suspect substance abuse in the family because of things a child reveals to you verbally or through recurring themes in dramatic play, stories or drawings. Decide together how your program or community might be able to support the family to aid recovery.

◆ **Recommend books**. If other family members reveal to you that there is a substance abuser in the family, recommend books about addiction that they could read to their children (see the resource section at the end of this chapter). This can help children realize that they are not the only ones who have these experiences. A child can learn the vocabulary to express himself and can also learn to understand her feelings toward the parent's addiction.

◆ **Support the parent**. If you have a friendly, supportive relationship with the parent, you might offer to go to an AA or Narcotics Anonymous meeting with her.

◆ **Go to meetings first**. If possible, visit such meetings first, so you can be sure you are recommending something that will be helpful.

Substance Abuse in the Family

RESOURCES FOR CHILDREN

Books

Before you read any of these books to children, discuss the issue with your supervisor. It might be best to have the books on hand to loan to families, but not have them in the classroom. If, on the other hand, everybody is aware of the situation and the parent is in a recovery program and knows the materials, it might be acceptable to read some of these books to children individually. Be very careful not to be critical of the parent to the child or undermine the parent-child relationship.

Laik, Judy. (1994). Illustrated by Rebekah Strecker. *Under Whose Influence?* Seattle, WA: Parenting Press, Inc. Jamie is at a friend's house. When the other kids, nine to twelve year olds, decide to sample the liquor cabinet Jamie must decide what to do.

Sanford, Doris. (1987). Illustrated by Graci Evans. *I Know the World's Worst Secret: A Child's Book About Living with an Alcoholic Parent.* Portland, OR: Multnomah Press. This is the story of how Elizabeth learns to grow and maintain her own life even though she has family responsibilities because her mother is an alcoholic.

Vigna, Judith. (1988). *I Wish Daddy Didn't Drink So Much.* Morton Grove, IL: Albert Whitman Publishers. After a disappointing Christmas, Lisa learns ways to deal with her father's alcoholism with the help of her mom and an older friend.

Vigna, Judith. (1990). *My Big Sister Takes Drugs.* Morton Grove, IL: Albert Whitman Publishers. When the police bring home Paul's sister Tina, who was found taking drugs in the park, a nightmare begins for the whole family.

RESOURCES FOR ADULTS

Books

Barth, R., Pietrzak, J., and Ramler, M.(Eds). (1993) *Families Living with Drugs and HIV: Intervention and Treatment Strategies.* New York: The Guilford Press. The book, written by various experts, explores ways agencies in a community can collaborate to best serve families in need. The articles give in-depth information for understanding the nature of addiction and how best to respond to parents, as well as their children.

Black, Claudia. (1987). *It Will Never Happen to Me*. New York: Ballantine Books, Inc. This book provides an insight into growing up in a family where there is alcohol abuse. It describes various personality types that emerge when substance abuse dominates a family. There is also a chapter on family violence and a section on available resources.

Finkelstein, Norma. (1990). *Getting Sober, Getting Well*. Cambridge, MA: The Women's Program. This treatment guide for caregivers who work with women has information about drug addiction and alcoholism. The guide also discusses parenting and contains useful training materials. Resources of the Cambridge and Somerville Program for Alcohol and Drug Addiction Rehabilitation (CASPAR) have contributed to this resource. To order the book contact The Women's Program, 6 Camelia Avenue, Cambridge, MA 02139.

Roberts, Dorothy. (1991). *Women, Pregnancy and Substance Abuse*. Center for Women Policy Studies, 1211 Connecticut Avenue NW, Suite 312, Washington, DC 20036. 202-872-1770. This report discusses the legal, social and medical aspects of the problem of substance abuse among women and proposes policy options that emphasize treatment. To order, contact the Center for Women Policy Studies. $15.

Sexton, Daniel A., (1992). *Healing the Wounds of Childhood, The Resource Guide for Adult Survivors of Childhood Abuse and Addictions*. Hollywood, CA: Childhelp U.S.A. This book lists literally hundreds of advocacy organizations, hot lines and publications related to any kind of child abuse. A good resource to have available for staff or parents who were abused as children.

Articles

Cohen, Abby. "Releasing a child to an adult 'under the influence' or a non-custodial adult." *Child Care Information Exchange.* March/April 1993, 15-16. What do you do when an inebriated parent comes to pick up her child? The article outlines your legal responsibilities and gives strategies for how to handle the situation with the parent.

Katz, Lilian G. "Misguided intentions in drug-abuse prevention." *Young Children*. March 1994. Should we be teaching children about drugs and alcohol, or is this an adult problem?

"Substance involved young children and their families." *Zero to Three*. 13(1), August/September 1992. This 40-page issue of the journal of the National Center for Clinical Infant Programs is devoted to substance abuse in parents of infants. It contains excellent articles on Fetal Alcohol Syndrome and treatment programs for addicted parents. To order a copy of this issue contact the National Center for Clinical Infant Programs, 2000 M Street NW, Suite 200, Washington, DC 20036. 202-638-1144. www.zerotothree.org. $6.00 plus $2.50 shipping and handling.

Alcohol, Child Abuse and Child Neglect. National Committee to Prevent Child Abuse, Fulfillment Center, 1 Community Place, South Deerfield, MA 01373-0200. 800-835-2671. www.channing-bete.com. The pamphlet describes alcohol-related abuse and neglect, and the price paid by each family member. It notes warning signs to watch for, identifies sources of help for families and individuals and outlines positive steps that can be taken.

Chandler, Carole. *Parenting and Substance Abuse Don't Mix*. National Committee to Prevent Child Abuse, Fulfillment Center, 1 Community Place, South Deerfield, MA 01373-0200. 414-359-1040. www.channing-bete.com. The author explains the link between substance abuse and child abuse, and the ways abuse occurs and how the cycle can be stopped. Substance abuse by pregnant mothers is also discussed.

Living in a House of Cards: The Chemically Dependent Family. Alliance for Children & Families, 11700 West Lake Park Drive, Milwaukee, WI 53224. 800-221-2681. www.alliance1.org. The pamphlet describes chemical dependency as a physical disease caused by abuse of alcohol or drugs. It also describes characteristics of children raised in a chemically dependent household and lists where to seek professional assistance. Single copies are available at no charge.

Resources for Alcohol and Other Drug Education Catalog. Hazelden Publishing and Education, 15251 Pleasant Valley Road, P.O. Box 176, Center City, MN 55012-0176. 800-328-9000. www.hazelden.org. This catalog has hundreds of resources for working with both children and adults in the areas of addiction. It has an especially good selection of videos for training purposes. The catalog also contains resources from other publishers. Call the toll-free number for a copy of the catalog.

Curriculum Materials

Newell, Patricia L., and Sheehan, Marguerite M. *I'm So Glad You Asked*. Vineyard Haven, MA: I'm So Glad You Asked, Inc. This curriculum, designed for preschool and kindergarten children, focuses on building strengths in children that will help them make appropriate decisions later in life. Scripts for puppet plays, songs, stories, parent pages and slides explore topics which include recognizing and expressing feelings, making mistakes, safe and unsafe substances and fears. Especially valuable is the basic information for adults about addiction and different drugs. This group also offers specialized on-site staff training on helping adults come to terms with abuse in their past and working with difficult parents who may be substance abusers. To order the curriculum call 413-549-3873. $185.

Putting the Family Together Again. (1993). Parent Child Services, 911 North Skidmore, Portland, OR 97217. 503-236-9389. www.ehspdx.org. This video presents the model and experiences of a Head Start program in Portland, Oregon that has had success in addressing the needs of parents and children in substance abusing families. It is especially helpful in gaining empathy for and understanding of parents who are recovering substance abusers as parents describe their own processes and thoughts. There is also discussion about supporting the staff as they learn to deal with difficult situations. $75 plus $5 shipping and handling.

Organizations & Hot Lines

Alcohol, Drug and Pregnancy Help Line. 800-638-BABY. The Hot Line provides resource information and treatment referral service.

Mt. Regis Center-Drug & Alcohol Treatment Center, 405 Kimball Avenue, Salem, VA 24153. 800-477-3447. www.mtregiscenter.com. Self-help 12-Step programs sponsored by Alcoholics Anonymous (AA) are the most affordable and often the most effective programs available, offering peer support and encouragement. Check the telephone directory for the listing of your local chapter.

Al-Anon Family Group Headquarters, Inc., 350 Broadway Street, Suite 404, New York, NY 10013. 212-941-0094. www.nycalanon.org. Associated with Alcoholics Anonymous (AA) groups, Al-Anon groups provide peer support for family members and close friends of alcoholics. Some groups are formed for teenagers. Other groups are designed for adults who as children lived with parents who were alcoholics. These groups include: Adult Children of Alcoholics (ACOA) and Adult Children Anonymous (ACA). Check the telephone directory for the listing of your local chapter. Al-Anon has an extensive publications list.

National Clearinghouse for Alcohol and Drug Information, P.O. Box 2345, Rockville, MD 20852. 800-729-6686. www.health.org. The Clearinghouse provides resource information about the abuse of alcohol, and drug and prescription drug abuse. An extensive publications catalog is available.

National Council on Alcoholism and Drug Dependence Hope Line. 800-NCA-CALL. The Hot Line provides the telephone number of the affiliate organization in the caller's local area.

National Cocaine Hot Line, 800-COCAINE. The Hot Line provides a listing of clinics, private practitioners, schools, hospitals and other sources of help in the caller's community. It also has a number to call for more information on children who were prenatally exposed to cocaine.

National Drug and Alcohol Treatment Routing Service Hot Line, 800-662-4357. www.health.org. The Hot Line provides a number of services including treatment options listed by state location, drug treatment referrals, printed material on alcohol and drug abuse, assistance with an alcohol problem and counseling on adolescent and family problems.

CHAPTER 14

COMMUNITY VIOLENCE

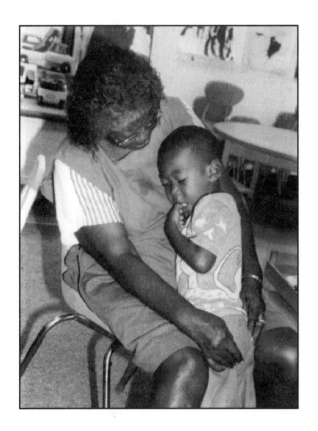

HERE'S AN EXAMPLE

Five year old Jason returned home with his divorced mother after going to a movie. When they entered their house, they surprised some burglars. Jason ran to a neighbor's house. After the incident, Jason went to live with his father who enrolled him in the local child care center. He was given psychological counseling for a time. He "graduated" from counseling when the psychologist felt he was doing fine. But his teacher, Shirley, isn't so sure everything is fine. Jason told her that he feels bad because he should have fought the people who robbed his house but he was too scared. His father's girlfriend told her that Jason is very afraid of the dark, is afraid to be in a room by himself and wakes up several times a night with bad dreams. But since his father doesn't feel he can afford to pay for more psychological counseling, and it isn't covered by his health insurance, Jason is going without help.

LET'S LOOK AT THE ISSUE

"Violence, and the fear of violence, is the most debilitating, corrosive force in the lives of our children. Kids who are scared cannot learn or develop properly." —Colorado Governor Roy Romer, October 1994.

Children are greatly harmed by their exposure to violence, either directly or indirectly. There is no argument about that. Teachers report that an increase in children exposed to violence is the greatest change in the last 20 years. They are seeing more fear, more rage, more aggressiveness, all of which interfere with learning, social adjustment and playing. All children today are victims, direct or indirect, of the violence that pervades our society.

The NAEYC Position Statement on Violence in the Lives of Children, states, "The causes and effects of violent behavior in society are complex and interrelated; much violence results from social injustice prevalent in our society. Among the significant contributors are poverty, racism, unemployment, substance abuse, proliferation of guns, inadequate or abusive parenting practices, adult models of violent problem solving behavior, and frequent exposure to violence through the media."

The models of violence children see in the media are discussed in chapter 15. Children also see role models in their lives, such as parents, people they know in the community and sports heroes who solve their problems by using violence.

Even though there is much media coverage and discussion about preventing violence with children, people don't often focus on young children and violence. Children are affected in different ways, depending on the type and amount of violence to which they have been exposed. Diane Levin in *Teaching Young Children in Violent Times* created the image of a pyramid of violence, showing how all children are impacted, and depending on the type of exposure, how serious the implications for the individual child are. At the base of the pyramid, where the greatest number of children are exposed to violence, is the general exposure to violence on television and other media. Fewer, but very significant numbers of children are at the middle level of the pyramid. These are children who have personally witnessed acts of violence, such as a shooting in the community. At the tip of the pyramid are those children who are experiencing chronic violence in their everyday lives, such as domestic violence and ongoing community violence. While all children experience heightened anxiety and stress as a result of exposure to violence, the higher you go on the pyramid the more severely affected the children are.

As we consider what to do, it is clear that the early childhood teacher cannot go out in society and solve these problems. Our question is, rather, how to respond to the individual children in front of us to build their resilience, their ability to recover from the psychological impact and continue to develop in a healthy fashion. As James Garbarino states in *Children in Danger*, "Although high-quality early childhood programs are not an inoculation against the destructive effects of violence, positive early school experiences and warm, nurturing relationships with teachers are known to be critical contributors to children's ability to cope with stress and trauma."

Increased aggression. When children have witnessed a lot of violence, they are more likely to use violence themselves as a means to get what they want or to solve problems. Increased aggression is one symptom of a violent environment.

Feeling powerless. Being aggressive is also one way children compensate for feeling powerless in their lives.

Aggressiveness inhibits children's social development, being able to solve problems and get along with others. These things are vital for later learning and developing supportive peer relationships that build resiliency.

Models of violent behavior, plus a lack of models for cooperative problem solving behavior increases the likelihood of children acting aggressively.

Quick to anger. Children exposed to violence may be more explosive and quick to anger.

Desensitized to violence. Children sometimes become desensitized to violence. They don't care, and don't empathize with the pain and suffering.

Children may become fearful and withdrawn and turn inward. They become emotionally numb to events happening in their lives that otherwise are overwhelming to them.

Infants at great risk. Some of the greatest damage may be to infants whose major emotional task is developing basic trust and bonding to caring adults. When parents and family members do not feel safe and are emotionally distracted by community violence and its related social problems, they are often unavailable to babies, unresponsive to children's cues.

Problems in the parent-child relationship. Parents may be overprotective and restrict the child's opportunities for recreation and independent play. They may be harsh and punitive in an attempt to steer children away from violent behavior or violent peers.

Adults may be less tolerant of children's behavior. Adults who are stressed because of danger in the environment are less tolerant of the constant testing of typical toddlers. Harsh reprimands come more quickly, ultimately inhibiting a child's inclinations to explore.

Children may feel overwhelmed and helpless. Children can suffer from post-traumatic stress, resulting from feelings of being overwhelmed and helpless.

Community Violence

WHEN TO SEEK HELP

Remember that all of the following may be present from time to time in all children. Knowing your children and their circumstances will help you determine when extra help is needed.

◆ **Overly vigilant**—the child feels very fearful, afraid to venture out, to play and is frightened or overly wary of new people and new experiences. The child startles easily.

◆ **Overly sensitive to sights, smells, sounds** that remind the child of a direct experience.

◆ **Nightmares** and other sleep disturbances.

◆ **Memory impairment,** difficulty concentrating.

◆ **Regression**. Children often show signs of regression—such as sucking thumb, returning to baby talk, loss of toileting skills and throwing temper tantrums.

◆ **Emotional numbing**. The child seems flat, doesn't care.

◆ **An excessive amount of aggressive behavior**.

◆ **Repetitive play involving violent themes**.

WHO CAN HELP

◆ Child psychologists and mental health professionals
◆ Play therapists
◆ Law enforcement agencies
◆ Concerned citizens in the community and neighborhood watch groups

HOW TO RESPOND

Obviously, no teacher in the classroom is going to solve these problems. Yet, the teacher must respond in a professional way when one of the children in her charge encounters such an incident. The teacher can provide one safe haven where the child can relax, deal with fears, and feel capable and powerful.

HOW TO RESPOND WITH THE STAFF

◆ **Staff meeting**. You might start by having a staff discussion about how violence has affected you all personally. Sometimes these issues need to be dealt with first on a personal level in order to think clearly about our responses to children. Some of your staff may themselves be living in violent environments and may be suffering just like the children.

◆ **Dangerous area**. If your program is located in a dangerous area, getting to and from work may be extremely stressful in the first place, and staff may feel like prisoners in the setting, afraid to go out for lunch or on breaks. Perhaps some creative problem solving will be possible.

HOW TO RESPOND WITH THE CHILD

◆ **Find out what the child experienced**. In order to respond appropriately, you need to know what the child experienced. Find out as much as you can about what happened, what the child witnessed and how the child reacted. What was the child told? Who was there with the child?

◆ **Let the child talk about it**. Don't pretend that nothing happened and go on as usual. Without prying or forcing the issue, let the child know that you know about what happened and that you are available to talk about it. "I heard some people got hurt in front of your house last night. Would you like to talk about it? No? Well, if you change your mind, just let me know and we can find a quiet place where we can talk about it."

◆ **Talk about what to do if it happens again**. Depending on the type of incident, talk about how the child might respond or act if it happens again. What can he do? Where can he go?

◆ **Make a list of people she can talk to**. Ask the child to make a list of people she can talk to about violence.

◆ **List places where he feels safe**. Help the child list places where he feels safe in his neighborhood.

◆ **Draw or dictate**. Encourage the child to draw about the scary things she has witnessed or is worried about. Very young children might just scribble, but you can ask the child to tell you about the scribbles and take dictation.

◆ **Encourage dramatic play**. Young children often replay a traumatic scene over and over in their play. While a child doesn't need to replay the scene to recover from it, if he does, you can act as a soothing force.

◆ **Offer many calming activities**. Find out what is comforting to this particular child such as playing with clay, sand or water, looking at books, doing puzzles or painting.

◆ **Include opportunities for self-expression**. Activities such as squeezing clay, creative movement and dramatic play as well as verbal activities help the child express what feelings are dominating (see chapter 23).

HOW TO RESPOND WITH THE OTHER CHILDREN

◆ **Find out what the other children know**. If they are not aware, consult with your director about whether to tell them. Rumors among children spread quickly and often it is better to simply address the situation, state what happened and talk about it. If not, the rumors that children come up with can be more bizarre than what really happened.

◆ **Talk to the children about their concerns**. Depending on the situation, you may be able to help reassure them of their safety.

◆ **Make the children feel safe**. Offer a stable, consistent routine with no surprises. The children need to know what to expect every day. That helps them feel secure (see chapter 22).

◆ **Review and practice class rules**. Frequently review and practice class rules in neutral or pretend settings, such as acting them out in circle time, or letting children remind a forgetful puppet in your group meeting time.

◆ **Develop friendship skills**. Support children as they learn friendship skills so that they can develop strong peer relationships.

◆ **Always stop verbal or physical aggression**. Intervene in play when you notice verbal or physical aggression and the children don't seem to be moving in constructive ways.

◆ **Be a good role model**. Be very conscious of your interactions with other staff, parents and children, both in conflict resolution and in general social situations because a child may not have had appropriate models in his life.

◆ **Build a sense of group and belonging**. Communicate in many ways that all the children in the group are valued and that you all care about each other. Talk with the children about a child who is absent, about how the class is looking forward to the child returning to the class.

◆ **Invite a police officer to come and talk to the children** about how to stay safe in their neighborhood. It is important that children learn to see police as safe people they can trust.

Community Violence

HOW TO RESPOND WITH INFANTS AND TODDLERS

◆ **Infants and toddlers are very vulnerable**. Infants and toddlers are most affected by the reaction of the adults around them. If a trusted adult is traumatized by the violence, the child will feel it, become more tense and may develop eating and sleeping problems. This can, in turn, feed the tension in the family.

◆ **Remind parents**. Remind parents that it is important to comfort and reassure babies and be as playful and interactive with them as possible.

◆ **Developmental delays are possible**. In unsafe environments, toddlers and young children are often confined and unable to explore their environment, a vital step in cognitive development. They may have few opportunities to really play, engage in gross motor activities and have social interactions with other children. So there is a greater likelihood of developmental delays from simple lack of practice and opportunity. Be sure to offer them many opportunities in your setting.

◆ **Brainstorm with parents**. Therefore, help parents brainstorm and figure out ways the child may have the practice and developmentally appropriate activities needed to thrive. Give ideas for adding safety to the environment for the child, simple activities to offer at home and places to take the child.

HOW TO RESPOND WITH THE PARENTS

◆ **Recommend social supports**. Parents are undoubtedly feeling the same effects that their children are, if they are exposed to chronic violence. Feeling safe comes first on their needs list, before they can devote energy to their children. Be sure to link them up with any social supports that your program or community offers.

◆ **Reaffirm family bonds**. Times of community violence are times when it is extremely important to reaffirm family bonds. Encourage parents to spend extra time with their children to let them know they are loved and cared for.

◆ **Become an advocate**. Either individually, or as a whole staff, push to get the support in the community you need to provide a safe environment for children.

RESOURCES FOR CHILDREN

Books

Angelou, Maya. (1978). Illustrated by Jean-Michel Basquiat. *Life Doesn't Frighten Me*. New York, NY: Stewart, Tabori & Chang. Maya Angelou's poem celebrates the courage within each of us. Fearsome images are summoned and dispelled by the power of faith in ourselves.

Bunting, Eve. (1994). Illustrated by David Diaz. *Smoky Night*. New York, NY: Harcourt Brace & Company. *Smoky Night* is a story about cats and people who couldn't get along until a night of rioting. This book was the winner of the 1994 Caldecott Medal.

Bunting, Eve. (1990). Illustrated by Ronald Himler. *The Wall*. New York, NY: Clarion Books. A boy and his dad come from far away to visit the Vietnam Memorial in Washington and find the name of the boy's grandfather.

Guy, Rosa. (1991). Illustrated by Caroline Binch. *Billy the Great.* New York, NY: Bantam Doubleday Dell Publishing Group, Inc. Billy definitely has a mind of his own. When new neighbors move in and tempers flare, Billy proves that sometimes parents can learn from their children.

Heide, Florence Parry and Gilliland, Judith Heide. (1992). Illustrated by Ted Lewin. *Sami and the Time of the Troubles*. New York, NY: Clarion Books. A ten year old Lebanese boy goes to school, helps his mother with chores and lives with his family in a basement shelter when bombings occur and fighting begins.

Keens-Douglas, Richardo. (1992). Illustrated by Anouchka Galouchko. *The Nutmeg Princess*. Buffalo, NY: Firefly Books Inc. A beautifully illustrated story about the impor- tance of trust and integrity in relationships.

Levine, Arthur A. (1993). Illustrated by Robert Roth. *Pearl Moscowitz's Last Stand.* New York, NY: Tambourine Books. Pearl Moscowitz takes a stand when the city government tries to chop down the last gingko tree on her street.

Morimoto, Junko. (1987). *My Hiroshima*. New York, NY: Viking Childrens Books. When the war came there were some things that changed. But when the bomb fell, everything changed, including the life of one small girl.

Naylor, Phyllis Reynolds. (1994). Illustrated by Nola Langner Malone. *King of the Playground*. New York, NY: Macmillan. With his dad's help, Kevin overcomes his fear of the "King of the Playground" who has threatened to tie him to the slide.

Tsuchiya, Yukio. (1988). Illustrated by Ted Lewin. *Faithful Elephants: A True Story of Animals, People and War.* Boston, MA: Houghton Mifflin Company. This story recounts how three elephants in a Tokyo Zoo were put to death because of the war, focusing on the pain shared by the elephant and the keepers.

RESOURCES FOR ADULTS

Books

Carlsson-Paige, Nancy and Levin, Diane E. (1987). *The War Play Dilemma: Balancing Needs and Values in the Early Childhood Classroom*. New York: Teacher's College Press. This book includes useful suggestions for parent involvement.

Carlsson-Paige, Nancy and Levin, Diane E. (1994). *Who's Calling the Shots: How to Respond Effectively to Children's Fascination with War Play and War Toys*. Philadelphia, PA: New Society Publishers. These books will help you think about what to do regarding children's dramatic play involving guns.

Eth, Spencer and Pynoos, Robert S. (Eds.). (1985). *Post-Traumatic Stress Disorder in Children*. Washington, DC: American Psychiatric Press, Inc. Chapter Two deals with children traumatized by witnessing acts of personal violence. Other chapters give the broad picture of post-traumatic stress disorder caused by different situations in children's lives.

Garbarino, James, Dubrow, Nancy, Kostelny, Kathleen and Pardo, Carole. (1992). *Children in Danger, Coping with the Consequences of Community Violence*. San Francisco, CA: Jossey-Bass Publishers. This book is a valuable resource for persons working with children experiencing chronic community violence. In addition to case descriptions, there are discussions of program designs that augment children's resilience. It will give you a broader understanding of the issue along with some strategies for responding.

Kotlowitz, Alex. (1991). *There Are No Children Here: The Story of Two Boys Growing Up in the Other America*. New York: Doubleday & Company, Inc. This book is especially valuable reading for persons for whom inner city violence, gangs, poverty and despair seem like distant problems, or problems with clear solutions. The book is a narrative that reads like a novel, but traces the real lives of two little boys living in Chicago's projects. It gives you a chance to get inside their lives and feel what it is like to grow up in that environment. The book is also available on audio cassette.

Levin, Diane E. (1994). *Teaching Children in Violent Times: Building a Peaceable Classroom*. Cambridge, MA: Educators for Social Responsibility. This excellent resource has much discussion of getting children to solve their differences in peaceful ways.

Osofsky, Joy D. and Fenichel, Emily, (Eds.). (1994). *Caring for Infants and Toddlers in Violent Environments: Hurt, Healing, and Hope*. Arlington, VA: Zero to Three National Center for Clinical Infant Programs. A series of articles and case studies which give insight to the impact of violence on the development of very young children. Available from Zero to Three National Center for Clinical Infant Programs, 2000 14th Street North, Suite 380, Arlington, VA 22201-2500. $4.95.

Articles

Brodkin, Adele M. "Roundtable: Children and Violence." *Early Childhood Today*. New York: Scholastic Inc., March 1994, 46. A discussion with James Garbarino, President of the Erikson Institute in Chicago; Beverly Robertson Jackson, Director of Public Policy and Education at Zero to Three National Center for Clinical Infant Programs in Arlington, VA; and Joy D. Osofsky, professor of pediatrics and psychiatry at the University of New Orleans on the impact of violence on young children.

Gelman, David. "The Miracle of Resiliency: How Kids Grow." *Newsweek*. Special issue, Summer 1991, 44.

Gobel, Carla B. and Bomba, Anne K. "A Parent Meeting: Young Children and Firearm Safety." *Young Children*. 50(2), January 1995, 81.

Wallach, Lorraine B. "Helping Children Cope with Violence." *Young Children*. May 1993, 48(6), 4-11.

Booklets & Pamphlets

Can They Hope to Feel Safe Again? The Impact of Community Violence on our Infants, Toddlers, their Families, and Practitioners. The report of the 8th Annual Conference of the National Center for Clinical Infant Programs. Dec. 1991.

Helping Children Cope: A Guide to Helping Children Cope With the Stress of the Oklahoma City Explosion. American Psychological Association, Practice Directorate, 750 First Street, NE, Washington, DC 20002. 202-336-5898. www.apa.org. The American Psychological Association (APA) has compiled guidelines to help parents, caregivers and teachers give children the support and reassurance they need to get through the difficult period which follows a disaster. The free material may be duplicated without permission, as long as no changes are made and credit is given to APA.

NAEYC Position Statement on Violence in the Lives of Children. National Association for the Education of Young Children, 1509 16th Street, NW, Washington, DC 20036-1426. 800-424-2460. www.naeyc.org. The document provides an overview of violence and its effect on young children. It is an excellent resource for an early childhood staff to discuss in gaining a common knowledge base.

Being Healthy and Safe With McGruff and Scruff: Activity Book for Preschool, Head Start, and Other Child Care Programs. National Crime Prevention Council, 1000 Connecticut Avenue, NW, Washington, DC 20036. 202-466-6272. www.ncpc.org. This colorful activity book provides 20 separate activities (plus dozens of adaptations and variations) that are developmentally appropriate for young children. The book uses songs, games, crafts, and stories to convey a variety of important ideas and skills including good health habits, sense of family and community, making decisions, differentiating fantasy and reality, and building self-esteem. Sample letters to parents which suggest reinforcement activities are included. $24.95.

Cops Helping Kids: Teaching Preschoolers Violence Prevention and Safety. National Crime Prevention Council, 1000 Connecticut Avenue, NW, Washington, DC 20036. 202-466-6272. www.ncpc.org. The book offers suggestions on effective ways to communicate with young children and provides reproducible materials for activities that help police officers introduce themselves, build rapport and convey prevention messages. The activities address concerns as bullies, inappropriate touches, medicines versus drugs, what to do if separated from parents, calling for help in emergencies, awareness of strangers and how to avoid danger from guns or other weapons. $19.95.

Garbarino, James. (1993). *Let's Talk About Living in a World With Violence: An Activity Book for School-Age Children*. Erikson Institute, 420 North Wabash Avenue, Chicago, IL 60611. Although this workbook is designed for use with school-aged children it is easily adaptable for use with verbal four and five year olds. It does call for a lot of representational drawing, but many older children can begin to do that. It will give you some good ideas for discussion starters and activities as well. The teacher's guide also offers the opportunity to write to the Erikson Institute for specific guidance. The parent's guide is very helpful. The materials are available in both English and Spanish.

Smith, Charles. (1993). *The Peaceful Classroom: 162 Easy Activities to Teach Prechoolers Compassion and Cooperation*. Beltsville, MD: Gryphon House. Filled with over 150 activities to help teachers develop children's cooperation, compassion, friendship and problem solving skills, this is an excellent resource. Activities include relevant children's books and ways to involve parents.

Helping Kids Handle Conflict: A Guide for Those Teaching Children. National Crime Prevention Council, 1000 Connecticut Avenue, NW, Washington, DC 20036. 202-466-6272. www.ncpc.org. The guide provides activities for primary grade students about subjects that often generate or aggravate conflict among children in kindergarten through fifth grade. The guide is designed to assist school personnel in making it possible for young people to learn nonviolent ways to handle anger and disagreements and to develop a caring school climate. The activities deal with issues of bullying, cultural differences, gender conflicts, media violence and weapons. The 104-page guide is reproducible. $24.95.

Scruff Beats the Scary Streets. National Crime Prevention Council, 1000 Connecticut Avenue, NW, Washington, DC 20036. 202-466-6272. www.ncpc.org. This comic book is interspersed with activities to engage young readers in learning how to deal with bullies and with other possible problems around the neighborhood. Single copies of this 20-page book are available to any child or adult who requests in writing to McGruff, Chicago, IL 60652. Multiple copies are available at bulk prices from the National Crime Prevention Council. The book is available in both English and Spanish.

Second Step: A Violence Prevention Curriculum for Preschool--Grade 8. Committee for Children, 568 First Avenue, Suite 600, Seattle, WA 98104-2804. 800-634-4449. www.cfchildren.org. *Second Step* is a violence prevention curriculum that teaches children to change the attitudes and behaviors that contribute to violence. The curriculum teaches skills to reduce impulsive and aggressive behavior in children and increase their level of social competence. *Second Step* school and family components are important parts of any comprehensive plan to reduce violence. The content of the lessons varies according to the grade level, and the skills targeted for practice are designed to be developmentally appropriate. At all grade levels, *Second Step* provides opportunities for modeling, practice and reinforcement of the new skills.

Straight Talk about Risks: A Pre K-12th Grade Curriculum for Preventing Gun Violence (STAR). (1993). Center to Prevent Handgun Violence, 1225 Eye Street, NW, Suite 1100, Washington, DC 20005. 202-289-7319. www.bradycampaign.org. STAR is a comprehensive school-based program to teach children of all ages the dangers associated with playing with, carrying or using guns. Star also teaches children how to stay safe when encountering guns, how to resist peer pressure to play with or carry guns, and how to distinguish between real-life and television violence. Through STAR, students learn how to make better, safer decisions and resolve conflicts without violence.

Organizations & Hot Lines

Children's Defense Fund, 25 E Street NW, Washington, DC 20001. 202-628-8787. www.childrensdefense.org. This nonprofit organization's main purpose is to provide advocacy for children, especially for poor, minority and disabled children. They have an extensive publications list and maintain current statistics and information. They also publish a newsletter, *CDF Reports*, with monthly messages from Marian Wright Edelman and updates on current issues.

Coalition to Stop Gun Violence, 1023 15th Street, NW, Suite 600, NE, Washington, DC 20005. 202-408-0061. www.gunfree.org. The Coalition to Stop Gun Violence (CSGV) was founded in 1974 to combat the growing gun violence problem in the United States. CSGV's many activities include lobbying elected officials, conducting research and public education projects, and coordinating local activists and grassroots organizations. CSGV offers a variety of resource materials.

The Brady Campaign, 1225 Eye Street, NW, Suite 1100, Washington, DC 20005. 202-898-0792. www.bradycampaign.org. Founded in 1974 by victims of handgun violence, the Brady Campaign works to pass federal and state legislation to reduce gun violence. It's educational counterpart, the Center to Prevent Handgun Violence, researches gun violence issues and provides educational materials. Activities of the Center include implementation of the school based curriculum for gun violence prevention, *Straight Talk About Risks*, listed in the curriculum materials section of this chapter.

National Crime Prevention Council, 1000 Connecticut Avenue, NW, Washington, DC 20036. 202-466-6272. www.ncpc.org. The National Crime Prevention Council (NCPC) is a private, nonprofit organization whose mission is to enable people to prevent crime and build safer, more caring communities. NCPC sponsors the National Citizens' Crime Prevention Campaign, operates demonstration programs with schools and neighborhood groups, publishes books including children's activity books, kits of camera-ready program materials and posters. NCPC also offers training and technical assistance. For more information and a publications list call 800-627-2911.

Violence Policy Center, 1140 19th Street, NW, Suite 600, Washington, DC 20036. 202-822-8200. The Violence Policy Center is a national nonprofit education foundation that conducts research on firearms violence and works to develop policies and proposals to reduce violence. A publications list is available.

CHAPTER 15

TELEVISION VIOLENCE

HERE'S AN EXAMPLE

Matthew spent the morning aggressively chasing and threatening the other children, and several times his family child care provider tried to slow him down. Finally, when she was at the other end of the yard, he hurt Martin by kicking him. She later asked him why he had kicked Martin. "Because that's what they do on television," he responded, showing no remorse.

LET'S LOOK AT THE ISSUE

You only need to spend a few hours watching children's cartoons on television to see that in recent years (since the Federal Communications Commission's decision to deregulate children's commercial television in 1982) the images they present to children are increasingly more violent, especially the action cartoon shows. Teachers report that children mimic the violence they see on television.

Weapon toys directly connected to violent television shows are now being actively marketed to children. These toys encourage violent play.

Many studies show that aggressive behavior in children increases when they watch violent television shows. But those studies are no surprise to teachers who deal with such behaviors on a daily basis. Across the country, teachers of young children are reporting a distressing change in the quality of their socio-dramatic play. Instead of taking on pretend roles and acting out scenarios from their imaginations, children now are taking on roles of power figures they have seen on television. As a result, children today are losing much of the intrinsic value of socio-dramatic play (see chapter 24).

Unfortunately, it is simplistic to say that parents should simply not allow their children to watch certain television shows. The images are so pervasive that children will be exposed to them through advertisements, toys and play with other children regardless of parental rules about television watching.

INSIGHTS FROM CHILD DEVELOPMENT

Fantasy or reality? Even if they live in a nonviolent environment, young children who see violence on television can still be negatively affected by it because they may have difficulty separating fantasy from reality.

Commercial or program? Young children cannot distinguish commercials from programs. In fact, many children's entertainment shows seem to be half-hour long commercials for specific toys.

Re-enactment in dramatic play. Children often re-enact frightening scenes in dramatic play in order to gain a sense of power and control over the frightening situation.

Feelings of aggression. Even without commercially made war toys, children will often play out battle scenes, even creating their own weapons. Long before violent shows on television, children enjoyed monster play and other scary games. Through this type of play, children come to terms with their own feelings of aggression.

Imitation or imagination? Re-enacting scenes of violence witnessed on television does not have the same value as true dramatic play, where a child takes on a role and develops a plot with other children. Time spent in mere imitation play robs children, taking away the time they could have spent on more valuable dramatic play.

Creativity and language skills. Television affects creativity and language skills. Children who spend a great deal of time watching television have less time for playing, reading and talking with other children and adults. Language skills are best fostered through reading and active two-way participation in conversations and play activities.

Feeling powerful. Children naturally identify with the power roles of superheroes, which is not all bad. Children have very little power in the world around them, and by pretending to have super powers, they can temporarily reduce some of their anxieties.

Television Violence

◆ **Extreme imitation of television**. When children's dramatic play seems to be mere repetition or imitation of violent scenes from television cartoon shows.

◆ **Hurting**. When war play escalates into actual hurting behavior.

WHO CAN HELP

◆ Parents by

Limiting the number of hours children watch television.
Selecting. Helping the child select shows that are appropriate for young children and have little or no violence.
Watching television with their child and discussing what they see.
Thinking critically. Helping children think critically about commercials.
Formulating policies. A parent group can have great influence by formulating policies for your program about war toys and encouraging other parents to monitor what children watch on television.

HOW TO RESPOND

HOW TO RESPOND WITH THE STAFF

◆ **Discuss problem at staff meetings**. This is a good focus topic for a staff meeting. Discuss specific incidents when the children have imitated television violence. Brainstorm responses and ways to extend children's play in creative ways.

◆ **Know what children are watching at home**. Be aware of what the children are watching at home. Watch those shows yourself so you are familiar with the characters and typical story lines. Then you can intervene more effectively.

◆ **Banish television in the classroom**. Do not have a television in your early childhood classroom. In the case of family child care providers where a television set is in most environments, limit it specifically to educational programming designed for young children.

◆ **Prohibit toy guns**. Many centers have a written policy that prohibits children from bringing toy guns and other war toys to the center, even for show and tell.

Television Violence

◆ **Tell stories!** Start by telling parents how their children's play is affected by what they watch on television. Be specific.

◆ **Raise awareness**. Consider writing a story about this for your local newspaper to raise awareness.

◆ **Write to your legislators**. Share specific stories of children's violent behaviors caused by television and urge legislators to push for regulation of children's television programming.

◆ **Become an advocate**. Together with parents call local television stations and commercial sponsors when you don't like what you see in their programming. Also let them know when you do like what they air.

HOW TO RESPOND WITH THE CHILDREN

◆ **Encourage imaginative dramatic play**. Do not prohibit war play or superhero play, but expand and enhance the quality of the dramatic play by encouraging children to act out their own ideas.

◆ **Play with the children**. You might join in by taking on a role yourself. Follow the lead of the children in the play theme, but ask questions or act out your role in ways that add depth to the characters and make children elaborate the plot.

◆ **Put limits on superhero play**. Do not allow children to hurt or scare other children. Because this kind of play is very active in nature, it is easy for children to cross the line and really become aggressive. A pretend punch can easily become a real punch. The adult needs to stay alert to signs that the play is getting out of hand and help the children calm down.

◆ **Respect the child's role**. Address children within their roles. Use the character or role names, not the children's names, to encourage them to be careful and to calm down.

◆ **Move beyond imitation**. See if you can get children to move beyond mere imitation of television scenes. Ask them about the character. "What kind of person is the current superhero? What do you think he would do right now if he came to our school?"

◆ **Discuss the positive side**.

◆ **How are superheroes helpful?** Help children think about the positive side of the superhero's role, which involves protecting and helping others.

◆ **Talk about commercials**. Have a discussion with children about commercials. Ask if any of them have ever gotten a toy that they saw on a commercial and were disappointed by it. How was the toy different from what they saw? Tell them that toy companies pay the actors they see on commercials to try to convince people to buy their toys.

HOW TO RESPOND WITH THE OTHER CHILDREN

◆ **Create a safe place**. Create a place in the classroom and outside where superheroes cannot go. This provides a haven for children who do not want to participate in this type of play.

◆ **Talk about feeling safe when playing**. During group time, teach the children to tell their friends when they do not feel safe. When you notice a child looking frightened or overwhelmed by superhero play, ask the child, "Do you feel safe?" Then help that child tell the others.

HOW TO RESPOND WITH THE PARENTS

◆ **Collect nonviolent resources**. Think about developing a nonviolent toy and book library. Parents can borrow from the library and suggest things to add to it. One teacher included a card with each toy or book telling how the child benefits when playing with the toy and how the adult can be involved in the child's play.

WHERE TO FIND MORE INFORMATION

RESOURCES FOR ADULTS

Books

Carlsson-Paige, Nancy & Levin, Diane E. (1985). *Helping Young Children Understand Peace, War and the Nuclear Threat*. Washington, DC: National Association for the Education of Young Children. Although this book does not talk directly about television, the topic is very relevant and involves issues they will see on television. There is a very useful discussion on how children think about and perceive situations of violence. Some very good advice for helping children to interact in peace-promoting ways.

Carlsson-Paige, Nancy, and Levin, Diane E. (1987). *The War Play Dilemma: Balancing Needs and Values in the Early Childhood Classroom*. New York: Teachers College Press. This book focuses specifically on children playing war and shooting, rather than television violence as such. The authors examine the issue of war play with four possible solutions: banning war play; taking a laissez-faire approach; allowing war play, with specific limits; and actively facilitating war play. Very useful suggestions for parent involvement.

Carlsson-Paige, Nancy & Levin, Diane E. (1990). *Who's Calling the Shots: How to Respond Effectively to Children's Fascination with War Play and War Toys.* Philadelphia, PA: New Society Publishers. This book is written with parents as the primary audience. The authors explore how the toy manufacturers' advertising and children's television programming have collaborated to create a market for children's dramatic play toys that have violence as a theme. Strategies for parents for dealing with war play are suggested as well as resources and advocacy groups.

Levin, Diane E. (1994). *Teaching Young Children in Violent Times: Building a Peaceable Classroom Environment*. Philadelphia, PA: New Society Publishers. A very useful book with the theme of media violence woven throughout. There is also a chapter specifically devoted to the negative influence of media and media linked toys.

Paley, Vivian Gussin. (1986). *Boys & Girls: Superheros in the Doll Corner*. Chicago: University of Chicago Press. Within this book that explores the differences in the play of boys and girls, the author also discusses the influence of television shows on their dramatic play. This kindergarten teacher helped children explore the characters by encouraging them to act out stories of their own involving the characters.

Rogers, Fred and Head, Barry. (1983). *Mister Rogers Talks with Parents*. Winona MN: Hal Leonard Publishing Corporation. This general resource for parents has a chapter on the influence of television on children. Children's fears and emotional development is one theme of the book which provides a context for this chapter.

Smith, Charles. (1993). *The Peaceful Classroom: 162 Easy Activities to Teach Preschoolers Compassion and Cooperation.* Beltsville, MD: Gryphon House. This excellent resource helps children learn through activities the important social skills of friendship, compassion, cooperation and kindness. Strategies for involving parents in this process are also included.

Articles

"Beginnings workshop: Dealing with violence". *Child Care Information Exchange*. March 1995.

Gronlund, Gaye, "Coping with Ninja Turtle play in my kindergarten classroom". *Young Children*. August 1994, 3-6. A teacher turns a negative into a positive by understanding the characters and getting involved in the play.

Kostelnik, M.J., Whiren, A.P., and Stein, S.C. "Living with He-Man: Managing super-hero fantasy play." *Young Children*. 4(4), 1986, 3-9. Describes potential benefits of superhero play and how teachers can support it without letting it get out of hand.

Levin, Diane E. and Carlsson-Paige, Nancy. "Developmentally appropriate television:

Putting children first." **Young Children**. August 1994, 38-44. The article spells out reasons violent children's shows are harmful to children, what television programs should and could look like and how to explain the impact of television to parents.

"Morphing May Be Hazardous to Your Teacher." **Wall Street Journal**. December 7, 1994. The article discusses the negative influence of a children's cartoon show in breeding aggression in young children.

"NAEYC position statement on media violence in children's lives." **Young Children**. 45(5), 1990, 18-21. The article outlines the reasons television violence is bad for children and what early childhood professionals and parents can do to raise awareness.

Booklet

Media Violence and Children: A Guide for Parents. National Association for the Education of Young Children, 1509 Sixteenth Street, NW, Washington, DC 20036-1426. 800-424-2460. Provides information about the effects associated with children's repeated viewing of television violence and offers guidelines for parents.

Organizations & Hot Lines

Campaign for Kid's TV, Center for Media Education, 2121 L Street, NW., Suite 200, Washington, DC 20037. 202-331-7833. www.cme.org. The Center maintains statistics on children's television watching and the number of acts of violence on television.

Coalition for Quality Children's Video, 112 West San Francisco Street, Suite 305A, Santa Fe, NM 87501. 505-989-8076. www.kidsfirstinternet.org. The Coalition publishes Kids First! newsletter and Kids First! Directory, which contains a complete list of all titles endorsed by a screening jury and by children, with information on where the titles are available.

National Foundation to Improve Television, 60 Congress Street, Suite 925, Boston, MA 02109. 617-523-5521. The Foundation has developed a number of initiatives which, if adopted by the Federal Communications Commission (FCC), would reduce the amount of dramatized television violence viewed by small children. In addition, the Foundation is active in a number of projects to use television as a powerful tool to reduce television violence.

CHAPTER 16

INCLUDING CHILDREN WITH SPECIAL NEEDS

HERE'S AN EXAMPLE

"Birthday parties! That's what I want for my little boy. Birthday parties. I want him to be one of the gang. I want him to have friends. I want someone to like him who's not paid to like him." This is what the father of three year old Travis said when he enrolled his son in the center. Travis has Cerebral Palsy and cannot stand or walk or talk. He uses a wheelchair and a special adaptive chair and stander. The staff at the center received some special training from Travis's occupational therapist, who also helped the other children learn how to understand his way of communicating. A community agency also provided a volunteer in the mornings to help Travis change positions and to be an extra pair of hands in the active classroom. Travis's personality soon blossomed and the other three year olds quickly overcame the language barrier and were even skillful at telling the teachers what he wanted. And, yes, he was invited to many birthday parties.

LET'S LOOK AT THE ISSUE

Having a child with special needs in your class is not a crisis, but a challenge. Handled well, it can be a positive challenge and everyone involved will benefit. In the above example, the child required special assistance. The center approached the challenge positively, encouraging Travis to take part fully in their program. The idea of having a volunteer help with Travis resulted from a staff problem solving session. However, many children who have special needs do not require extra adult assistance and can fit right in.

The Americans with Disabilities Act, which went into effect in 1992, requires that equal access to all facilities and services be provided to individuals with disabilities. Child care is a service often needed by families who have a child with special needs. Most early childhood programs are enrolling at least one or more children who have developmental delays or some type of disability. This is no longer a remote issue. And while including special needs children in programs for typically developing children is now common, it is not always done well. However, with the right kind of staff training and support, it certainly can be done well and benefit everyone involved.

BENEFITS TO CHILDREN WITH SPECIAL NEEDS

◆ **Increased potential**. Children with special needs benefit from a group setting when they learn to feel good about themselves in relation to others. Their potential for social involvement is improved.

◆ **Peer role models**. The child with special needs will benefit from the positive role models presented by peers.

BENEFITS TO TYPICALLY DEVELOPING CHILDREN

◆ **Developing tolerance**. Typically developing children and adults learn to feel socially comfortable with people who have disabilities.

◆ **Learning to nurture**. Many typically developing children will practice caring and nurturing skills as a result of interacting with peers who have special needs.

BARRIERS

◆ **Classroom management challenges**. Managing a classroom with diverse abilities can be challenging and require some special planning.

◆ **Collaborative effort**. To be most effective, teachers should work as part of a team by collaborating with the parents and other professionals involved with the child. This can be time consuming and require flexibility on everyone's part. These meetings don't always have to be face to face. Contact people by telephone, and take good notes.

TERMINOLOGY

There has been much discussion about what to call individuals with special needs. Terms used in the past like "handicapped children" and "special education children" are no longer acceptable. The terms we use now attempt to focus on the whole child rather than the child's particular disability. Therefore instead of saying "special needs child," put the adjective after the child and say, "child with special needs"; instead of "cerebral palsy child," say "child who has cerebral palsy." Instead of referring to "normal" children, say "typically developing" children, because a child who has special needs may, indeed, be "normal" in many respects. Calling other children "normal" in contrast implies that the child with special needs is abnormal. All of this is done with the intent of treating individuals fairly and seeing them as whole, functioning human beings. Often the best thing is to ask the parents of the child how they refer to their child's condition and the terms they would like you to use.

Although this child may require some extra work until everyone gets into a comfortable routine, you will probably learn a lot from the experience. It will likely be an enriching experience for everyone involved.

INSIGHTS FROM CHILD DEVELOPMENT

Curiosity and openness. Young children haven't yet learned not to stare. They are likely to ask their questions right in front of the child with special needs. Or you may notice their interest and curiosity or fear in the way they look at the other child.

Worries about "catching it." Young children worry that the condition may be catching and that if they play with a child wearing a brace, they may end up needing a brace as well.

Familiarity with the problem. Children may initially be afraid of the child with the disability, especially if the child looks different or has a special apparatus. The fear will disappear when the child becomes used to being around the child.

WHEN TO SEEK HELP

The following are signals that including children with special needs requires further intervention on your part.

◆ **Fear or discomfort**. Typically developing children avoid contact with the child, showing fear or discomfort.

◆ **Name calling, staring or excluding child from play** by typically developing children.

◆ **Isolation**. There is minimal or no social contact between the child with special needs and typically developing children.

◆ **Excessive separation anxiety**. The child with special needs has great difficulty separating from his parent.

◆ **Failure to achieve goals**. The child with special needs fails to make progress or achieve goals.

WHO CAN HELP

◆ Child Find. Public school personnel can help identify children you suspect may have some special need.
◆ Child's pediatrician
◆ Occupational therapist
◆ Language therapist
◆ Child phychologist, or other professionals who have worked or are working with the child
◆ Your local professional association may be helpful in referring you to people who do workshops or staff training.
◆ The child's parents

HOW TO RESPOND

HOW TO RESPOND WITH THE STAFF

◆ **Think about attitudes**. As a group, discuss your attitudes toward people with disabilities. Share any experiences you've had dealing with people who have disabilities.

◆ **Support may be needed**. In some cases, staff will need support to work with a child who has special needs. This support may come from the parents or other professionals, and may include training in how to manage special equipment or handling specific behaviors. All adults who are expected to interact with this child should be included.

◆ **Start by making the environment accessible**, even if no children with special needs are presently enrolled. Being prepared shows parents your willingness to include all children in your program.

◆ **Look at the whole child**. Guard against seeing the child only in terms of his disability. Instead, work hard to see the child as a whole person first.

◆ **Learn about the condition**. While you are not expected to be an expert in all areas of special needs, you should find out as much as you can about the condition affecting the particular child in your group. Start by asking the parents or other professionals working with the child if they can recommend some reading. Do not hesitate about asking the meaning of unfamiliar terms. Remember that there is a wide range of functioning with any particular syndrome or condition.

◆ **Guard against generalizing**. Realize that children with special needs are individuals and different from each other. Find out as much as possible about a particular child. What are her strengths? What frustrates her quickly? Where does she need help? Are there any particular ways you can adapt your environment to help this child?

HOW TO RESPOND WITH THE CHILD

◆ **Let the child get used to the program gradually**. Encourage the child and parent to visit together for a short period of time. Then have the child stay for increasing lengths of time without the parent. Follow up by talking to the parent.

◆ **Don't do too much for the child**. Give the child every opportunity to accomplish a task on his own, but be sensitive to when the child may be passing his tolerance for frustration.

◆ **Know when adult intervention is needed**. The social benefits expected with inclusion don't happen without adult intervention. Facilitate friendships and social development. This may be the most important educational aspect of the program (see chapter 24). You might get the child used to interacting with just one other child in some very simple activity. Gradually involve the child in more small group activities, like blowing bubbles, that are simple and fun for everyone.

◆ **Model accepting behavior**. You might try playing with the child in view of the other children, even if it means getting down on the floor. A lot of games and activities that children enjoy can be done on the floor.

◆ **Include music in your program**. Music appeals to almost all children, even those with hearing impairments. Children enjoy it on several different levels. They can sit in a circle and use simple instruments such as shakers.

◆ **Include art in your program**. Manipulative mediums such as clay appeal to most children even those with motor impairments

◆ **Plan interactions**. Facilitate situations in which interactions with other children are successful and fun.

◆ **Plan opportunities that allow the child choices**. Art activities when the child can select colors are especially good.

◆ **Build on what a child knows**. Build on what the child already knows and does well.

◆ **Encourage children to express feelings**. Children with special needs are often encouraged to be nice and not create problems. Encourage them to just be themselves and help them learn to express their feelings in appropriate ways. For example, if name calling is a problem, help the child figure out the best ways to respond.

◆ **Set behavior limits.** Do put behavior limits on the child, just as you would for all the other children. Sometimes adults, because they feel sorry for the child, will let her misbehave without consequences. This leads the other children to resent the child with special needs, and will certainly not help that child learn socially acceptable behavior.

◆ **Find related children's books**. Look for books and pictures that show people with special needs engaged in a whole range of activities. The child needs to see himself reflected in at least some of the images present in the classroom.

◆ **Make a a scrapbook of success**. Create a scrapbook for the child acknowledging every accomplishment made in your program. This will help the child feel more confident and increase his self-esteem. Include photographs of the child participating and her accomplishments, but always ask the parent's permission to photograph the child. Even better, have the child make her own scrapbook or portfolio of creative endeavors.

◆ **Be consistent with discipline**. When children who have disabilities exhibit behavior problems, work with the other adults in the child's life—such as parents and therapists—to develop consistency in discipline techniques.

◆ **Practice special procedures beforehand**. If you have to do a special procedure with the child, or manipulate special equipment, practice first with the child when the parent is present. Also ask what might happen if you used the equipment incorrectly. Practice until you feel comfortable and competent.

◆ **Have alternatives if the child's equipment should break** or be damaged. Know who to call when repairs are needed.

Adapting your environment

◆ **Modify your classroom** to optimize the child's ability to function. The following are general suggestions. Ask the parent and occupational therapist working with the child for more specific suggestions.

◆ **Make materials accessible**. If toys and materials are out of the child's reach, she may see this as a negative statement.

HOW TO RESPOND WITH CHILDREN WITH MOTOR CHALLENGES

◆ **Widen space between furniture**. You may need to widen the space between furniture to accommodate a wheelchair or other special equipment.

◆ **Raise or lower tables**.

◆ **Make things easier to grasp**. Put knobs on some puzzles, for instance.

HOW TO RESPOND WITH CHILDREN WITH VISUAL IMPAIRMENTS

◆ **Adjust light level**. Children with visual impairments may need the light level adjusted, either brighter or dimmer, according to their sensitivity.

◆ **Round or pad corners on furniture**.

◆ **Use Velcro strips as guides** for children with visual impairments.

◆ **Have other tactile objects or clues in the environment** for identification of areas and objects.

HOW TO RESPOND WITH THE OTHER CHILDREN

◆ **Model accepting behavior**. Without your support and encouragement, typically developing children may shun the child, eliminating the social benefits on both sides. You will need to help them learn ways to approach each other. Be supportive and empathetic. Lead the way. If you choose to sit by the child, play with the child and seek the child's opinions, the other children are more likely to do the same.

◆ **Encourage children's questions**. They may need to ask a lot of questions about the child with the disability. Answer questions simply and accurately, with a respectful attitude toward the special child.

◆ **Focus on what the children have in common**. Emphasize to the other children that although the special child is different from them in one area, she is like them in many other ways. Focus on what they all have in common. Perhaps you could make a chart of common interests.

◆ **Always ask if the child wants help**. Children often want to do too much for the child with special needs. Help them learn to ask if the child wants help and allow the child to do as much as possible for himself.

◆ **Let the child help others**. When a child with a disability is especially good at something, like singing or naming colors and shapes, allow that child to teach the others. This shows everyone that the child is a capable individual.

◆ **Ask permission before touching a child's equipment**. The *Anti-Bias Curriculum* cautions that while children are curious about special equipment such as a wheelchair or a brace, they should be taught to ask permission (from the child or other adult) before touching it. Always supervise when a child touches another child's equipment because it may be expensive to fix or replace. Another option is to borrow or rent similar equipment for the other children to explore.

◆ **Stop all name calling**. Do not permit children to use words such as cripple, retard, idiot. This is verbal aggression. Intervene immediately, just as you would with physical aggression.

◆ **Encourage children to include the child in their play**. Do not permit children to exclude the child with special needs from their play because of the child's disability. If necessary, help the other children figure out how to adapt their play so the child with special needs can be included.

◆ **Invite adults with disabilities to visit your class** so children can see them as people who work, have families and live full lives. Make sure these adults are comfortable with children's direct questions and curiosity.

◆ **Invite adults with disabilities who have special talents** such as an art, music or acting to provice role models for children.

◆ **Develop children's empathy**. Young children are learning the concept of fair and unfair. Use this as a starting point when you try to help them empathize with people who have disabilities.

◆ **Help identify undiagnosed needs**. Help to identify any child in your group who might have an undiagnosed special need. You don't need to conduct formal assessments unless you have had very specialized training. However, your experience with children in this age group has probably helped you develop a sense of the norm for certain behaviors and skills. When you see a child who acts in an unusual way, pay attention. Ask yourself why this child seems different to you. Take some notes and observe the child's play and interactions. Ask another colleague to observe the child as well. Together, decide whether to mention something to the parent and recommend further professional assessment.

HOW TO RESPOND WITH SIBLINGS

Siblings of a child with special needs have their own special needs.

◆ **They may express resentment**. Their siblings with special needs attract so much attention from others that they might feel left out. This might cause feelings of resentment, which could be followed by feelings of guilt. Let the child know that it is okay to have all kinds of feelings and that people can feel many different ways about the same person.

◆ **They may act out to get attention**. She might see the new environment as a place where she can get the attention she doesn't get at home. Be sure to give her lots of positive attention for the good things she does.

HOW TO RESPOND WITH THE PARENTS

◆ **Parents should be your prime consultants**. They are the experts on this child and may know a great deal about the child's condition as well.

◆ **Parents are under personal stress**. Understand that the parent of a child with special needs has been under personal stress, perhaps since the child's birth. They may be very assertive because they have always had to fight battles to ensure that their child gets needed services. They may also seem impatient.

◆ **Parents may be concerned that their child will not be able to learn** in the new environment. Meet with the parents to find out specifically what their goals are and together decide how you will proceed to meet these goals. Contact other professionals, such as speech therapists and occupational therapists, who may be working with the child. Try to follow their guidelines for consistency.

◆ **Ask the parents how they answer questions about their child**, and use their explanation when discussing the child's condition with other adults and children who ask.

◆ **Invite the parent to talk to the other children about their child**. They will probably be able to answer the children's questions in the best way. They can also share things about the child that the other children will be interested in—what his favorite toys are, what he likes to do best.

◆ **Parents may be socially isolated**. Parents of children with special needs are often socially isolated because of the demands of caring for their child. They may appreciate social events where they can interact with the staff and other parents.

◆ **Get support before talking with parents**. Suggesting to parents that their child should be evaluated for special needs is an extremely sensitive issue. Never do this on your own, without extensive discussions with your supervisor. Do not guess what you think the problem is.

◆ **Be familiar with resources in your community**. Refer parents when appropriate.

◆ **Other parents may have concerns**. They might fear that their own child will be afraid of the child with special needs, or won't get as much attention from staff. They might worry that their child will pick up behaviors of the child with special needs, or be injured by her. Usually it is possible to address these concerns to everyone's satisfaction. Tell the parents how their own children will benefit by being in a class with the child, and explain your plan for classroom management so that everyone will benefit fully from your program.

WHERE TO FIND MORE INFORMATION

RESOURCES FOR CHILDREN

Books

Booth, Barbara D. (1991). Illustrated by Jim Lamarche. *Mandy*. New York, NY: Lothrop, Lee & Shephard Books. Mandy, who is hearing-impaired, risks going out into the scary night, during an impending storm, to look for her grandmother's lost pin.

Bunnett, Rochelle. (1995). *Friends at School*. New York, NY: Star Bright Publishers. In this story, school is a fun place for children who have different needs and abilities. Illustrated with lovely color photographs.

Cairo, Shelley, et. al. (1985). Photographs by Irene McNeil. *Our Brother Has Down's Syndrome: An Introduction for Children*. Toronto, Canada: Annick Press Ltd. Mostly Jai is like every other brother or sister in the world. Sometimes he's fun and sometimes he's not. But, no matter what, his family loves him very much.

Carlson, Nancy. (1990). *Arnie and the New Kid.* New York, NY: Viking. Arnie discovers that you can be different and still be a lot alike, and that is what being friends is all about.

Caseley, Judith. (1991). *Harry and Willy and Carrothead*. New York, NY: Greenwillow Books. Three boys overcome prejudicial ideas about appearances and become friends. One of the boys was born with no left hand. He wears a prosthesis.

Rabe, Berniece. (1988). Photographs by Diane Schmidt. *Where's Chimpy?* Morton Grove, IL: Albert Whitman Publishers. Misty, a little girl with Down's Syndrome, and her father review her day's activities in their search for Chimpy.

Rankin, Laura. (1991). *The Handmade Alphabet*. New York, NY: Dial Books. This book presents the manual alphabet used in the American Sign Language. Beautiful illustrations.

Rosenberg, Maxine B. (1983). Photographs by George Ancona. *My Friend Leslie: The Story of a Handicapped Child*. New York, NY: Lothrop, Lee & Shephard Books. *My Friend Leslie* presents a kindergarten child with multiple handicaps, who is well accepted by her classmates.

Russo, Marisabina. (1992). *Alex Is My Friend*. New York, NY: Greenwillow Books. Even though Alex is a dwarf and sometimes has to use a wheelchair because of the operation he had on his back, his friend does not mind because they still have good times together.

RESOURCES FOR ADULTS

Books

Chandler, Phyllis A. (1994). *A Place for Me, Including Children With Special Needs in Early Care and Education Settings*. Washington, DC: National Association for the Education of Young Children. This book explores the attitudes of early childhood teachers when they learn that a child with special needs will be in their class. This book includes many useful insights and suggestions, and has an extensive resource section.

Derman-Sparks, Louise, and the A.B.C. Task Force. (1989). *The Anti-Bias Curriculum: Tools for Empowering Young Children*. Washington, DC: National Association for the Education of Young Children. Chapter Five, "Learning About Disabilities," describes developmental tasks of children, their understandings, as well as specific guidelines and activities for the classroom teacher. This book includes suggestions on helping staff and children repect each other as individuals.

Froschl, Merle, Colon, Linda, Rubin, Ellen, and Sprung, Barbara. (1984). *Including All of Us: An Early Childhood Curriculum About Disability*. New York: Educational Equity Concepts, Inc. *Including All of Us* is a guide for creating an early childhood curriculum that is inclusive, one that is nonsexist, multicultural, and incorporates role models of children and adults with disabilities. It fosters children's cognitive, social and emotional growth by expanding their world view to include people with disabilities and by teaching appreciation of and respect for human differences. For example, activities are described which model experiences for hearing, visual and mobility impairment.

Mitchell, Grace and Dewsnap, Lois. (1995). *Common Sense Discipline: Building Self-Esteem in Young Children, Stories From Life*. Glen Burnie, MD: Telshare Publishing Company. Much more than a discipline book, this insightful resource has a section about including children with special needs.

Neugebauer, Bonnie, (Ed.). (1992). *Alike and Different: Exploring Our Humanity With Young Children*. Washington, DC: National Association for the Education of Young Children. This excellent resource is a collection of chapters on differences—cultural, racial, and capabilities. The book includes practical suggestions and has an extensive resource section.

Simons, Robin. (1987). *After the Tears: Parents Tell About Raising a Child With a Disability*. San Diego, CA: Harcourt Brace and Company. Parents of children with a variety of special needs describe their feelings, from their first reactions of anger, denial and grief to their coping strategies and personal growth. An excellent, interesting, easy to read book that gives insight to being a parent of a child with special needs.

Turecki, Stanley K., and Tanner, Leslie. (1989). *The Difficult Child*. New York: Bantam Books, Inc. The author discusses what is and is not hyperactivity, attention-deficit disorder (ADD), attention-deficit hyperactivity disorder (ADHD), and other disorders. Useful discipline strategies are discussed.

Wolery, Mark and Wilbers, Jan S., (Eds.). (1994). *Including Children with Special Needs in Early Childhood Programs*. Washington, DC: National Association for the Education of Young Children. A careful examination of the issue of including children with special needs in programs with typically developing children. It includes a historical perspective as well as many references to specific research studies.

Articles

Abbott, Carole F. and Gold, Susan. "Conferring with parents when you're concerned that their child needs special services." *Young Children*. 46(4), May 1991, 10-14. The authors address issues concerning the refferal procedure for assesssing a child who may have special needs.

Gross, Anne L. and Oritz, Libby Wyatt. "Using children's literature to facilitate inclusion in kindergarten and the primary grades." *Young Children*. 49(3), March 1994, 32-35. The authors describe how children's literature can be used to develop positive attitudes toward people with disabilities and to encourage positive peer relationships among children of differing abilities.

Ross, Helen W. "Integrating infants with disabilities? Can 'ordinary' caregivers do it?" *Young Children*. 47(3), March 1992, 65-71. The article outlines a basic infant program, focusing on safety and developmental appropriateness, which meets the needs of all infants. The parent education and support program incorporated in a mainstreamed infant program is described.

The Exceptional Parent. 209 Harvard Street, Suite 303, Brookline, MA 02146. 617-730-5800. This magazine is an excellent publication for families of children with special needs.

Booklet

Understanding the Americans with Disabilities Act: Information for Early Childhood Programs. National Association for the Education of Young Children, 1509 16th Street, NW, Washington, DC 20036-1426. 800-424-2460. www.naeyc.org. This booklet provides introductory information on the Americans with Disabilities Act as it relates to eary childhood programs, including a list of resources for technical information. $.50 per copy. Quantity discount, $10 for 100 copies.

Videos

Anti-Bias Curriculum. Pacific Oaks Bookstore, 5 Westmoreland Place, Pasadena, CA 91103. 626-397-1330. www.pacificoaks.edu/bookstore.html. 30 min. Featuring Louise Derman-Sparks and other members of the A.B.C. Task Force that developed *Anti-Bias Curriculum: Tools for Empowering Young Children*, this video is excellent to use in introducing the philosophy to new staff and parents. The video gives an overview of child development and classroom practices which support inclusion of children with disabilities.

Children and Families with Special Needs. Educational Productions, Inc., 9000 Southwest Gemini Drive, Beaverton, OR 97008. 800-950-4949. www.edpro.com. A set of four video training modules which provide valuable insights into families with special needs children. Additional video training resources are listed in the Educational Productions, Inc. catalog including videos on language development, play and social development, which are relevant to children with special needs and typically developing children.

Organizations & Hot Lines

Many disabilities are supported by national associations with toll-free numbers to call for resource materials. The child's doctor or local hospital libraries will probably have information about local or state chapters of the associations. The national offices of several associations are listed.

Alexander Graham Bell Association for the Deaf, 3417 Volta Place NW, Washington, DC 20007. 800-255-4817. www.agbell.org.

American Association on Mental Retardation, 444 North Capitol Street NW, Suite 846, Washington, DC 20001. 800-424-3688. www.aamr.org.

American Foundation for the Blind (AFB), 11 Penn Plaza, Suite 300, New York, NY 10001. 800 AFB-LINE. www.afb.org.

American Speech Language Hearing Association, 10801 Rockville Pike, Rockville, MD 20852. 800-638-8255. www.asha.org.

Association for Retarded Citizens (The Arc) National Headquarters 1010 Wayne Avenue, Suite 650, Silver Spring, MD 20910. 800-433-5255. www.thearc.org.

Attention Deficit Disorder Association (ADDA), PO Box 972, Mentor, OH 44061.

ERIC Clearinghouse on Disability and Gifted Children, Council for Exceptional Children, 1110 North Glebe Road, Arlington, VA 22201-5704. 800-328-0272. www.ericec.org.

Epilepsy Foundation of America. 4351 Garden City Drive, Landover, MD 20785. 800-332-1000. www.epilepsyfoundation.org.

Learning Disabilities Association, 4156 Library Road, Pittsburgh, PA 15234. 412-341-8077. www.ldaamerica.org.

National Down Syndrome Society, 666 Broadway, Suite 800, New York, NY 10012. 800-221-4602. www.ndss.org.

National Information Center for Children and Youth with Disabilities, P.O. Box 1492, Washington, DC 20013. 800-695-0285. www.nichcy.org.

National Mental Health Association, 1021 Prince Street, Alexandria, VA 22314-2971. 800-969-6642. www.nmha.org.

Spina Bifida Association of America, 4590 MacArthur Boulevard, Suite 250, Washington, DC 20007-4226. 800-621-3141. www.sbaa.org.

United Cerebral Palsy Association, 1660 L Street, NW, Suite 700, Washington, DC 20036-5602. 800-872-5827. www.ucp.org.

CHAPTER 17

RACISM & PREJUDICE

HERE'S AN EXAMPLE

Theresa, the teacher of three year olds, overhears blond, blue-eyed Elizabeth announce in the doll corner: "I don't want to play with that black doll. She's ugly!" Nicole, a shy African-American child, looks on. Theresa knocks on the door of the play area and creates a role for herself. "Hi, I'm your neighbor. Thank you for babysitting my beautiful little girl," and goes over and picks up the black doll. "How is my little girl with the beautiful brown skin? Did you have a good time playing with our neighbors today?" Later, with everyone gathered around the lunch table, Theresa points out the many beautiful colors of skin the children have and comments positively about every one.

LET'S LOOK AT THE ISSUE

Young children generally play with each other regardless of skin color. While they notice skin color or racial differences, they usually don't attach the same importance to these differences. However, their attitudes are forming and they may begin to develop a kind of "pre-prejudice" that will eventually turn into racism.

In the book *We Can All Get Along* (see the resource section at the end of this chapter), racism is defined as "any action or attitude, conscious or unconscious, that subordinates an individual or group based on skin color or race." Racism is about power and who has access to privilege and opportunity. It is at the root of many societies' problems.

Children form attitudes about race early in life, learning from the important adults in their lives. An educator's goal should be to take advantage of children's natural curiosity and help them see differences in individuals as interesting, exciting and enriching. Unfortunately, children will be confronted with racist messages and images. If important adults such as parents and teachers take a proactive stance against unfair and hurtful practices, they can help prevent the development of racist attitudes.

It is important not to oversimplify when we speak of differences and focus only on race. A family's culture, economic status, education, presence of extended family and community supports, religion and many other variables help determine a child's sense of himself and his self-esteem.

One thing is certain: our country is becoming more and more multiracial. Being tolerant and respectful of people of different ethnic backgrounds and races is essential in our society.

INSIGHTS FROM CHILD DEVELOPMENT

Fair and no-fair. Children know about fair and no-fair, and about hurt feelings.

Inclusion and exclusion. These are themes in all childhoods, regardless of race.

Self-esteem, so vital in learning and later success in life, is very much connected to competence. Young children must feel valued for who they are. A cherished teacher has an important role in helping a child believe he is beautiful, "just right" and competent.

Physical characteristics. Young children, in establishing their own identity, are busy sorting out the world. They notice and talk about physical characteristics such as skin color, eye shape and hair type.

Awareness of differences. Contrary to popular belief, young children do notice physical differences associated with racial identity.

Skin color words. Words adults use are confusing to children. "Black" skin isn't black, "white" skin isn't white, "yellow" skin isn't yellow, and "red" skin isn't red.

Understanding geography. Terms such as African American, European American, Asian American and Native American name a child's group identity. Young children will not yet understand the geographic meaning of these terms, but they can grasp that they refer to a larger group of which their family is part.

Accepting those different from themselves. As children get older, more and more they seek out friends who are as much like themselves as possible. This can lead to hurtful excluding of others. If they have early, positive experiences with all kinds of people, they will be more flexible in their thinking and accepting of children who are different.

SPECIAL ISSUES FOR CHILDREN OF MIXED RACIAL HERITAGE

Children who have parents of different racial or cultural background are becoming more and more numerous. While they share similar developmental processes with all children, they also face some specific issues.

To develop their self-identity, they have to sort out more pieces in relation to their racial background and may feel confusion about where they fit.

To develop a clear sense of identity, mixed heritage children need consistency between home and school in the naming and supporting of who they are.

Parents of mixed heritage children may choose different ways of thinking about their child's identity. Some choose to focus on one heritage. Other parents consider all aspects of their background as equally important and want their child to have biracial identity. Some parents are not sure or disagree about what identity they want their child to develop and need support sorting out their own decisions.

Mixed heritage children are raised in varying contexts: some by both parents, some by one of their parents, some with support from both extended families, some with support from only one extended family, some by adoptive parents of a different racial background. All can provide their child with a strong identity, but each context has its own dynamics and specific challenges.

WHEN TO SEEK HELP

Although racism and prejudice are ongoing problems in our society, the following situations indicate when specific intervention is needed.

◆ **Negative behaviors** and statements of children become a problem.

◆ **Child is excluded**. A child excluded another child from play because of color or culture.

◆ **Children refuse to sit next to a child because of color or culture**.

◆ **Children say racist things** such as, "I don't like her. She has ugly skin." "His eyes are funny. He's weird."

◆ **Direct ethnic slurs** and name calling.

WHO CAN HELP

◆ Early childhood education professionals trained in the Anti-Bias Curriculum. Check with local colleges and professional associations.

HOW TO RESPOND

HOW TO RESPOND WITH THE STAFF

◆ **Encourage training and awareness.** This issue merits special attention by staff.

◆ **The *Anti-Bias Curriculum*** (see the resource section at the end of this chapter) offers specific staff training and discussion topics.

◆ **Remember their own childhood experiences.** Encourage staff members to think about their own first awareness of racial differences and experiences with prejudice.

◆ **Explore their own cultural identity.** Through storytelling, encourage staff to identify the important underlying values and rules of behavior they learned from their families and what aspects of their culture give them strength and support.

◆ **Discuss incidents.** At regular staff meetings encourage people to bring up difficult situations they have encountered, especially if they were unsure of how to respond. Discussing the incidents in a supportive environment can give people insights to use in future situations.

◆ **Do not reinforce stereotypes.** As you plan themes and curriculum activities, be sure not to reinforce stereotypes. Be on guard for stereotypical images in purchased classroom materials or decorations. Watch for these images especially in books and holiday decorations.

◆ **Work on this issue every day.** Countering early racism and prejudice should not be a theme or a unit, but rather a philosophy woven into your everyday interactions with children.

HOW TO RESPOND WITH THE CHILDREN

◆ **Use teachable moments**. Be alert for comments that reveal racial misunderstandings on the children's part either about themselves or others. Use these teachable moments. Do not ignore them.

◆ **Intervene immediately**. Prejudicial statements need immediate contradiction by the adult present. "Timmy, I heard you say that Mai's eyes look `funny.' Mai's eyes are different from yours but they are not `funny.' Mai's eyes are shaped like her family's eyes and the eyes of millions of people who live in the part of the world where Mai's family comes from. They are beautiful eyes, and they are just right for her."

◆ **It's not all right to hurt someone's feelings**. Alert children when their remarks might hurt someone's feelings, and remind them that it's not okay to say such things.

◆ **Stop racial slurs**. When you sense that children's remarks are racial slurs purposely meant to hurt another child, treat this the same as you would any other type of aggression. Intervene, comfort the victim, address the situation and state strongly that it is not okay to hurt people with words or with actions in the classroom or at home.

◆ **Admire differences**. Speak openly and with interest and admiration about people's different skin colors, eyes and hair. If you ignore race or change the subject when it comes up, children may gain the attitude that it is something to be ashamed of or avoided.

◆ **Give accurate, positive information**. Even if you hear no remarks about racial identity, bring the subject up. Children may hear racial comments at another time or place. They need accurate, positive information.

◆ **Use puppets or dolls with different skin colors** to talk to each other or the children about how their feelings were hurt when someone wouldn't let them play or said unkind remarks about their skin color. The children can talk about how it was unfair. This type of activity builds empathy in a neutral setting, without embarrassing anyone.

◆ **Be sensitive to children's feelings**. As children approach elementary school age, they try very hard not to be different. If only one of the children in the group is of a different race, avoid singling that child out for observation. Instead, talk about everyone's skin color. Comment positively on all the children's skin color.

◆ **Notice with wonder different skin colors**. Collect photos and magazine pictures of people with many different colors of skin. Make a book or a collage that you can look at often with the children. Let them compare their skin color to those in the photos.

◆ **Notice the great variety of skin tones**. In classrooms with all European American children, there is still a great variety of skin tones, eye and hair color. Expand the discussion to include the other types of racial characteristics people might have.

◆ **Invite people of different races to visit your class**, especially if all of your children are of the same racial group. Find out if these visiting adults would let the children touch their hair, compare their skin colors and talk openly with them about the differences they see. If these visitors can do something fun with the children, like play an instrument, cook something or play with blocks, the children will quickly learn that they are no different than anyone else.

◆ **Bring in pictures**. Have all the children bring in pictures of their immediate family and other relatives if possible.

◆ **Collect pictures showing eyes of different shapes and colors**. Your interest and appreciation for the variety will foster children's positive attitudes.

◆ **Do body tracings**. Create a body tracing for each child. Let the children choose the colors of paint or crayons they feel is closest to their own skin, eye and hair color. Put the tracings on the wall with a title, "We Come in Many Colors."

◆ **Collect samples or pictures of different types of hair**. Perhaps people you know will donate little snippets of their hair for a poster. If not, you might make a book of photographs showing hair of many colors and textures.

◆ **Classroom materials should reflect the children**. Children should see images of their own race as well as other children's races reflected in the posters, books, toys and other materials in the classroom.

◆ **Collect pictures of adults of different races at work**. Include all types of jobs. Perhaps put the pictures in a book about occupations.

◆ **Collect children's books** that have beautiful illustrations of children of different races as main characters, but are first and foremost good children's literature (some favorites are listed at the end of this chapter.) After enjoying the story together, ask the children, "Do you think she'd be fun to play with? Wouldn't it be fun to have her in our class?"

◆ **Intervene when appropriate**. If you hear children say that brown or black are ugly colors, collect beautiful things that are black or brown. Let children know by your words and actions that you think all shades of brown and black are beautiful.

◆ **Clear up misconceptions**. Children may have misconceptions about skin color and think that it was colored or painted on, or more commonly, that dark skin color is dirty. You need to correct such misconceptions. One simple explanation is that people get their skin colors from their birth mother and father.

◆ **Avoid complicated explanations**. Explaining skin color to children in terms of geography or melanin can be difficult. However, the book *All the Colors We Are*, listed in the resource section at the end of this chapter, is a good place to start. Introducing the concept now will do no harm, and children will understand it better when they are older.

◆ **Discuss adopted children**. When an adopted child is of a different race than her family members, children may ask for an explanation. Say that the adopted child was born to people who look like her.

HOW TO RESPOND WITH THE PARENTS

It's important that parents know how you address issues of racial bias with children so that messages at home are consistent with what children are hearing at school or in the child care setting.

◆ **Communicate your philosophy**. Either in a newsletter or parent meeting, explain to parents that you believe in talking about all races in positive terms and addressing related issues with their children. The *Anti-Bias Curriculum* video listed in the resource section at the end of this chapter is a useful tool for introducing the topic.

◆ **Have a parent meeting** on ways to prevent prejudice. Share with parents some of the typical questions and issues that can come up in an early childhood classroom and brainstorm appropriate responses. Describe how children develop negative attitudes and misconceptions about race, and what adults can do to overcome them. Also describe strategies for building tolerance in children, such as providing opportunities for positive interactions with people of different races and talking with children when you notice examples of unfairness and prejudice.

◆ **Consult the *Anti-Bias Curriculum***. Chapter 11 of the *Anti-Bias Curriculum* listed in the resource section at the end of this chapter gives useful strategies for a parent meeting.

◆ **Build positive attitudes**. Some parents may respond, "They're so young and innocent. Do we have to burden them with this so soon?" You may need to let parents know that children as young as two notice and comment on different skin colors and other racial characteristics, and that now is the time to build positive attitudes toward people who may look different.

◆ **Use family photos**. Encourage parents to send in family photos so that children can see that they get their colors from their families.

◆ **Be consistent**. Ask parents how they have explained ethnicity to their child so you can be consistent. Be sensitive to the needs of adopted children and children of mixed heritage.

◆ **Invite parents to the classroom**. Invite parents who represent different races and cultures to visit your classroom and interact with the children.

◆ **Involve parents when dealing with prejudicial remarks**. Involve them whether their child is the victim or the offender. Describe what happened, and how you responded. See if you can figure out together how best to handle the situation. Discuss how the parents will handle it at home so you can reinforce each other's efforts.

◆ **Remember that few problems are solely related to race**. Resist ascribing the child's or the family's problems to their racial or cultural heritage. In reality, very few of their problems may be related to race or culture.

WHERE TO FIND MORE INFORMATION

RESOURCES FOR CHILDREN

Books

Coles, Robert.(1995). Illustrated by George Ford. *The Story of Ruby Bridges*. New York, NY: Scholastic, Inc. For months, six year old Ruby Bridges must confront the hostility of segregationists when she becomes the first African American girl to integrate Frantz Elementary School in New Orleans in 1960.

Hamanaka, Sheila. (1994). *All the Colors of the Earth*. New York, NY: Morrow Junior Books. This book reveals in verse that despite outward differences, children everywhere are essentially the same and all are lovable.

Johnson, Dolores. (1993). *Now Let Me Fly: The Story of a Slave Family*. New York, NY: Macmillan Publishing Company. A fictionalized account of the life of Minna, kidnapped as a girl in Africa, as she endures the harsh life of a slave on a Southern plantaion in the 1800's and tries to help her family survive.

Lacapa, Kathleen and Lacapa, Michael. (1994). Illustrated by Michael Lacapa. *Less Than Half, More Than Whole*. Flagstaff, AZ: Northland Publishing. A young Native American boy playing with his friends at the lake suddenly recognizes that he is different from them.

Mockizuki, Ken. (1993). Illustrated by Dom Lee. *Baseball Saved Us*. New York, NY: Lee & Low Books, Inc. A Japanese American boy learns to play baseball when he and his family are forced to live in an internment camp during World War II. It gave him a purpose while enduring injustice and humiliation in the camp.

Nikola-Lisa, W. (1994). Illustrated by Michael Bryant. *Bein' with You This Way*. New York, NY: Lee & Low Books, Inc. On a beautiful day, a little girl rounds up a group of her friends for fun and games. As they play they discover that despite individual physical differences, they are all really the same.

Polacco, Patricia. (1992). *Mrs. Katz and Tush*. New York, NY: Bantam Books. A long-lasting friendship develops when Larnel, a young African American, presents Mrs. Katz, a lonely Jewish widow, with a scrawny kitten without a tail.

Rosen, Michael J. (1992). Illustrated by Aminah Brenda Lynn Robinson. *Elijah's Angel*. San Diego, CA: Harcourt Brace & Company. At Christmas and Hanukkah time, a Christian woodcarver gives a carved angel to a young Jewish friend, who struggles with accepting the Christmas gift until he realizes that friendship means the same thing in any religion.

Shelby, Anne. (1991). Illustrated by Irene Trivas. *Potluck*. New York, NY: Orchard Books. More than thirty kids from many cultures bring their favorite foods to a scrumptious meal. Children like the way the words trip off the tongue.

Wild, Margaret. (1991). Illustrated by Julie Vivas. *Let the Celebrations BEGIN!* New York, NY: Orchard Books. A child, who remembers life at home before life in a concentration camp, makes toys with the women to give to the other children at the very special party they are going to have when the soldiers arrive to liberate the camp.

RESOURCES FOR ADULTS

Books

Derman-Sparks, Louise, and the A.B.C. Task Force. (1989). *Anti-Bias Curriculum: Tools for Empowering Young Children*. Washington, DC: National Association for the Education of Young Children. The first and most complete discussion of issues of bias, this book should be the center point of every professional library addressing racism, prejudice and diversity in our society.

Ford, Clyde W. (1994). *We Can All Get Along: 50 Steps You Can Take to Help End Racism at Home, at Work, In Your Community*. New York: Bantam Doubleday Dell Publishing Group, Inc. This is a basic primer on the issue of racism in general. It is recommended reading for all staff prior to group discussion on the topic. Easy to read, the text is brought to a personal level providing possible responses in different situations.

Neugebauer, Bonnie, (Ed.). (1992). *Alike and Different: Exploring Our Humanity With Young Children*. Washington, DC: National Association for the Education of Young Children. This excellent resource is a collection of chapters on differences—cultural, racial and capabilities. It includes practical suggestions and has an extensive resource section. There is an excellent chapter by Francis Wardle on biracial children.

Paley, Vivian Gussin. (1990). *White Teacher*. Cambridge, MA: Harvard University Press. Definitely worth reading! A skillful and sensitive kindergarten teacher describes classroom scenarios as she explores her own development in being able to handle race issues.

Thompson, Barbara J. (1992). *Words Can Hurt You; Beginning a Program of Anti-Bias Education*. Mainly Park, CA: Addison Wesley. An excellent resource for teachers, especially in the early elementary grades.

Articles

Ramsey, Patricia G. "Research in review: Growing up with the contradictions of race and class." *Young Children*. 52 (6), September 1995, 18-22.

Wardle, Francis. "Are you sensitive to interracial children's special identity needs?" *Young Children*. 42(2), January 1987, 53-59.

Booklet

Teaching Young Children to Resist Bias: What Parents Can Do. National Association for the Education of Young Children, 1509 16th Street, NW, Washington, DC 20036-1426. 800-424-2460. www.naeyc.org. This booklet includes suggestions for teachers and parents to help children appreciate diversity and deal with others' biases. The booklet is available in both English and Spanish. $.50 per copy. Quantity discount is $10 for 100 copies.

Curriculum Materials

Teaching Tolerance. Southern Poverty Law Center, 400 Washington Avenue, Montgomery, AL 36104. Fax 205-264-3121. The first issue of this curriculum publication was developed in 1991. Current issues are mailed twice a year at no charge to educators on the mailing list. *Teaching Tolerance* is published by the Southern Poverty Law Center, a nonprofit legal and education foundation, to provide teachers with resources and ideas

Racism & Prejudice

to help promote harmony in the classroom. Send your name and address to the Southern Poverty Law Center to be placed on the mailing list.

Crayons and paints reflecting a wide range of skin tones. Available from most school suppliers.

Dolls and puppets for dramatic play, puzzles and posters that represent people of different races are available from most school suppliers.

Videos

Culture and Education of Young Children. National Association for the Education of Young Children, 1509 16th Street, NW, Washington, DC 20036-1426. 800-424-2460. www.naeyc.org, 16min. $39. Early childhood educator, Carol Phillips, discusses how programs can show respect for cultural diversity and use this richness to enhance children's learning.

Louise Derman-Sparks. ***Anti-Bias Curriculum***. Pacific Oaks Bookstore, 5 Westmoreland Place, Pasadena, CA 91103. 626-397-1300. www.pacificoaks.edu/bookstore.html. 30 min. This excellent video gives an overview of children's development and classroom practices related to preventing racial, gender and disability prejudice. A good tool for introducing the concepts to parents or new staff.

Organizations & Hot Lines

Culturally Relevant Anti-Bias Education Leadership Project. Pacific Oaks College, 5 Westmoreland Place, Pasadena, CA 91103. 626-397-1300. www.pacificoaks.edu/bookstore.html. Louise Derman-Sparks, Director. The Project provides technical assistance, training services and consultations to early childhood educators and programs. Educators learn how to teach other adults how to provide culturally relevant anti-bias education with children, and how to work with community groups on social justice issues.

Mid-Atlantic Equity Consortium, 5454 Wisconsin Avenue, Suite 655, Chevy Chase, MD 20815. 301-657-7741. www.maec.org. The Consortium was founded to assist organizations and schools to address issues of cultural diversity, race and gender equity, cross-cultural communication and the establishment of multicultural programs and work environments. The staff provides technical assistance and training services without charge to schools in the Mid-Atlantic region in three program areas: race, gender and national origin desegregation. They have an extensive list of publications which are disseminated nationally at cost to cover printing and shipping expenses.

The Prejudice Institute, 2743 Maryland Avenue, Baltimore, MD 21218. 410-366-9654. www.prejudiceinstitute.org. The institute provides resources fro activists, lawyers, and social scientists. It is devoted to policy research and education on all dimensions of prejudice, discrimination, and ethnoviolence.

The Center for the Study of Biracial Children, 2300 South Kremaria Street, Denver, CO 80222. 303-692-9008. www.csbc.cncfamily.com. The Mission of the Study of Biracial Children is to enhance the lives of interracial families and biracial children by providing information, training, materials, presentations and advocacy. We work with families, child care programs, interracial organizations, schools, universities and the media.

Racism & Prejudice

CHAPTER 18

SEXISM

HERE'S AN EXAMPLE

Four year olds Jimmy, Justin and Tommy, usually kings of the block corner, were lured into the housekeeping area by beautiful, new dress-up clothes their teacher had brought in that morning. They giggled and pranced around in feather boas, sequined evening dresses, silver high heels and broad rimmed hats, admiring themselves in the mirror. Their teacher, Debbie, was so proud of them for crossing the barrier between "girls' play and boys' play" that she took a Polaroid picture of them proudly modeling their finery for the class scrapbook. Tommy's father arrived at that moment, and Debbie was dumbfounded when Tommy's father was outraged to see his son in women's clothes. "What are you trying to do to my son?" he shouted. He told Tommy, "Take that stuff off. You look like a sissy." Later, at a private parent meeting, Debbie tried to explain to Tommy's father and mother that when children are four years old they often enjoy trying different roles and engaging in fantasy play. But her remarks seemed to make no impression on the parents, although they didn't try to argue with her. The point was clear to Tommy. He never ventured near the housekeeping area again.

LET'S LOOK AT THE ISSUE

The example above reflects an attitude that is prevalent in our society. The teacher is in an uncomfortable dilemma. Her decision to talk to the parents in a private meeting is wise. Even though she felt she was not effective in getting Tommy to feel free to dress-up, she made an effort to defuse the anger of the parents and to understand their feelings. She can still make sure Tommy has many rich dramatic play opportunities in different settings.

Parents (and grandparents, siblings, aunts, uncles) sometimes feel that they must nurture "boyness" or "girlness" in their children in order for them to develop the proper sex role identification. They may do this without consciously thinking about it. From the beginning, many girl babies and boy babies may be treated differently by parents. Girls may be perceived as delicate and fragile, boys as robust and strong. As they progress through the toddler years, girls may be praised for how they look, while boys are praised for their accomplishments.

On the other hand, it is a mistake to pretend that boys and girls are just the same except for their physical differences. Boys do seem to gravitate toward playing with vehicles and blocks. The nurturing side of girls shows up very early in their play with dolls and stuffed animals. Is this genetics or environment? It's hard to say how much of this is due to the roles they see in their families and the type of toys they have been given, and how much of it is biological.

What is important to keep in mind is that both boys and girls generally like all kinds of play. Even if they spend more time in one area than in others, they should always have a wide variety of options. Boys enjoy dramatic play, if not always in the housekeeping area. Girls enjoy constructing things. Make sure that your classroom or home environment does not develop "exclusion zones."

Showing respect for the opposite sex is a problem in our society. There have even been lawsuits over sexual harassment on the elementary school level. The education department in Minnesota is developing written guidelines to assist staff in recognizing and stopping sexual harassment among children. Whether it is sexual harassment lawsuits or sexual discrimination in the job market or individuals limited because of gender, sexism is an aspect of our society.

However, some gender differences are a reality. We need to be cognizant of them to make curriculum and programs work well for boys as well as girls.

INSIGHTS FROM CHILD DEVELOPMENT

Sense of identity. Sometime in the second year, young children figure out that they are either a boy or a girl and then are intent upon determining what makes them a boy or girl and how the rest of the world fits into these powerful categories. They don't realize that it is body parts that determine gender.

Misunderstandings. Hair styles, clothing and activities are highly visible to young children, so they tend to think these are the distinguishing characteristics.

Gender cannot change. Children may not realize that they will always be a boy or girl, and that changing hair length or clothes does not make their sex change. The understanding that gender does not change over time also has to develop.

Quick to stereotype. Young children, with their limited experience, are very quick to stereotype based on models they have been exposed to. They may ignore, or at least resist, evidence that doesn't agree with what they have personally experienced. Cognitive development takes care of some overstereotyping, but the role of teachers and parents in encouraging multiple perspectives is important.

Roles for men and women. Young children are rather rigid in what they believe men and women can or should do. This is due to their recent acquisition of the concepts "men" and "women." They are actively sorting out who goes with what. Three year olds in particular ascribe very traditional roles to adults. As they gain experience in diverse roles, they expand the list of what they consider acceptable roles for men and women.

Same-sex play. Children, once they are beyond the age of two, may develop strong preferences for playing with same-sex peers. Because this tendency seems to occur across different cultures, there might be a biological basis. Perhaps boys and girls are more comfortable with same-sex peers because of similar play styles. This play preference can become a problem when children are excluded by those of the opposite sex from joining in their play.

WHEN TO SEEK HELP

Since sexism is endemic in our lives, it should be addressed on a daily basis. The following are a few warning signs indicating that additional intervention is needed.

◆ **Strong exclusion statements**, "Girls can't climb," "You can't play here because you're a boy," indicate that you need to devote some specific attention to this issue.

◆ **Reluctance to try new roles**. A child is reluctant to try anything not strictly in traditional sex roles. Boys won't try cooking, for instance, or girls won't use tools at the workbench.

◆ **Bullying**. A child may bully, trying to solve all problems by dominating others.

◆ **Timidity**. A child may seem very timid, unwilling to try new things, passive, whining often, afraid to get dirty.

◆ **Strong statements by parents about sex roles**. Some parents tell their children what is okay to play with and what is not, especially warning boys to stay away from "sissy" activities.

◆   Experienced early childhood professionals

◆   Children's librarian to help you find resources and children's books that counter stereotypes

HOW TO RESPOND

HOW TO RESPOND WITH THE STAFF

◆   **Observe children's play patterns**. Start by observing the play patterns of the children in your group. Who likes to play where, with whom? Take some time to formally observe your classroom. Every five minutes during free play time write down who is playing where. Review your notations. You might be surprised.

◆   **Model play that is not typical of your own gender**. If you are female, play in the block corner or at the woodworking bench and show that you enjoy the materials. If you are a male, play with dolls and dishes. Your example shows children it is okay to play with everything in the environment.

HOW TO RESPOND WITH THE CHILDREN

◆   **Be proactive**. Teachers will have to be proactive on this issue, not just intervene when they hear some stereotyped comment from children. You may have to show children over and over that certain activities and roles are not just for one gender or the other.

◆   **What makes you male or female?** Emphasize to children, who may think that dress, length of hair or play preferences are what makes them male or female, "What makes you a boy is that you have a penis. What makes you a girl is that you have a vagina." If you are uncomfortable using the terms "penis" and "vagina," say "boy private parts" and "girl private parts." Accurately illustrated children's books and anatomically correct dolls are useful.

◆   **Explain that a person's gender will never change**. Children should be told that, no matter how they dress or wear their hair, they will always remain a boy or a girl because of their special boy or girl body parts.

◆   **Everyone can play with everything**. With input from the children, create the rule for your classroom or child care home: Everyone can play with everything.

◆ **Intervene quickly, directly and tactfully** when you hear children being excluded from an activity because of their gender. This is really a form of aggression—verbal aggression—and you should treat it the same as you would treat physical aggression. Comfort the victim, discuss the situation and help the children solve problems without hurting anyone.

◆ **Comment on mixed-gender play**. When you see boys and girls playing cooperatively with each other, say something like "Manuel and Julia are making a city in the sand box." Pointing them out to the class gives the message that you approve of this type of play.

◆ **Encourage children**. Some children will need specific encouragement or an invitation to try certain activities. Engaging in parallel play with them also helps them feel more comfortable.

◆ **Present traditional and nontraditional role models**. Look for and present to children models of capable, confident, caring individuals in traditional and nontraditional roles. Find these models in children's stories, illustrations, photos and magazine pictures.

◆ **Invite visitors who work in nontraditional roles**, such as women electricians and male cooks, to visit your classroom or center. Start with parents to find such models.

◆ **Encourage chidren to think beyond stereotypes**. Point out exceptions to stereotypes. When you hear, for instance, "Girls don't like bugs," you could respond, "It may be true that some girls don't like bugs. But some girls think insects are very interesting. I'm a girl, and I like to study insects."

◆ **Counter stereotypical statements**. Counter children's stereotypical statements with contradictions from their own experience. "Girls can't fix things." "Miss Marsha is a girl, and she just fixed our toilet."

◆ **Read books** like *William's Doll* to the children and then get their comments. This gives you a chance to tell children that it's okay for boys to play with dolls and that lots of boys like to do this. Also encourage girls to talk about the "boys' toys" they like to play with. Talk about what you liked to play with when you were a child that might not fit into the stereotype.

◆ **Riding toys and dramatic play**. Make sure girls have equal access to riding toys outside. Create dramatic play settings outside that attract both boys and girls and that can incorporate riding toys.

◆ **Make a class book** about activities that the children's parents do in and out of the home. Then point out and talk about the diversity of roles.

◆ **Make sure that boys as well as girls help the teacher**. All children should have the privilege and responsibility of helping the teacher with classroom chores, such as clean-up time and setting the table.

◆ **Arrange the classroom**. For example, placing the doll corner furniture right next to the block corner can encourage more cooperative play between boys and girls.

◆ **Place the woodworking bench next to the art area**. Encourage children to blend the materials. Both boys and girls will be drawn to it.

◆ **Use themes**. Create dramatic play areas around themes other than housekeeping. How about a restaurant, a grocery store, a hardware store, a hospital, a firehouse? Diverse props attract diverse children.

HOW TO MAKE YOUR PROGRAM MORE COMFORTABLE FOR ALL CHILDREN

◆ **Reduce group sitting time**. Limit time spent on activities such as circle time where you require children to sit still and pay attention. Instead of always reading to a large group, for instance, read with one or two children in a cozy corner.

◆ **Look for books that will appeal to active learners**—books about construction, workers and tools, vehicles, imagination and adventures.

◆ **Provide language enrichment activities**. Bring language learning into the block corner. Offer to take dictation from the children about what they built. Provide writing materials so they can create signs.

◆ **Enlarge the block corner**. This area could be enlarged to make room for more boys and girls.

◆ **Set up a workbench**.

◆ **Provide dress-ups for male and female roles**. Hats of all types are popular. Also include capes, belts, worker props such as tool boxes and lunch boxes, and clip boards.

HOW TO RESPOND WITH THE PARENTS

◆ **Discuss how children benefit from different kinds of toys**. Bring up the subject at parent meetings and in newsletters.

◆ **Encourage parents to get a nurturing object toy for their sons and daughters**— if not a doll, then a stuffed animal that they can tenderly care for and play with, give rides to and pretend to feed. Encourage dramatic play, "Oh look, bunny feels sad because he is on the floor behind the door. He'd much rather be snuggled up next to big bear." Point out how this type of play helps boys develop empathy and tenderness.

◆ **Stress the importance of play clothes**. Encourage parents to dress both boys and girls in play clothes that can get dirty.

◆ **Collect stereotypical images**. Develop a collection of male and female stereotyped images from magazines and cards. Use this to raise parents' awareness of images their children are seeing, even if they are not modeling this in their own lives.

◆ **Help parents counter stereotyping**. Suggest words they can use to counter male and female stereotyping they encounter in the media, toy packaging, greeting cards and books.

WHERE TO FIND MORE INFORMATION

RESOURCES FOR CHILDREN

Books

Danish, Barbara. (1971). *The Dragon and the Doctor.* New York, NY: The Feminist Press. Doctor Judy has an unusual patient—a dragon with a sore tail. With Nurse Benjamin's help, Doctor Judy cures Dragon and together they celebrate with Dragon's many friends.

Hoffman, Mary. (1991). Illustrated by Caroline Binch. *Amazing Grace*. New York, NY: Dial Books for Young Readers. Although classmates say she cannot play Peter Pan in the school play because she is black and a girl, Grace discovers she can do anything she sets her mind to do.

Hudson, Wade. (1992). Illustrated by Culverson Blair. *I'm Gonna Be!* Orange, NJ: Just Us Books. The Afro-Bets kids discuss what they're going to be when they grow up. African American role models are presented, both men and women, and brief descriptions of their occupations.

Phelps, Ethel Johnston. (1978). Illustrated by Pamela Baldwin Ford. *Tatterhood and Other Tales*. New York, NY: The Feminist Press. Accustomed as we have all been to great derring-do tales of heroes and handmaidens, it is a pleasure to enjoy these folk tales where the central characters are clever, strong, resourceful and successful females.

Zolotow, Charlotte. (1972). Illustrated by William Pène Du Bois. *William's Doll*. New York, NY: Harper Trophy. William goes through a lot with his family before he finally gets the doll he has wanted for so long.

Books

Carlsson-Paige, Nancy and Levin, Diane E. (1990). ***Who's Calling the Shots: How to Respond Effectively to Children's Fascination with War Play and War Toys***. Philadelphia, PA: New Society Publishers. This book has an informative chapter that discusses how children gain their sex role identities and how television programming and advertising, along with toy manufacturers, are promoting blatant sexist thinking in boys and girls.

Derman-Sparks, Louise, and the A.B.C. Task Force. (1989). ***Anti-Bias Curriculum: Tools for Empowering Young Children***. Washington, DC: National Association for the Education of Young Children. Chapter Six is entitled "Learning About Gender Identity." It contains many useful insights and practical suggestions.

Edwards, Carolyn Pope. (1986). ***Promoting Social and Moral Development in Young Children: Creative Approaches for the Classroom Environment***. New York: Teachers College Press.

Helping Children Love Themselves and Others: Resource Guide to Equity Materials for Young Children. (1994). Washington, DC: The Children's Foundation. Parents, teachers, librarians and trainers will find this newly revised guide, which is available in both English and Spanish, a useful resource. The guide contains a checklist of books, toys and materials to assist in determining equity resources; annotated bibliographies of children's literature and resources for adults that include books, curricula, magazines, newsletters and pamphlets; a listing of companies with anti-bias and/or multicultural books and materials available; and a listing of national support organizations. To order send check or money order for $11.50 to The Children's Foundation, 725 Fifteenth Street, NW, Suite 505, Washington, DC 20005-2109. 202-347-3300.

Miller, Karen. (1989). ***The Outside Play and Learning Book: Activities for Young Children***. Beltsville MD: Gryphon House. This book has chapters on dramatic play involving wheel toys outside, sand play and other active play that will attract both boys and girls, providing opportunities for cooperative play.

Neugebauer, Bonnie, (Ed). (1992). ***Alike and Different: Exploring Our Humanity With Young Children***. Washington, DC: National Association for the Education of Young Children. The chapter by Judith Leipzig exposes unconscious sexist attitudes of adults in caring for infants and toddlers. Other discussion of sexism is throughout the book.

Paley, Vivian Gussin. (1986). ***Boys & Girls: Superheros in the Doll Corner***. Chicago: University of Chicago Press. This highly readable book shows a sensitive teacher's obser vations on the nature of boys' play and girls' play, though very different, are equally powerful, and how boys and girls act on one another's turf.

Paley, Vivian. (1992). *You Can't Say You Can't Play*. Cambridge, MA: Harvard University Press. This book reads like a novel, and has an allegorical tale woven through it. The theme is exclusion. Paley describes how she dealt with the issue of girls and boys excluding others in their play.

Thomas, Marlo. (1974). *Free to Be You and Me*. New York: McGraw-Hill Book Company. This feminist classic is a collection of great poems, stories and songs that are about children reaching their potential. The selections about feelings, including the poem and song, "It's All Right to Cry," are also available on audio cassette and record.

Curriculum Materials

Community helper figures for block play in nontraditional sex roles.

Puzzles that picture nontraditional work roles.

Anatomically correct dolls.

Videos

Moving Machines. Bo Peep Productions, P.O. Box 982, Eureka, MT 59917. An excellent video that shows both boys and girls enjoying playing with toy vehicles and machines and watching real earth movers and other large machines.

Preschool Power, More Preschool Power, Preschool Power 3. Concept Associates, Bethesda, MD 20814. A series of three videos which show two- to six-year-olds of both sexes having a wonderful time doing all sorts of things: cooking, dancing, dress-ups, gardening.

Organizations & Hot Lines

Mid-Atlantic Equity Consortium, 5454 Wisconsin Avenue, Suite 655, Chevy Chase, MD 20815. 301-657-7741. www.maec.org. The Consortium was founded to assist organizations and schools to address issues of cultural diversity, race and gender equity, cross-cultural communication and the establishment of multicultural programs and work environments. The staff provides technical assistance and training services without charge to schools in the Mid-Atlantic region in three program areas: race, gender and national origin desegregation. They have an extensive list of publications which are disseminated nationally at cost to cover printing and shipping expenses.

The Children's Foundation, 725 15th Street, NW, Suite 505, Washington, DC 20005-2109. 202-347-3300. www.childrensfoundation.net. Since its founding in 1969, The Foundation has worked to improve the lives of children and those who care for them. They provide training for child care providers and publish a family child care bulletin. Their extensive list of publications include equity materials which are available in both English and Spanish.

Women's Action Alliance, 370 Lexington Ave., New York, NY 10017. This organization publishes a newsletter, called *Equal Play*, twice a year.

Sexism

INCLUDING CHILDREN FROM MANY CULTURES

HERE ARE TWO EXAMPLES

Four year old Pedro and his mother and father had just arrived in Massachusetts from Portugal. Both the mother and father found work immediately, so Pedro was enrolled in the local child care center. His teachers, Karen and Vivien, did not speak Portuguese, but the assistant director at the center was Portuguese and acted as an interpreter for the teachers while they showed the family the classroom and explained what Pedro's days would be like. The assistant director also translated daily notes home describing what Pedro did each day. Vivien explained to the other children that Pedro could not understand them and talk to them yet, but he would learn and they could help. On the first day, Karen read them a funny picture book story, and Pedro laughed at one of the pictures. Another child announced happily, "Pedro laughs in English!" An outgoing child, Pedro happily joined in all the play options of the classroom and especially enjoyed building with the other boys in the block corner and playing outside. Karen made time each day to settle down with Pedro and one or two friends to do a language activity, like identifying pictures in a book. Everyone was amazed at the speed at which Pedro picked up English. He started with words of greeting and routines such as "Hi!," "Bye-bye!," "Go outside," "Clean-up time," and "Lunch!" He was especially proud when his mother came and cooked with the other children one day. After six months, Pedro's language developed rapidly.

Barb enrolled her four year old daughter, Melissa, in a preschool program in a Detroit suburb. Upon visiting, she found a chaotic situation. About half of the children in the class were Japanese. The fathers of the children were here for a year on an exchange with executives from an American firm. Because the teacher had no idea how to communicate with the Japanese children, there was no order or routine in the classroom. The teacher was at her wit's end. Also, Barb observed that the American children and the Japanese children did not play together. She sensed that there were many missed opportunities. So Barb decided to form a mothers' club. With the aid of one Japanese mother who spoke both English and Japanese, she invited everyone to a tea at her house while the children were in school. They talked about the problems in the classroom and devised ways to help. The Japanese mothers didn't realize they would be welcome to volunteer and help in the classroom. Many of them knew a little English but were shy and didn't want to make mistakes. The teacher later assured them that they would be most welcome and that their help was much appreciated. Barb also encouraged the American mothers to invite one Japanese child and mother to come over to their houses to play after school, thus building friendships between the children and the parents. Before long, the Japanese mothers were actively sharing their culture in the classroom from time to time, and everybody benefited from their unique situation.

LET'S LOOK AT THE ISSUE

According to the 1992 Census, one in eleven inhabitants of the United States is foreign born. Given this statistic, you are likely to have a child in your class who is from another culture and doesn't speak English. While this situation is filled with exciting opportunities, it is not without its special challenges. How do you help this child adjust, and how do you help him learn to communicate with you and the other children?

Your challenge is not just linguistic, communicating with the child and the family, it is also cultural. You will need to make a special effort to make the family feel welcome, and recognize and value their culture. Often the child's family is in transition. They have left their homeland, sometimes under dramatic circumstances and are trying to start a new life. Even under the best of circumstances, the family will probably be under stress.

The parents may have a hard time trusting you. When people search for child care, they instinctively look for people as much like themselves as they can find, people who reflect their own values and culture. Some parents fear that if their children learn English, they will forget their native language and will not want to identify with their native culture and values.

Actually, this situation is a marvelous opportunity to enrich your program and your life. But it will take some extra effort at first.

Strong separation anxiety. A child from a different culture is likely to experience strong separation anxiety. Not only is he being left with strangers, but you might look different from people he knows. You certainly sound different! The food might taste different. And nobody can comfort him and reassure him that his parent will return.

Parental anxiety. The child may also reflect the considerable anxiety many parents feel leaving their children with someone they don't know, haven't yet learned to trust, and with whom they cannot communicate.

Communication. Remember that words are only one part of communicating. Tone of voice, intonation, facial expression, body language, gestures and touch are all important ways human beings communicate with each other, and even very young children understand these things very well.

Language capacity. Young children have an amazing capacity to learn language. Be aware that receptive language, hearing and understanding words and phrases, comes first. Productive language, producing words and phrases to communicate, is usually harder and comes a little late. In other words, a child understands more than she can speak.

Differences. Young children have little understanding of cultures, but they do notice differences. If the new child not only sounds different, but looks different from the other children in the group, you need to talk about it with the other children. Be open as you talk about skin color, hair type, the color of eyes and other differences. Collect pictures of people of different cultures. Invite visitors to the class that represent different cultures, if you don't have a diverse population in your class or center, so children become comfortable with diversity (see chapter 17 on racism).

Respect. Do not allow people to talk about the child or the family (especially if there are problems) in the child's presence, thinking the child does not understand. Even though the child may not understand every word, he will probably sense that you are talking about him and will pick up on the tone.

WHEN TO SEEK HELP

◆ **Extreme separation anxiety**. The child may continue for a long period of time to exhibit extreme separation anxiety. Do not ignore this situation because it may not resolve itself without your help. If the child cries and clings to the parent and then clings to you all the time instead of participating, and the parent seems anguished, talk with the parent. Home visits often help a great deal in such situations. You will have to judge each

Children from Many Cultures

situation individually to decide how long normal separation anxiety behaviors can go on, and when it needs more attention. Discuss it with your supervisor.

◆ **Social interactions**. The child may be withdrawn, aggressive, or have trouble making friends. This behavior may be related to language development, feeling isolated, insecure or frustrated. Work with the child to ease social interactions.

◆ **Irregular attendance** may indicate family anxieties. Be proactive. Reach out to find out why the child is absent and what else you might do to make the parents and child feel more comfortable.

WHO CAN HELP

◆ Regional Access Project (RAP) for Head Start may have resources to assist with a particular culture. Check local listings.
◆ English as a Second Language (ESL) teachers and specialists in your local school district.
◆ The education department at a local university may also be a resource.
◆ Someone who speaks English from that child's cultural community. It's ideal if your program can locate someone who is well respected in that community who can act as an interpreter and liaison for you and the parents. Unless there is no other alternative, avoid using an older child as an interpreter.

HOW TO RESPOND

HOW TO RESPOND WITH THE STAFF

◆ **Read about the family's culture**. The local librarian can help you find resources. Then check details with the family. "I read this about your culture. Is it true? Tell me more about it." Parents will react warmly when they sense that you are trying to learn more about them.

◆ **Learn key words and phrases in the child's language**. Of course, nobody expects caregivers to be multi-lingual, but you can learn greeting, parting and social words, like "hi", "good morning," "good-bye" and "thank you." Survival phrases are important for you to understand, such as "hungry," "tired," "thirsty" and "go to the bathroom." You might develop a list of these phrases, written out the way they are pronounced, to have in the child's file.

◆ **Add a staff person from that culture**. If many children come from a particular culture in your program, it is ideal if you can add a staff person or volunteer from that culture.

HOW TO RESPOND WITH THE CHILD

◆ **Be the child's "anchor."** Like all new children to your program, the child needs to develop a trusting relationship with one adult first and can then extend this trust to others. This child may need much holding and comforting. Stay close. Like a toddler in a new environment, eventually the child will venture out and play a little, and come back to touch you at intervals, to make sure you are still there. If you provide this extra accessibility when it is critically needed at the beginning, the child will develop confidence and independence more quickly.

◆ **Represent the child's culture in pictures and materials**. Make sure the child's culture is represented in pictures and materials you have available in your classroom. Perhaps the family can be of help. Ask them to save food boxes or dress-up clothes for the housekeeping corner. Try to find pictures, books, music and other items representative of the culture.

◆ **Use recorded music**. If possible, find recorded music from that child's culture to play for the whole class.

◆ **Be a good language model for the child**. Speak slowly, simply, and clearly (but not more loudly), and in full sentences. Describe what you are doing, and what the child is doing.

◆ **Talk to the child as though he understands you**, and help him understand you by doing what you are talking about. For instance, say, "Peter, it's time to go to the table and eat lunch." Then take him by the hand and lead him over to the table and sit down with him.

◆ **Extend the child's single word utterances** when they start. If she says, "Shoes," and points, say, "Yes, I see you have new red shoes on today!"

◆ **Play simple language games** that involve understanding (receptive language) while also involving other children to develop the child's social contacts.

> **Puppet packs his suitcase**. Have a puppet tell the child and a friend or two, "I'm going to Grandma's house, and I need to put some things in my suitcase to bring along." Then have the puppet name things from the room and ask the children to go and get them for him. The puppet can talk about each object before it is put into the suitcase. "That's a shiny, red truck."
>
> **Puppet unpacks his suitcase**. When the puppet "returns from Grandma's" the next day, he can bring the packed toys as well as a few other objects out of the suitcase to talk about. "Here's the red truck. You

can put it back now. Thank you." "Look what else my Grandma gave me, a nice, soft pillow."

Point to the picture. Find a picture book with many pictures on a page. Magazines and catalogs work well too. Ask the child, "Where is a cat?" "Where is a television?" Let the child point to the objects. If she does not know, take her finger and put it on the correct picture and say, "There is the cat!" Then a few questions later, ask her to find the same thing again. An English-speaking friend will enjoy playing along and praising the friend for getting the correct answer, or helping her find it.

Picture to thing. Cut out pictures of objects in your room and mount the pictures on cards covered with transparent self-adhesive paper. Hand the card to the child and a friend. Say, "This is a ball. Bring the picture to the real ball." Later the child will be able to do this independently. Before long, you will be able to point to the object or the picture and ask, "What's this?," and the child will be able to name it in English.

Flannel board. Cut out a number of pictures of common objects and back them with felt, sandpaper or Velcro. Place them in front of the flannel board. While working with a small group of children, ask them to pick up the picture of a certain object and put it on the board one at a time. With the child who speaks limited English, choose something you are sure he knows, or have him pick up the last one and put it on the board. Take the pictures down again in the same fashion.

◆ **Build vocabulary**. Clean-up time can be a great vocabulary builder. Simply stay with the child and name the things you are putting away together. Or let a puppet help.

◆ **Read familiar books** over and over.

◆ **Create simple rituals**. Often the first words a child says out loud are social words such as "hi," "bye-bye" and "thank you." Encourage all the children to say "hi" or "good-morning" and "bye" when someone leaves, and "thank you." "Yes," "no" and "okay" are other common early words. Think about including other ritual phrases.

◆ **Interpret early efforts to communicate**. Read the child's nonverbal communication and supply it with words. The child points at the pitcher and makes a noise. "Oh, you want more juice? I'll be glad to pour you some juice." You are helping the child connect useful words to feelings. "Maria is sad because she can't find her hat."

◆ **Use singing**. Songs with repeated phrases are good to use. "E-i-e-i-o" is easy to master, and fun to sing. Singing is much easier than talking. The words usually come out slower and are more predictable. It is good practice with productive language (speaking and producing words). Musical games involving body parts, such as "Hokey Pokey" are ideal. Perhaps the child, with a parent, can teach the other children familiar songs like "Happy Birthday" in their own language.

◆ **Use firm, gentle guidance and consistent limits**. Whatever the culture, children will feel most secure with firm, gentle guidance and consistent limits. Sometimes children will pretend not to understand messages long after they really do understand. Remember, nonverbal messages of a discipline situation are always understood, so make your tone of voice and facial expression match your words. If a child is doing something unacceptable like taking a toy away from another child, simply get down on the child's level, hold his shoulders, look into his eyes and shake your head while saying, "No, that's not okay." Use the same positive techniques you use with the other children of praising good behavior and redirecting unacceptable behavior.

◆ **Increase open-ended activities.** Luckily, many of the activities in a typical early childhood curriculum do not require strong language skills on the part of the child. Just like all the other children, the child who does not speak English will need many experiences of success and fun to develop a feeling of self-worth. So, provide plenty of experiences using art materials, clay, playdough, manipulatives, blocks and dramatic play. Children pick up language from their parallel play with other children, and you can describe with interest what they are doing.

◆ **Let the child help you create her own word book**. In a homemade book, put pictures or drawings of words that the child knows in English. You might also say the word in the child's native language. It's a good idea to do this in a loose-leaf binder so it can grow and grow!

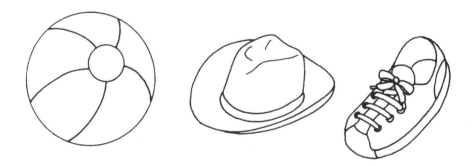

◆ **Record progress**. Keep a record of the new words and phrases the child learns. It will be interesting to see what comes first, probably some of the things most important to the child. Also make note of what the child enjoys doing and with whom the child likes to play. Keep the parents well informed and share the pleasures and successes.

HOW TO RESPOND WITH THE OTHER CHILDREN

◆ **Encourage interaction**. Talk to the other children about how their new friend cannot understand their words, but does understand what their bodies are saying. Let them think of ways they can use their bodies to "talk" to their friend such as smiles, head nods or shakes and taking the child's hand.

◆ **Interpret interactions**. Likewise, help the other children "read" their new friend's gestures. "Mariko is shaking her head. She doesn't want to go with you right now."

◆ **Encourage friendships**. Brainstorm with the children how they can be a friend to someone without being able to talk to them. The children might think of things like sharing playdough, sitting next to each other, playing with dolls, looking at pictures in a book together, playing follow the leader, holding hands and greeting their friend with a warm hug.

◆ **Let the new child teach words from his language** to the other children. The English-speaking friends will enjoy learning greeting words in another language as well as the words for common objects in the room. The child who does not speak English will probably enjoy teaching these words, possibly with the help of a parent, and it will show respect for the child and his culture.

HOW TO RESPOND WITH INFANTS AND TODDLERS

◆ **Anticipate greater anxiety**. Parents may have greater anxiety leaving an infant or toddler than when leaving an older child. They may feel that the child is particularly vulnerable because she is so young and cannot express herself. Have an adult interpreter present to facilitate communication with these parents, if possible.

◆ **Note how the parent interacts with the child**. Notice how the parent holds and comforts the baby and try to adopt that style yourself.

◆ **Invite the parent to spend the day with you and the baby,** caring for the child. Try to imitate the parent's gestures and ways of communicating with the baby.

◆ **Arrange for a consistent caregiver**. Having the same, consistent primary caregiver is especially important for babies from a different culture so that they only have to get used to one new thing at a time.

HOW TO RESPOND WITH THE PARENTS

◆ **Get acquainted with the parents**. Make the effort to get acquainted with the family and help them feel comfortable. Take your time with the intake interview. Use this as the first opportunity to make the parents feel welcome and supported.

◆ **Invite the parents into the classroom**. Invite the parent to spend a day or more in the classroom, with or without the child, just to see what goes on and to become comfortable with you. He or she might then have more specific questions. Assure the parents that they do not need to know English to be welcome in your program.

◆ **Visit the home**, if this is agreeable to the parents. You can learn a great deal about the child and about the culture. Plus, in meeting them in their home, you develop a sense of ease and friendship with the family. It might be easier for a mother to express her concerns and fears as well as her hopes and wishes when she is sitting in her own kitchen.

◆ **Maintain a warm social relationship with the family**. Be conscious of your facial expressions, body language and tone of voice when you see parents. Greet them warmly and with respect. Share the joy of their child. Laugh. Develop and attend social events for families like pot luck dinners and parties that include children. When you have a social rapport with parents, it is easier to talk about any conflicts or concerns that arise, and you avoid creating mountains out of molehills.

◆ **Find an interpreter from their culture to be present at all conferences** and get-acquainted sessions with the family. All of the program's written policies should be translated for them into their language.

◆ **Encourage parents to bring in pictures of their families**, family celebrations, vacations or other events, as well as pictures of their homeland, if possible. It gives the new child some comfort in a strange situation, as well as sharing the culture. Do this with all of your children. It's also a good idea to send pictures of you and the children in the class home with the new child. If they do not have pictures, offer to take photos of the family yourself. Explain how you will use them.

◆ **Share the culture**. Invite family members to come in and spend time with you, and as much as they are able, share their culture. Doing a cooking project is fun. Perhaps a family member could teach a children's song from that culture. If they know some English, they might be able to tell the children one of their folk tales, in English, or show them a children's picture book from their country and tell the other children what it says on each page. Again, make them know you would welcome their participation, even if they cannot speak English. A non-English-speaking parent could sit at the clay table and play with the children, or look at picture books with them. The child will be proud that his parent visited.

◆ **Translate the lunch menu**. Send a translated version of the lunch menu home a week ahead of time. Talk to the parents about the child's food preferences and introduce new foods gradually. Allow parents to bring in substitute food items when they don't think their child will eat what is planned.

◆ **Establish a daily routine that you can share with parents** so that they can prepare the child. Knowing the routines is comforting to the child.

◆ **Help parents understand the calendar.** Make a special effort to ensure parents understand events on the calendar (especially when school might be closed).

WHERE TO FIND MORE INFORMATION

RESOURCES FOR CHILDREN

Books

Anno, Mitsumasa. (1981). *Anno's Journey*. New York, NY: Philomel Books. This wordless picture book follows a character through a number of scenes depicting Northern Europe. The pictures are filled with details and a child doesn't need to know English to enjoy it.

Avery, Charles E. (1992). *Everybody Has Feelings*. Seattle, WA: Open Hand Publishing Inc. A book of photographs of children from many cultures exploring a wide range of human emotions. Limited text in both English and Spanish.

Day, Alexandra. (1993). *Carl Goes to Day Care*. New York, NY: Farrar, Straus & Giroux, Inc. Alexandra Day's illustrations are filled with humor as Carl goes to the day care center and delights the children with his antics. A wordless book.

Fassler, David and Danforth, Kimberly. (1992). *Coming to America: The Kid's Book About Immigration*. Burlington, VT: Waterfront Books. *Coming to America* can help refugee children discuss their personal experiences, of leaving their country and coming to a new one.

Martin, Jr., Bill. (1983). Illustrated by Eric Carle. *Brown Bear, Brown Bear, What Do You See?* New York, NY: Henry Holt. The simple text in this almost wordless book is repeated again and again. Children love to say the refrain together as the story is read to them. This classic is loved by young children.

Martin, Jr., Bill. (1983). Illustrated by Eric Carle. *Polar Bear, Polar Bear, What Do You Hear?* New York, NY: Henry Holt. This book explores the sounds that animals make. Children love to join in on the refrain on each page. Just as delightful as *Brown Bear, Brown Bear, What do You See?*.

Raffi and Pike, Debi. (1985). Illustrated by Lillian Hoban. *Like Me and You*. New York, NY: Crown Publishers, Inc. Raffi celebrates children around the world, as they send letters from one country to another, singing, reading and learning each other's names.

Robinson, Marc. (1993). Illustrated by Steve Jenkins. *Cock-A-Doodle-Doo!: What Does It Sound Like to You?* New York, NY: Stewart, Tabori & Chang. This fun-filled book is filled with animal sounds in many languages. A unique look at language diversity for young children.

Shaw, Charles. (1988). *It Looked Like Spilt Milk*. New York, NY: HarperCollins. Sometimes it looked like spilt milk, but it wasn't spilt milk. Sometimes it looked like a bird, but it wasn't a bird. What was it? A stimulating wordless book which encourages conversation.

RESOURCES FOR ADULTS

Books

Derman-Sparks, Lousie. (1989). *Anti-Bias Curriculum: Tools for Empowering Young Children*. Washington, DC: National Association for the Education of Young Children. The first and most complete discussion of issues concerning bias, this book should be the center point of every professional library addressing racism, prejudice and diversity in our society.

Gonzales-Mena, Jante. (1993). *Multicultural Issues in Child Care*. Mountain View, CA: Mayfield Publishers. An especially good resource for people working with infants and toddlers.

Neugebauer, Bonnie, (Ed.). (1992). *Alike and Different: Exploring Our Humanity With Young Children*. Washington, D.C.: National Association for the Education of Young Children. This excellent resource is a collection of chapters on all types of differences including culture, race and capabilities. It is full of good advice and practical ideas and has an extensive resource section.

Ramsey, Patricia G. *(1987)*. *Teaching and Learning in a Diverse World: Multicultural Education for Young Children*. New York: Teachers College Press.

Diversity, Independence and Individuality; Diversity: Contrasting Perspectives; Diversity and Communication; Diversity and Conflict Management. Magna Systems, 101 N. Virginia Street, Suite 105, Crystal Lake, IL 60014. 800-203-7060. These four videos, written by the highly regarded Janet Gonzales-Mena, are part of the Early Childhood Training Series: Diversity. $89.95 for each title in the series, $295 for the series.

Essential Connections: Ten Keys to Culturally Sensitive Child Care. California Department of Education, Bureau of Publications, Sales Unit, P.O. Box 271, Sacramento, CA. 95812-0271. This video, which includes interviews with Louise Derman-Sparks, Yolanda Torres and Carol Phillips, shows the anxiety of families from different cultures as they enroll their children in child care. With a focus on infant and toddler care, the viewer is exposed to strategies to make the family feel comfortable. The video was produced by the Far West Laboratory in collaboration with California Department of Education. 36 min. $65.

Organizations & Hot Lines

American Indian Resource Center, 6518 Miles Avenue, Huntington Park, CA 90255. 323-583-1461.

Cross Cultural Communication Centre (CCCC), 965 Bloor Street W., Toronto, Ontario, Canada M6H 1L7.

ERIC Clearinghouse on Elementary and Early Childhood Education, University of Illinois, 51 Gerty Dr., Champaign, IL 61820. 800-583-4135. www.ericec.org.

Information Center on Children's Cultures, United States Committee for UNICEF, 333 E. 38th Street, New York, NY 10016. 212-686-5522. www.unicefusa.org.

National Clearinghouse for English Language Acquisitions, 2121 K Street NW, Suite 260, Washington, DC 20037. 800-321-6223. www.ncela.gwu.edu.

National Latino Children's Institute, Corporate Fund for Children, 1325 N. Flores Street, Suite 114, San Antonio, TX 78212. 210-228-9997. www.nlci.org.

Teachers of English to Speakers of Other Languages, Inc. (TESOL), 700 South Washington Street, Suite 200, Alexandria, VA 22314. 703-518-2527. www.tesol.org.

Community Education Development Center, 55 Chapel Street, Newton, MA 02458-1060. 617-969-7100. www.edc.org.

CHAPTER **20**

POVERTY & UNEMPLOYMENT

HERE'S AN EXAMPLE

Beth had a rough year. She discovered her husband was a substance abuser, which explained why there never seemed to be enough money to pay the rent and buy food for her four year old son, Jamie and three year old daughter, Sarah. After their divorce, Beth applied for public assistance to help her with child care and other living expenses while she went to school to become a bookkeeper. She also worked part-time at a local convenience store in the evenings while a neighbor watched the children. Jamie and Sarah were small for their age and somewhat listless, and both exhibited extreme separation problems in the morning. They were also often unkempt and hungry. When the staff made a home visit, they came away feeling that this was a mother who loved her children but who was simply at the "end of her rope," trying desperately to get some stability in her life.

After a few months at the center, the children began to thrive. They clearly benefited from the good nutrition at the center, and from the relationships they formed with their teachers and peers. The teachers made friendly contact with Beth, reporting the many positive experiences her children were having and noting their progress. Beth later told them that the support she had from the child care teachers was the boost she needed to regain her self-esteem and climb out of her depression.

A year later she landed a bookkeeping job but lost the public assistance that supported her child care expenses. She noted with a shake of her head that now that she had to pay for child care, she was only a few dollars ahead of where she had been. However, there was a huge improvement in her state of mind and in the well-being of the children. They were getting by. She still got their clothing at a local thrift shop, but she knew that things would get better in a few years once the children were in school. She felt confident that she could handle things and appreciated the ongoing friendship and support of the staff at the child care center.

LET'S LOOK AT THE ISSUE

Marian Wright Edelman, in her introduction to the book, *Wasting America's Future* (see the resource section at the end of this chapter), states: "Poverty steals children's potential and in doing so steals from all of us."

People are poor for many different reasons—bad luck, substance abuse, industry layoffs, teen pregnancy, divorce, etc. Surely, poverty is one of the most complex issues discussed in this book. At best, it is possible only to look at the effects of poverty. The child care provider certainly cannot be expected to solve a family's financial crisis, but good child care can be one factor that helps a family climb out of poverty.

It's important to distinguish between poverty and neglect. Both may lead to a child not having the basic necessities of life, such as food, clothing, shelter and medical care. However, the interventions and supports needed are different for each. Neglect is a form of child abuse (see chapter 10) that you are required to report to your local child abuse agency. Neglect indicates an "emotional absence" of the caregiver and is extremely devastating to a child's development. Although many neglected children are from poverty-stricken families, not all poor children are neglected. Many are loved and emotionally valued by their families. A family living in poverty often receives social supports such as job training, food and housing assistance. While poverty and neglect may exist together, this is not always the case.

Poverty is often a "blame the victim" situation in our society, but one thing is certain—children don't deserve the circumstances of poverty that often deprive them of the opportunities they need to overcome life's hardships.

Increased stress in the family. The very circumstance of poverty in a child's life almost always translates to an environment of high stress in the family. High stress may lead to increased domestic violence, child abuse, neglect or substance abuse.

Self-esteem and poverty. As children get older and compare their circumstances to those of peers, they may feel that they are not as good as others. This may be reinforced if their peers look down on them unfairly.

Lag in social and academic areas. Poverty can exclude children from many enriching social and educational experiences. The child may begin to lag in social and academic skills.

Divorce or separation may often plunge a family into poverty. Children will need your help in coming to terms with their feelings of abandonment and worthlessness, especially when the custodial parent is feeling depressed and therefore not as emotionally available to the child.

Resignation. Children may feel less worthy than their peers. They may learn to think of themselves and their families as losers. Frustration turns into hopeless resignation, and they stop trying.

WHEN TO SEEK HELP

◆ **The child lacks basic necessities**—food, clothing, shelter.

◆ **The child is tired**, falls asleep during the day.

◆ **The child may be insecure**, fearful, possessive, clinging to a coat or any small possessions.

◆ **The child is withdrawn and depressed**. Because of enormous stress, the parent may be emotionally unavailable to the child. The child may become withdrawn and depressed.

WHO CAN HELP

◆ Local social service agency
◆ Job training programs

Poverty & Unemployment

HOW TO RESPOND WITH THE STAFF

◆ **Working poor**. Child care workers may be themselves part of the working poor. The issue of poverty may be painfully close to home for many teachers. The National Association for the Education of Young Children (NAEYC) has information that can help programs examine ways to improve salaries and benefits. Work as a collaborative group with the administration to address this issue.

◆ **Local resources**. Make sure staff members are aware of local resources for assistance with food, clothing and shelter in case parents need this information.

HOW TO RESPOND WITH THE CHILD

◆ **Address hunger first**. Head Start programs and other programs specifically designed to serve poor and homeless children include good nutrition. If you have just a few poor children in your program and do not normally offer breakfast or other meals, see if you can arrange to do so. Perhaps these children can go to another room to eat so they will not be embarrassed. Hunger impacts every other aspect of a child's experience. Good nutrition must be the starting point.

◆ **Provide a cubby or special place**. Children need a place of their own in the classroom—their own cubby or other place for their possessions.

◆ **Create a safe, stable environment**. Because children from poor families often live in unstable, even chaotic environments, take extra steps to make your environment feel stable, safe and predictable for the child.

◆ **Understand possessiveness**. A child may be very possessive about toys and materials, and sharing may be more difficult. This requires sensitive intervention on your part. Don't always require a child to share. Sometimes the need to feel "ownership" of a toy, even for a little while, outweighs the social value of learning to share.

HOW TO RESPOND WITH THE OTHER CHILDREN

◆ **Encourage children to include everyone**. Try to prevent children from being excluded from play with others because they don't have a certain toy or are dressed differently.

◆ **Discourage showing off**. Eliminate the "bring and brag" type of show-and-tell from the daily routine.

◆ **Build children's talents**. Many skills don't depend on material possessions. Offer many opportunities to use art materials, for instance.

◆ **Offer your support**. The support and encouragement of one adult can make a difference. When a child feels respected by a beloved teacher, he will be more secure and optimistic.

HOW TO RESPOND WITH THE PARENTS

◆ **Provide information on community support**. Help put parents in contact with community agencies and services that offer various forms of support. Find out about services that exist in your community, what they offer, who can take advantage of them and what people must do to participate.

◆ **Respect parents**. Parents need to feel your respect, empathy and support before they can fully benefit from the services of your program. Your friendship, pleasant greetings and sharing of good news about their child can be very encouraging to them. Knowing their children are well cared for, they can put their energy into job training or other activities that will help them pull things together for the family. There will be one less worry, one thing that is going right in their lives. They can build on that.

WHERE TO FIND MORE INFORMATION

RESOURCES FOR CHILDREN

Books

Ackerman, Karen. (1994). Illustrated by Catherine Stock. *By the Dawn's Early Light*. New York, NY: Atheneum Macmillan Publishing Company. Just about dawn Rachel's mom comes home from working the midnight shift. Rachel and Josh get up and have a quiet time with their mom to talk about school and work.

Altman, Linda Jacobs. (1993). Illustrated by Enrique O. Sanchez. *Amelia's Road*. New York, NY: Lee & Low Books Inc. An inspiring story of a young girl from a migrant family who overcomes the hardship of their frequent moves by creating a special place for herself.

Covault, Ruth M. (1994). Illustrated by Francisco Mora. *Pablo and Pimienta*. Flagstaff, AZ: Northland Publishing. Pablo is riding in the back of his papa's old truck on the way to melon fields in Arizona with his father and uncle. Suddenly he is bounced out and the truck keeps on going. Pablo has an adventure he will never forget.

Dobrin, Arnold. (1973). *Josephine's 'Magination: A Tale of Haiti*. New York, NY: Scholastic. Josephine, a Haitian child heeds the advice of the peddler who told her to use her 'magination. She makes the brooms into dolls and has greater success in the market place.

Kalifon, Mary. (1995). *Mom Doesn't Work There Anymore*. Los Angeles, CA: Cedars-Sinai Medical Center. When a single mother loses her job, things can get a little scary for her and her children. This book helps them understand and cope. Includes a parent guide.

Kalifon, Mary. (1995). *My Dad Lost His Job*. Los Angeles, CA: Cedars-Sinai Medical Center. The loss of a dad's job changes a family's life. This book helps both parents and children sail through the tough times with love and courage.

Mills, Lauren. (1991). *The Rag Coat.* Boston, MA: Little, Brown and Company. This story is set in the Appalachian region. Minna wears her new coat made of clothing scraps to school, where the other children laugh at her until she tells them the stories behind the scraps.

Shea, Pegi Deitz. (1995). Illustrated by Riggio. *The Whispering Cloth*. Honesdale, PA: Boyds Mills Press. A young girl in a Thai refugee camp finds the story within herself to create her own pa'ndau, which is a tapestry similar to American quilting.

Sonneborn, Ruth A. (1970). Illustrated by Emily A. McCully. *Friday Night Is Papa Night*. New York, NY: Puffin Books. Pedro's dad works two jobs far away from home, so he only comes home on Friday night.

Thomas, Jane Resh. (1994). Illustrated by Michael Dooling. *Lights on the River*. New York, NY: Hyperion Books for Children. Teresa's memory of her grandmother in Mexico helps her get through the hard life of a migrant worker.

RESOURCES FOR ADULTS

Books

McLoyd, Vonnie, C. and Flanagan, Constance A. (Eds.). (1990). *Economic Stress: Effects of Family Life and Child Development*. San Francisco: Jossey-Bass, Inc. The book describes how poverty affects children's development and thinking and its impact on society.

Sherman, Arloc. (1994). *Wasting America's Future: The Children's Defense Fund on the Costs of Child Poverty*. Boston: Beacon Press. Do you need statistics and demographics to help you make your point? Do you need actual examples of how poverty affects lives? Do you need comparisons of different groups of society and analysis of the

Poverty & Unemployment

relationships between poverty, stress, violence and other negative factors? This book gives you all this and more in compelling, readable fashion.

Sunley, Robert and Sheek, G. W. (1986). *Serving the Unemployed and Their Families*. Milwaukee, WI: Families International Incorporated. The book explains how to increase services to the unemployed through providing information on model programs, research and survey findings. To order contact Families International, Inc. 11700 W. Lake Drive, Milwaukee, WI 53224. 414-359-1040. www.alliance1.org.

Booklet

Nuta, Virginia R. *Stress and the Single Parent*. National Committee to Prevent Child Abuse, Fulfillment Center, 200 State Road, South Deerfield, MA 01373-0200. 800-835-2671. www.preventchildabuse.org. This booklet describes the isolation and economic hardship of single parenthood and has practical suggestions for improving one's situation.

Organizations & Hot Lines

Children's Defense Fund, 25 E Street NW, Washington, DC 20001. 202-628-8787. www.childrensdefense.org. This organization is an excellent resource when you need information, statistics and support about issues of child poverty. They have excellent publications on a wide range of topics and the most current information. They also publish a newsletter, *CDF Reports*, with monthly messages and inspiration from Marian Wright Edelman and updates on current issues.

Center for Women Policy Studies, 1211 Connecticut Avenue NW, Suite 312, Washington, DC 20036. 202-872-1770. www.centerwomenpolicy.org. The Center is a policy research and advocacy institution which examines the connections among women's educational opportunities, employment options, economic status, and work and family roles through a series of programs. For more information concerning the specific programs contact the Center.

Food Research and Action Center, 1875 Connecticut Avenue, NW, Suite 540, Washington, DC 20009. 202-986-2200. www.frac.org. The Center, a nonprofit organization, sponsors the Campaign to End Childhood Hunger, and provides information and advocacy tools to groups across the country. Call the Center to locate an affiliate program in your area.

National Center for Children in Poverty, 154 Haven Avenue, New York, NY 10032. 212-304-7100. www.nccp.org. Located at the School of Public Health, Columbia University this organization exists to enhance the health and development of children under six living in poverty. The Center conducts interdisciplinary analyses and disseminates information. In addition to publishing a newsletter, the Center also has a catalog of publications and monographs.

CHAPTER 21

HOMELESSNESS

HERE'S AN EXAMPLE

Marguerite was very surprised to find herself classified as "homeless" when she landed in a shelter for battered women with her three children, aged 18 months, three and six. She had always thought homeless people were mentally ill or substance abusers. Through her own experiences, she found out that people are homeless for may reasons. Abused by her spouse, afraid, and with nowhere to go in her small community, she fled to a large city. She could not afford the deposit on an apartment and had no job. The shelter that took her in offered child care while she looked for a job. The shelter helped her apply for AFDC and got her into transitional housing while she attended school to get job training. She says she feels stressed out and overwhelmed much of the time. She also feels annoyed by the stigma she feels from being homeless, that others look down on her. She has had quite a hard time with her children. Much to her amazement, they say they miss their dad! The older one especially misses his toys, friends and other relatives and is often beligerent and hard to handle. The baby seems okay, but somewhat listless. The three year old is very quiet and withdrawn but is starting to play with other children at the child care center run by the shelter.

Homelessness

Homelessness is a growing problem all over the United States. People are homeless for many reasons. It may be a temporary situation, as in the example described above, as women escape dangerous situations of domestic violence and try to get their feet on the ground, or relocate to other areas and start all over again. Or wage earners lose their jobs and get evicted because of the inability to pay rent. Some homeless people are college students who run out of funds. And yes, there are those who have emotional problems, mental illnesses and problems with addictions.

The article in *Young Children* cited in the resource section at the end of this chapter describes the following common characteristics associated with parents in homeless families (a large percentage of them single mothers). Keep in mind that these are generalizations and by no means indicate that all homeless parents have these characteristics.

Drug and alcohol abuse. Maternal drug and alcohol abuse and psychiatric problems much greater than are found among mothers living in public or private subsidized housing.

A history of abuse as children, and battering as adults.

Fragmented support networks. Homeless parents may have few, if any, long term support networks.

No health care. A greater likelihood of having neither health insurance coverage nor preventive health care.

Homeless parents desperately need and want respect. They need a lift, a break; they need support, humor and friendship because they are looked down upon, even by some of the very people who help them. These parents and especially their children, are often innocent victims of life's circumstances. Many may be escaping abusive situations and are desperately trying to make positive improvements in their lives. Not all homeless people are substance abusers or mentally ill. Those who have been affected by these problems may be trying hard to make changes.

Do not confuse the deprivation they experience as a family with the issue of child neglect, a form of child abuse. Both situations require intervention.

Many parents are afraid that their children will be taken away from them, so it may be difficult to develop warm, trusting relationships with them.

Homelessness

In addition to stable housing arrangements, **families need help finding permanent places** for their children in early childhood programs and schools. They need nutrition assistance, health care assistance, transportation assistance, job training and parenting and counseling sessions. This is not a one-dimensional problem. The growing problem of homelessness requires a multifaceted societal response.

The child care program can be an enormous positive influence in the life of the family. The child may have his first opportunity to play, paint, dig, have friends and feel safe. The parent may feel supported for the first time and, consequently, feel optimistic about the future. With children well cared for, parents can look for work and take advantage of job training, counseling and other services to get their lives on track. Your friendship and respect for the parent and for the child can have a subtle yet great impact.

INSIGHTS FROM CHILD DEVELOPMENT

The child may suffer extreme separation anxiety.

Changes in a child's life add stress. The child has gone through a lot of changes lately, none of which he had any control over. This may make the child very insecure and frightened.

The child may have had traumatic experiences. The child may have been a witness to violence or have had other traumatic experiences. Try to find out as much as you can about what the child has been through so you can respond sensitively and interpret behaviors.

The child may be aggressive. A child who has witnessed domestic violence may identify with the aggressor and be aggressive himself. The parent is likely to be very stressed, tired, and perhaps finding it hard to focus on the child.

The child may have had few previous opportunities to play. The child comes from a frightening, serious world where there is little opportunity for humor or play.

The child may have special needs. Because of very difficult life circumstances, homeless children have a higher percentage of special needs than children in the general population. Because they have lacked a nurturing, stimulating environment, they may be suffering developmental delays and language delays.

The child may have difficulty sharing. Homeless children can lack a sense of permanency, fearing that everyone and everything in their lives will disappear. Hoarding toys and the inability to share are common behavioral responses.

General characteristics of homeless children. McCormick and Holden's article in *Young Children* (see the resource section at the end of the chapter) describes the following characteristics of the general population of homeless children as compared to children who are not homeless, citing various research studies.

- ◆ Higher levels of problem behaviors
- ◆ One or more developmental delays serious enough to warrant referral
- ◆ Severe depression, anxiety and learning difficulties
- ◆ Sleep problems and extreme resistance to napping
- ◆ Shyness and withdrawal
- ◆ More aggression
- ◆ Severe separation problems
- ◆ Severe anxiety interfering with the ability to participate in routine activities
- ◆ Poor quality (superficial) relationships
- ◆ Short attention span
- ◆ Signs of emotional disturbance, including severe tantrums, dangerously aggressive and destructive behavior, extreme withdrawal, elective muteness, violent mood swings, and oppositional and manipulative behavior
- ◆ Gross motor developmental delays
- ◆ Speech and language delays
- ◆ Cognitive developmental delays

These characteristics are not surprising considering what life has been like for many homeless children. All of the above sounds pretty grim, to be sure. Keep in mind though that this doesn't mean that all homeless children embody all of the above characteristics. One thing, however, is certain. The children from homeless families and their parents have suffered extreme amounts of stress and trauma. Life has been very, very hard for them.

Also remember that children are quite resilient and with consistent and sensitive help, they can make amazing improvements. You are the starting point.

WHEN TO SEEK HELP

Most of the time, programs know when homeless children are enrolled. So, the warning signs you look for are those that indicate that the child has suffered some severe psychological or developmental delays from his life circumstances. Be conscious of the characteristics described above and sensitive to any behaviors that indicate that the child needs more help or more specific intervention.

WHO CAN HELP

- ◆ Community agencies that provide services for homeless families
- ◆ Mental health and family service centers
- ◆ Food, clothing and household support services

HOW TO RESPOND

HOW TO RESPOND WITH THE CHILD

◆ **Establish trust**. Because this is a family in transition, you may only have the child for a few weeks. This is not much time to establish trust and build a relationship. Nevertheless, try hard to establish trust on the part of the child. Be there for the child. Spend as much one-on-one time with the child as is possible.

◆ **Take an instant picture of the parent** to help ease separation anxiety. The child can keep the picture with her all day. It might also help if the child can also keep some small thing that belongs to the parent.

◆ **Establish a consistent and stable routine.** Provide consistency and stability in the child care environment. A few full time, stable adult caregivers is better than a host of part time staff and volunteers. Use the same room all the time and keep the furniture in the same arrangement for an extended length of time. Maintain great consistency in your daily schedule. These things allow the child to predict the future and have a sense of safety and control.

◆ **Let the child make choices**. Give the child many opportunities to feel in control, to make choices, to decide what will happen. Free play time is important, when the child can decide where he will play, with what, with whom, and for how long. Avoid making all the decisions for the child.

◆ **Help the child feel valued and special**. Homeless children need reinforcement of their self-esteem. They may be feeling helpless, worthless, confused or insecure. You have an opportunity to make them feel valued and special. Greet them warmly, talk with them, play with them, ask for their help, and show pleasure in their ideas and positive interactions.

◆ **Give the child opportunities to express himself**. Give the child many opportunities to express himself with beautiful, open-ended, creative art materials.

◆ **Offer many opportunities to play**. Homeless children have a special need for play. They may not have any other opportunities to play in their lives. Provide rich opportunities for dramatic play and block play; tactile play with water, sand, clay and playdough; play with toys and manipulatives; riding toys and active outdoor play.

◆ **Help with socialization skills**. Homeless children often need extra help with socialization skills. Because of the chaos in their lives they often have not had the experience of forming friendships with peers.

◆ **Help with problem solving skills**. Some children may need special help solving problems in ways that do not involve physical aggresion.

◆ **Rethink birthdays and celebrations**. Rethink what you do about birthdays and other celebrations if there are homeless children in your group. Asking parents to bring in baked goods presents a real hardship. And if these are the only families you don't ask, the children may be embarrassed or made to feel different.

◆ **Prepare the child to move on to another program**. Because homeless children are still in transition they are likely to be with you only a short time. When the family establishes permanent housing and the child is being transferred to another early childhood program, make an effort to prepare the child for the move and even talk to the next teacher. It's especially helpful if you can maintain a friendship with the child and the family.

WHERE TO FIND MORE INFORMATION

RESOURCES FOR CHILDREN

Books

Bunting, Eve. (1991). Illustrated by Ronald Himler. *Fly Away Home*. New York, NY: Clarion Books. A little boy and his father are homeless. They live in an airport, moving from terminal to terminal, trying not to be noticed. A very interesting story of homelessness as told by the little boy.

Chalofsky, Margie et. al. (1992). Illustrated by Ingrid Klass. *Changing Places: A Kid's View of Shelter Living*. Beltsville, MD: Gryphon House. This book helps children who are homeless validate the wide range of emotions they might be feeling. It helps children to see the shelter as a safe place, a place to help them.

Di-Salvo-Ryan, Dyanne. (1991). *Uncle Willie and the Soup Kitchen*. New York, NY: William Morrow Jr. Books. Uncle Willie understands the importance of showing respect to all people, and giving personal resources to your community.

Goble, Paul. (1993). *The Lost Children*. New York, NY: Bradbury Press. This Blackfoot Indian story, told by the great storyteller, Paul Goble, is a timeless reminder about the dangers of neglecting children.

Guthrie, Donna. (1988). Illustrated by Dennis Hockerman. *A Rose for Abby*. Nashville, TN: Abingdon Press. After Abby becomes aware that there are people without homes she tries to help people who are homeless.

Wild, Margaret. (1992). Illustrated by Gregory Rogers. *Space Travellers*. New York, NY: Scholastic Inc. A very sensitive portrayal of what it is like for a little boy and his mother to be homeless in the city.

RESOURCES FOR ADULTS

Books

De Woody, Madelyn. (1992). *Confronting Homelessness Among American Families: Federal Programs and Strategies*. Washington, DC: Child Welfare League of America. Aimed at child welfare and social service agencies that administer programs for the homeless. This resource provides specific information about a wide variety of services for children and families. $12.95.

Homelessness: The Impact on Child Welfare in the '90s : Recommendations from a CWLA Colloquium. (1991). Washington, DC: Child Welfare League of America. This report summarizes the Child Welfare League of America Colloquim held on the importance of linking child welfare with a housing service in order to address the growing problem of housing families with young children and youths. A broad range of service options, model programs, planning and coordination designs, legislative initiatives and advocacy strategies are included. $6.95.

Goins, Brad and Cesarone, Bernard. *Homeless Children: Meeting the Educational Challenges.* ERIC Digest. Urbana IL: University of Illinois. This volume of the *ERIC Digest* may be obtained from the ERIC Clearinghouse on Elementary and Early Childhood, University of Illinois, 51 Gerty Drive, Champaign, IL 61820-7469. 800-583-4135. www.ericeece.org.

Article

McCormick, Linda and Holden, Rita. (1992). "Homeless children: A special challenge." *Young Children*. 47(6), 61-67.

Videos

A Place Called Home. Child Welfare League of America, 440 First Street, NW, Suite 310, Washington, DC 20001-2085. 202-638-2952. www.cwla.org. This award-winning documentary records the efforts of one concerned group of citizens who reached out to a group of homeless children in their community. Working in tandem, a social worker and a local theater director produced plays with shelter residents, who held performances all over the city. An intimate portrait of impoverished children and their parents as they find new sources of hope and self esteem. The accompanying discussion guide is co-written by CWLA staff members.

Rewind: It Could Have Been Me. National Coalition for the Homeless, 1012 14th Street, NW, Suite 600, Washington DC 20005-3471. 202-737-6444. www.nationalhomeless.org. The animated video portrays the story of a homeless mother. Music by Holly Near. 13 min. $14.

Organizations & Hot Lines

Child Welfare League of America, 440 First Street, NW, Suite 310, Washington, DC 20001-2085. 202-638-2952. www.cwla.org. The Child Welfare League of America (CWLA) publishes an extensive list of books and monographs on a wide variety of topics. Ask for their catalog.

Children's Defense Fund, 25 E Street NW, Washington, DC 20001. 202-628-8787. www.childrensdefense.org. This nonprofit organization (funded by foundations, corporate grants and individual donations) exists to provide a lobby—a voice for poor, minority and disabled children. They have a wide variety of helpful publications and maintain current statistics and media support.

Habitat for Humanity International, 121 Habitat Street, Americus, GA 31709-3498. 229-924-6935. www.habitat.org. This nonprofit organization brings community members together to build, renovate and sell homes to families and individuals in need.

National Alliance to End Homelessness, Inc., 1518 K Street NW, Suite 206, Washington, DC 20005. 202-638-1526. www.naeh.org. The Alliance works with nonprofit organizations, public officials, business leaders, homeless and formerly homeless people to implement the solutions to homelessness—affordable housing, adequate incomes and services. The Alliance has published research on the relationship between foster care and homelessness and provides information on Congressional developments, funding opportunities, and resources through its monthly newsletter, *Alliance*.

National Coalition for the Homeless, 1012 14th Street, NW, Suite 600, Washington, DC 20005-3471. 202-737-6444. www.nationalhomeless.org. The National Coalition for the Homeless (NCH) is a federation of individuals and organizations—federal, state and local—committed to ending homelessness. NCH staff publishes a newsletter and provides technical assistance and support to state and local groups. Call the national office to obtain a publications list and to locate a coalition for the homeless in your state.

National Coalition for Homeless Veterans, 333½ Pennsylvania Avenue SE, Washington DC 20003-1148. 800-VET-HELP. www.nchv.org. The National Coalition for Homeless Veterans (NCHV) is operated exclusively as a charitable and educational organization to service the needs of homeless veterans, veterans on the verge of becoming homeless and organizations and agencies who assist these veterans. NCHV services and resources include maintaining the nation's clearinghouse for information on the needs of veterans and publishing a bi-monthly newsletter featuring updates of research, funding opportunities, public and private initiatives and program development.

3
PART

CRISIS AND CURRICULUM

CHAPTER 22

PROGRAM DESIGN

CREATE A STABLE ROUTINE

To help children feel safe in the classroom environment, try to create a stable routine. Children whose lives at home are unpredictable will find a stable routine to be reassuring.

Program Design

MAKE EVENTS PREDICTABLE

Think about the regular events in your daily schedule, such as arrival and greeting time, circle time, free play time, clean-up time, snack time, outside time, lunch time, rest time and closing and departure time. Do these things in the same order each day. If snack time always comes right after clean-up time, if going outside always comes right after circle time, the child begins to feel secure. "I can handle this," she thinks, "I know what's going to happen here." Other suggestions include:

◆ **Create a chart** where children can read together the regular routine of the day. Use photographs of children engaged in all the various aspects of the daily schedule. If you arrange these from left to right, you are also reinforcing a reading skill. Post this at the children's eye level.

 Welcome

 Circle Time

 Lunch Time

 Nap Time

◆ **Review the chart frequently** with children. It's a nice way to open a conversation with a new child in your program. "Come on over here. I'd like to show you what we do here each day."

◆ **Talk about modification.** If you've planned some modification in the routine on a particular day, such as a special visitor, go over to the chart and point to the place where the change will occur.

◆ **Review the chart each morning.** Describe for the children all the things that will happen within the normal routine—what play choices there will be, what will be served for snack.

CREATE RITUALS

Children like ritual—doing certain things in certain ways every day. Although some children might seem rigid in their need for ritual, remember that rituals give them something to hang onto and help them feel secure. These can be very simple things, such as saying the same greeting poem as soon as everyone is gathered for circle time, or singing a certain song together before you eat lunch, or having one book and one stuffed animal at rest time.

You may notice that some children create their own rituals. For instance, every morning a child might put her coat in her cubby, say hello to the pet guinea pig and draw a picture. Give the children power. Let them help you create the group's rituals. You could develop a special greeting together and decide what the signals will be for various routines of the day. You might ring a bell, sing a song or clap a pattern to indicate the start of a particular segment of your program. These are all subtle ways to give children power and a sense of control.

KEEP SPECIAL EVENTS TO A MINIMUM

Field trips, exciting visitors and other special events should probably be kept to a minimum when you have traumatized, insecure children. Even happy events like birthday parties should be kept low-key because they, too, can cause stress for some children.

Don't create events that are stressful by their very nature, like having children put on a show for parents, memorize lines or speak before a group of strangers. Parent functions are important but should be informal and fun.

Invite parents to come to the program with their child. Let each child show his parents around the room. Encourage parents to participate in their child's favorite activities, such as easel painting, clay, dress-up play or block building.

TIPS FOR THE DAILY SCHEDULE

Greeting time

Greet each child warmly and make physical contact as soon as the child comes in. Touch the child with a pat on the back, a hand shake, a hug, an arm on the shoulder—whatever the child seems to prefer. This human contact tells the child that she is valued and acknowledged.

Some teachers find it helpful to begin the day with structured activities and allow more freedom as the morning progresses. Instead of having all the centers open, for instance, you might have just a few enticing, calm play choices set out on table tops for the child to select. Suggestions include warm playdough with interesting objects to press into it on one table, special manipulatives saved just for this time of day on a second table and drawing materials on a third table.

Have a brief group greeting ritual soon after all the children have arrived each morning. You might sing the same greeting song every time. Do one or more activities that mention each child's name, such as singing a song or having a pet puppet come out and greet each child. The puppet could also describe plans for the day.

A fun way to take attendance that builds a feeling of group cohesiveness is to fill a box with individual photographs and then take them out, one at a time. Ask, "Who is this?" Describe the child in the photo in complimentary ways: "Here is a girl with pretty black hair and blue eyes. Who could this be?" When a child identifies the photo, he hangs it on a "Who's Here Today?" chart. Also identify the children who are not present and express concern for them. "I hope Tara will get better soon." This builds a warm feeling of belonging as you indicate that each friend is important.

Morning group time can also set the tone for the day. Tell children what activities will be available that day, and anything else that will be happening.

Free play time

Knowing what is expected of them makes children feel comfortable and secure. They should know where they can play, what they can do with the materials and how to put things away again.

Some children will have a difficult time choosing where to settle down. You may notice that a few children prefer to watch others play at first. Give them the time to do this. Later, when they are used to the program, help them make a choice.

You may decide to limit the number of children who can play in one center or area at a time to avoid overcrowding the space. Do this with care and only if you feel it is really necessary. It can be extremely frustrating for a child when she's finally made a choice and then is not allowed to go there. This child may then need your help to choose an alternative play choice. A waiting list helps. Put the child's name, photo or symbol on a sign-up board so you can remember that she is waiting for a turn. Be sure to let the child know when there is a space.

Clean-up time

Clean-up time may be a new experience for some children who do not have a clean-up routine at home. In addition, many children resist any change in activities, especially if they are not ready to stop what they are doing. Have something fun to do next to increase motivation. Food works best! "As soon as our room is cleaned up, we can have our snack."

Give children a two or three minute warning before clean-up time begins so they can finish up what they are working on and feel prepared for the change. The block corner may need a little more time to clean up, so you can get them started earlier. (See the section on block play in chapter 23 for more specific clean-up strategies.)

Develop a sense of pride in the room. When everything is picked up, look around and admire the good job they did and how nice everything looks.

There is a real value in developing orderliness in your environment to counter chaos in children's lives. Having a labeled place for everything and special containers that are easy to find and use makes clean-up time go more smoothly.

Snack time

Food is very important to children under stress for several reasons. Aside from its nutritional value, food symbolizes nurturing. Some programs have developed a snack center where snack foods are put during free play time and where children can help themselves. This works fine for many children. However, some children who are very insecure or very hungry, or who have problems with sharing or hoarding, may tend to grab or guard their food. In that case, a more formal snack time may be best. The main thing is to have plenty of food and to keep things relaxed.

Going outside

Parents often marvel at how teachers can get hats, coats and boots on a whole group of children in ten minutes. It seems like magic! One approach is to encourage each child to do it by himself. Also, teach children to ask each other for help. This allows a child with skills to feel competent and valued. Cut down on passive waiting time as much as possible. Try to have one adult go outside with the children who are ready first so they do not have to wait. Otherwise, have something for the waiting children to do like looking at a collection of greeting cards or laminated pictures.

Lunch time

Sitting down at the lunch table and enjoying a meal together may be another new activity for some children. Develop a lunch time ritual to help children feel secure. Whatever serving routine you choose, try to keep it the same every day. Although it may be more convenient to have the food dished out on plates before the children get to the table, this may cause the children to miss some important opportunities. A better option is to introduce the food, describe what is in each bowl and then pass it around. Let children help themselves and tell them how much they can take for their first helping. You can also tell children to put at least a little bit of everything on their plates.

It's very important for the adults to eat at the table with the children. Although you need not stress manners, you can be an important model of good manners for children. You can also be the social director, keeping pleasant conversation going and talking about what the children did that day or what will happen after rest time.

An important part of the lunch ritual is what happens when the children are finished eating. It is not advisable to make everyone stay at the table until the last person is finished eating. Too much waiting time invites restlessness and trouble. Develop a routine for what they should do—scrape and stack their plates, put their utensils in a special container, throw their napkins away.

Lunch to rest transition

This transition period, which should be a time for everyone to calm down, is often the most chaotic time of the day. During lunch, talk about rest time in a pleasant way. "Ah, soon we will all be able to stretch out on our cots with our blankets and hug our stuffed animals and rest. It will feel so good."

Make a ritual out of what is expected. Find the sequence of events that works for you and for the children. Some programs have one adult settle down for a calm story time, perhaps using a puppet that is very sleepy and keeps yawning, while the other adults clean up the lunch table. That teacher then calls one or two children at a time to use the bathroom, wash hands and brush teeth before settling down on their cots.

Rest time

Although some children like napping at school, others find it very difficult. It may just be a matter of temperament, but children who are experiencing trauma in their lives may be especially resistant to falling asleep. It takes trust to allow yourself to slip into a subconscious state in a room full of people! If you have a child who strongly resists napping, consider the individual and what is going on in her life.

Keep the atmosphere calm and comforting. Sing each child a lullaby, incorporating his name into the song while you rub his back, for example, "Hush little Patrick don't say a word..." This is the time to bring out special security toys brought from home.

If a child does not fall asleep after about 30 minutes, have a place where the child can get up and play quietly, ideally in another room. Quiet play choices such as reading books, coloring pictures or putting together rubber puzzles are good.

Closure

It's good to have a closing ritual before children go home. Schedule a late afternoon group meeting when all the children are still there. You can talk about what you did that day, what was the most fun, new accomplishments or what is planned for tomorrow—always emphasizing the positive. Again, mention each child's name, and perhaps sing a special song or hold hands in the circle. This is your final way of acknowledging and honoring each child in the group and building a sense of belonging before everyone goes home.

RETHINK CIRCLE TIME

Large group time, or circle time, is such a traditional aspect of the early childhood curriculum that sometimes people engage in it automatically without truly examining its values. It warrants a good look.

CHALLENGES OF CIRCLE TIME

The adult is less available

When the teacher is conducting circle time, she is not very accessible to individual children. She is intent on controlling the whole group and keeping everyone focused and engaged. Because each child is unique, it may be difficult to reach all the children at the same time. The more time you spend in circle time, the less time you have to spend with individual children.

Behavior problems emerge

Circle time is often the least successful time of day for troubled children who may have difficulty paying attention, sitting still and blending into the group. They may not want to feel like part of the group. Much of their behavior cries out, "Notice me!" Often emotionally needy children will get negative feedback from adults trying to get them to settle down during this part of the daily routine. Consider making circle time optional or not worrying if a child chooses not to sit down with the others as long as he is not disruptive and can still be supervised.

VALUE OF CIRCLE TIME

This is not to say that circle time has no value for children or that you should discontinue it. There are some major advantages to circle time.

A sense of belonging

A major value of circle time is to develop a sense of belonging or togetherness for the children. Circle time builds a sense of community for the children.

A neutral arena

You can bring up sensitive topics in a neutral, nonthreatening way using books, puppets, pictures or the flannel board. In this way, children learn that they are not alone in their experiences.

The joy of music

Music activities, which are important opportunities for self-expression, are often best taught and enjoyed in group time. Knowing the same songs makes children feel like they belong to a group. Don't be surprised if you hear the children singing these songs spontaneously while they play.

Shared pleasures of language and literature

During group time, you can share with children a beautiful folktale, poem or picture book. You can read out loud in a way that emphasizes the rhythmic flow of sounds or words.

Problem solving

This can also be a valuable time for group problem solving. The teacher can say, "We have a situation here that we need to talk about. I'd like some of your good ideas about what we should do." Be sure to use this time to congratulate each other when a problem is finally solved.

Should this be a circle time activity

For everything you plan to do in circle time, get in the habit of asking yourself, "Does this really need to be done with the large group? Might it be more effective with one child at a time or with an informal small group during free play time?" Often it is much more effective to read a book to two or three children snuggled together on your lap, for instance, or to have a puppet talk to an individual child.

THE IMPORTANCE OF FREE PLAY

MAKE THE MOST OF FREE PLAY TIME

The greatest learning takes place during free play time, when children choose or initiate the activity. That is when you will see children exhibiting concentrated attention. This is also a time when questions emerge and communication skills are practiced. More important for our purposes, you are able to settle down with a few children at that time, rather than being in charge of the whole group.

WHAT IS FREE PLAY

There has always been some confusion about the term free play. For some teachers, the term brings to mind a chaotic time, or free-for-all. They prefer terms like free choice or center time. Some people think that during free play time, the teacher sits back and does nothing while the kids just play. Actually, for free play time to work well, the teacher has to do quite a bit of planning and must always stay alert.

Plan your environment. Arrange furniture in the space you have available to its best advantage. Plan which materials will be available to the children and how to display these materials so they are easily accessible.

HOW DOES A TEACHER INDIVIDUALIZE DURING FREE PLAY

During free play time, the teacher is able to settle down with a small group of children, either facilitating a project such as an art or cooking activity, or observing children's play, noting how children interact with each other, what issues they work on in their play, how they use language to express themselves and which materials each child seems to enjoy most. At times, the teacher may join in the play but should always follow the children's lead.

During free play time, the teacher is available to talk to a particular child, read a book to one or two children or just play with a small group of children, making them feel valued and accepted.

In short, it is during free play time that the teacher can truly concentrate on what is happening with individual children and build relationships with them.

WHY IS FREE PLAY VALUABLE

The main premise behind free play time is that children almost always choose the very activity that is just right for them on that given day, provided the environment is rich and varied with many appropriate choices. So make it truly free choice time and don't try to rotate children from one area to another or force them to do everything. Allowing children to choose how they want to spend their time respects them as individuals and gives them a sense of power. Remember that children learn from everything in your environment. Trust them to select what they need!

Keep things interesting by including a variety of choices, including puzzles and manipulatives, dramatic play accessories, books and a wide assortment of materials for creative expression and sensory play. Vary what is available. However, it is also good to have consistency, making many of the same materials and favorite toys available from day to day. This makes children feel safe; they know what to expect and where to find favorite things.

Plan special projects such as cooking or art experiences to be a choice during free play time. Although many children may choose to participate in the specially planned project, allow those who do not to play somewhere else.

If all the children are new to the setting, or many of the children are easily distracted (one outcome of excessive stress in their lives), it is best to start with a limited number of play choices so you do not overwhelm them. Let them have a chance to get to know each new toy or material without feeling pressured to go on to the next thing.

MAKE THE MOST OF OUTDOOR TIME

Don't forget that outdoor time is a valuable portion of free play time when different types of play and learning can occur. Teachers often neglect outside time. They may fail to involve themselves in the play or maximize the possibilities for valuable, expressive play. More socio-dramatic play goes on outside than inside, especially for boys. Sand and water play opportunities outside mean less mess to clean up and give children chances for free expression. Active, gross motor play allows children to release energy and feel powerful. Plan in order to make the most of this valuable portion of your day.

RESOURCES

CURRICULUM PLANNING

Bredekamp, Sue. (Ed.). (1993). *Developmentally Appropriate Practice in Early Childhood Programs Serving Children From Birth Through Age 8*. (exp. ed.). Washington, DC: National Association for the Education of Young Children.

Jones, Elizabeth, and Nimmo, John. (1994). *Emergent Curriculum*. Washington, DC: National Association for the Education of Young Children.

CLASSROOM ENVIRONMENT

Greenman, Jim. (1988). *Caring Spaces, Learning Places: Creating Environments That Work.* Redmond, WA: Exchange Press.

Isbell, Rebecca. (1995). *The Complete Learning Center Book: A Guide to 36 Early Childhood Learning Centers.* Beltsville, MD: Gryphon House.

Slaby, Ronald et al. (1995). *Early Violence Prevention, Tools for Teachers of Young Children*. Washington, DC: National Association for the Education of Young Children. The chapters include designing the physical and programmatic environment and selecting materials.

GROUP SIZE AND STAFF RATIOS

Willer, Barbara. (1989). *Quality, Compensation, and Affordability: An Action Kit*. Washington, DC: National Association for the Education of Young Children.

OUTSIDE PLAY

Miller, Karen. (1989). *The Outside Play and Learning Book: Activities for Young Children*. Beltsville, MD: Gryphon House.

CHAPTER 23

CURRICULUM IDEAS & ACTIVITIES

DRAMATIC PLAY IDEAS AND ACTIVITIES

Dramatic play is an extremely important part of the early childhood curriculum and is often undervalued by both teachers and parents. Perhaps this is because children who have spent a morning engaged in dramatic play or pretend play have nothing to show for it — no concrete product. In our results-oriented adult thinking, that may be viewed as wasted time. To the contrary, the kind of play where the child takes on a role pretending to be somebody else, and interacts with other children from within that role, is very valuable.

VALUE OF DRAMATIC PLAY

Relief from emotional tension

When adults experience a traumatic event in their lives, like the death of a friend or relative or witnessing a terrible accident, they may cope with it through conversation, retelling the event over and over. Children, however, tend to replay the event in their dramatic play rather than talk about it.

I witnessed children in a Los Angeles inner-city child care program for homeless children screaming, running toward a small set of stairs, scrambling over the stairs, then running and hiding behind a partition. A teacher later told me that they were playing "run across the border," a game in which they re-enacted recent and frightening events in their lives.

If a child attends a funeral, she is likely to "play funeral" afterwards with friends, dolls and stuffed animals. Children who have experienced an earthquake like to "play earthquake," making the floor rumble and running for cover. If a child witnesses a car accident on the way to school, she might spend the morning in the block corner making toy cars collide with each other, or crash her tricycle into someone else's on the playground.

Children feel powerful

When children re-enact frightening experiences, they usually put themselves in a position of power. They often choose the role of mommy or daddy, the most powerful people in their lives. When they play earthquake they are the ones who make the earthquake start and stop. When they play hospital, they are the ones who give the shots. Children often feel powerless, especially when faced with a crisis. This leads to extreme frustration, fear and feelings of dependency and helplessness. In pretend play, all things are possible. A child can punish the aggressor she is afraid of in real life. Wishes can come true.

Empathy and social interaction

Dramatic play offers children valuable opportunities to see things from someone else's point of view. When they have make-believe experiences where they have put themselves in someone else's shoes, they become better able to do it in real life. This role-playing ability is especially useful in developing conflict resolution and problem solving skills.

When children interact with each other in their roles, they also learn to negotiate and work together. You may hear much discussion about who is going to do what and how.

Language development

Language development is fostered by dramatic play. Expressive language is augmented when children are motivated to make their wishes known to other children and speak from within their roles. It may be in the dramatic play area that you hear your first real expressive language from shy, withdrawn or frightened children. Receptive language is also enhanced as children pick up vocabulary from other children.

When children have had many experiences acting out the story line of their own dramas, they become better able to follow the sequence of events in a story book. They learn about sequential thinking—that events take place in a certain order.

Use of symbols

When children have many opportunities to create and use symbols of their own making, they gradually become better able to use other symbols, like letters, words and numbers. For younger children, or children who have not had much experience with pretend play, the props available have to be very concrete. The object has to look like a telephone for a two year old child to use it like a telephone. A four year old child, however, who is experienced in dramatic play, can use a block or even a hand gesture to represent a telephone. A doll is a symbol for a baby, or even the child herself. A paper plate might become a steering wheel. Slips of paper become money. A stick or extended finger becomes a gun. A piece of fabric tied on the back becomes a cape symbolizing supernatural power.

Sorting out fantasy and reality

It is obvious that dramatic play helps children sort out fantasy and reality when they announce, "I'm just pretending!" When they are sure that everyone present knows this, they feel safe to explore the possibilities of the role. You will also hear them change their voices into exaggerated inflections as a signal that they are playing a role.

THE ROLE OF THE ADULT

Provide time

The key element is to provide enough time for children to get deeply involved in their play. Children need time to decide what they are playing, who has what roles, what dress-up clothes and props they will need, and how to negotiate the action. If they are frustrated in their attempts to get started, they may be discouraged from engaging in dramatic play. Generally, play time of 45 minutes to one hour at a stretch is needed to foster good play.

Provide space and materials

◆ **Typical housekeeping equipment**. This should include a table and chairs, stove, refrigerator, sink, dishes, telephones, dolls, doll beds and standard home accessories.

◆ **Dress-up clothes** for both traditional and nontraditional male and female roles.

◆ **Relevant props**. Whenever possible, provide props relevant to the crisis the child is experiencing, such as a pretend veterinarian's office if the child's pet has died.

◆ **Other kinds of props**. Provide objects and materials that children can use in many different ways when engaging in dramatic play.

Suitcases
Containers of all types, such as shopping bags, boxes, barrels
Telephones in different styles, walkie-talkies, beepers
Large pieces of fabric, tablecloths, or blankets
Writing materials, such as paper, note pads, marker pens, tape
Art materials they can use to create other props they need.

Help children plan

◆ **Involve children** in gathering and creating props for their play. Later on, they will do it for themselves. "What would we need to make a hospital?" "What could we use?" "Do you think we could make that out of something?"

◆ **What do they want to play?** Find out which children want to play pretend. Ask them what roles or situations they think they will want to act out. Help them decide what things might happen (enriching the theme), what props they will need and where they can play so they won't disturb the other children. You don't want to take away their spontaneity, but you do want to encourage them to organize their thoughts so their dramatic play will be a better experience.

When the children are finished playing, talk to them informally about what they played. Can they describe the scene and the action? Were there any problems? Do they think they will play this again or add some variation the next time? This builds self-awareness and problem solving on the part of the children and also tells them that you are interested in play that comes from their own ideas.

Observe the action

Observe children's play and think about how each child is involved.

◆ **Favorite themes**. What kinds of pretend situations does the child seem to prefer?

◆ **Solitary play or not?** Does the child engage mostly in solitary play or is he able to include others?

◆ **Frequent playmates**. With whom does the child usually want to play?

◆ **Create props or not?** Does the child simply use the props in front of her, or is she creative in making her own props or improvising?

◆ **Discuss and negotiate?** Does the child discuss the play with others and negotiate what will go on and who will do what?

◆ **Leader or follower?** Is the child a leader or a follower in deciding play themes and determining the action?

Extend the play

◆ **Don't edit**. The play belongs to the children and they should be able to play out themes of interest to them, with the exception of sexual activity or exploitation. In that case, stop the play and involve the child in something else (see chapter 11 on child sexual abuse).

◆ **Ask the children what they are playing**. See if they can describe the situation to you. Ask them questions that might further define roles. "Is the bad person always bad?"

◆ **Ask questions that will extend play**. "How will someone know your store is open?" "Will your passengers need any money?"

◆ **Add a simple prop**. Sometimes adding a simple prop related to the play theme will make it more interesting for the children.

◆ **Take on a role**. On occasion, play with the children and use your role to support the other players. Do not take the dominant role. Be a passenger rather than the driver, a patient rather than the doctor. Follow the children's lead and don't dictate the action. You can even ask them how you should act. "Should I pretend to be afraid?"

◆ **Redirect violent play**. If you notice that the play is imitative of violent television shows, you could either take on a role yourself to redirect the play, or ask questions to give the play more depth. "Boy, it looks like that guy got hurt. Should we call 911?" (see chapter 17 on television violence).

◆ **Is the child fixated on a certain role?** A good time for you to take on a role is when a child becomes fixated on a particular role or plays the same thing in the same way over and over again. As a fellow player, you can help the child develop new roles and subplots.

What to do if the topic concerns you

◆ **Be careful not to overinterpret**. When you see troubling play themes such as beating up a doll or acting out some form of substance abuse, do not assume they signify a real problem. The child may, for instance, be re-enacting something seen on television or in the play of other children.

◆ **Ask questions or make a comment**. "It looks like the mommy is really mad at that baby."

◆ **Be careful with the child's feelings**. If you feel a need to stop the play or change its theme, tone down the intensity of your response so the child does not feel ashamed.

◆ **Observe over a period of time**. If the troubling play themes continue in spite of your efforts, talk to your supervisor about the problem. You may decide to seek the advice of other professionals such as a child psychologist or social worker.

◆ **Stop rough play**. If the play gets rough, you can ask the players, "Do you feel safe?" Then remind the players that everyone has a right to feel safe in the classroom.

◆ **Stop hurtful play**. If the play involves sexism or hurtful words or actions, make a statement that affirms everyone's rights and dignity. "In our classroom, play cannot hurt someone's feelings."

◆ **Superhero play**. For a discussion of superhero and war play, see chapter 15 on television violence.

MINIATURE PLAY

Another kind of pretend play that has great value is the kind that goes on in the block corner, the sandbox and the doll house. In this type of play, the child literally becomes a giant, able to create a miniature world and manipulate all the characters within it. Is it any wonder that this type of play has such appeal to children?

Value of miniature play

◆ **Power**. The child assumes a position of total power, which may relieve feelings of frustration that come from being powerless in an adult world.

◆ **Storytelling**. Miniature play gives children a way to tell their stories. Many children do not have the language skills to tell their stories any other way.

◆ **Use of symbols**. Miniature people and objects symbolize real people and objects for the child. In some cases, the child creates her own symbols to add to the other available objects. Blocks are used to build rooms or highways. Boxes become rooms. Pieces of fabric become tents or roofs.

◆ **Creativity and imagination**. The child learns that his ideas are valued. As he creates props and scenes, he uses materials in new ways. He learns to ask the question, "What could I use for...?"

◆ **Problem solving**. The child learns to experiment with ways to create a certain scene or effect.

◆ **Solitary or group play**. The child can play alone or with others. When playing as a group, children will practice language, negotiation, communication, and conflict resolution skills.

◆ **Character identification**. "This doll is me," the child thinks. Through this type of play, she can put herself in the middle of a situation in a nonthreatening way.

◆ **More control than dress-up play.** Miniature play gives the child even more control than the dress-up pretend play because the child can take on several roles simultaneously.

BLOCK PLAY

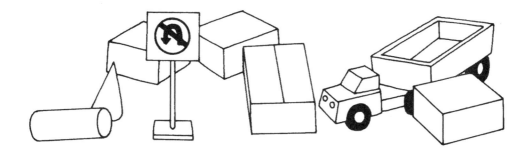

People usually think of play with wooden unit blocks as constructive play, and that certainly is one aspect of their use. Children use blocks to construct things, and in doing so gain all the benefits of that type of play—developing problem-solving skills, absorbing mathematical concepts, and learning concepts of space, size and location. However, depending on the accessories available, dramatic play is equally dominant. In fact, the block corner is where the indoor dramatic play of most boys takes place.

To enrich the dramatic play potentials in block play, provide a variety of accessories.

Purchased accessories

Early childhood suppliers offer a wide variety of high quality, durable accessories for block play that are sturdier than those you might find at garage sales and toy stores. Toys designed for use in the home are usually not durable enough to stand up to rough use by multiple children, they may also be stereotypical. Be careful what you make available.

Vehicle—cars, trucks, fire engines, police cars, ambulances

Accessories relevant to the children's culture. For example, Head Start programs serving Alaskan Natives have wooden float planes, snow mobiles, boats and caribou figures in their block corners.

Small people. It is possible to order small wooden or plastic people with different skin colors from school suppliers. Also, look for figures that represent both men and women in various work roles. Small, flexible doll house families also make good block corner accessories.

Small animals. Beautifully made and sturdy replicas of farm and wild animals are available. Farm accessories such as barns and fences are also available.

Dinosaurs. Although young children may not have a true understanding of dinosaurs and prehistoric times, toy dinosaurs are valuable because they symbolize scary things. By using them in their play, children can confront danger and conquer frightening situations.

Improvised accessories

There are many kinds of objects that can add to children's play in the block corner. Again, involve the children by asking them what they might need to create something and help them locate materials. Also bring abstract props into the block corner and ask the children, "How do you think you could use these?"

Shoe boxes and other small containers
Cardboard tubes
Flexible plastic tubing (such as aquarium tubing)
Coffee can lids
Canning rings
Aluminum foil
Large pieces of fabric
Plastic berry baskets
Flashlights
Yarn
Masking tape
Writing materials

Dress-ups

Adding a few items for the child to put on as he plays can enhance miniature play. Perhaps dressing up helps the child to concentrate and put himself into the role.

Worker hats including hard hats
Head phones
Beepers and pretend mobile phones

Tips for clean-up time

One reason the block corner can be an unpopular place for teachers and some children is the clean-up time hassle. Here are some tips:

◆ **Make sure the children have had enough time to play**. When children feel like they're right in the middle of a project, they will be more reluctant to dismantle it to put the blocks away. Free play periods should be at least 45 minutes long.

◆ **Keep track of who played there**. Children may spend most of the play period in the block corner and then suddenly change centers at the very end, just before clean-up time. They can be told to go back and help clean up.

◆ **Notice their constructions**. Children are often reluctant to tear down something that they've made. It may help to take a photo or make a drawing of the construction first. Sometimes it's enough if the teacher just takes the time to look at the construction and discuss it with the children.

◆ **Give block builders a few extra minutes for clean-up**. Start them a little earlier than the others and give them a few minutes of warning so they can put the finishing touches on their building project.

◆ **Consider leaving the construction up**. You probably can't do this all the time, but every now and then you might put a "Please leave this up" or "Please do not disturb" sign on the building so the child can go back to it during the next play period. Have the children put away the extra blocks they did not use.

◆ **Outline the building**. Make a masking tape line around the perimeter of the building so that the children can attempt to rebuild the structure in the same place during the next play period.

◆ **Use a puppet role model**. A sock or other type of puppet that can pick up things with its mouth or hands can be a useful helper and elicit eager cooperation from children. The puppet can pick up blocks, ask children to hand him other blocks and talk about how much fun clean-up time can be when everyone pitches in.

◆ **Create an assembly line**. This can turn drudgery into fun. Position a child who is good at organizing and recognizing shapes next to the shelf. Have the other children form a line from her to the block corner. They should be spaced an arm's length apart. Then have the children hand the blocks down the line. The child by the shelf stacks the blocks according to shape.

◆ **Divide and conquer**. Put one block of each shape in a can or bag. Have each child reach into a can and pick out a shape to put away. One child puts away all the triangles, another all the squares, etc.

◆ **Use a small wagon or big truck**. Children enjoy filling the back of a truck or wagon with blocks, then pushing it over to the shelf and unloading it.

◆ **Express admiration and appreciation** for a job well done! Comment on how nice the block corner looks with everything in order. Talk about the reason for this as well. "Now you will be able to easily find the things you need when you play there again."

When a child seems "stuck" in the block corner

Teachers may worry when a child spends all of his free play time in the block corner, but this is really not cause for concern. The learning potential of block play is so great that there is almost no place else a child could settle that would be more beneficial. Add variety to the experience by bringing in different props and creative materials like writing and art supplies for making signs and props. Bring books or measuring tools and scales to the block corner. Also remember that free play time is only one segment of the daily schedule, and children learn from everything that happens during the day.

Provide enough unit blocks

In my experience, early childhood programs usually do not have enough unit blocks available for children's play. They are an expensive, up-front purchase when setting up a program, and there are many other demands on the budget. However, without an adequate supply and variety of blocks, the value of the play will be diminished. Early childhood suppliers often recommend numbers of blocks for various ages. Also consult the books listed in the resources section at the end of this chapter for recommended numbers. It is worth an extra fundraiser or two to upgrade the block centers.

DOLL HOUSE PLAY

Doll houses are very useful to have in classrooms where children are experiencing trauma or crises in their lives. So many crises center around the family. A doll house gives the child a setting to play out scenes and control the drama.

Unfortunately, doll houses made for home use and the furniture and accessories that go with them are generally not sturdy enough to withstand the play of many children in group settings. So it's definitely advisable to buy doll houses and accessories from early childhood suppliers where the materials are designed for child care and early childhood education settings.

◆ **Children can create their own rooms using blocks**. If you do not have a doll house and cannot afford one, ask the children to help you create rooms from cardboard boxes. Wallpaper the rooms with patterned self-adhesive paper or wallpaper samples and glue a carpet or flooring sample to the floor. Add windows, curtains and other trimmings. The children will have fun looking through magazines and finding little pictures for the walls that they can cut out and add. A series of small boxes could even be arranged by the child to make his own house configuration or neighborhood.

◆ **Use sturdy, purchased doll house furniture** in these homemade rooms, or let older children make the furniture from small boxes, paper cups and other materials of their choosing.

◆ **Represent different races and cultures**. School suppliers all carry doll house families representing different races. Provide doll house dolls that represent all the children and families in your group.

◆ **Make homemade doll house dolls**. These can be made by bending and twisting pipe cleaners (chenille stems) and then wrapping this wire frame with adhesive tape. Make the heads from fabric stretched over cotton balls. Features can be drawn on with permanent markers. Sew on some yarn hair.

SAND PLAY

The outdoor sand area or indoor sensory table can be a great setting for miniature dramatic play.

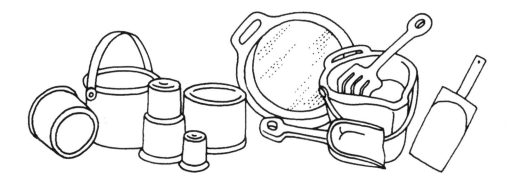

◆ **Dampen sand**. Sand that is a little damp can be molded into shapes more easily. It also keeps its shape as roads, rivers and mountains are built. Try giving children spray bottles with a small amount of water so they can dampen their own sand.

◆ **Accessorize the sand box**. In addition to traditional sand toys like shovels, spoon, and buckets, provide children with some of the miniature play accessories such as little people, animals, plastic berry basket "cages," fences, vehicles and even doll house furniture. Plastic dinosaurs are particularly popular. Children like burying and digging them up and creating attack dramas. Indoors and out, use objects from nature such as pine cones and sticks to create trees and other landscape features.

◆ **Display accessories**. Indoors, keep a group of miniature accessories on a shelf next to the sensory table. Let children help themselves to the accessories they want to use rather than dumping everything into the sensory table.

◆ **Try a sand tray**. A large commercial sized baking pan with sides that are 3 to 4 inches high makes a good sand tray. It can be filled with an inch or two of sand and set on a table top for the child to use with miniature accessories, then emptied and put away again if necessary.

OTHER OPPORTUNITIES FOR MINIATURE PLAY

Sensory table play

Play with water, cornmeal, clay and other materials can easily involve miniature people and accessories.

Shaving cream on table top

Smearing large, soft, fragrant gobs of shaving cream on a table top is a favorite activity in early childhood classrooms. Increase the fun by adding plastic animals and dinosaurs, berry box "cages," plastic vehicles and other small accessories. Give each child a styrofoam or paper cup and show them how to invert it and push it through the shaving cream to create roads.

People dolls

Take a photo of each child in your group (whole body, not just face), or cut out pictures from magazines and catalogs representing different types of people. Include people of different races and ages. Let the children help you search for suitable pictures. Cut out and mount the photos or magazine pictures on sturdy cardboard or thin wood and laminate. These figures can be made to stand up in lumps of modelling clay or play dough. For a more permanent result, mix up plaster of Paris and pour it in spray can tops. Then stick the people figures in this and allow to set. Children might use these like stick puppets, having them talk to each other, or they might move them around in a doll house or block setting.

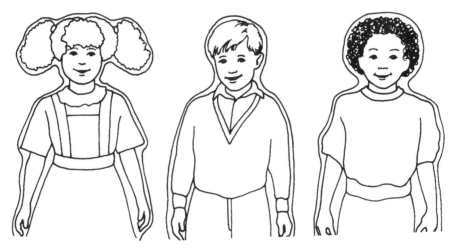

Spontaneous miniature play

You will see children engaging in this type of play in every imaginable setting, planned or unplanned. A child might "drive" a crayon up one arm and down another, crashing in various places along the way.

ROLE OF THE TEACHER IN MINIATURE PLAY

◆ **Observe, don't edit.** The play belongs to the child and she should be allowed to play out any theme she wishes with the materials provided. Make note of the play themes that might bother you and discuss these with your supervisor if you feel you need to.

◆ **Provide materials** and help the child gather what he needs.

◆ **Organize materials** so they are easy for the child to find.

◆ **Make creative art materials available** in case the child needs to create something to enhance the scene.

◆ **Help the child think about the play**. Ask the child to describe what she is playing. Ask extending, open-ended questions. Usually a child is eager to describe the action to an interested adult. But be careful not to be intrusive. You won't want to do this every time the child plays.

◆ **Offer to be a recorder for the child**. You could take dictation as the child describes what is going on. Later, the child might like to illustrate this description of his own play. Perhaps it can be something to share with parents.

CREATIVE ART IDEAS AND ACTIVITIES

Children need many ways to tell their story, express their emotions and influence their environment. Dramatic play and playing with blocks are some of the ways children can express themselves in an early childhood education environment. Painting, scribbling, drawing, playing with clay, singing, dancing, making things and using words are other ways. Words are important. Young children grow rapidly in their ability to express themselves verbally, but verbal expression is often not a child's most effective way of communicating.

A teacher's challenge is to offer children many different ways to express themselves and many interesting materials to use. Another challenge is to allow children freedom of expression, and to be accepting of that expression.

OPEN-ENDED ACTIVITIES

Resist suggesting to children what they should draw or make. If a teacher tells a child to draw a dog and it doesn't end up looking like a dog, the child will feel like she failed and will be less interested in trying things in the future. If a teacher produces an example of what a craft project should look like, and the child's efforts fall short, the child again feels like a failure. This can erode self-esteem.

However, when a child is given interesting, beautiful materials and encouragement to express himself, he has an opportunity to feel successful and to develop potential talents. Do value the product a child comes up with on his own, whether it is a block building, a clay animal, a painting of abstract shapes, a new way of moving to music or an elaborate drawing. Show children you value their work in many ways.

◆ **Show interest**. Look with appreciation at what they did. Comment on the physical characteristics of what you see. "I see you used mostly rectangle blocks and made both sides the same." "You used lots of yellow today." "You used round stickers for the wheels of your car!"

◆ **Be careful with their work**. If children make something tangible, such as a painting or collage, help them find a place where it can dry or be stored without being damaged.

◆ **Display children's work attractively**. An ever changing display of children's art near the entrance of your room will show children and visitors that you value the work. If a child insists on taking her art work home, try asking her to make another one for you to put up in the room because you like it so much. A child is often proud to comply with such a request.

◆ **Invite (but don't require) the child to tell you about his work**. Offer to take dictation and create a descriptive label for it.

◆ **Don't edit**. Sometimes teachers are tempted to alter, improve or correct a child's work. Avoid doing this. A child should not be made to feel that his work is not good enough.

◆ **Help others, especially parents, notice and appreciate the child's work**. Describe how children benefit from such an activity. A photo of the child engaged in the process of creating it is especially meaningful.

◆ **Occasionally photograph nonpermanent creativity.** Catch a child involved in creative movement. Surprise actors in the middle of their dramatic play with a camera. Take a snapshot of that great block building before it must be put away. Display these pictures or put them in your class scrapbook for parents to see.

All of this tells the child, "I think you are interesting. You have good ideas." This builds self-esteem and encourages the child to communicate more.

CREATIVE ART

The process of creating art can help build a sense of self-worth and identity in a child. When she makes a drawing, sculpture or collage, she puts something of herself into it. She has made a mark, altered the world a little bit. Sometimes children are able to work out unconscious feelings through art work, either through the pure physical motion of smearing paint across the page, which can serve as a release of tension, or through using symbols.

Play therapists have long used children's drawings to try to figure out their emotions. Early childhood teachers are not usually trained in this skill, and I caution you against overinterpreting children's artwork. A child may be using a lot of black and red in a painting because he is feeling depressed, or has a lot of rage, or because he really likes bold colors! He may draw himself tiny when he draws his family because he feels small and insignificant, or because he didn't think he left enough room on the page. Don't worry about interpreting children's drawings, although you might save some in the child's file. Creative art is autotherapeutic. It has value all by itself without any interpretation. It's fun. It makes pretty colors. It feels good.

When planning art activities, keep in mind that the child should be able to do the entire project herself. If the adult has to do any part of it, question if it is really appropriate for this age.

Do not use coloring books or predrawn patterns for children to color or paint. The object is to get children to express themselves, and these items inhibit self-expression. It's the illustrator's ideas that are on the page and not the ideas of the child. Coloring book patterns also inhibit creativity in other ways. Children are less likely to draw things in their own way when they have seen the model in a pattern. There is a greater possibility of failure and comparison. It is very difficult for young children to stay within the lines. Other children might be quick to point out where a child went out of the lines. Children do not learn anything at all about the object depicted in a two-dimensional line drawing, so there is virtually no learning value to coloring books and reproduced patterns.

Help-yourself art

Certain materials should always be available for children to express their ideas with, even if there is no planned art project that day. The particular items you make available on a daily basis might vary from group to group, but they should be consistent for that group. The older and more capable children should have a greater variety of items to choose from.

A help-yourself art shelf could contain:
- Writing implements
  Pencils, black and colored
  Ball-point and felt-tipped pens
  Wide-tipped felt markers

- ◆ Paper
    - Inexpensive newsprint
    - Scrap paper from offices and printing shops
    - Construction paper in various colors
- ◆ Sticking agents
    - Several types of tape
    - Glue sticks
    - Paste
    - Small bottles of white glue
- ◆ Children's round-tipped scissors
- ◆ A collage box with a variety of interesting materials to glue
- ◆ Cardboard, paper plates and other things to use as collage bases

Work to build children's independence with art materials

When you teach children to work independently with art materials, you make them feel more capable. You also give yourself more free time to interact with the children because you do not have to oversee everything.

◆ **Show children how to use materials properly**. You could do this as a circle time activity. For instance, you could demonstrate how to dip a brush in paint, wipe it against the side of the cup to remove excess paint, use it on the paper and then return it to the same paint cup.

◆ **Teach children to put materials away properly**. Each item should have a specific spot on the shelf. It helps to label the spot with a picture of the object.

◆ **Teach children to put on their own smocks,** or ask a friend for help.

◆ **Older children can learn to put paper on the easel**, remove it when they are finished and take it to a drying rack.

Gather interesting materials

Another way you can show children that you respect them is by giving them beautiful, high quality materials to work with. Offer children a wide variety of materials, including standard items that are always available. Be on the lookout for interesting materials the children might enjoy. If a certain item is a big hit, budget to purchase more in the future so that it becomes a standard item.

◆ **Mix paints well**. If you use powdered tempera paints, be sure to mix them well. Try using baby powder as a paint extender. It creates a creamy consistency and sparkles a little when dry. Discard paint that gets muddy from mixed colors.

◆ **Find beautiful colors for children to use**. Let them choose the colors they want to paint with from a wide assortment.

◆ **Include different skin tone colors**. Tempera paint, crayons and marker pens now come in many different skin colors.

◆ **Collect interesting brushes and rollers** for children to use in their painting projects.

◆ **Collect paper scraps**. Print shops often have scraps of interesting paper to give away.

◆ **Visit a recycling center**. Your local children's museum may have a recycling center where teachers can pick up unique industry throw-aways that can be used for art projects and other activities in your classroom.

BASIC PROCESSES

Drawing

Some children will begin representational drawing as young as three years of age, telling the adult proudly what it is they have represented on paper. Other children will simply experiment with lines and patterns. Young children should not be pressured to make or draw something that looks like a particular person or object.

Very young children enjoy the pure pleasure of scribbling. They are learning that they can make marks and are discovering the relationship of their arm and hand movements to where the marks go. It takes a lot of scribbling practice before children can control their movements and make marks that are more systematic. Also, it is difficult for children under three to do two different things with their hands. Because drawing requires that the child hold the paper with one hand and move the drawing implement with the other, it helps to tape the paper to the table top, wall or easel.

Crayons have distinct advantages over other drawing materials for young children. Crayons are the only medium that responds to the pressure the child exerts. Light pressure makes a fine, pastel line and heavy pressure makes a dark, bold line. Children can use the tip and the broad side of a crayon. Old and broken crayons can be peeled, melted in muffin tins in a warm oven and cooled to make "hockey puck" crayons. Plus they come in every color imaginable. Have both fat and thin crayons on hand so children can experiment to see which is easiest to use.

Felt-tipped marking pens are also interesting to use because with very little pressure they make a bright, vivid line that is very satisfying to children. Use them on finger paint paper or coated shelf paper. If the child wants to pound with the markers, however, she will quickly destroy them so in some cases they are not appropriate. Supervise the use of markers with very young children because they sometimes like to suck on them. Safety note: Pen and marker caps are just the right size for choking. Discard pen caps. Sink marker caps, open side up, into wet plaster of Paris that is poured into a small container. Place the caps so they stick up about half an inch above the surface of the plaster of Paris. These caps now cannot be swallowed, and you will not lose them.

Suggestions for supplies to include in a Drawing Center:

- Fat and thin crayons
- Wide-tipped felt markers
- Fine-tipped marking pens
- Colored and white chalk and a chalkboard
- Various types of pencils and erasers
- Colored pencils
- Oil crayons
- Ball-point pens
- Several types of paper
- Small writing pads
- Clip boards

Painting

Children who are under stress often find painting to be a very satisfying release. Try to make this art activity available as an everyday choice. Control messiness by teaching children how to use the paint and brushes properly. Teach the children to put on a smock and be independent in the process. Children often love the job of washing out the brushes at the sink under a running stream of water, watching the color come out and gradually fade.

Some children will really thrive on consistency—having the same kind of paint and the same colors available all the time. But if you sense the children need a change, bring variety to the painting process by changing the medium, the tools or the surface used to paint on. Here are some ideas.

The medium:
- ◆ Offer different combinations of colors.
- ◆ Mix paint thick one day, thin the next.
- ◆ Use watercolor paints.
- ◆ Mix different things into the paint—for example, baby powder, coffee grounds, sawdust.

The tools:
- ◆ Standard easel brushes
- ◆ Short-handled paint trim brushes from the hardware store
- ◆ Wide house painting brushes
- ◆ Fine, watercolor brushes
- ◆ Make-up brushes
- ◆ Sponges of various textures
- ◆ Small paint rollers from the hardware store

The surface:
- ◆ Easel paper and butcher paper
- ◆ Aluminum foil
- ◆ Plastic wrap
- ◆ Wax paper
- ◆ Cardboard boxes of all shapes
- ◆ Wood scraps

Finger painting is a very valuable process to offer children. It is messy and requires supervision and planning. Some children will be reluctant to try it and get their hands dirty. These children might be more comfortable finger painting with shaving cream on a table top. Make sure children are wearing smocks and have sleeves pushed up. Coated finger paint paper works best, allowing the smooth paint to glide across the glossy surface. Coated shelf paper can also be used. You might consider allowing children to finger paint directly on the surface of the table or on a cookie sheet.

Water color trays are interesting and appropriate for older children. The child must wet the brush in water, swirl it on the paint pad, make the mark on paper, and then remember to rinse the brush and wipe excess water off before using a second color. Children do like the control and variety they can get from this type of paint, but it is not for beginners.

Face painting is wonderful fun and a good self-image activity. Mix up your own face paints by putting globs of cold cream in the compartments of a plastic egg carton or ice cube tray. Mix a little tempera paint into each compartment. Place a long mirror sideways on a table top and position chairs and paints in front of it. Let children sit side by side and paint their own faces with small paint brushes. This face paint will wipe off with a tissue.

Children enjoy all kinds of cutting, pasting and gluing activities. The main challenge is to gather a rich variety of materials with different shapes, textures and colors for children to use. The greater the variety of materials, the more imaginative children's productions will be. Keep a large compartmentalized collage box on the art shelf, or create a separate Collage Center. As you collect things, think about the three variables: 1) the bases upon which children can stick things, 2) the stuff that they can stick on, and 3) the sticking agent.

Suggestions for a Collage Center

Bases
   ◆ Precut pieces of heavy cardboard
   ◆ Paper plates
   ◆ Plastic coffee can lids
   ◆ Corrugated cardboard
   ◆ Cardboard boxes
   ◆ Small, flat pieces of wood
   ◆ Poster board or matte board

Stuff to cut and stick
   ◆ Old greeting cards
   ◆ Old magazines
   ◆ Ribbon scraps
   ◆ Yarn scraps
   ◆ Lace scraps
   ◆ Fabric scraps
   ◆ String
   ◆ Wire
   ◆ Buttons
   ◆ Fake fur pieces
   ◆ Colored paper scraps
   ◆ Odd puzzle pieces
   ◆ Colored sand

Sticking agents
   ◆ Small bottles of white glue
   ◆ School paste
   ◆ Homemade paste
   ◆ Glue sticks
   ◆ Masking tape
   ◆ Transparent tape

◆ Colored electrical tape

In addition, provide children's round-tipped scissors. Children might also use some of the writing materials to add lines or color to their collages.

Sticky picture

An easy and nonmessy way to offer a collage activity is to cut self-adhesive paper into picture-size pieces. Peel off the backing and affix a construction paper frame to the sticky side. Let children stick collage pieces onto the sticky side to make a picture.

Sticky Picture

Sticky wall

Sticky Wall

Attach to the wall a large piece of self-adhesive paper, sticky side out, at the children's height. Remove the backing. Add a border if you like. Hang a bucket of fabric scraps and other interesting things like yogurt container tops in front of it. Let the children stick the objects onto the wall and peel them off again. You could also attach a photo of each child to a yogurt top so the children can put their friends' pictures on the sticky wall.

A few more thoughts about creative art

There are, of course, many more art processes besides those described here (see the art books in the resource section at the end of this chapter for more ideas). Just remember to search out interesting processes and materials you think your children might enjoy. Stay away from telling them what to make and any form of patterned work where everybody's product ends up looking the same.

Art should be offered to children individually or in small groups during free play time when they also have plenty of other play choices. Never sit the whole group down at once to do

Curriculum Ideas & Activities

a project. This causes too much waiting, and does not show respect for children's individual interests. Children will be much more relaxed in a small group and have more opportunity for conversation with you about what they are doing. It actually does not take longer this way because there is less wasted time. If children have a hard time waiting their turn to do an art project, offer them a sign-up sheet so they can be sure they will have art time, too.

Also keep in mind that sometimes boys stay away from the art center. If pressed, they will do one quick sample to please the teacher and then head somewhere else. To entice reluctant boys, invite several to the art center at the same time. Try bringing art outside where children can make a mess with great abandon. A different setting may attract children who are reluctant to paint indoors.

Finally, do not feel pressure to offer something new and different every day. Children enjoy doing the same process again and again. A child who has done seven paintings in a row gets more out of the experience than the child who is forced to move on after only one painting. Some children just like to sample a project, while others want to repeat it many times.

Save samples of children's creative artwork and date them. It's exciting to see scribbles turn into suns and spiders and people. This is one concrete way to share with parents the child's progress. A child's artwork might also be of interest to a psychologist or play therapist who is working with the child.

WOODWORKING IDEAS AND ACTIVITIES

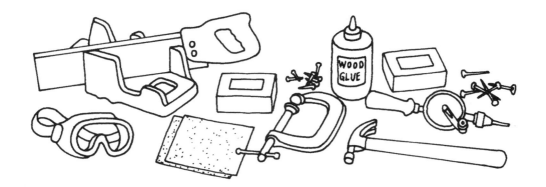

Many teachers are hesitant to include woodworking in their classrooms. "Put a hammer in the children's hands? No way!" So carpentry benches sit unused in many classrooms. Although you might not choose to offer this type of activity to children who have severe problems with aggression, it can be a very satisfying creative activity for children if there is proper planning and set-up.

If possible, wait to introduce woodworking until all the children are familiar with each other and the program, and you feel that you know individual children well. Open the workbench area when you are free to supervise and are not deeply involved in other activities.

VALUES OF WOODWORKING

◆ **Pounding and making a loud noise in an acceptable way** can relieve physical tension caused by stress.

◆ **It offers good redirection**. Pounding at the workbench can be a satisfying redirection when a child is inclined to hit another.

◆ **A child feels powerful** as she makes dents and cuts in wood.

◆ **A child enjoys using real tools** and develops fine motor skills in the process.

SET-UP

Place a child-sized workbench in a corner of the room where noise will not disturb others. It should not be near the library center or other quiet area, for instance. You might put it next to the art area because children often like to use art materials such as glue, paint, string and various collage materials along with the wood.

To reduce the noise, try carpeting the workbench by nailing on carpet samples. These can easily be replaced. One teacher placed a large box on the workbench, the open side facing the children. Children hammered inside the box, reducing the noise.

Keep a good supply of small wood scraps in a box nearby. Provide a variety of shapes and sizes. Ask a secondary school woodworking teacher if her students could cut up their scraps into small pieces for your class. Lumber yards and cabinet or furniture making shops are other good places to find wood scraps.

Store tools in a tool box or hang them on a peg board near the workbench.

Limit participation to one or two children at a time. Create a sign-up system if necessary.

INTRODUCING THE CHILDREN TO WOODWORKING

Children should be "checked off" on each tool before they are allowed to use it. To "check off" a child, show her how to use the tool safely and properly, then have her demonstrate the tool's use to you. At the same time, have the child show you that she knows how to put the tool away properly.

Learn how to use the tools yourself first. You may need to find someone to teach you how to use them.

START WITH SIMPLE HAMMERING

Just pounding directly on wood (with no nails) is very satisfying for children. You might start by letting them pound on styrofoam sheets or blocks, first using light wooden mallets from toy pounding benches, then later using real hammers. Children enjoy seeing the marks left on the surface by the hammer. Draw little Xs on the surface for them to aim at if you wish. Some children might enjoy painting these round depressions in the art corner.

HAMMERING WITH NAILS

To prevent children from hammering on their thumbs, punch a nail through one end of an index card. Let them position the nail where they want it, then hold the other end of the card while they hammer. Short nails with large flat heads are best to use.

After they have had some experience with the index card, show them how to hold the nail and tap it lightly to make it stick in the wood. Tell them to let go of the nail and hold the side of the board before pounding it in further.

SAWING

You need either a vise or a C-clamp to firmly attach the board to the workbench before a child can use a saw effectively. Show the child how to put the wood into the vise and screw the vise shut. This can be fun. Then show them how to use the saw and how to keep it at a proper angle.

TAKING THINGS APART

Children enjoy using screwdrivers, tweezers and other tools to take things apart. Collect telephones, radios, alarm clocks and other small machines that are no longer usable for children to take apart. This builds fine motor skills, sparks curiosity and makes children feel powerful.

DON'T WORRY ABOUT FINAL PRODUCTS

Young children are very satisfied just using the tools and seldom care if they have a finished product at the end. They like making the noise, seeing the nail sink into the wood, feeling the saw's vibrations and touching the pile of sawdust that accumulates. Sometimes a child will want to make something specific, like a sign for a block structure, and may even ask for help. Act as an advisor and help where needed, but allow the child to do everything possible for himself.

Music and movement are an essential part of any early childhood classroom. The values of music and movement for children in crisis include:

◆   **It is another form of expression**, a way for children to show emotions without having to use words.

◆   **It allows an energy release**. Moving to music allows an acceptable release of energy.

◆   **It strengthens cultural identity** when music from the child's culture is included in classroom.

◆   **It encourages children to feel happy**. Singing and dancing is fun and can lift the mood of the children.

◆   **Music develops a sense of belonging**, a sense of being part of a group. Singing is something people do together. When children know the words to the same songs and enjoy them together, they feel that they are all part of the same group. That is one reason to let children enjoy singing the same songs over and over, all year.

SING ANYTIME

There are certainly many fine children's recordings on the market, but do sing along with the recordings. And don't always use recordings. Children need real live models to learn to sing. Use music as a handy tool, something you can pull out any time without the use of a tape recorder or record player. It is one of the best things in life and it is free! Here are some ways to model spontaneous music making.

◆   **Make up songs for various routines of the day**. Weave children's names into the song as they perform the routines.

◆ **Make up songs or simple chants to sing when there are special events**. Simply fit words to familiar tunes. For example, sing the following to "Mary Had a Little Lamb."

Henry got new shoes today,

Shoes today, shoes today.

Henry got new shoes today,

He likes them very much!

◆ **Encourage children to make up their own songs** and sing them for you. You might record them on a cassette tape or invite the child to teach the song to the group. This is a great activity for increasing self-esteem.

◆ **Sing the child's song with him**. When you hear a child chanting, as some children will do spontaneously, chant along with him.

◆ **Sing anytime**. If you have to wait between activities, if lunch is late, or if it's a beautiful day and you're outside, just start singing one of the songs you all know and see who joins you.

◆ **Develop a collection of favorite songs**. These could be made-up songs, songs from recordings or songs from song books. As you teach these to children, write down the words and add them to a loose leaf notebook called The Class Song Book. Illustrate the songs, or add children's illustrations. Place this book on a low table or in the music area. It won't take long for children to learn these songs if they can read the words as they sing.

Songs about feelings

There are many good children's songs about feelings, starting with "If You're Happy and You Know It." My personal favorites are Mister Rogers' songs such as, "Sometimes People Are Good," "Good People Sometimes Do Bad Things," "What Do You Do With the Mad That You Feel" and "Wishes Don't Make Things Come True."

Make stick puppets that illustrate facial expressions for various emotions that children could hold up as they sing.

Mood music

Search for instrumental music that reflects various emotions. Classical music offers a wide range to choose from. Some ideas: A Hayden symphony often sounds happy and light-hearted; Moussorsky's "Night on a Bald Mountain" can sound angry; Pachelbel's "Canon" has a peaceful sound. Of course, you'll find plenty of examples in popular music as well, but sometimes the words in the songs are not appropriate. Occasionally put on one of these recordings and ask the children, "Listen to this music. How does it make you feel?" You might invite children to scribble or paint while they listen.

Use lullabies at rest time

Soft recorded lullaby music is nice to play at rest time. There are a number of good recordings available. This does help drown out background noise and reduce distractions as children' try to relax. It is especially nice if you offer to sing each child a special lullaby. Have several to choose from.

Haul out the band

Some teachers avoid using rhythm instruments because they can create chaos. That need not be the case. Using rhythm instruments with children gives them a legitimate opportunity to make noise.

Here are hints to get the most value out of these materials.

◆ **Use instruments without music**. In the beginning of the year, use rhythm instruments without any other music so children can concentrate on the sound they make. Also, use rhythm instruments as a small rather than large group activity.

◆ **Start with the body as the first instrument**. "How many different ways can you make a sound using your body?" Explore how it sounds when you all clap your hands, hit the top of your heads, open and close your mouths while tapping your cheeks, slap your thighs, stomp your feet or tap a table with your finger tips.

◆ **Practice body sounds**. Let children practice controlling the sounds they make using their bodies. See if they can clap going from soft to loud to soft again. Then practice going from slow to fast and back to slow again.

◆ **Start by giving all children the same instrument**. There will be less competition for favored instruments and the children can concentrate on just one sound. Introduce the instruments to a small group of children.

◆ **Add one more instrument at a time**. Create groups of two, then three different instruments. See if children can start and stop playing their instrument when you give them a signal like a band leader. Later children can take on this conductor role.

◆ **Finally, add music**. When children have learned about the sounds of all the different instruments, add music.

◆ **Homemade instruments** are fun to add in. They include everything from coffee can drums to hollow tubes to wooden blocks.

It's loud, it's fun, it's something you do together with your friends.

Moving to music is another way to express oneself. Dancing is a good large group activity. Collect a wide variety of recorded music that is fun to move to, such as classical ballet music, marches, polkas and rock and roll. Don't bother with choosing partners or teaching dance steps. Keep it as free and open-ended as possible. Simply invite children to move the way the music makes them feel. Bring out scarves, crepe paper streamers or pompons to use when dancing.

SENSORY MATERIALS IDEAS AND ACTIVITIES

This kind of play is about things that squish and drip and ooze and pour. These materials just feel good, and they are especially good for children in crisis for the following reasons.

◆ **A child can make things happen**. A child can mold these materials, and this makes her feel powerful.

◆ **Messes are acceptable**. The child has a legitimate way to make a controlled mess.

◆ **These materials offer easy social interaction**. They are especially good for children who are not very skilled at making friends or playing with others. When children play near each other, they may share ideas, comment on each other's projects and occasionally practice sharing and taking turns.

◆ **A child's imagination is stimulated**. These materials encourage the child's use of imagination. Listen for the stories that might emerge.

◆ **Tactile materials offer cognitive benefits**. By playing with these materials, children gradually absorb the concept of conservation of matter—that the amount remains the same even though the shape may change.

◆ **The activities provide fine motor practice** as the children fill and pour.

◆ **They are calming activities**. Another benefit of tactile materials is that they are often soothing and calming. The child focuses less on what's happening in the environment and more on the sensations in her fingertips. If you sense that a child is very tense, this would be a good way to help her settle down.

◆ **Tactile materials lend themselves to miniature play**. Children might even create stories with them.

When you join in the play with sensory materials, copy the children's actions rather than showing them what to do. Be sure to model the proper way to handle the materials—not throwing sand, keeping the water in the water table.

Some children like tactile materials. Other children may have tactile sensitivity and may not like the feel of certain kinds of materials. Never force tactile materials on children. A much better strategy is to set them up in the classroom and let the children decide if they care to use them.

Try to offer at least one of the following tactile play options as one choice during every free play time.

WATER

Setting up

Some people hesitate to set up water play because cleaning up is too much work. Even with the rule, "Keep the water in the water table (or sink, or dish pan)," some drips are inevitable. But remember that the children might actually enjoy using a mop to help clean up.

Protect children's clothing with waterproof smocks. Hang smocks nearby at the children's height. Show them how to put the smocks on themselves or ask a friend to help.

To minimize drips on the floor, try setting dish pans of water inside the table or inside a small child's plastic wading pool set on a low table. Most of the drips then go into the water table or pool, rather than onto the floor, and each child has her own defined space. Or try standing the whole water table inside a large plastic wading pool placed on the floor.

Start with fresh water for each play period. During cold season, keep children with runny noses away from this play choice.

Place water play accessories on a nearby shelf. Let the children choose for themselves which accessories they want to use that day.

Also remember that water play is a great outdoor activity on a warm day.

Possible water play accessories

Things for pouring:
- ◆ Plastic containers of many shapes and sizes
- ◆ Small plastic pitchers
- ◆ Funnels
- ◆ Plastic bottles

Things for experimenting:
- ◆ Turkey basters
- ◆ Clear plastic plumbing tubing pieces
- ◆ Plastic eyedroppers
- ◆ Sponges of several types
- ◆ Collected junk for float and sink experiments
- ◆ Spray can tops and jar lids
- ◆ Containers with small holes punched in the bottom

Things for dramatic play:
- ◆ Little people
- ◆ Plastic boats
- ◆ Plastic plates to create islands
- ◆ Plastic animals and dinosaurs

From time to time, offer to add other things to the water, such as fluffy islands of shaving cream, food coloring or ice cubes. Let the children decide what to add.

Blowing bubbles

Blowing bubbles is one variation of water play that the child who avoids tactile play might enjoy. The deep breathing required to blow out the bubbles helps relieve tension. Bubble blowing usually puts children in a good mood. Bubbles are beautiful! The children are thrilled at their shapes and rainbow colors.

Bubbles can also be an exciting, tension-raising activity, depending on what you do with them. If you blow bubbles across the room and have children chase them and stomp on them, you raise the activity level and create competition and sometimes collisions. You might want to do this type of activity when the children seem sluggish or in need of exercise. In that case, let children chase bubbles outside on a windy day.

A good bubble solution is about eight tablespoons of liquid dish detergent to one quart of water. You can add a little glycerine to create stronger bubbles, but this really isn't necessary.

Start by showing children how to blow through a straw rather than suck on the straw. Have all the children demonstrate that they can do this. Then give each child a small dish containing about one-fourth of the bubble solution. Let them blow a big froth of bubbles.

Later let children experiment making bubbles using a variety of different materials.

◆ **Dip the end of a paper towel tube** in the solution and blow slowly and steadily on the other end to make a big bubble.

◆ **Cut the inside out of a plastic coffee can lid** to make a ring. Dip this in the solution and wave it through the air to make a long tube bubble.

◆ **Let children twist pipe cleaners** into loops of various shapes, dip them in the bubble solution and blow on them.

◆ **Pour the bubble solution into a large baking pan**. Twist a wire coat hanger into a circle and dip it fully into the solution so that the whole space is covered with bubble film. (This might take several tries.) Then wave this through the air to make a really huge bubble.

◆ **Experiment with other things that have holes**. Plastic berry boxes, slotted spoons, tea strainers, key rings and funnels are just a few ideas.

◆ **Check out the book about bubbles** listed in the resource section at the end of this chapter for really elaborate bubble fun for older children.

Yes, bubbles are messy! Little puddles of soapy water will get all over the place and the floor might get slippery. So limit bubble blowing to a certain area of the classroom, and let the children have the pleasure of cleaning up the floor when they are finished.

SAND AND MORE SAND

Sand table play has many of the same benefits as water play and the set-up can be very similar. Even the accessories are similar, except add toy vehicles and sifters. Provide a broom and dust pan in place of the mop for clean-up.

There are a couple types of sand to consider. Fine, soft sand, like beach sand, feels wonderful falling through your fingers and pours easily through a funnel. It is very soothing. On the other hand, it's not very good for molding and sculpting and making roads. Coarser sand, like what builders use for making concrete, is great for making roads, mountains and tunnels. Perhaps you could put one kind of sand indoors in the sand table and another type outside in the sandbox.

Many different things can be put in sensory tables besides water or sand. These include birdseed, paper "holes" from hole punches, confetti, cotton balls, packing materials like shredded paper or huge mounds of shaving cream. Each provides a different texture to explore. Involve the children in deciding what to put in the table from week to week. Some programs avoid using food materials. Do not use styrofoam beads or packing materials. Small particles can float in the air when they are stirred up and can cause serious damage to lungs. Avoid any other substance that children can choke on.

Create mud

It's fantastic to have mud days in the heat of the summer and flood part of the playground. Children can wear bathing suits and spend the whole day outside playing with hoses and sprinklers, creating lakes and mud puddles and rivers. But it is also possible to give children a more controlled mud play experience any time of year, indoors or outdoors.

Put a plastic wading pool on a low table. In this, or in the water table, place several dish pans—one filled with water and the others filled with sand and dirt. Let children experiment on their own combining different quantities of water, sand and dirt. Also supply play dishes, large spoons and containers for scooping and pouring.

Clay

Try potters clay! It's a natural product—cool, soft, and recyclable. It comes in several different colors. It's "clean" dirt. Store it in a plastic garbage bag inside a pail with a lid. To keep it moist, add a little water to the bag, twist the bag closed and put the lid on the can. If it gets too gooey (not necessarily undesirable), let it dry out a bit in open air. If it hardens into solid pieces, these can be reconstituted by putting them in a bag with water. Clay cleans up easily with wet sponges. If you do not find this kind of clay in school supply catalogs or stores, look in artist supply or ceramic supply stores. It comes either in powder form or in premixed blocks. I recommend getting the premixed blocks.

Put clay in the sensory table and simply cover it with plastic when not in use, or let children use it on a table top. To minimize mess, let children play with the clay on cookie sheets or cafeteria trays.

Some children love to pound clay with little wooden hammers or with their hands. This is a good release of tension.

Many people make the mistake of encouraging children to create permanent objects out of clay to take home. Clay is very fragile when it dries and must be fired in a kiln. Even the oven-bake variety is still fragile after it is fired. The objects break easily. Remember, young children are not as interested in the final product as they are in just messing around with the materials. Don't put pressure on them to make something. Instead let them just enjoy poking, punching, squeezing and rolling. They are learning they can change the shape of a material. It is the pure sensory pleasure of the material—the way it feels when you play with it—that is its major value.

When joining children who are playing with clay, just imitate what they are doing—poking, patting and rolling.

Fun accessories to include with clay are textured objects that leave an interesting pattern when pressed into it, such as onion bags and berry boxes, as well as plastic knives and popsicle sticks to carve and mold with, and plastic people and animals to stand up in it. Remember, though, that clay is fun to play with using no accessories at all.

PLASTICENE

Plasticene, or modeling clay as it is sometimes called, is a common early childhood play material. It comes in many bright colors and doesn't dry out. Although it is cleaner than potter's clay, it can get stuck in crevices of textured things and cannot be washed out as easily as potter's clay. It is difficult and frustrating to use when it is cold, and it only becomes malleable when children have held it in their hands for awhile. For all these reasons, clay is preferable to plasticene.

PLAYDOUGH

Playdough, the early childhood classroom standard, is wonderful for its variety. In addition to the commercial product, there are many different recipes for satisfying playdough, each with a slightly different texture. You can add food coloring or powdered gelatin mixes for color and fragrance, or various cooking extracts and plastic glitter for variety.

Although people automatically bring out rolling pins and cookie cutters for accessories, playdough is great fun to use with the toy extruding machines that squeeze the dough through a shaped hole. Use a garlic press for a similar effect. Younger children love poking things into the playdough, such as plastic drinking straws and birthday candles.

Make a huge amount of playdough and then let children combine it with small plastic people, animals and vehicles to create miniature dramatic play scenes.

GOOEY STUFF

The following materials are favorites of many teachers and children. They are soothing and allow children to use their imagination. You can see the tension drain from children as they play with these materials and utter sounds of delight.

Shaving cream

Is it safe to let children play with shaving cream? The cans say, "Keep out of the reach of children." The manufacturers and poison control people I contacted said that once it is out of the can it is simply soap. If a child were to consume great quantities of it, she would get a stomachache. (I have never seen children take more than one little taste.) Like any soap, it can irritate the eyes. If a child's eyes come in contact with it, wash them out with water. Be sure to supervise the use of shaving cream. Push up children's sleeves so that the substance doesn't stay in cuffs and irritate the skin underneath. Avoid using the mentholated kind.

Some things to do with shaving cream:

◆ **Let children finger paint** with it directly on the table top. Later, add a little food coloring or powdered tempera paint to create pastels.

◆ **Give them little people and animals** to use with the shaving cream.

◆ **Invert a styrofoam cup** and scrape it along the surface where they have spread the shaving cream. This will create "roads." Then give the children small vehicles to drive along these roads.

◆ **Let them finger paint with it on an unbreakable mirror**. They like covering and uncovering their reflections.

◆ **Make "islands" of shaving cream** that float in the water table.

Make "aggression bags"

Help the children fill small, zip-closure plastic bags with shaving cream. Now let each child choose two different colors of food coloring. Put a squirt of each into the bag and zip it closed. If desired, tape the bag closed with duct tape. Now let the child squeeze the bag to mix the food coloring into the shaving cream. This makes beautiful pastels, and squeezing it is very satisfying and soothing.

Cornstarch and water goop

Pour a box of cornstarch into a large bowl or dish tub. Mix in just enough water to make it the consistency of yogurt. This magic substance can be picked up and squeezed. It will turn warm and more solid when the child squeezes it. When the child releases his hand, it will turn liquid again and dribble between his fingers.

White glue and starch putty

Mix together roughly two parts of white glue to one part of blue liquid laundry starch, such as Sta-Flo. Squeeze it and knead it a little bit to get a springy consistency. If it becomes too slippery and stringy and doesn't stick together, add more glue. If it is too gooey and sticks to hands or the table top, add more starch.

This congeals into a viscous substance that is neither liquid nor solid. It slowly takes the shape of the container it is in. Children love to hold it up and let it stretch down into long sheets or strings. It's fun to poke holes in it and watch the holes gradually dissolve.

After a couple days of playing with this substance, let one child poke holes in it. Put several drops of one color in each hole and then seal it over. Let the children squeeze and roll the putty to mix the color in. It marbleizes into beautiful swirls before it mixes all the way through, showing children how colors mix. Because it is a white substance, beautiful pastels appear when you add color.

Some rules for putty play:
- ◆ Wash hands first.
- ◆ Use it at a table over a tile floor.
- ◆ Don't throw it.
- ◆ Don't put it in your pockets!

If it gets into clothing, it will soak out in water, but it is hard to get out of a carpet.

It keeps indefinitely if stored in a zip-closure bag or covered plastic container in the refrigerator. A little water may form on the surface while it is stored. Just work it back in. You may need to add a little more starch if it gets too sticky. It will harden if it is left out in the air.

It is a very soothing, relaxing and satisfying activity.

BOOKS AND STORIES

The wide variety of excellent children's books available today are a valuable resource. In addition to the children's books listed in these chapters, the children's librarian at your local public library can suggest books on particular topics.

Reading a book about a topic you know a child is struggling with can be an ideal way to open up a conversation without prying. The child may spontaneously bring up the parallels in his own life. Or, depending on the situation, you could ask, "How is the book different from what happened to you?" or "Do you feel that way sometimes?"

Although books are very helpful, they are not a substitute for real conversation with the child about a situation. Do not assume that the child has come to terms with the topic just because you have read the book or she makes no comments.

Books can help children make the discovery that they are not the only ones who have ever had a particular problem. They may feel relieved to discover this.

As well as books on specific problems, find books and stories that display role models of strong, brave children. Examples are: *Jack and the Beanstalk*; *The Paper Bag Princess*, by Charles Munsch; and *Ramona the Brave*, by Beverly Cleary.

SOME HINTS

◆ **Read to a group or an individual**. You will have to make the decision whether to read the book to a group of children or to one child in a more private setting. Books about feelings, general problems and adventures are good for everyone. A book about a particular situation or a sensitive issue might embarrass a child if read to the whole group.

◆ **Choose a time and place** when it will be easy for the child to concentrate.

◆ **Read the book before you read it to the children**.

◆ **If necessary, modify the book as you read it**, simplifying the language or leaving out certain concepts you feel the child is not ready to hear. Or, use the framework of the book to tell your own story.

◆ **Allow the child to interrupt** and add comments or ask questions. Take your time.

◆ **Make story cassettes available**, or record books yourself. Read the story and make a sound signal when the child should turn the page. Children can take the cassette player, cassette and book into a nook and listen to it by themselves. It's best, of course, to read the book to the child in person. But children like to hear stories over and over again. This allows that to happen even when you are busy.

THINGS TO DO AFTER READING BOOKS

After children are quite familiar with a particular book or story, try some of these activities.

◆ **Invite the children to act out the story**. Assign particular character roles to children in the group. While you read, they pantomime what the character is doing. Gather any props needed ahead of time.

◆ **Create stick puppets for the main characters**. Older children might even enjoy illustrating the characters. With the help of the children, cut them out, mount them on cardboard and attach them to short sticks such as tongue depressors. Give the stick puppets to the children. (You could have multiples of the same character.) As you read the story, each child holds up his stick puppet when he hears you read about that character.

◆ **Create a flannel board representation of the story**. Mount pictures of main characters and objects in the story on tag board and back with Velcro or felt. Let the children help you place these illustrations on the flannel board as you read the story. Leave these out in the book area during free play time.

◆ **Invite the children to change the ending** or other details in the story if they wish. Then read their versions.

◆ **Substitute a child's name for that of the main character**.

Once upon a time...

Storytelling is the most direct art form. There is nothing that comes between the teller and the listener. And it is the ultimate way to customize the curriculum! If you model storytelling, soon the children will become storytellers as well. You are also giving them a valuable tool for self-expression—a critical skill for all children, but especially those in crisis.

When listening to a story, children have no pictures for cues, so they stare intently at your face while forming pictures in their minds.

You don't have to be a master storyteller to tell stories children will enjoy. And there are some great, easy techniques to get children involved in the telling.

The story of our day

Simply frame the morning's events in story language. Settle down with the children and announce that you have a story to tell them. Use a special storytelling voice. Make eye contact with everyone. Then start, "Once upon a time, on a (your weather) day in April in the little town called (your town), there was a teacher named (your name) in a school called (your program). Then simply describe the events that actually happened in your day. "Timmy was the first to arrive, just as Miss Susan had finished mixing the paint for the easel. He said, `Guess what, Miss Susan?'." Describe the rest of the day or morning, mentioning other children. End your story with, "And they all lived happily ever after."

Your children won't mind the weaknesses in the plot. They'll love hearing their names in the story and might even correct details as you go.

Depending on the situation and the children's sense of humor, you might add funny details from your own imagination. "Noah walked over to the wall, walked up the wall, and then walked across the ceiling upside down!" "Keisha was running so fast outside, suddenly the wind picked her up and she started to fly!" Some groups will want you to stick strictly to the details of the truth, while others will love flights of fantasy.

Curriculum Ideas & Activities

Real-life heroes

Tell true stories about children in the class who bravely survived some ordeal (only if it is appropriate to talk about, of course). "Once there was a little boy named Derek. One morning he woke up feeling very, very sick. His mother felt his forehead and said, `I think we better take you to the doctor.'"

A funny thing happened on the way to the office

Tell the children about something you saw on the way to work, or something funny that happened at home. If you tell stories like this, children will start telling you stories as well. First they have to know what a story is.

Offer to take dictation

When you pull out a pencil and a pad of paper, children's stories become more elaborate. They feel important and valued. Invite them to tell you their stories, "Would you like to tell me a story? I'll write down your words."

Vivian Paley, a kindergarten teacher who has written many wonderful books about teaching, writes down children's stories every day. She sits at a "story table" where children can come during their free play time and dictate their stories to her. Later in the day, she invites these children to act out their own stories, with their friends taking on roles.

Fill-in-the-blank stories

This is great fun. You supply the story framework, the connecting phrases and the transitions, and the children provide the details. You can do this individually or with a small group. Play a tape recorder while you do this and write the story down later. These will become some of the children's favorite stories to hear again and again! One possibility is:

Teacher:	*Once upon a time there was a...*
Children:	*Bear (or whatever the children say)*
Teacher:	*This bear was very, very...*
Children:	*Clumsy (tired, hungry, ...)*
Teacher:	*He was so clumsy that he couldn't even...*
Children:	*Stand up (climb a tree, run...)*
Teacher:	*Now this bear realized he had a problem! So he decided to call his good friend...*
Children:	*The hummingbird (the giraffe, Miss Smith...)*
Teacher:	*Hummingbird said, "Why Mr. Bear, why are you so upset?"*

Continue the story until you run out of time or ideas.

These stories are great fun, and every one is different. You never know where they're going. Best of all, the adult must follow the lead of the children. The only difficulty is that sometimes they are hard to end! Don't worry, the character can always fall asleep.

Tell a story, then read it

Find a good story in a children's book that the children have not heard before. Learn the story and tell it without using the book. Then pull out the book. "Look. Here's a book of the same story I just told you. I'm going to read you the book now." Read it and show children the pictures. Then ask them, "When you had to see the pictures in your mind, how were they different from the pictures you see in the book?"

By doing this, you reinforce the idea that the pictures they make in their own minds are just as good as the pictures the illustrator thought up.

Parallel stories

Start with a simple story that the children all know, like "The Three Billy Goats Gruff" or "Goldilocks." Invite them to help you retell the story by changing all the details. You might end up with four gentle rabbits and a wolf who lives under the bridge. Again, with this process, you are valuing children's ideas and showing them that they have something interesting to say.

Create your own album of collected stories

Children love to hear their own stories over and over again. Make little books out of each story, or write them down and keep them in a large binder. Some of the children might be motivated to illustrate their stories.

PUPPETRY IDEAS AND ACTIVITIES

Everyone knows that puppets are magic. What starts out as a small piece of cloth and

scraps suddenly takes on a personality and a life of its own. They add charm and fun to a program, and it's truly amazing what a child will tell a puppet!

Puppets are also great teaching tools. They are extremely good at holding children's attention, possibly because children are trying to figure out what is fantasy and what is reality. With puppets, you can present social and emotional concepts in a neutral way.

PUPPETS FOR CHILDREN TO USE

It's good to have puppets on hand for children to put on and use during their play time. By talking for the puppet on their hand, children learn to put themselves in someone else's shoes and consider a different point of view. A shy child sometimes talks more freely through a puppet because everyone's eyes are on the puppet instead of the child. A child who stutters may be able to make a puppet talk without stuttering. A child who is afraid or worried might be able to express fears through a puppet. A child's puppet can have a conversation with an adult's puppet. Two or more children will enjoy having their puppets interact. So it's good to have a nice variety of puppets for children to choose from.

Early childhood suppliers now have a great variety of multi-racial puppets depicting all types of people and occupations. Homemade sock puppets and animal puppets are great additions, too.

Children will also enjoy making their own fanciful paper bag puppets. Perhaps they could create monster puppets to go along with the story, *Where the Wild Things Are* by Maurice Sendak.

Stick puppets are easy to make by cutting out magazine pictures of people, gluing them to cardboard backing and attaching them to short sticks. Ask the children to find characters for stick puppets. A great source for stick puppet figures is outdated sewing pattern books that fabric stores might donate.

PUPPETS FOR ADULTS TO USE

There are special benefits to having a Pet Puppet that is only for the teacher to use. A puppet can be like a teaching assistant, doing all sorts of useful chores for you. They aren't human, so they can make silly mistakes for the children to correct. They can discuss problems they are having, allowing you to address children's problems without getting personal. They can introduce new concepts and ask children questions, giving them a valuable review of experiences. They are wonderful poets, musicians and storytellers. And if they sing off key or forget part of the story, the teacher doesn't feel like a fool. Best of all, they add an element of humor and imagination to the classroom.

PET PUPPET ACTIVITIES

Give the Pet Puppet a special name, voice and personality. Although you can have other puppets for the children to play with, don't let them play with the Pet Puppet. Keep the personality of the Pet Puppet strong and never changing. Children will also pay attention to the Pet Puppet if he comes out only at special times. There are many wonderful ways to involve the Pet Puppet in the classroom. Here are some starters.

Morning greetings

The puppet takes attendance by calling each child's name in turn. When the child hears his name, he goes over and gets a kiss from the puppet. If he wants, he can give the puppet a hug. Even very young children enjoy this game. It helps them learn everybody else's name.

Describe each child

After the Pet Puppet comes out in the morning, he can suggest that you play a guessing game. He describes one child at a time, in admiring ways, and the children have to guess who he is describing. "I see someone who has long, brown braids and beautiful, brown eyes. She is wearing pink sneakers and has buttons on the front of her shirt. Who is it?" "Right! It's Flora." This builds vocabulary as well as enhances self-esteem and a feeling of belonging.

Forgetful puppet

In a variation of the above, Pet Puppet is forgetful and is quite embarrassed that he can't remember the children's names. So you ask him to describe the person he can't remember until the children are able to tell him who he is thinking of.

Or, Pet Puppet asks you who a particular child is. You describe the child. "Manuel has black hair and brown eyes and today he is wearing a shirt with green stripes." The puppet can then examine each child, out loud, until he comes to the right conclusion. "Let's see. This person has blond hair, so that can't be Manuel. This person has black hair, but he has on a blue shirt so that can't be Manuel. This person has black hair and big brown eyes, and a shirt with green strips, so this must be Manuel! Hi, Manuel!"

Shy puppet

This puppet is very shy and afraid of loud noises. He peeks out and then ducks back in his bag. You coax him out and he shakes in fear. You ask him what's the matter. He whispers something to you. You say out loud, "You're afraid of these children? Why?" He whispers something else to you. You say, "Because it is so noisy? You'll be quiet won't you, boys and girls?" The puppet can then proceed to whisper a series of questions to you that you can then relay to the children. If the children ask him a question, he can respond to you in a whisper. He never talks because he's so shy. You never have to be a ventriloquist, and the children usually stay quiet and strain to hear what he is whispering. This can be a calming activity when the children have been noisy.

Review the morning

Your puppet has been asleep all morning and has missed out on everything that went on. So he asks the children, one at a time, what they did that morning. He can ask questions to get the children to expand on their remarks. "You played with blocks? What did you build? What shapes did you use? Was anyone playing with you?"

Make silly mistakes

The puppet can show misunderstanding of a basic concept. For instance, he can pull a ping pong ball out of his bag and announce proudly that he has a great big ball. If the children don't correct him spontaneously, you can call their attention to his mistake. "Is that really a big ball?" Then you can say to the puppet, "You don't seem to understand the difference between big and small. We'll help you." Then you can have children teach the puppet by finding things in the room that are big for one pile and things that are small for another. You could do this with many concepts: colors, hard and soft, round and square.

True and false game

The puppet can make a series of statements and the children call out whether the statement is true or false. "Cars have tires." "Cars drink milk." "Cows say, `Moo.'" "Cows live in chicken coops." The sillier the better!

Where is it

This is a good receptive language game. It can be used to find out what words the children understand but do not speak. The puppet challenges children to find certain things in the room. "Where is there a picture of a turtle in our room?" "Where is there a flower in our room?"

Puppet packs a bag

On a Friday, our puppet shows up with a small suitcase. (Children are fascinated by suitcases.) He is all excited because he's going to visit his Grandma. But he wants to bring some stuff with him because there are not many toys at Grandma's. So he asks children, one at a time, to go and get certain things in the room for him to borrow over the weekend. This is an excellent receptive language game, because the children simply have to understand what he wants. For older children, you could make this more advanced by having the puppet forget the name of the toy and describe it instead. "I want to borrow the toy that has lots of pieces and when you put them together the right way, they make a picture." Or he could describe certain attributes. "I want to bring along soft things."

Puppet's surprise bag

Pet Puppet returns from visiting Grandma and is all excited because he has something special from her house in his bag. He can bring out any common object—a rubber glove, a hand mixer, wire whisk, wallet or book—and discuss it with the children. "What is this? Do you know what it's for? Guess what room in her house I found it in." For older children, make a guessing game out of it. The puppet gives hints or clues about the object and challenges the children to guess what it is before he pulls it out. Or, the object is in a cloth bag and the children guess what it is by feeling through the bag first.

Guess what

The puppet can lead simple guessing games. Every time Pet Puppet comes out this could be part of his ritual. "Guess what I did this morning! It has to do with food." Or the simple, "I spy" game. "I spy something that's used to keep people's coats from falling on the floor." After you have played this type of game many times with children and they are thoroughly familiar with it, ask the children to think of something the puppet has to guess. "Guess what we did this morning." It may be difficult for children to come up with clues that don't give it away, so play this with older children.

What do you know

Use Pet Puppet to ask children questions about a topic to see what they already know about it. This can be very useful before you go on a field trip or at the very beginning of a theme unit. "Tell me about fire engines. What are they for? Why do they make so much noise? Why do they have those scary lights on them? Why do they have those ladders?" "Tell me what you know about a circus. I have a hard time remembering. Can you (teacher) write down some of the things that they say so I can remember?"

Tell me about it

Pet Puppet didn't get to go along on the field trip, or he slept through a special event. He wants the children to tell him all about what they saw and did. The puppet can ask questions to expand the children's answers. "Did the fire fighters have any special clothes?"

Help with show and tell

Show and Tell can be a difficult time, especially for children who have a sudden wave of shyness when addressing all of their playmates. Instead, let them show the puppet what they brought and answer the puppet's questions about it. The puppet can pick who is next, choosing good listeners.

Supervise clean-up time

Have a special puppet whose job it is to supervise clean-up time. He could start out by going to each center and notifying children that clean-up time will start in five minutes. (Give the children in the block corner a little extra warning time.) Then he could go to each area and help organize the children. "You put the boxes back on the shelf, and you line up the shoes, and you hang up the dress-up clothes." Then he could join various groups of children and help them for a time, cheering them on and encouraging them. When the job is done he might admire the appearance of the room and congratulate individual children for a job well done.

Dismiss children

At the end of group time, Pet Puppet could pick one child at a time to come up and tell him a secret, give him a hug and then go on to the next part of the day (wash hands to get ready for lunch) or start playing in a chosen center at the beginning of free play time.

Tuck children in at nap time

Pet Puppet is very tired and keeps yawning and stretching. He says he can't wait to curl up in his nice, cozy bed and have a good dream. But first, he will go around and tuck children in and sing them an individual lullaby. However, he will only go to children who show they are ready by lying quietly.

Puppet has a problem

Pet Puppet can have a problem similar to those of children in the group. He is afraid of the dark, for instance. He might ask, "Have any of you ever been afraid of the dark when you go to bed at night? What do you do?" Or he might be upset that his friends won't play with him because he's purple. Maybe he's ashamed because he was mean to his friend or little brother and feels bad about it, but doesn't know what to do now. He needs advice about how to make up. Let the children advise him and weigh the merit of various solutions.

Pet Puppet can also talk with one child at a time. Sometimes children will tell a puppet things they are afraid or reluctant to tell a person. Using puppets in this way is especially useful when working with children in crisis.

Curriculum Ideas & Activities

Create a home for Pet Puppet

As a class project, create and decorate a special home for Pet Puppet. The puppet could be there to say what his preferences are, in case there is disagreement. Would he like a square dog house? Would a basket with a lid be better? Does he want it to be soft inside? What should the outside look like? Whenever Pet Puppet is not being used, place this puppet in a home on a high shelf, out of reach of the children, so he can sleep in peace.

All these ideas are just here for starters. If you use your pet puppet with children on a daily basis, he will develop many more games and jobs. You'll be amazed at how he comes to life!

RESOURCES

ART

Cherry, Clare. (1990). *Creative Art for the Developing Child* (2d ed.). New York: Simon & Schuster.

Hereford, Nancy Jo, and Schall, Jane. (1991). *Art: A Practical Guide for Teaching Young Children*. New York: Scholastic Inc.

Kohl, MaryAnn. (1994). *Preschool Art: It's the Process, Not the Product*.. Beltsville, MD: Gryphon House.

Lasky, Lila, and Mukerji-Bergeson, Rose. (1980). *Art: Basic for Young Children*. Washington, DC: National Association for the Education of Young Children.

BLOCK PLAY

Church, Ellen B., and Miller, Karen. (1990). *Blocks: A Practical Guide for Teaching Young Children*. New York: Scholastic, Inc.

Hirsch, Elisabeth S. (1984). (Ed.). *The Block Book*. Washington, DC: National Association for the Education of Young Children.

BOOKS AND STORYTELLING

Maguire, Jack. (1985). *Creative Storytelling: Choosing, Inventing, and Sharing Tales for Children*. New York: McGraw-Hill.

Raines, Shirley C., and Canady, Robert J. (1989). *Story S-t-r-e-t-c-h-e-r-s: Activities to Expand Children's Favorite Books*. Beltsville, MD: Gryphon House.

ibid. (1991). *MORE Story S-t-r-e-t-c-h-e-r-s: More Activities to Expand Children's Favorite Books*. Beltsville, MD: Gryphon House.

ibid. (1992). *Story S-t-r-e-t-c-h-e-r-s for the Primary Grades: Activities to Expand Children's Favorite Books*. Beltsville, MD: Gryphon House.

Raines, Shirley C. (1992). *450 More Story S-t-r-e-t-c-h-e-r-s for the Primary Grades: Activities to Expand Children's Favorite Books*. Beltsville, MD: Gryphon House.

DRAMATIC PLAY

Klugman, Edgar, and Smilansky, Sara. (1990). *Children's Play and Learning*. New York: Teachers College Press.

Monighan-Nourot, Patricia, Scales, Barbara, and Van Hoorn, Judith. (1987). *Looking At Children's Play: A Bridge Between Theory and Practice*. New York: Teachers College Press.

Paley, Vivian Gussin. (1984). *Boys & Girls: Superheros in the Doll Corner*. Chicago: The University of Chicago Press.

Segal, Marilyn, and Adcock, Don. (1981). *Just Pretending: Ways to Help Children Grow Through Imaginative Play*. Englewood Cliffs, NJ: Prentice Hall, Inc.

MUSIC AND MOVEMENT

McDonald, D.T. (1993). *Music in Our Lives: The Early Years*. Washington, DC: National Association for the Education of Young Children.

Beall, Pamela C., and Nipp, Susan H. (1982). *Wee Sing Silly Songs*. Los Angeles: Price Stern Sloan.

SENSORY MATERIALS

Hill, D.M. (1993). *Mud, Sand and Water*. Washington, DC: National Association for the Education of Young Children.

Zubrowski, Bernie. (1979). *Bubbles*. Boston: Little, Brown and Company.

Block Play: Constructing Realities. (1994). National Association for the Education of Young Children, 1509 Sixteenth Street, NW, Washington, DC 20036-1426. 800-424-2460. www.naeyc.org. $39. (Video)

CHAPTER 24

HELPING CHILDREN LEARN TO MANAGE THEIR BEHAVIOR

Nobody is surprised when children who are experiencing trauma in their lives act in ways that may be difficult for a teacher to handle. Their feelings, their frustrations, their fears must get expressed. Very young children are more likely to use actions rather than words to express themselves.

Sensitive and caring guidance from a trusted teacher can have a very positive impact on how children cope. Giving this guidance may be the most difficult thing you have to do. Because each situation and each child is different, nothing works for every child or situation. This chapter will give you strategies to try and ideas to think about as you approach each situation.

It is useful to think about what you are trying to accomplish when you help children learn to manage their behavior. There are really two major goals: 1) to maintain a safe classroom so that all the children can thrive; and 2) to help the individual child express feelings and interact with the other children in positive ways. Teachers constantly work to balance these two goals.

As a professional, you have a responsibility to maximize the experience for all of the children. Most important is that children feel safe and respected. This is the baseline. If they worry about physical or verbal attacks from other children, they cannot relax and benefit from the learning environment and activities you have prepared. Teachers and parents can feel very frustrated when one child seems to absorb much more than his share of the teacher's attention because of difficult behavior. Teachers and parents also express concern that one child can be a bad example for others and undesirable behavior can spread to other children if it is not handled quickly and appropriately.

An equally important goal of behavior management is to build coping skills and competence in each individual child. So, while the immediate goal is to stop the offending behavior, be it hitting, verbal attacks or tantrums, the ultimate, long-term goal is to teach the child other, acceptable behavior for expressing the same emotions.

It is very important to generate curriculum that is sensitive to the needs of the children. Only then will it be developmentally appropriate. Flexibility is essential. The teacher must see interactions as centrally important. Learning how to get along with others and develop friendships is an important aspect of all the children's education. They must have these skills in order to succeed in school and in life.

The following may help you enjoy the process of teaching children to manage their behavior.

◆ **Create roles for yourself**. Think of yourself as a coach working to teach children appropriate strategies for dealing with hurt, anger and frustration.

◆ **Think of the classroom as a human interactions lab** in which children have endless opportunities to learn skills. Each encounter or conflict between children is an opportunity for them to exercise their abilities.

◆ **Celebrate successes**. Most teachers report that seeing children's progress is the one thing that makes behavior management activities enjoyable. It is wonderful when you hear a child using a conflict resolution technique you taught her rather than an aggressive action. So watch for these successes. Praise the children. Record the successes in your journal and in the child's file. Share them with parents. Focus on these successful experiences, and be sure to pat yourself on the back!

◆ **Don't be discouraged** when the child resorts to previous behavior. He needs your support. As with all other types of learning, he will make mistakes along the way. Help him build on his successes.

◆ **Show you care**. Realize that the children have to like you first before they can care about your reaction to a situation. So work on building friendly, affectionate relationships. Laugh with children. Let them know that they are important people to you.

◆ **Everyone benefits when children learn how to control their behavior**. When you worry that you are taking time away from other children, remember that they will benefit from watching you help their classmate. From your model they learn kindness, empathy,

Learning to Manage Behavior

understanding and a vocabulary about feelings.

Be careful not to blame the victim. It is easy to do! When a child repeatedly spoils your plans, tries to hurt other children, embarrasses you in front of colleagues and parents and makes you feel ineffective, it's easy to feel angry at that child. But young children are not calculating. They do not make plans and lay traps. They just act and react. It is tempting to ascribe negative characteristics to the child and make dire predictions for her future. And we correctly fear for the child's future, unless effective intervention is possible. The hopeful part, however, is that in early childhood, there is still time to help. Children are still malleable. We can still make a difference.

USE PROFESSIONAL SUPPORTS

Really difficult behavior on the part of children can leave teachers feeling overwhelmed. It can be a prime burnout factor. When nothing you try seems to help, you can end up feeling ineffective. Your professional self-esteem suffers. It is extremely important to have the support of other professionals, so take advantage of your team. Let's look at how various team members might help.

OTHER STAFF

When several people look at the problem together, they can brainstorm and perhaps come up with more resources and ideas than an individual can working alone.

You might do some advance planning together if you know of a problem ahead of time. For instance, a four year old boy who had been asked to leave three different child care centers for incorrigible biting had been referred to a new center as a last-ditch effort. The staff brainstormed what to do. Their plan:

1) They would work hard to teach him how to deal with frustration.
2) They would be careful to greet him warmly every day and give him lots of loving, special attention.
3) They would give him a special "lovey"—a stuffed animal to carry around that would be just his.
4) They would focus on meeting his emotional needs, reading his moods and supporting him as much as possible.

It was no surprise that, after a few false starts, the plan was successful.

Your coworkers can be useful in other ways. Ask someone who does not teach in your room to come in and observe a child. Sometimes they can notice subtle things that lead up to a child's actions.

Discussing a particular child with a group (never in front of her) allows you to tap into the insights and experiences of other professionals. Some centers do this in a routine, systematic way with very good results. One teacher or team of teachers presents a case study describing the child, the child's background and situation, the behavior that is causing difficulty and what has been tried. Then the rest of the staff brainstorms with them. The teacher or team goes back and tries the suggestions. They report at the next meeting and either congratulate themselves for their collective success or go back to the drawing board.

THE CHILD'S PARENTS

Depending on the situation, the parents may be your best resource when figuring out what is bothering their child. Regard them as expert consultants.

At first, you may have to make special efforts to break down their defensiveness. Often parents know that their child has behavior problems that need to be worked on. When you call to discuss them, they might be afraid that you are going to ask them to remove their child from your program. And they probably fear that their child's behavior reflects on their skills as parents, and that you will be critical of them.

Consider the following when working with parents.

◆ **They are part of the team**. Help them understand that you see them as vital members of the team.

◆ **Ask for their insights**. Why do they think their child is acting a particular way? What light can they shed on the subject?

◆ **They are the experts on their own child**. Parents know their child better than anyone else; they are the experts on that particular child. You know about child development, positive discipline and various strategies that could be tried. With the help of all involved, a complete plan is possible.

◆ **Regular communication**. After you decide how to handle a situation, make a date to meet again and evaluate progress. This helps everyone feel included and successful. The child benefits, and you and the parents have formed a collaborative bond.

THE OTHER CHILDREN

Don't forget about the other children who know the situation very well. Teachers are often surprised at the positive effect of group problem solving. "I have a problem. I'd like your ideas about what might solve this problem." Diane Levin, in *Teaching Young Children in Violent Times* (listed in the resource section at the end of this chapter), describes a group meeting technique in which children generate ideas that the teacher writes down. This might work best when it concerns group behavior. In one example cited, the teacher said she got grouchy in the afternoon when everyone wanted her attention at once and people had a hard time waiting for their turn. The teacher wrote down the children's ideas of what she might do. They decided to try several strategies for awhile and then meet again to discuss them. This allowed children to practice problem solving and evaluation. The teaching techniques involved in this approach are described in detail in that resource.

Teachers have also reported success with younger children, even when the situation required dealing with the behavior of a particular child. A group of three year olds sat down to talk about a child who bites other children. With the biter present, they discussed ways to deal with the situation. In a very supportive and respectful way, the teacher told the children, "Sean has a problem. He gets mad sometimes when he wants something and before he knows it, he ends up biting someone!" (Everyone, including Sean, nods in recognition of the situation.) "What can we do to help Sean remember not to bite?" The children decided that whenever it seemed that Sean was getting mad and might bite them, they would say, "No biting!" They even practiced saying it forcefully a few times. Success! This peer support helped the child stop biting. The children became aware of Sean's moods and "invested" themselves in the problem.

OTHER PROFESSIONALS

Whenever necessary, consider inviting other professionals such as a child psychologist to observe the child in the environment of your classroom. Or, if that is impossible, see if you and the parents can meet with the professional. Of course, you must consult with the director and the parents first, and this is not something most programs can do frequently.

FAMILY CHILD CARE PROVIDERS—YOU ARE NOT ALONE

Of course, you can just as easily use parents and other professionals as described above. Also connect with the local family child care professional association and the local resource and referral agency. When you have concerns about a particular child and don't know what to try next, you might find that these agencies can offer suggestions. Your local public school's Child Find function might also offer valuable consultation services.

HOW TO IDENTIFY AND ANALYZE BEHAVIOR PROBLEMS

When you have a specific method for identifying and analyzing a problem behavior and work systematically to resolve it, you will feel less overwhelmed. In essence, you are saying to yourself and others, "This is my best effort," and you know that you are making a sincere attempt to help the child.

OBSERVE AND GET THE FACTS

◆ **Write down a description** of the problem behavior. Be specific and narrow it down. Instead of telling yourself, "This child is out of control," focus on the specific behavior you want to modify. Observe the child for a couple of days. When does the behavior occur? What leads up to it? Who is the child interacting with at the time? Is it the same indoors and outdoors?

◆ **Be a detective**. While exercising good professional ethics, find out as much as you can about the child's situation. Is the child going through a crisis or trauma? What are the family dynamics? Look for insights to help explain the child's behavior. In some cases this may influence how you handle it.

◆ **Look at the environment**. Take another look at the environment, schedule and program design to make sure it is not causing or worsening some problems. Is there too much waiting time? Does the child need to sit still too long? Does the child feel crowded and need to protect his personal space?

RECORD WHAT HAPPENS

◆ **Keep a journal**. You can add this information to the regular observation files you keep on each child or, even better, create a separate notebook. The first entry could be the description of the problem and the background information described above.

◆ **Write down the plan of action** you will try when the behavior occurs.

◆ **Record incidents as they occur**. Include time of day, location, other children involved, possible events that precipitated it, how you responded, what the child did and the aftermath. Do this consistently so that you can notice any patterns that might emerge. You could even develop a frequency graph. This will help you notice small decreases in the behavior that you might otherwise miss.

◆ **Record preventive activities**. In addition to writing about how you reacted to an incident, record other preventive activities you try with the child that might decrease the behavior—offering more sensory play to relax the child, reading a book on a particular topic or playing near the child when the behavior is most likely to happen.

USE THIS JOURNAL WHEN YOU INVOLVE OTHER ADULTS

◆ **Everyone benefits from clear notes**. Another staff member, parent or outside professional will benefit from a clear picture of what has gone on before.

Learning to Manage Behavior

◆ **Continue adding to the journal**, including involvement and interaction with any other person. That person could add to it by noting thoughts and observations.

BRAINSTORM WITH OTHERS

◆ **Generate possibilities**. Work with the other person to generate possible strategies and then narrow them down, deciding what you will do first.

◆ **Record successes or failures**. Analyze. Decide what to try next.

CELEBRATE SUCCESSES

◆ **See the results of your efforts**. This journaling process allows you to look back and see real progress with the child. It helps you realize the results of your efforts. Pat yourself on the back.

◆ **Respectfully help the child**. Quietly, and with respect, help the child feel the satisfaction of mastering a behavior. "You two have really learned how to be friends and use words to solve your problems."

And if the interventions are not successful.

◆ **Recognize your best effort**. No matter what happens, you will know that you gave it your best professional effort.

◆ **You will have valuable background information** for other professionals who will work with the child.

CHILD DEVELOPMENT FACTORS THAT INFLUENCE BEHAVIOR

There are child development factors to keep in mind when figuring out how to approach behavior problems of young children.

EGOCENTRISM

Young children are egocentric. The term "egocentrism" does not have the same negative connotation that it has when applied to adults, meaning that the person is selfish and inconsiderate. With young children, egocentrism is natural and understandable. They come into this world knowing only their own body sensations. Their world gradually expands to include those who care for them. Young children have not had enough time on the planet to consider that other people have feelings independent of their own feelings. In fact, they assume that everyone else has the same perceptions and feelings they do. That is why they are so impatient when another child doesn't hand a toy over immediately, and why they work so hard to be the center of attention. Helping them grow out of their egocentrism and learn to consider other people's points of view is one of the major social tasks of the early childhood years. Even when the young child does learn to share and engage in social situations, she may still act according to egocentric reasons: "because then he will be my friend," or "because then she will invite me to her birthday party."

Another aspect of egocentric thinking is the child's perception that all events happen for or because of her. We are amused when a child tells a father he can turn the ocean waves off now because she wants to go home. But when a child thinks she is the cause of her father's drinking, or parents' fighting, or grandmother's death, difficulties occur. Even though adults say over and over again, "It's not your fault. You had nothing to do with what happened," the child doesn't quite believe it.

ALL OR NOTHING

It's difficult for young children to consider that someone or something can be both good and bad at the same time. Someone is all good or all bad. Johnny who hits is a bad boy. The teenage brother who plays ball with the child cannot possibly be "bad" because he sells drugs. A child cannot look at both sides of a question or easily consider a situation from a different point of view.

ANCHORED IN THE PRESENT

The young child considers a situation only from her immediate perspective. She has difficulty thinking about events that led up to something, or what might happen in the future because of it. Understanding cause and effect requires abstract thinking, and the young child is still in a very concrete mode.

FOCUS ON THE PHYSICAL

The young child has to be able to perceive something with his senses to understand it. Responses to behavior have to be immediate. Waiting until the end of the day to discuss a problem with a child is much less effective. The child is not skilled at hypothetical thinking. The following response to a child's aggression, "How would you like it if someone did that to you?" is usually completely ineffective. The child doesn't understand. In fact, the child may even perceive such a comment as a threat that someone will do the same thing to him.

MAGICAL THINKING

The young child has a difficult time sorting out fantasy and reality. Images on television, even cartoons, seem real to the child. Bodies spring back to life. Punches don't hurt. The child may also believe that wishing something makes it come true. This doesn't usually cause problems until the child wishes for something negative, such as wanting a bad thing to happen to a sibling. If a real tragedy does occur, then the child can be overwhelmed by guilt.

VULNERABILITY

Young children are vulnerable and dependent. They learn to depend on the adults around them. In early years, they focus on ways to get the adults to attend to their needs. Infants learn to cry when they are uncomfortable, hungry or bored, and—like magic—someone appears. Toddlers learn to whine. Two year olds learn how to throw tantrums. Three year olds learn how to manipulate. This is why the issue of trust is such a major one. If a child's needs are met with relative consistency, the child can relax and enjoy the world. If they are not, the child will become tense. When children have not been able to trust the important adults in their lives, or when they feel betrayed, they become more fearful and clinging. Children need ways to feel more powerful to counteract feelings of helplessness. Children who feel helpless may become bossy, belligerent and aggressive, and may challenge rules and limits.

DIFFERENT TEMPERAMENTS

The basic temperament a child is born with will also influence how she adjusts to circumstances and what kinds of interventions work best. Although there are different labels, three basic personality types have been identified: 1) easy or flexible; 2) feisty or difficult; and 3) fearful or sensitive.

Every teacher knows that some children enter the classroom eager to learn and make friends, while others hang on to the teacher's leg and only gradually venture out. Some children can take a lot of abuse from other children and roll with the punches, while others blow up at the least provocation.

It is useful to consider the child's temperament when you think of different possible intervention strategies. Adjust your responses to the personality. Some sensitive children are very cautious about trying anything new. Letting the child approach new material on his own terms works better than sitting the child down and insisting he try something. A flexible child can be paired with a feisty child to help the feisty child learn give-and-take. But one needs to avoid ignoring "easy" children because they don't cause waves. A feisty child needs advance warning of transitions in your daily schedule. A fearful child needs reassurances and contact with a safe adult when there is a special visitor.

Two resources listed at the end of this chapter offer more information about the influences of temperament on behavior and the kinds of interventions that work best. They are: *The Difficult Child* by Stanley Turecki and Leslie Tanner, and *Flexible, Fearful, or Feisty: The Different Temperaments of Infants and Toddlers* (a video produced by the California State Department of Education).

Remember that difficult behavior is a sign that a child needs something. Try to figure out what that need is—attention, security, control, feeling valued—and try to fill the need so that the child won't continue to act in undesirable ways.

BUILDING SELF-ESTEEM

Children's self-esteem often suffers at times of crisis. They may think that they have caused the bad things that have happened to them, be it their parents' divorce, the death of their baby brother or an earthquake. When parents' patience wears thin and they lash out at the child because of their own stress, the child may become even more convinced that he is bad. In addition, when adults are consumed with a particular crisis, they may not have much emotional energy left over for the child. As a result, the child may feel worthless and abandoned. Children also feel powerless and helpless in many crisis situations, further eroding their self-esteem. When children have low self-esteem, they tend to act in ways that reinforce this image, often alienating people who might be their friends and supporters. It is important to try to break this negative cycle.

You can tell a child's self-esteem is low when:

- ◆ He has problems interacting with peers and has no friends.
- ◆ She whines or throws tantrums to demand her way.
- ◆ He has low tolerance for frustration.
- ◆ She misbehaves to gain attention.
- ◆ He is overly fearful.
- ◆ She is bossy and bullies other children.

When children have high self-esteem, they are generally more flexible and willing to take risks. Children who feel confident and capable of handling themselves in various situations are less aggressive than children who feel helpless. The bully in your classroom often turns out to be the child who has the weakest self-image.

Much of a child's self-esteem is built on successful interactions with adults and other children. Self-esteem can be eroded when adults make the child feel bad about himself. So, while you want to stop or change behavior, it is important to figure out how to do that and still leave the child feeling valued or respected. Besides being careful with the words you use, try to establish a caring, friendly relationship with the child.

Although a child's self-esteem is most strongly influenced by his parents and family, there

Learning to Manage Behavior

is much that a caregiver can do to make him feel like a worthy, capable person.

FEELING VALUED AND HAVING FRIENDS

◆ **Be kind, gentle and supportive**. The most important way to build a child's self esteem is to be kind, gentle, supportive, available, responsive.

◆ **Pay attention to the child**. Give her a warm greeting when she arrives. Take time to listen when she wants to tell you something.

◆ **Engage in conversations with the child**. Talk with the child rather than just telling him what to do or offering simple praise.

◆ **Avoid judgmental statements** such as, "You shouldn't feel that way." The child needs to feel that you are on his side.

◆ **Help children play together**. One of the most important ways children develop self-esteem is by having good relationships with their peers. All children want to have friends, but sometimes young children are quite clumsy in their efforts. By helping children learn how to play, solve problems, work together, and negotiate conflicts with other children, you can enhance their ability to make friends and keep them.

◆ **Create a "Who's Here Today?" board**. Take a photo of each child. Punch a hole in the top and write the child's name on a label at the bottom. Title a piece of poster board, "Who's Here Today?" Put pockets, hooks or Velcro on the board so the child can find her picture and attach it to the board at arrival time. This board gives the child a feeling that she is an important member of the group.

◆ **Talk about who is missing**. Look at this chart, or some variation of it, every morning with the children. Talk about who is here and who is missing. When a child returns after an absence, make sure the group welcomes her back.

◆ **Use a puppet to greet each child in the group**. The puppet should use the child's name and say something pleasant to her.

◆ **Children love to help**, especially if this gives them one-on-one time with a significant adult. Create jobs that a child can help you with, such as setting the table, cleaning up after lunch, feeding classroom pets, watering plants, setting out cots or folding notes to parents. After the child has helped you, be sure to express your appreciation and compliment him on a job well done. This will make him feel special.

◆ **Encourage children to help each other**. When possible, ask a child to help a class-mate with such tasks as zipping up a jacket, tying shoes, carrying something or opening a door. Children feel good about themselves when they help others.

◆ **Involve children in arranging the environment**. When you feel a need to rearrange furniture, solicit suggestions from the children. Then let them help you push the furniture around. They also love to decorate. Let them help put up seasonal decorations or artwork.

◆ **Support the child's ideas**. "I noticed you arranged the shapes in an interesting pattern."

◆ **Recognize efforts**. Even when children try something and do not succeed, comment on their willingness to make an effort. "Good try!"

◆ **Teach children how to act in different social settings**. Children also gain self-esteem by knowing how to act in different situations. For example, they may need to know how to behave at a wedding or funeral, or when visiting someone who is ill. They may also need to learn how to call for help when there's an emergency. In some cases, rehearsing these scenes ahead of time can help.

FEELING POWERFUL

◆ **Give children choices**. Give children many opportunities to make choices and direct their own activities during the day. Offer plenty of free play time and don't require that children rotate centers or do everything that is offered.

◆ **Create a self-regulating system for centers**. A sign-up system for popular centers can help children be self-regulating. A child can then relax and enjoy the activity rather than worrying about defending his right to be there.

Learning to Manage Behavior

◆ **Let children help decide what activities will be available**. How long shall we stay outside? Shall we put out clay or water?

◆ **Ask and heed their opinion**. Where do you think I should hang this picture?

THE ROLE OF LANGUAGE DEVELOPMENT

It's hard to overemphasize the role of language development in learning to manage emotions and behavior. Just look at the difference between two and three year olds. In general, two year olds are more likely to hit, pull another child's hair and scream when they don't get their way. Three year olds tend to use verbal weapons: "I won't be your friend." "I won't invite you to my birthday party."

Children who are frustrated because they cannot communicate their needs and wishes may act aggressively. This is true for older children who for one reason or another have lags in their language development. Neglected and abused children who have not been talked to and encouraged to express themselves fall into this group as well as children with developmental delays, hearing impairments or other communication difficulties.

All of the activities that encourage language development also relate to behavior management. Children must understand language in order to get the messages others are trying to communicate. And they need productive vocabulary to express their opinions and wishes.

CONSIDER NONVERBAL COMMUNICATION FIRST

With nonverbal children, demonstrate what you want them to do while saying the words you want them to use in the future. If you see a two year old reaching for the hair of a playmate, for instance, stop him. Say, "Touch gently." Then demonstrate by touching the other child's hair gently. Let the more aggressive child touch your hair and the other child's hair gently (if the other child is willing).

A non-English-speaking child or a toddler can learn vocabulary on the spot, connecting words to your actions. You can stop a child's hitting motion and say firmly, "No hitting." The child will see by your facial expression, body language and action that hitting is not allowed.

SIMPLIFY YOUR LANGUAGE

Although most parents and experienced teachers do this without thinking, it may take some practice for new teachers to simplify language and use words children understand. Give one direction at a time rather than stringing them together. For instance, "Push in your chair, scrape your plate in the garbage and go sit on your cot until I call you to come to the bathroom to brush your teeth," is too complicated for young children. Adults must also learn to speak at a slower pace than they normally would.

"No" is a word that enters a child's usable vocabulary very early on, but sometimes it triggers an emotional response and causes the child to assert her autonomy. You might find that the word, "Wait!" works better to stop an action, allowing you time to move in close.

MODEL APPROPRIATE RESPONSES

Even children who have productive language may not know how to string the words together to say what they want, especially if they don't have experience playing cooperatively with others. Give them words to repeat.

> "Susan, when that happens again you can say, `Stop. I don't like that!' Let me hear you say that. Good!"
> When you hear a scream of protest say, "Mark, tell Jason, `I'm playing with this now.'"

INTERPRET INTERACTIONS

You can help a nonverbal or timid child be understood.

> "Caitlin, you didn't hear Kristen. She said that she doesn't want to wear that hat."
> "Daniel, Kevin is screaming. That means he doesn't want you to push his chair."

HELP CHILDREN TALK IT OVER

Once children have a fair facility with language, you can help them learn to communicate effectively. Children who do have language may still need help expressing themselves. When an altercation between two children occurs, you can ask them to explain the situation to you. Rather than trying to fix it for them, see if they can come up with the solution themselves. Sometimes your presence will help them remember what they have heard many times before. And you can help each child hear the other's point of view.

> "But Danielle said she didn't want to build a road. She needed the long blocks for the side of her house."
> "Danielle, Jonathan said only the long blocks would go over his bridge."
> "Can you two think of any way to solve this problem?" You are not taking sides. You are demonstrating your support to help them solve their problem in a way they both think is fair.

All children thrive in environments with consistent rules and routines, but children in crisis especially need them. They find comfort in having one place where they can count on having limits. Ways to develop predictable routines are discussed in chapter 22. Solid rules for good behavior also help create a safe environment.

The younger the children are in your group, the simpler the rules should be. You might have just two: "No hurting people," and "No breaking things." With older children you can be more specific. Rules generally fall into three categories: treatment of others, safety issues and classroom policies. How to treat people includes not hurting people either physically or through verbal taunting, sharing and taking turns. The safety rules include no running in the hall, no playing right in front of the door and other things specific to the environment. The classroom rules concern handling of toys and materials, pitching in at clean-up time and taking turns at the learning centers. You can have rules for certain types of materials or activities as well. For example: "No splashing at the water table," or "Wear a smock when you paint."

◆ **Try to involve the children in creating the rules**. "We had a problem at the water table today. Jennifer got all wet, the floor got slippery because there was water all over it and Jose fell down. What do you think we should do?" As children generate ideas, write them down. You might decide to give several of the suggestions a try during the next play period and then decide what the final rules will be.

◆ **Rules are worth repeating**. Don't assume that all the children know or remember the rules. It does help if they are involved in making rules. But rules are worth repeating on a regular basis. As a prereading exercise, you and the children could read the rules each morning when you gather for your first group time.

◆ **Review rules**. When you bring out special materials or equipment that are not used on a regular basis, review with the children how to handle the materials and how to clean up when they are finished.

◆ **Stay neutral**. Children are often quick to recite a rule when a child disregards it. If you must intervene, try to stay neutral. "This is our rule. I expect you to do your best to remember it. I think you can do this."

◆ **Consistency is important**. Because of children's "all or nothing" thinking, they are more comfortable when the rule is enforced all the time.

◆ **Don't bend rules** because you feel sorry for a child. Sometimes when a child is going through a traumatic situation, adults feel sorry for her and bend the rules. This teaches the child how to be manipulative and may actually make her feel less secure.

Learning to Manage Behavior

◆ **Change rules when it makes sense**. Involve the children in the discussion and perhaps take a vote. All this makes them feel secure, respected and powerful.

THE TERRITORIAL IMPERATIVE

Children's squabbling in early childhood classrooms often involves the territorial imperative—defending space or materials. The younger the children, the more this is the case. Young children are more egocentric and may simply not see the other child's point of view. Fighting over possessions can also be a way of asserting power. "I am what I possess."

When a child in a stressful situation has a shaky self-esteem, sharing can be a more difficult issue than it would otherwise. When a child's life is in turmoil, he may have little generosity of spirit left over. And children shouldn't always be required to share or take turns. Sometimes they have a strong need to possess something, even if it's just in the classroom.

A starting point is to have plenty of equipment so that there is enough for everyone and waiting is minimized.

◆ **Some children are inexperienced in play**. Younger children (toddlers through three year olds) and children who are not accustomed to playing with other children may be impulsive. If they see another child playing with something that looks like fun, they may try to take it away so they can have fun, too.

◆ **Some children are surprised when others protest**. Because they think that everyone sees the world the way they do, they are sometimes genuinely surprised when there is a protest at the other end of the object they are grabbing.

◆ **Provide duplicates of the same toy.** The teacher can redirect the child by showing him the duplicate toy. This might lead to productive parallel play.

◆ **Note issues of dominance and power**. However, sometimes children want what the other child has, even if there is an identical one close at hand. Then you know you are dealing with issues of dominance and power, not just impulsiveness.

◆ **Learning to take turns is important**. Even if a program could afford to have one identical tricycle for each child, this would probably be unwise. Children benefit from your guidance as they learn to negotiate, consider other children's desires and practice taking turns.

SHARING

Heather Wenig, a teacher of toddlers, shares the following scenario, which illustrates children's thinking about sharing.

Josh is playing with the school bus (a favorite toy in the toddler room). Lisa decides she would enjoy playing with the bus as well and tries to take it away from Josh. (Enter the cries: "Mine! Mine!") The teacher tells Josh, "You need to share," and allows Lisa to have the bus.

What have Josh and Lisa learned? Josh loses his possession and learns to aggressively protect his playthings, while Lisa learns that she may take whatever she wants from others, and sharing has become a negative concept. What do you suppose the teacher really expected? It is my opinion that many adults, quite inadvertently, expect sacrifice when they use the word share. The difference? Children experience loss rather than mutual gain. In situations like these, when children are struggling over a toy, I have found it best to ask the original possessor, "Could Lisa play with your toy when you are finished? This question will quite often satisfy Lisa and prompt Josh to be generous. This simple method assures Josh that his rights will be protected and allows him to be in control of the decision. In addition, both children have a positive experience taking turns.

◆ **What does sharing mean?** Heather's scenario points out that children may not even know what sharing means (and in this case, the teacher doesn't seem to know, either). To share really means that two or more children use the same materials at the same time. Taking turns means alternating use of a toy. We have to make sure that sharing does not translate to giving up in the mind of the child.

◆ **Use share in context**. Notice when children do share. "Marcus and Shelly are sharing the playdough."

◆ **Be a good role model**. "I brought some stickers to share with you today. We can all have some."

◆ **Set up situations where children share naturally** and then comment. For instance, put a bowl of crayons between two children who are coloring and say, "You two can share these crayons."

◆ **Point out the reaction of the other child** when sharing happens. "You made Lisa happy when you shared your cracker with her."

ISSUES OF SPACE

For some children, especially those who are tense or very active, space issues can be a problem. One child might crowd another child or accidentally knock down a block construction. Children often don't realize a bump is an accident, and they react with distress and aggressiveness. You can try helping the two children work it out together, with one understanding that the incident was unintentional, and the other working to repair the damage. But some children need a clearer definition of their space. Try these ideas.

◆ **Give children hula hoops** or small rugs to help define their space. Tell the child that the materials are to stay within that defined space. This will make it easier for other children to recognize the boundaries.

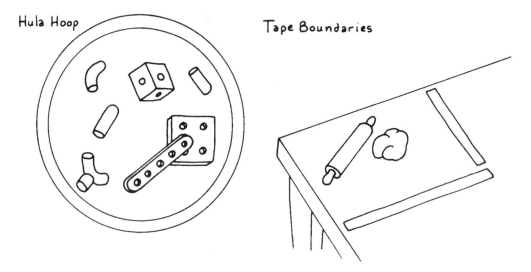

Hula Hoop   Tape Boundaries

◆ **Put lines of masking tape on a table top** or in the block center to define a child's work space.

◆ **Give children individual dish pans of water**, sand or other sensory materials to play with. These can be placed inside the larger water table, in a plastic wading pool or on a table top. Children benefit from parallel play without having to share the materials so directly.

Learning to Manage Behavior

TAKING TURNS

Taking turns is not exactly the same thing as sharing, although some of the same issues are involved. When children share crayons, each child gets some, but when children share a tricycle, only one child can ride at a time. Taking turns can build social skills as children learn to give and take. The following suggestions, taken from *The Outside Play and Learning Book: Activities for Young Children*, show how to facilitate turn taking, in this case with a tricycle:

◆ **Teach children how to ask for a turn**. With younger or less experienced children, you might even have to give them the words. "Say `Tiffany, I want to have a turn on the tricycle when you are finished.'"

◆ **Help the asker be heard**. Repeat the child's request clearly to the rider. "Stacy would like a turn on the tricycle. Will you give her this tricycle in a few minutes when you are finished with your turn?"

◆ **Leave it in the hands of the children**. If possible, let the rider give up the tricycle on her own terms. This sometimes happens very quickly. If you force it, on the other hand, you are more likely to encounter resistance or even a tantrum.

◆ **Have alternative activities for both children**. "Here, Stacy. While you are waiting to ride the tricycle you can pump gas over here at the gas station."

◆ **Express appreciation**. When the rider gives up the toy, express appreciation if the other child doesn't. "You made Stacy happy when you let her have a turn on the tricycle. Would you like to pump gas now?"

You can also help children figure out other ways to take turns, such as using a timer or signing up for something ahead of time. All of this gives them valuable experience with social give-and-take.

TEACHING CHILDREN CONFLICT RESOLUTION SKILLS

Teaching children to resolve conflicts peacefully is challenging under any circumstances, but teaching these skills to children in stressful life situations is extra challenging because they may have difficulty focusing on the needs and wishes of others. Consider also that some children, especially those from violent homes, may never have seen people working their problems out peacefully.

Keep in mind that you cannot get children to talk through a problem and come to a cooperative agreement in a highly charged emotional situation. If one child is frightened or extremely angry, let her calm down first. Perhaps you will need to separate the children or encourage them to sit down quietly for a few minutes before they can think.

Teachers often ask how much they should intervene when they see two children struggling. There are a number of different options, each appropriate in different situations.

◆ **You direct the behavior**. With this option, the adult is acknowledged as the most powerful person. This is probably the most common response of adults. "Lisa, give Jared the truck back." It can solve the problem of the moment, but probably isn't teaching the children very much, except that they can trust you when they need help. You aren't teaching them any skills. If you don't have time to sit down and talk to the children, you might resort to this approach. Maybe you can bring them back together to talk about it later, when you have more time. However, children learn best when the situation is in the immediate.

◆ **You are a coach, a facilitator**. Move in close and help children clarify their meanings and wishes. Nudge them in the right direction to come to a mutually satisfactory solution. "There seems to be a problem here. What are some of the solutions you can think of? Let me help you figure out what to do." You might have to help them understand how the other person feels, and to express themselves clearly. When they come to a satisfactory conclusion, help them notice how good it feels. "I'm glad you figured how you can both play with the truck. Now you are both having fun." You do this when you think the children might not come up with a nonaggressive solution on their own.

◆ **You are the cheerleader**. Just move in close and say nothing. The children are aware of your presence. They have heard your advice and guidance before. Your physical presence reminds them of what they already know, that they should work it out and come to a solution without your active intervention. You can either move away and say nothing, or act as a cheerleader. "I see you two really know how to work out a problem. Good work!" Obviously, this approach works only when children already have been exposed to the skills.

◆ **Ignore the children and keep your distance**, listening with one ear. You might do this when you think your presence could undermine the resolution process. The children might expect you to solve the conflict for them, or they might seek your support or sympathy for one side or the other.

FEELINGS

Weave the discussion of feelings into group activities. Rather than doing a theme unit on feelings, bring up the subject frequently when doing all kinds of things with the children. Young children need to learn about feelings. They need to recognize the different emotions that they have and understand also that everyone has and is entitled to a whole range of feelings.

First, acknowledge that children have a right to their emotions. Sometimes adults have an idealized vision of childhood, or what they think childhood should be—a time of blissful happiness and innocence. Of course, this has never been the case, but children who are experiencing stress in their lives need to have their emotions defined for them and acknowledged. They must know that it is not bad to feel angry, jealous, sad or frustrated.

As we help children identify and acknowledge their feelings, we also need to help children learn what to do with them. Teachers can help children see many different ways to respond to certain situations or to control their impulses.

This is not to say that we should pry or try to force children to talk about stressful situations in their lives. Teachers often wonder, "Should I bring up the topic if the child doesn't?" You can let the child know that you are aware of a particular situation and are there to talk about it if they want to. Some children will be relieved to know that they can share a problem with someone they trust. Other children will prefer to keep their thoughts to themselves, and we must respect that. In either case you can talk about emotions in more neutral ways by including general activities and discussions about feelings in your curriculum.

Knowing about the range of emotions people can have helps children talk about how they are feeling. Be aware of how you enable children to express their feelings and thoughts. Develop a wide repertoire of options.

HERE ARE A FEW IDEAS

◆ **Teach children a vocabulary about feelings**. Use words about feelings in context. Talk about your own feelings. "I'm feeling sad today because I really miss my Dad, who died last year." "I got very angry this morning when I missed the bus." Also describe children's emotions as you see them happening. "Marsha is sad. She is crying because she misses her mommy. Did you ever feel that way?"

◆ **Sing children's songs about feelings**. "If You're Happy And You Know It Clap Your Hands," is one familiar example. You are at least naming various emotions and making children familiar with the concept. You can precede or follow the song with a group discussion of the things that make them feel happy, sad, mad, etc. Fred Rogers (Mister Rogers) has created many excellent songs that focus on specific emotions. "What Do You Do With the Mad That You Feel," "Wishes Don't Make Things Come True" and "Sometimes People Are Good" are a few examples.

◆ **Have a puppet express emotions**. A classroom Puppet Pal can talk to the children about his feelings. "My name is Sam and I have a problem. My mom just had a new baby and now she doesn't pay any attention to me anymore. Everyone thinks my new brother is so cute, but I think he is ugly and all he does is cry. My mom doesn't love me anymore." Ask the children, "Have you ever felt that way? What do you think Sam can do? What might help him?" Then talk to the puppet. "You see, Sam, everyone feels that way sometimes. But Kathy found out that her mom really does love her very much, but she was just very tired and busy. Your mom loves you, too."

◆ **Create a picture file of feelings**. Find magazine pictures of faces that exemplify different emotions or of situations that elicit emotions. Mount the pictures on construction paper or cardboard and cover with clear self-adhesive paper or laminate them for durability. Then you can ask children, "What's going on here? Why do you think the little boy has that expression on his face? Do you think he is scared?" This activity helps children identify various emotions and talk about when they have felt them, too. They learn that they are not the only ones who have ever felt a certain way.

◆ **Have children sort pictures of feelings**. Collect pictures of people expressing a range of different emotions. Mount them on individual cards and let children sort them according to the feelings represented. Then ask the child what the piles represent (the emotions the child has identified) and why he sorted the pictures the way he did.

◆ **Make masks of feelings**. Mask making can be a wonderful creative experience for older preschoolers and elementary school-aged children. Children can make masks out of many different materials, including paper plates with tongue depressor handles glued on, paper bags, construction paper and papier-mâché. Talk about feelings first, and let the child identify a feeling for which he would like to make a mask. Provide glue, paint and a rich variety of collage materials and scraps for the child to use for features. The child will probably need help in deciding where to put eye holes on the mask and in actually cutting the holes. Older children might enjoy creating skits in which they can use their masks. Younger children might simply hold up their masks and tell friends about the feeling they represent.

◆ **Use creative movement**. Start with simple walking. Have all the children walk randomly around in a space, perhaps while you are beating a drum. Then announce, "Now walk like you are angry." After a few minutes, change the emotion. "Now walk like you are happy..." "...afraid...," etc. This gives you an opportunity to talk about emotions and how to tell what someone is feeling.

◆ **Dance a feeling.** Find a variety of music for children to dance to that brings to mind different emotions. Classical music often lends itself to different moods. Don't tell children how to move, or what they should be doing. Just let them express themselves freely. Add large squares of chiffon for them to wave around for extra expression. After each dance, you might ask the children what the music reminded them of.

◆ **Children's books.** Collect favorite children's books about feelings and read them to the children. Invite the child to find a book about how she is feeling after she is familiar with your collection and offer to read it to her. Children might even like to act out the story.

BOOKS ABOUT FEELINGS

Alexander and the Terrible, Horrible, No Good, Very Bad Day by Judith Viorst
All My Feelings at Preschool: Nathan Day by Susan Conlin and Susan Levine
Even I Did Something Awful by Barbara Shook Hazen
Feelings by Joanne B. Murphy
I Was So Mad by Norma Simon
Sometimes I Like to Cry by Elizabeth and Harry Stanton
The Temper Tantrum Book by Edna Preston Mitchell

Anger

Anger as an emotion needs special focus. It is the emotion that is most upsetting to adults when they see it in children. We want to stop its expression, sometimes at all costs. Anger is frightening, both to the child who is angry and to the people around him. And anger can be dangerous when it leads to destructive behavior. Yet, children need to know that it is natural for everyone to feel angry from time to time and to have occasional squabbles. We need to find ways to allow children to recognize their anger, express it appropriately and move through their anger to a more productive emotion.

When a conflict arises, and also during neutral times such as circle time, talk to the children about appropriate things to do when they are angry. Work with the children to generate a list of possible actions.

◆ **Talk it over**. Encourage the child to say out loud, "I'm angry," or I'm mad." This should be one of the first things he does when he feels very angry. Children must know that it is okay to use these words.

◆ **Use a puppet**. Lead a discussion about anger with a puppet. A puppet could talk about something that made him mad, and the children could give the puppet suggestions of what he might do. Or a puppet might act as an "anger consultant." The children tell him why they are angry, and the puppet helps the children think of how to respond.

◆ **Offer lots of active play opportunities**. Outdoor time is very important and should not be cut short (unless, of course, weather dictates.) Running, shouting, jumping, climbing, riding wheel toys all expend physical energy and release tensions. Make provisions for active physical play inside as well.

It's-okay-to-be-mad center

Create an "angry center." Because anger is an emotion that causes such physical tension, you might have a special place in the room where children can go to express anger appropriately. You might decide not to call it an "angry center" though, because you don't want children to think that they must be angry to use the materials in this place. Maybe call it the "express yourself center." In it could be such things as:

◆ **Things to punch** such as large pillows, punching balls or punching clowns so children can release their physical tension.

◆ **Tactile play materials** that tend to be soothing and comforting such as water; cool, moist potters clay; fine, smooth sand; and shaving cream to smear around.

◆ **Things to pound**. If supervised adequately, a woodworking bench is a great addition. Many programs have woodworking as an outside activity. Children also enjoy using small wooden mallets to pound playdough or clay or sheets of styrofoam. Pounding golf tees into a block of styrofoam with a wooden mallet also has great appeal.

◆ **Aggression bags**. Help children squirt shaving cream into sandwich-size, zip-close bags. Then let them choose two bottles of food coloring and put a squirt of each in the bag. Zip the bag closed. Now let the children squeeze the bag to their heart's delight to mix the colors. This is a good tension reliever.

◆ **Painting at an easel**. Set up an easel with bright, bold colors (including black and red) of creamy tempera paint to encourage the children's creative expression. Especially with a child in crisis, let her make painting after painting rather than stopping her after one painting so that others get a turn.

◆ **Art materials**. Include other expressive art materials. Bright marking pens, crayons, colored pencils, a rich collection of collage materials, glue and paper invite children to make marks that express how they feel.

◆ **Things to destroy**. Include newspapers and old magazines to cut or tear up, fabric to rip and other collected junk for children to take apart.

◆ **An unbreakable mirror** for making angry faces.

◆ **Soft balls to squeeze**.

◆ **Noise makers**—shakers, cookie sheets to bang wooden spoons against.

◆ **Target and beanbags**. Put a target on the wall and let children throw beanbags against it as hard as they can.

◆ **A yelling box**. Work with the children to paint a large cardboard appliance box on the outside and decorate it on the inside. Cut a door in one side. Invite children to go inside the box, close the door and yell or roar like a lion when they need to let off steam.

◆ **Teddy bears to hug** or tell their problems to.

◆ **Books about feelings**. Have children's books on hand that talk about anger such as *Alexander and the Terrible, Horrible, No Good, Very Bad Day* by Judith Viorst.

Keep in mind that all of these activities are not intended to get rid of the feeling of anger, or other emotions, but to acknowledge it, express it and learn to deal with it in a healthy and constructive way. These are all autotherapeutic activities. They are beneficial in and of themselves and do not need adult interpretation or mediation to make them effective.

UNDERSTANDING AND DEALING WITH AGGRESSION

Aggression is defined as any act that causes physical or psychological harm to someone else. Aggression is frightening for everyone involved, including the aggressor. Because most aggression in early childhood classrooms grows out of frustration, it makes sense to try to reduce some of the frustration children might feel in the environment. If you can reduce the amount of direct competition among children in your room, you may have fewer situations where children feel the need to be aggressive.

A common type of aggression is when a child uses physical force to obtain an object or keep the object she currently possesses. For young children it seems often to be the quickest means to an end.

Another type of aggression is hostile aggression. This is when a child purposely says or does something to hurt another individual. Retaliation and jealousy are often the causes. This type of aggression can take the form of hitting, tripping someone, scratching or hair pulling. Name calling and humiliating another child is more common with older children.

Because children see aggressive models of problem solving around them, both in life and on television, we should not be surprised when they imitate a negative behavior that seems to work well for others. Sometimes children are even taught to be aggressive. This is especially true of boys. "Stand up for yourself." "Hit 'em back!" One teacher reported an incident in which two children got into a fight while the class was on a field trip. When the parents were told about the child's fight, their first question was, "Did he win?"

Do not ignore physical or verbal aggression, as doing so actually increases aggression with young children. Remember, young children think everyone sees the situation the same way they do. If the teacher ignores it, the child actually comes to think that the adult approves of, or even expects, the behavior. You have the formidable task of showing them another way. It is not hopeless. If children could think of a better way of dealing with their frustration, they would use it. They want to be successful. Grabbing someone's toy or kicking someone to get them out of the way may seem to work. If they discover another way that works even better, they will use it.

STRATEGIES TO TRY

◆ **Establish eye contact.** Make sure you have the child's attention when you are trying to get him to respond.

◆ **Catch it before it happens**. Catch aggression as it is building. Once you know the children well, you can read their moods. As frustration builds, approach the child. Divert her attention if possible. Of course, aggressive behavior can happen very fast. "Wait!" is a good word to use.

◆ **Use sensory play**. Try to dissipate some of the child's tensions in sensory play or other calming, soothing activities. Use the calming effects of water, clay or playdough.

◆ **Deal with the underlying tension**. Although dissipating the child's tension is useful, don't forget to deal with the underlying emotion. Help the child figure out what to do with the mad feelings she has.

◆ **Empathize with the child's feelings**. Validate the feelings. "You're mad. It's okay to feel mad. Shelly hurt your feelings and that's not okay. You really want to let her know you are mad, but I can't let you hurt her. I will help you think of another way to tell her you are mad. People need to feel safe here. I won't let anyone hurt you, or let you hurt anyone."

◆ **Teach children to use words instead of actions**. Then, keeping both children together, teach them the words to use to express their feelings. If they are fighting over a toy, help them learn the words they need to negotiate a turn or a trade.

◆ **Be consistent in your interventions**. If you stop a child the first time he pokes someone, then let him get away with it later, you are actually increasing the likelihood that the child will poke or hurt children more often. It's the "gambling response," also called intermittent reinforcement. It becomes a game with children, and they, in effect, say to themselves, "I wonder how long she'll go this time before she blows her top."

◆ **Praise children when they try nonaggressive solutions**. "Good try!" Although children's nonviolent attempts at negotiation may not always be successful, aggressive children should not always get the most attention. If children are successful at attracting your attention and approval by trying conciliatory modes, they are more likely to try again.

◆ **Teach kindness**. You may have to teach children how to be kind and empathetic to each other. If a child is crying, of course, you model kindness and try to comfort the child. But you could also involve the other children. "What do you think we could do to make Manuel feel better?"

VICTIM CHILD

We all know the victim child. This is the child who everybody bullies, the child whom crumbles easily under aggressions and is constantly on the losing end of the stick. Victims feel they have two choices: either yield to the aggressor, which reinforces the behavior of the aggressor, or become desperate and counterattack. You can teach the victim to use words. "Tell him you don't like it when he takes things from you." Teach the child how to get mad at other children acceptably. "Susie, say,`Stop hitting me! I don't like it!'" You can also teach the child how to ignore aggressive children and walk away from them or come to an adult for help. When children learn effective ways of dealing with other aggressive children, they are less likely to become frustrated and aggressive themselves. You are building their own sense of self-esteem and control.

WHEN A CHILD HURTS A TEACHER

The child must learn that it is not okay to hurt you in any way. A child who is allowed to hurt an adult will ultimately feel unsafe and guilty. Other children in the room will not feel safe, either, if they think the adult is not in control. Teachers are also included in the rule, "Everyone needs to feel safe here."

DEALING WITH SWEARING

Foul language is everywhere in our culture. Children hear it on prime time television, in movies, from older kids and sometimes from their parents. Because young children are imitators, we should not be surprised when they use expletives. Teachers wonder what to do about it, and what parents will think of them if they do not stop it.

The key to dealing with young children who use foul language is to focus on the intent, not the content. Is the child using the language out of frustration or to hurt someone? When a child drops his lunch on the floor or accidentally knocks over a block structure and then uses an expletive, don't immediately lecture the child about the appropriate use of language. Instead, simply address the situation. "You were really hungry and now your lunch is on the floor. I can see you're upset. Let me help you clean this up and then we can get you more food to eat." If the child consistently uses curse words, wait until the child is calm to talk about it. Coach the child, "I understand you were really frustrated when your building fell over before. But using that word (say the word here) can really upset other people around you. Let's think of another word you can say when you feel like that."

When a child uses bad language to hurt someone's feelings, the situation should be dealt with the same way you deal with other types of aggression. It is important not to ignore verbal aggression. "In this classroom it is not okay to hurt people's feelings by calling them names."

When a child is angry enough to curse at you, this is not the time to lecture her. Later, when her temper has cooled, you can address the situation. "I understand you were really mad at me, but it's not okay to use (say the word)." Another response for the moment is, "You're calling me _____ but my name is Sandra."

One teacher takes the power out of the word by using it herself in context. "I heard the word _____ over here. What's going on?" A center director put a child who had been sent to her office for swearing (not a recommended practice) on her lap and said, "I heard you are saying _____ a lot lately. Does that mean you're mad?" When the adult says the word out loud in this manner, it takes some of the power out of it. Then address the situation that made the child angry or frustrated and how you would like the child to express herself in the future.

Even if a child is attempting to curse at you or another child and it comes out funny or is a word that doesn't offend adults, do not smile or ignore it if it was meant to be hurtful. Stupid and baby are aggressive swear words for young children. When a child screams, "You doo-doo head!" the intent is still there. Treat the child's anger seriously. Find out why

Learning to Manage Behavior

the child is angry, and help her deal with it.

Often children who frequently use swear words have a limited facility with language. We want to help children become adept at using language to communicate. You might ask the child, "What were you trying to say? Let me help you find some better words that really say what you mean." You can also have an intellectual discussion about swear words with children at some neutral moment, like during circle time. "Isn't it interesting that just saying certain words, making certain sounds come out of your mouth, can make people so upset?"

Some teachers worry that correcting a child's language—when the child probably learned the language at home—is the same as criticizing the family. This can be a sensitive issue. It's a lie, of course, to tell him that "nice people" don't curse. Yet, you don't want other children to pick up the swear word. One solution is to simply explain in a nonjudgmental way that in school those words are not used.

When a child comes to you and tattles about another child who has used a curse word, teach the child to be proactive. "Tell Michael you don't like it when he says that, or calls you that."

TEMPER OUTBURSTS

Some children, especially those in crisis, have real trouble "putting on the brakes." When frustrated, they quickly turn to temper tantrums or uncontrolled behavior as a way of expressing the feeling. This may be a difficult situation for the teacher to handle and can be frightening for both the out of control child and the other children.

◆ **Catch it before the child is out of control**. Intervene as early as you can. This means that the adults in charge must be very aware of this child's problem. One strategy is to assign one adult on the teaching team to stay close to the child without being too obvious.

◆ **Diffuse and redirect the child's frustration** when you see it building. Enter the play yourself. Add a little lightness and humor (not sarcasm or teasing). Invite the child to join you in an activity that offers a physical release of tension, such as dancing or running around outside. It might be best to get the child away from the stimulation of other children for a little while. Offer quiet solitary activities such as looking at books with or without you, listing to music on a headset or doing simple puzzles. Sometimes offering a small snack can help.

◆ **Find special training**. See if you can find special training on techniques for handling children who are truly out of control. Touch can be very calming but it has to be done right. Some experts feel that light touch can actually cause the child to increase his negative behavior. But if you get behind the child and put your arms around him with firm pressure on his sternum, you might be better able to calm him down. Another technique you might try is to put firm downward pressure on the child's shoulders. Again, it is best to receive specific training so that you do not apply too much pressure, or in some other way harm the child. Ask the local school district or community mental health agency for more information.

◆ **Be wise to manipulation.** When dealing with temper tantrums, try to distinguish between a tantrum to manipulate adults and a tantrum that occurs out of pure frustration. Treat these differently. Sometimes it is hard to distinguish between the two, especially if you're dealing with a combination of reasons. If you are sure the child is throwing the tantrum just to get his way, you can say, "This is not going to work. I will not let you have this, no matter how you act." Later, when the child has calmed down, you can tell him that he will never get his way with you by throwing a tantrum. If the child has a tantrum because he couldn't handle his frustration, you can be empathetic but firm. "I know it's hard for you to change activities. But it'll be all right." Later you can work with the child to deal with the stressful situation. In both cases, see that the child doesn't hurt himself or others.

ENCOURAGING POSITIVE SOCIAL SKILLS

Learning to control behavior and respond to social stresses in acceptable ways is hard work for children. Their progress won't be continuous. They will occasionally slip back to earlier forms of expression. You can help them with positive words to give them encouragement.

◆ **Acknowledge success.** When the child does achieve some success, it's important to acknowledge his efforts, not by raving ecstatically about every minor accomplishment, but by letting him know in a loving way that you've noticed he is trying harder.

◆ **Meaningful praise.** Children catch on quickly to empty praise. For example, when a teacher says, "Oh, how wonderful!" to everything, even if it isn't wonderful, praise loses its meaning. Instead, ask them how they feel about their work. "Are you pleased with the way your painting turned out?" "I bet you feel proud of that big building you made with the blocks." Some children are so hungry for compliments or praise that they create a quick scribble and bring it over to you to hear what you think about it. This is another situation where asking them how they feel about their work has more meaning.

◆ **Praise a child for hard work.** Rather than praising a child for appearance or possessions, praise the child for hard work or ideas.

◆ **Praise children for successful problem solving.** "You two came up with a great solution. Good work!"

◆ **Be genuine with your praise**. Try not to manipulate children through praise.

◆ **Catch children doing something right**, such as sharing with another child or cleaning up in a cooperative way. Instead of praising, notice. Smile. Mention it privately with the child.

◆ **Help children develop internal controls** and a sense of responsibility. You want a child to feel like she can handle things on her own.

CONCLUSION

Everyone wants a "cookbook" for handling behavior problems with young children. You look up the problem in the index, turn to page 47 and there is the recipe for how to handle it—satisfaction guaranteed! Of course there is no such "behavior cookbook" because we have no standard "ingredients." Each child is different, and the elements of the situation always vary according to how many people are involved, the time of day, what the child's morning was like and so on. The most we can do is to try to understand the variables and their impact on children's behavior. What works with one child or situation may not work with another. Our goal is not necessarily to solve the immediate problem, but rather to determine what will help the child become a competent, caring and successful human being.

Above all, don't forget your importance as a role model. For some children, you may be the only positive adult role model in their lives. Helping children learn to control their behavior is an art. Develop pride and mastery in the art. You have much to draw on, much to try. Even the most experienced teachers are constantly rethinking what they do, looking for better ways. Read what others have done, talk to colleagues, go to workshops, build support groups. It is always worth the effort.

RESOURCES

BOOKS

Family Communications, Inc., 4802 Fifth Avenue, Pittsburgh, PA 15213. 412-687-2990. www.misterrogers.org. Ask for their catalog which lists all of Mister Rogers' recordings and other excellent resources, practically all of which are centered on children's feelings.

Levin, Diane E. (1994). *Teaching Young Children in Violent Times: A Preschool — Grade Three Violence Prevention and Conflict Resolution Guide*. Cambridge, MA: Educators for Social Responsibility. This excellent resource discusses how to encourage children to solve their differences in peaceful ways. Relevant for young children and early elementary school-aged children.

Mitchell, Grace and Dewsnap, Lois. (1995). ***Common Sense Discipline: Building Self-Esteem in Young Children, Stories from Life***. Glen Burnie, MD: Telshare Publishing Company, Inc. This resource addresses discipline situations and suggests strategies for problems facing families. Among the many situations discussed are a divorced mother raising a child alone, grandparents raising a child and a child in foster care.

Mitchell, Grace and Dewsnap, Lois. (1993). ***HELP! What Do I Do About...? — Biting, Tantrums, and 47 Other Everyday Problems***. New York: Scholastic Inc. Compiled from Dr. Grace Mitchell's popular column in Scholastic's magazine *Early Childhood Today*. Behavior problems are listed in the table of contents. The book includes strategies for handling the situation, and using the four-step plan: anticipate, hesitate, investigate and communicate. The reader is given insight into why the child is behaving that way and how to understand and prevent the behavior in the future. A very useful resource.

Prutzman, Priscilla, Stern, Lee, Burger, M. Leonard, and Bodenhamer, Gretchen. (1988). ***The Friendly Classroom for a Small Planet: A Handbook on Creative Approaches to Living and Problem Solving for Children***. Philadelphia, PA: New Society Publishers. A valuable resource with strategies for developing a classroom where children feel safe and learn to cooperate. While most appropriate for slightly older children, there is much of value for early childhood classrooms.

Rogers, Fred and Head, Barry. (1993). ***Mister Rogers Talks With Parents***. Winona MN: Hal Leonard Corporation. This book discusses many of the more traumatic situations children encounter as well as their range of normal emotions. The words and music to Fred Rogers' songs that deal with emotions of childhood are in the back of the book.

Slaby, Ronald et al. (1995). ***Early Violence Prevention, Tools for Teachers of Young Children***. Washington, DC: National Association for the Education of Young Children. The chapters include structuring cooperative activities, responding in effective ways, helping children with aggressive behavior problems and teaching assertiveness.

Smith, Charles. (1993). ***The Peaceful Classroom: 162 Easy Activities to Teach Preschoolers Compassion and Cooperation***. Beltsville, MD: Gryphon House. An invaluable resource to teach children the skills of friendship, compassion, cooperation and kindness. In addition to offering activities to teach children these important life skills, the book also includes a listing of appropriate literature to read to children and suggestions to extend the learning to the home.

Turecki, Stanley K., and Tanner, Leslie. (1989). ***The Difficult Child***. New York: Bantam Books, Inc. Written for parents, this is an excellent book to recommend to parents of difficult children. A central theme is the role of temperament in how the child responds to situations and various intervention strategies.

ARTICLES

Fox, Robert A., Anderson, Rebecca C., Fox, Theresa, A., and Rodriguez. "STAR parenting: A model for helping parents effectively deal with behavioral difficulties." *Young Children*. 46(6), September 1991, 54-60. The authors describe the format and content of the parenting class which they developed. This approach to parent education brings together child development knowledge, behavior management principles, adult cognitive learning strategies and most importantly, common sense.

Furman, Robert A. "Helping children cope with stress and deal with feelings." *Young Children*. 50(2), January 1995, 33-41. The author explains that assisting a child to cope with stress is a crucial part of teachers' and caregivers' roles. This educational approach teaches a child to deal with the realities of the outside world as well as the feelings the child experiences.

Heath, Harriet A. "Dealing with difficult behaviors — teachers plan with parents." *Young Children*. 49(5), July 1994, 20-24. The author provides examples of parents and teacher working together on a child-guidance problem, including guidelines for evolving the guidance plan.

VIDEOS

Flexible, Fearful, or Feisty: The Different Temperaments of Infants and Toddlers. (1990). Sacramento, CA: California State Department of Education. Available from the Bureau of Publications, Sales Unit, California State Department of Education, P.O. Box 271, Sacramento, CA 95812-0271. 916-445-1260. This video gives clear visual images of how the different temperaments look in infants and toddlers and how adults can adjust their caregiving styles to meet the needs of children.

Hand in Hand: Supporting Children with Play Problems. Educational Productions, Inc., 9000 SW Gemini Drive, Beaverton, OR 97008. 800-950-4949. www.edpro.com. This set of seven video tape modules explores various play problems and possible teacher interventions. Each tape is about 30 minutes, and has an accompanying facilitator guide. This is an excellent tool to help teachers stand back and look at what is happening with children. Modules may be purchased separately at $295 each or as a set for $1,885. While expensive, they would be an excellent addition to a resource lending library. Titles include
>*When a Child Doesn't Play*
>*The Child Who Wonders*
>*The Child Who Dabbles*
>*The Child Who Appears Anxious*
>*The Child Who Appears Aloof*
>*The Child Who Is Ignored*
>*The Child Who Is Rejected*

INDEX

Index

Index

I

Index

S

Index

Index

Nailing Jelly to The Wall

Defining and Providing Technical Assistance in Early Childhood Education

Nancy P. Alexander

For experts in the field of early care and education, defining and providing technical assistance can be as difficult as nailing jelly to the wall. Learn to effectively coach, mentor, and train early childhood teachers and administrators with guided experiences, strategies, and activities to provide technical assistance in specific program areas like parent involvement, science, outdoor play, music. and art. 144 pages. 2012

ISBN 978-0-87659-413-1 | Gryphon House | 10034 PB

Socially Strong, Emotionally Secure

50 Activities to Promote Resilience in Young Children

Nefertiti Bruce, Karen Cairone

Now more than ever, adults must help children develop the skills necessary to navigate through life successfully. By focusing on building social and emotional strength, we increase children's resilience and prepare them to handle the challenges in life. The strategies and activities in *Socially Strong, Emotionally Secure* help children become socially and emotionally healthy for life. Organized into five chapters, the activities support and build resilience in children ages 3 to 8. 160 pages. 2011.

ISBN 978-0-87659-332-5 / Gryphon House / 10398 / PB